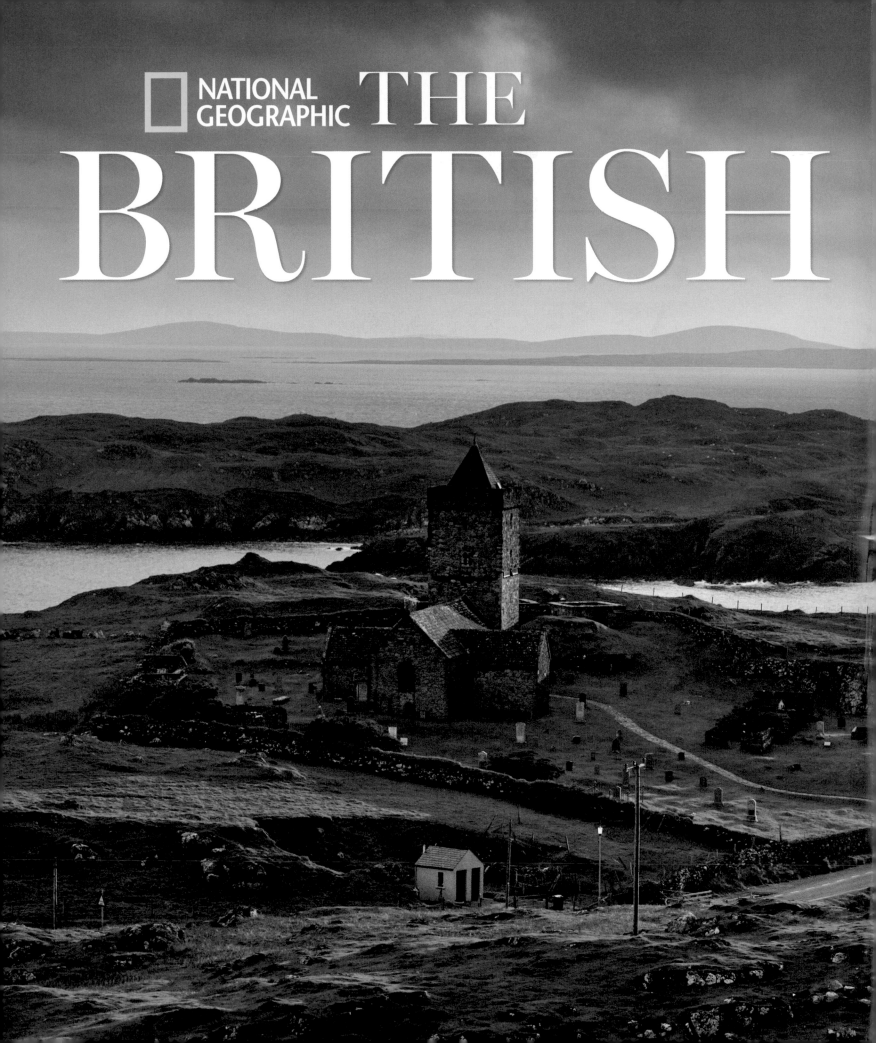

NATIONAL GEOGRAPHIC

THE
BRITISH

WORLD
AN ILLUSTRATED ATLAS

TIM JEPSON

National Geographic
WASHINGTON, D.C.

CONTENTS

Introduction 6

Chapter 1

PREHISTORY TO THE ROMANS 12
1,000,000 B.C.–A.D. 410

Chapter 2

SAXONS TO NORMANS 34
A.D. 410–1066

Chapter 3

THE MEDIEVAL AGE 60
1066–1485

Chapter 4

TUDOR BRITAIN 100
1485–1603

Chapter 5

THE STUARTS 146
1603–1714

Chapter 6

THE GEORGIAN ERA 190
1714–1815

Chapter 7

THE AGE OF EMPIRE 236
1815–1914

Chapter 8

THE MODERN AGE 284
1914–PRESENT

Appendix: Monarchs of Britain • 334 Further Resources • 336
About the Author and Other Contributors • 338
Acknowledgments • 338 Illustrations Credits • 339 Index • 342

INTRODUCTION

THE HISTORY OF THE BRITISH ISLES IS ONE OF THE RICHEST IN THE WORLD. Other cultures may be more ancient, or their memorials to a distant past more striking, but few contain the drama that has played out on these islands over the course of many millennia. And few have a legacy as profound or as far-reaching, the consequence of an empire that extended across almost a quarter of the Earth and continues to shape the lives of millions of people to this day.

It is a history with deep roots. It opens perhaps a million years ago, with unknowable groups of hunter-gatherers wandering an ancient shore. Moving through the ages of stone, bronze, and iron, it gathers pace as agriculture and trade and cultural exchange enrich a succession of ever more sophisticated peoples. Some two thousand years ago, it enters one of its many eras of blood and conquest, as first the Romans and then the Saxons and the Vikings are lured to Britain's prosperous shores.

All the while the vagaries of geography shape its course. For centuries, invaders balk at water or mountain. Ireland remains largely safe across its sea, while the wild uplands of Scotland and Wales become a redoubt for indigenous tribes and refugees from the ravaged lands to the south. And it is these lands to the south, more benign and already more prosperous, that will play a central role in the long story to come. In time, their green fields and busy settlements will become England, closer to Europe, and so more easily invaded, but also more fertile, and so more easily farmed and more easily settled.

Power and glory *page 1:* The Imperial State Crown, one of the United Kingdom's Crown Jewels; *pages 2–3:* Tùr Chliamhainn, or St. Clement's Church, set amid the wild landscape of Harris, off the west coast of Scotland; *page 4:* a portrait of Elizabeth I (ca 1600) in the golden robes worn at her coronation in 1559; *page 6:* St. Paul's Cathedral wreathed in smoke as London burned on December 29, 1940, during one of the worst nights of the Blitz.

From earliest times, therefore, before countries are named or borders settled, two powerful elements already shape the history of the British Isles. One is the fact that its narrative will contain the separate but tightly bound stories of Wales, Scotland, England, and Ireland. The second is the near certainty that this story will have a dominant character—the country most favored by geography and history's broad sweep: England.

England's dominance lasted at least a thousand years, based after its earliest blessings largely on trade, first with Europe and then with a wider empire. Invasion and civil war threw it off course, as did religious upheaval and the costly distractions of domestic and foreign wars. But through a combination of luck and longevity, of law, language, and institutions tempered by time and adversity, it eventually emerged as one of the most stable and prosperous nations on Earth.

To look at the history of the British Isles, we have divided *The British World* into eight chapters. The first three cover epochs of greater length, each bounded by war and invasion. Next come chapters devoted to the Tudors and the Stuarts, royal dynasties that saw Britain undergo some of the most profound changes in its history. Then come two chapters of briefer span, both filled with a rush of events as the changes of earlier centuries set the stage for Britain's march into the wider world. The final chapter, again rooted in the trauma of war, brings us to the present day.

Each of these chapters opens with a narrative overview designed to place the period's individuals and events in their broader chronological contexts. Each is accompanied by a time line of the chapter's key events and, after the first chapter, by a family tree that traces the often historically critical line of descent of England and Great Britain's and the United Kingdom's kings and queens. A summary of Scotland's monarchs is also included.

The sections following each narrative contain self-contained spreads over two or four pages, often with highly detailed accompanying maps. These spreads, again in roughly chronological order, look in more depth at a range of the period's most important aspects. Often they involve some of the many great names of British history, from leaders like Oliver Cromwell, Henry VIII, and Sir Winston Churchill to more singular icons such as Shakespeare, Darwin, and Sir Isaac Newton.

Just as often they involve battles—Trafalgar, Hastings, Agincourt, Waterloo, or the Somme—for Britain's history is nothing if not bloody. Also here are some of the other one-off events that crowd Britain's history: the catastrophe of the Black Death, the plague epidemic of 1348–1350 that killed hundreds of thousands; the Dissolution of the Monasteries after 1536, when the dispersal of church lands under Henry VIII changed the face of the British countryside forever; or the Gunpowder Plot of 1605, one of the many what-if moments of Britain's history, which, had it succeeded, would have changed the destiny of the British world in ways beyond imagining.

Elsewhere in the book, the emphasis is on more general themes, such as Britain's role in the slave trade, the mass emigration from the country's shores in the 19th century, the English Reformation of the 16th century, or the loss of the American colonies during the Revolutionary War. Often these themes develop threads across several chapters, most notably with the growth of empire, the rise of Britain as an industrial power, and the struggle for self-determination in Scotland and Ireland during their long and fractured relationship with England.

Other spreads address physical memorials to Britain's past. Some are artifacts, fragile and modest in a way that belies their historical importance—Magna Carta, for example, or the Domesday Book. Others are more obviously majestic and monumental—Stonehenge, Hadrian's Wall, Westminster Abbey, the Tower of London.

But even at more than 300 pages, *The British World* must bow before the sheer wealth of British and Irish history. Had space allowed, numerous other events might have been included, countless other individuals more fully described. Many more cultural and social issues would have been addressed. And more analysis would have been brought to bear, for few histories are as filled with controversy as those of these lands.

But this is one of the many beauties of the British world: that it is so rich and varied and endlessly debatable. Presenting and settling every argument is beyond the scope of this book. But that is not its purpose. Rather, it aims to be an introduction, an overview to whet the appetite, and above all a starting point that we hope will inspire readers to discover more about the people and events that have shaped both the British Isles and—for better or worse—much of the wider world in which we live. ∎

Shetland Islands

Orkney Islands

BRITISH ISLES

Great Britain

Ireland

Irish Sea

North

Celtic
Sea

ATLANTIC
OCEAN

English Channel

Bay of
Biscay

IBERIAN

PENINSULA

Pyrenees

Bale

Strait of Gibraltar

Alboran
Sea

Medi

PHYSICAL MAP
OF THE
BRITISH ISLES
AND
MAINLAND
EUROPE

PREHISTORY TO THE ROMANS

1,000,000 B.C. — A.D. 410

"*Because they knew no better, what the Britons called civilization . . . was but a part of their servitude.*"

TACITUS (A.D. CA 56–CA 120), ROMAN HISTORIAN

Early Times
Through
the Romans

Legend:
- Prehistoric monument
- Roman city
- Roman road
- Area under Roman civil government, first century A.D.
- Area under Roman military control, first century A.D.
- *Mide* — Celtic tribe

Shetland Islands
Broch of Mousa

Orkney Islands
Skara Brae
Ring of Brodgar

North Sea

Callanish Stones

Clava Cairns

Caledonii

Glenelg Brochs

Caterthun

A T L A N T I C

O C E A N

Temple Wood

Antonine Wall
Cairnpapple Hill

Damnonii

Hadrian's Wall
Luguvalium   Coriosopitum   Pons Aelius
Long Meg and   Concangis
Her Daughters

Carvetii

Grianan of Aileach
Beaghmore

Ulaid

Giant's Ring

Creevykeel Court Tomb
Carrowmore

Legananny

B R I T I S H   I S L E S

Isurium
Brigantum
Eboracum

Brigantes

Parisi
Petuaria

Connacht

Knowth
Newgrange
Mide
Hill of Tara

Irish Sea

Mamucium

I R E L A N D

Aquae Arnemetiae

Dún Aonghasa

Laigin

Barclodiad y Gawres
Segontium
Deceangli

Condate
Deva Victrix

Arbor Low

Lindum Colonia

Lough Gur

Mediolanum

Cornovii

Viroconium

Ratae Corieltauvorum

Corieltauvi

Happisburgh

Muman

Ordovices

Alauna

Lactodurum

Iceni

Staigue Fort

Pentre Ifan
Demetae
Moridunum

Y Garn Goch

Glevum

Dobunni

Corinium Dobunnorum

Catuvellauni

Verulamium

Trinovantes

Camulodunum

Silures

Isca Augusta
Venta Silurum

Celtic Sea

Aquae Sulis

Silbury Hill

Atrebates

Calleva

Kit's Coty House

Londinium

Durovernum Cantiacorum

Portus Dubris

Stonehenge

Belgae

Venta Belgarum

Regnenses

Cantiaci

Lindinis

Durotriges

Noviomagus Reginorum

Durnovaria

Dumnonii

Isca Dumnoniorum
Grimspound
Maiden Castle

The Hurlers

Chysauster

English Channel

miles
0   50   100

kilometers
0   50   100

EARLY BRITONS
AND FIRST CONQUEST

HISTORY IN THE BRITISH ISLES BEGAN WITH A SMALL FAMILY OF *HOMO ANTECESSOR*, a predecessor of our own species, wandering an ancient shore on England's east coast. A million or so years later, in 2013, violent winter storms revealed their preserved and long-hidden footprints—the earliest humanlike traces ever discovered in Britain and Ireland.

For a thousand millennia thereafter, a human presence in the islands ebbed and flowed, shaped by the glaciers of countless ice ages, cold forcing people south, warmth luring them back to a land rich in shelter and sustenance. Glacial ice also influenced the region's physical aspect, for Britain and Ireland were often not islands at all; rather, they were joined to Europe by a land bridge alternately lost and revealed by fluctuating postglacial sea levels.

Bison, mammoths, and other animals crossed this impermanent lifeline and helped sustain the small groups of Neanderthals and other hunter-gatherers who made up Britain's population until the appearance, around 45,000 years ago, of our own species, *Homo sapiens*. The new arrivals brought more sophisticated tools, such as flint blades and bone, ivory, and antler implements, along with more elaborate rituals of burial and worship. Among about 20 sites in the British Isles from this earliest era is Kents Cavern in Devon, home to a jaw fragment from 41,000 B.C.—Britain's earliest known remains of *Homo sapiens*.

Immense ice sheets pushed south into Britain around 25,000 B.C., but rising temperatures and sea levels around 13,000 B.C.

saw a return of hunter-gatherer groups, along with Britain's first known artists, who left work in the shape of etched animal bones and engraved cave paintings.

Since 8000 B.C., when the climate improved still further, Britain has been inhabited continuously. Ireland may also have been occupied during the same or previous periods, but the earliest human presence yet discovered on the island—at Mount Sandel in County Londonderry—probably dates from 8000 to 5000 B.C., the same period during which Britain and Ireland's coastline took on its present shape.

■ THE NEOLITHIC PERIOD

The Neolithic period (ca 4000–2400 B.C.) was a prehistoric watershed in Britain—the era when agriculture blossomed; when woodland was increasingly cleared; when pottery was made; and when pigs, sheep, and cattle were introduced, probably from Europe. Barley and early forms of wheat were planted, and simple ards, or scratch plows, were pioneered. Different settlement patterns also emerged, from isolated farmsteads and Ireland's communal longhouses to later village communities such as Skara Brae in the Orkney Islands.

Standing stones *(previous pages)* The Ring of Brodgar, a Neolithic stone circle on the Orkney Islands, off the northeast coast of mainland Scotland. Believed to date from 2500 to 2000 B.C., these stones, which had an unknown ritual purpose, make up the third-largest henge monument in Britain and Ireland. Like many prehistoric circles, such as Stonehenge, it stands at the heart of a much larger landscape of religious and ceremonial sites.

around 45,000 years ago
Homo sapiens arrive in Britain

25,000 B.C.
Immense ice sheets blanket Britain

13,000–10,000 B.C.
A warming climate ushers in return
of hunter-gatherer groups

6500–6000 B.C.
Britain's European land bridge disappears

ca 3000 B.C.
Creation of Stonehenge begins with circular
monument 375 feet in diameter

ca 2500 B.C.
Stonehenge second phase: Circles made
of sarsen stones and bluestones

1800–1500 B.C.
Stonehenge third phase:
two concentric pit rings

1000 B.C.
Ironworking arrives in Britain and Ireland

200 B.C.
An estimated two million people populate
Britain and Ireland

A.D. 43
Roman troops invade Britain. Defeat
English at the Battle of the Medway.

A.D. 60
Boudicca, queen of the Iceni, rises in revolt

A.D. 69
Emperor Vespasian launches campaign
to control mainland Britain

A.D. 120
Londinium (London) becomes capital of
Roman Britain

A.D. 128
Hadrian's Wall completed

A.D. 208–211
Emperor Septimius Severus pushes north
of Hadrian's Wall

A.D. 410–411
The Romans retreat from Britain

2013
Storms off England's east coast
reveal human footprints nearly
one million years old

The Neolithic was also the age of great monuments such as Stonehenge. The first began to emerge around 3800 B.C. in the shape of vast earthworks known as causewayed camps. Up to a hundred such camps have been found, mostly in southern and eastern England. Most probably had a ritual purpose rather than a residential one, and many have yielded artifacts from distant parts of Britain, thus suggesting far-flung networks of exchange.

Britain and Ireland's first significant grave monuments also date from this period. Archaeologists have identified two broad traditions: long mounds, or cairns, which echoed the hall-like longhouses of the living (and resemble similar monuments across northern Europe); and passage graves, consisting of a central chamber approached by a stone-roofed passage. The latter are especially common on Britain and Ireland's coasts, notably around the Boyne Valley in Ireland, where Knowth, Dowth, and Newgrange, among others, make up one of Europe's finest Neolithic landscapes.

Around 3200 B.C., Neolithic society experienced a dramatic shift as older passage graves and long mounds were closed, smaller settlements coalesced into larger communities, and a new form of incised and patterned pottery known as Grooved Ware developed. Archaeologists are unsure of the reasons for the change, but the result was more coherent and more sophisticated cultures. This in turn may explain the appearance of Stonehenge and the other large, labor-intensive "henge" (circular) monuments for which the era is famous (see page 22).

■ THE BRONZE AGE

The Bronze Age (ca 2400–800 B.C.) takes its name from the working of bronze, an alloy of tin and copper. During this era of gradual change, agriculture became progressively more sophisticated and settlement concentrated in ever larger communities. By the end of the period, most lowland Britons were probably living in clusters of simple dwellings edged by a patchwork of ordered fields, the lines of which can still be seen across much of southwest England and elsewhere.

> *"The barbarians had risen and were overrunning the country, carrying off booty and causing great destruction . . . for effective defence more troops or the presence of the Emperor was necessary."*
>
> LUCIUS ALFENUS SENECIO, GOVERNOR OF BRITANNIA FROM A.D. 207 TO 211

The hill forts that dominated the later Iron Age (see below) also began to take shape, accompanied by a proliferation of weapons, suggesting increased social pressures and competition for resources. The old henge monuments survived until around 2000 B.C. but eventually were superseded as belief systems tied to individual burial replaced the mass rituals of the Neolithic period.

Many of the burial sites connected to these newer beliefs have yielded funerary artifacts of remarkable similarity. This is especially true of the era's distinctive beaker-shaped pots, whose ubiquity suggests the ease with which beliefs and culture had begun to spread along emerging lines of trade and communication. In time, other goods and materials became coveted—gold from Wales and Ireland; tin from Cornwall; jet, a black gemstone, from Yorkshire; amber, coral, and other items from Europe—and were traded more easily and frequently, leading to an even more fluid proliferation of ideas and culture.

■ THE IRON AGE

The Iron Age (800–43 B.C.) in England and Wales was marked by the use of iron tools and the creation of more than 3,000 earth and timber hill forts—some defensive and settled, others used to store grain or to enclose livestock. Scotland also had forts, as well as striking single stone coastal dwellings known as brochs or duns. Toward the end of the period, the consolidation of many forts led to the development of more defined tribal kingdoms, along with larger settlements later known as *oppida*, sometimes as successors to the forts but often at new lowland sites on routes of trade and communication.

The Iron Age also saw an important and increased migration of culture, language, and possibly peoples from northern Europe and beyond. These peoples are conveniently referred to as Celts and their culture and languages as Celtic. Archaeologists once talked of a Celtic "invasion" of the British Isles, but more recent research suggests a process of assimilation and integration. As a result, by about 200 B.C. Britain and Ireland's population had risen to about two million, and those parts of Britain geographically suited to trade with Europe—notably the southeast—were thriving. This prosperity, and the links with Gaul (present-day France), were among the reasons Rome first turned its attentions north.

■ THE RISE AND FALL OF ROMAN BRITAIN

The Romans had long traded with the Celts, but they first took an aggressive interest in Britain—they would never reach Ireland—when Julius Caesar launched two raids in 55 and 54 B.C. (see page 28). The first serious and successful attempt at conquest took place in A.D. 43. Within ten years, the new Roman province of Britannia was secure, though Wales proved more resistant to the newcomers, and the province's northern frontier near the present Scottish border remained troublesome even after construction began on Hadrian's Wall in A.D. 122 (see page 32).

The Battersea Shield *(above)* Decorated with Celtic motifs of French origin and adorned with red glass, possibly from Italy, this first-century-B.C. bronze shield was found in the River Thames, where it probably was cast as a ritual object.

Praising pagan gods *(opposite)* Ritual and worship were important elements of life in prehistoric Britain and Ireland. Here, men light a pyre and raise burning torches to the moon in a Bronze Age funerary rite on the banks of the River Thames.

Set in stone *(above)* The cluster of eight houses at Skara Brae on the Orkney Islands represents Europe's best preserved stone village from the Neolithic period. Most other settlements from the era were built largely from wood and have not survived.

Rome's legacy *(opposite)* Remains of the Roman baths and thermal springs in the city of Bath in southwest England. The city was one of many settlements founded or expanded by the Romans during their almost 400 years in Britain.

By this date, much farther south, a walled colony on the River Thames known as Londinium had emerged as the Romans' capital, profiting from the Thames and its Europe-facing estuary for trade, as well as its position as the obvious focus for a burgeoning network of Roman roads between new or revitalized urban centers.

Roads were not the only legacy of the 367 years of foreign rule. Latin and many Roman customs, laws, and religious beliefs were introduced, along with all the beauties of classical art and architecture. The elite could also enjoy the many civilizing boons of Roman daily life—hygiene, sanitation, spas, under-floor heating, and more (see page 30).

Roman rule also brought taxes and tributes, but much of southern Britain was prosperous, and remained so until the fourth century, when Roman hegemony began to crumble. Britannia then became prey to Irish and Scottish raiders, along with Saxon and other peoples from Europe. A string of forts and periodic revivals in Roman fortunes kept the intruders at bay for a while, but in A.D. 410–411, Rome's troubles elsewhere caused the once great empire to withdraw from its northernmost territories, never to return. ■

"Stone Age . . . Bronze Age . . . Iron Age . . .
We define entire epochs of humanity by the technology they use."

WILMOT REED HASTINGS, JR., CEO, NETFLIX

PREHISTORY

From First Footsteps to the Creation of the British Isles

I n the spring of 2013, powerful storms lashed the coast of eastern England and scoured beaches of mud and sand that had covered them for millennia. Near Happisburgh in Norfolk, the erosion revealed a series of ancient footprints, mysterious marks that were all too quickly lost to the elements—but not before scientists confirmed them as the most important archaeological discovery in Britain for a generation.

Flint tools between 850,000 and 950,000 years old had already been discovered at Happisburgh in 2010, and at that point they were the oldest traces of human activity ever found in Britain and Ireland. The footprints on the beach—marks left by a small family group wandering a riverbank or estuary shore around a million years ago—may have been older. Only Africa has yielded older footprints.

The tracks probably belonged to *Homo antecessor*—a species some scientists believe was a predecessor of our own—who crossed to Norfolk on the land bridge that existed between Britain and mainland Europe for much of the million years of prehistory. In an age without powerful tools to clear trees, and in a place where much of the land was thickly forested, rivers and riverbanks provided a refuge and a route into the wilderness for the few thousand people who called Britain home.

Almost half a million years separate the Happisburgh footprints from Britain and Ireland's oldest physical human remains. These were found at an ancient hunters' site near West Sussex, close to a prehistoric watering hole, between 1993 and 1995. Here, among flint tools and the remains of butchered rhino and bison, were teeth and bone fragments belonging to *Homo heidelbergensis,* a species later than *Homo antecessor* that dates from around 500,000 B.C.

Homo heidelbergensis were present for almost 200,000 years, coming and going through all but the coldest eras of what is known as the Anglian ice age between 470,000 and 425,000 B.C. After the retreat of the ice—which penetrated deep into southern England—the Acheulean culture of this period came increasingly to the fore,

In for the kill The lives of early Britons revolved around hunting and scavenging, and remained essentially unchanged for almost a million years.

leaving sophisticated tools at sites such as Hoxne in Suffolk, in eastern England.

Little else then changed in Britons' hunter-scavenger way of life until around 250,000 B.C., when more widespread evidence of advanced tool-making techniques emerges. Where once pebbles had been used to shape chunks of flint, now hammer stones, wood, and antler were utilized to remove smaller flakes of rock to produce increasingly refined edges for cutting and sawing. Many archaeologists ascribe the appearance of these more sophisticated tools to the arrival in Britain of *Homo neanderthalensis*—Neanderthals.

Only a handful of Neanderthal tools or fossils have been discovered in Britain, notably at Pontnewydd Cave in Wales, Creswell Crags in Derbyshire, and, most recently (in 2010), near Dartford in Kent. However, the diffusion of flaked tools suggests that the Neanderthal or other peoples responsible for the implements were widespread, at least in England and Wales (no Neanderthal sites are known in Ireland or in the far north and west of Britain).

As with other peoples across the millennia, climate largely governed the broad cycles of Neanderthal presence in Britain. The periodic cooling associated with numerous ice ages saw prehistoric Britons retreat south, while the rise in sea levels of post–ice age warming submerged the ancient land bridge that allowed them to cross between Britain and mainland Europe.

Yet the Neanderthals remained hunter-gatherers for at least 150,000 years. Their way of life only changed around 45,000 years ago, with the appearance in Europe of our species, *Homo sapiens.* Much mystery surrounds the emergence of *Homo sapiens,* along with uncertainty as to how the new species interacted with *Homo neanderthalensis.* By around 10,000 to 13,000 years ago, however, "modern" humans were established, and the last major ice sheet had retreated from the British Isles. The period from 6000 to 6500 B.C. also saw the final disappearance of Britain's European land bridge, and with it the emergence of something close to the present coastline of the British Isles. ∎

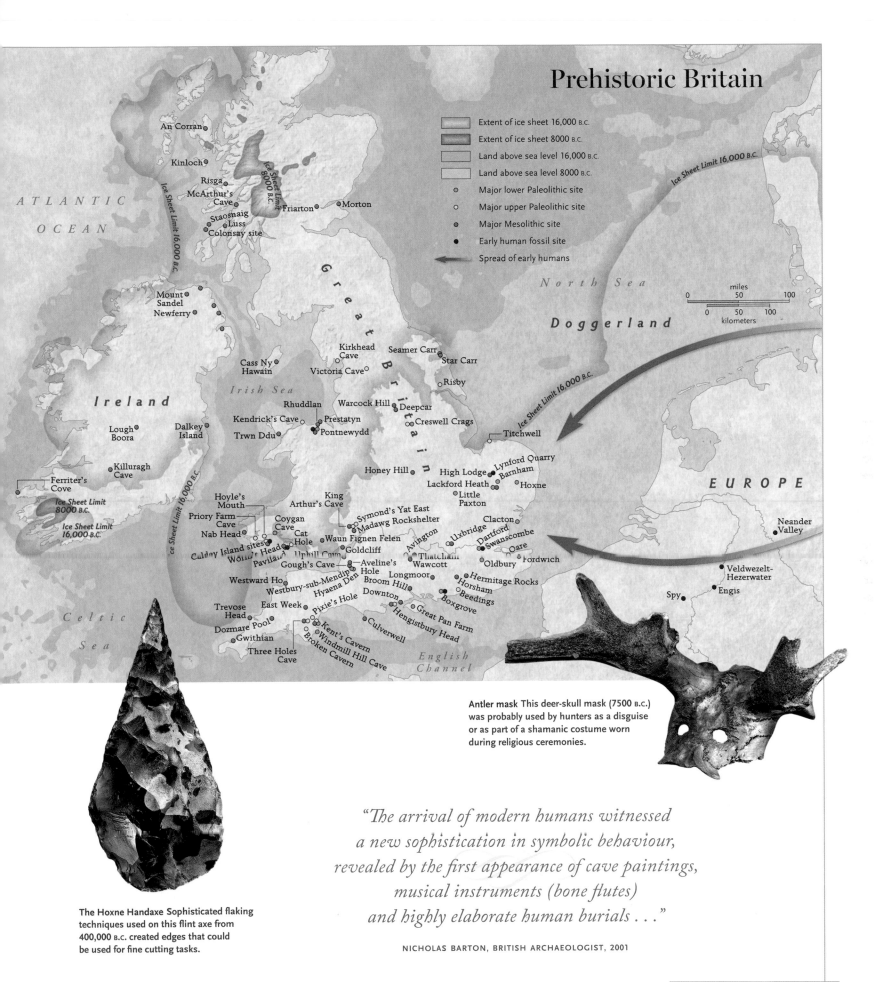

Prehistoric Britain

Extent of ice sheet 16,000 B.C.
Extent of ice sheet 8000 B.C.
Land above sea level 16,000 B.C.
Land above sea level 8000 B.C.

○ Major lower Paleolithic site
○ Major upper Paleolithic site
○ Major Mesolithic site
● Early human fossil site
→ Spread of early humans

ATLANTIC OCEAN

North Sea

Doggerland

An Corran

Kinloch

Risga
McArthur's Cave
Staosnaig
Luss
Colonsay site
Friarton
Morton

Ice Sheet Limit 8000 B.C.

Ice Sheet Limit 16,000 B.C.

Ice Sheet Limit 16,000 B.C.

Mount Sandel
Newferry

Ireland

Irish Sea

Cass Ny Hawain

Kirkhead Cave
Victoria Cave
Seamer Carr
Star Carr
Risby

Lough Boora
Dalkey Island

Killuragh Cave

Ferriter's Cove

Ice Sheet Limit 8000 B.C.
Ice Sheet Limit 16,000 B.C.

Ice Sheet Limit 16,000 B.C.

Rhuddlan
Kendrick's Cave
Prestatyn
Trwn Ddu
Pontnewydd

Warcock Hill
Deepcar
Creswell Crags

Titchwell

Great Britain

Honey Hill
High Lodge
Lackford Heath
Little Paxton
Lynford Quarry
Barnham
Hoxne

Hoyle's Mouth
King Arthur's Cave
Priory Farm Cave
Nab Head
Coygan Cave
Cat Hole
Culdey Island sites
Womb's Head
Pavilard
Gough's Cave
Westward Ho
Westbury-sub-Mendip
Hyaena Den
Trevose Head
East Week
Dozmare Pool
Gwithian
Three Holes Cave

Symond's Yat East
Madawg Rockshelter
Waun Fignen Felen
Goldcliff
Uphill Cave
Aveline's Hole
Broom Hill
Pixie's Hole
Kent's Cavern
Windmill Hill Cave
Broken Cavern

Avington
Thatcham
Wawcott
Longmoor
Downton
Culverwell

Uxbridge
Dartford
Swanscombe
Oare
Oldbury
Fordwich
Hermitage Rocks
Horsham
Beedings
Boxgrove
Great Pan Farm
Hengistbury Head

Clacton

EUROPE

Neander Valley

Veldwezelt-Hezerwater

Spy
Engis

Celtic Sea

English Channel

Antler mask This deer-skull mask (7500 B.C.) was probably used by hunters as a disguise or as part of a shamanic costume worn during religious ceremonies.

The Hoxne Handaxe Sophisticated flaking techniques used on this flint axe from 400,000 B.C. created edges that could be used for fine cutting tasks.

"The arrival of modern humans witnessed a new sophistication in symbolic behaviour, revealed by the first appearance of cave paintings, musical instruments (bone flutes) and highly elaborate human burials . . ."

NICHOLAS BARTON, BRITISH ARCHAEOLOGIST, 2001

THE NEOLITHIC

The Rise of Agriculture and the Age of Stonehenge

The Neolithic (4000–2400 B.C.) is the period in which British and Irish history springs to life, not least because it is the era that bequeathed some of the world's most majestic prehistoric monuments. It is also the age that saw increasingly advanced forms of agriculture replace the hunting and scavenging that had sustained humans for more than a million years. The two developments are linked, for the societies that created the monumental landscapes of Stonehenge and elsewhere were also the societies in which farming had created the larger and more coherent populations necessary to coordinate such vast projects.

Archaeologists believe settlers from Europe probably imported the techniques that improved British agriculture, along with better-bred domestic animals such as sheep, pigs, and horses. With improved resources came new belief systems, as well as improvements in trade and communication over longer distances. At the same time, vestiges of an earlier age also survived, notably the use of stone tools, which prevailed until ironworking arrived in Britain and Ireland around 1000 B.C.

Human habitation in the Neolithic varied over time and according to how the land was used. At the start of the era short-term individual homesteads were based around seasonal grazing or cultivation. Over hundreds of years these homesteads evolved into clustered

Village life *(above)* A re-creation of the Neolithic village at Durrington Walls, two miles northeast of Stonehenge. The settlement consisted of up to a thousand dwellings and was home to 4,000 people.

Work and worship *(below)* Stone axe heads dating from 4000 to 2400 B.C., found near Exeter in Devon, in southwest England. Most Neolithic axes were used as tools, but some may also have had a ritual purpose.

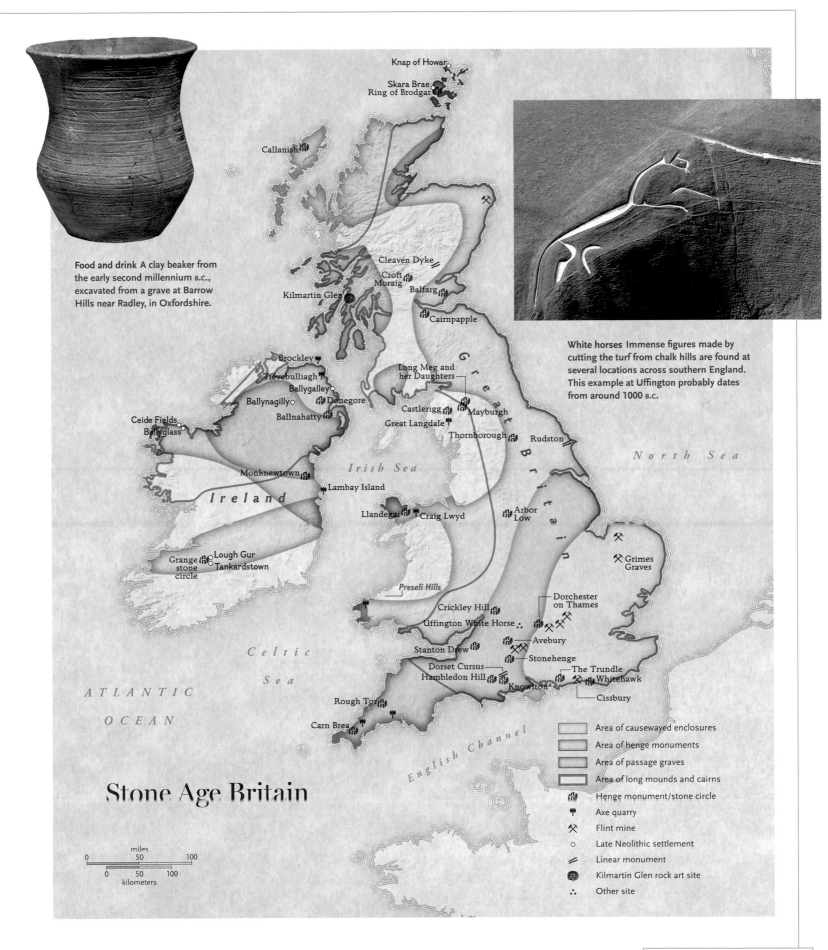

Food and drink A clay beaker from the early second millennium B.C., excavated from a grave at Barrow Hills near Radley, in Oxfordshire.

White horses Immense figures made by cutting the turf from chalk hills are found at several locations across southern England. This example at Uffington probably dates from around 1000 B.C.

Knap of Howar
Skara Brae
Ring of Brodgar

Callanish

Cleaven Dyke
Croft Moraig
Balfarg
Kilmartin Glen
Cairnpapple

Brockley
Tievebulliagh
Ballygalley
Ballynagilly
Donegore
Ballnahatty
Ceide Fields
Ballyglass

Long Meg and her Daughters
Castlerigg
Mayburgh
Great Langdale
Thornborough
Rudston

Great Britain

North Sea

Irish Sea

Monknewtown
Lambay Island

Ireland

Llandegai
Craig Lwyd
Arbor Low

Grimes Graves

Grange stone circle
Lough Gur
Tankardstown

Preseli Hills

Dorchester on Thames

Crickley Hill
Uffington White Horse
Avebury
Stanton Drew
Stonehenge
Dorset Cursus
Hambledon Hill
Knowlton
The Trundle
Whitehawk
Cissbury

Celtic Sea

ATLANTIC OCEAN

Rough Tor
Carn Brea

English Channel

Stone Age Britain

	Area of causewayed enclosures
	Area of henge monuments
	Area of passage graves
	Area of long mounds and cairns

🛕 Henge monument/stone circle
⚒ Axe quarry
⚒ Flint mine
○ Late Neolithic settlement
╱ Linear monument
◉ Kilmartin Glen rock art site
∴ Other site

miles
0   50   100

0   50   100
kilometers

villages edged with plowed fields and cleared woodlands. Most settlements were made of timber, mud, and straw, though remarkable stone settlements have also survived, notably in the Orkney Islands off the northeast coast of Scotland.

As Neolithic settlements grew, their populations acquired tribal characteristics. Political structures, leaders, and hierarchies also emerged. These in turn created the organizational and physical resources required to build Stonehenge and the other great monuments of the age.

■ THE BIRTH OF MONUMENTAL LANDSCAPES

Like the improvements in agriculture, the models for many monuments probably came from Europe. The earliest British models, which date from around 3800 B.C., consisted of earthwork causewayed camps or enclosures. Most were probably used for ritual purposes, though the degree to which ritual and domestic life were separated in this period's monuments has long vexed archaeologists.

More sophisticated structures called long mounds and cursuses—linear and other ditched enclosures—appeared around 3400 B.C., along with a wide variety of monuments to the dead. The first henge monuments—circular structures in wood and stone—followed around 3000 B.C. and, by 2500 B.C., were found across much of Britain and Ireland. Some, such as Stonehenge, were linked to the movements of the sun (and possibly the moon), though their precise ritual purpose, despite considerable conjecture, remains unknown.

■ THE CREATION OF STONEHENGE

Europe's most famous prehistoric monument lies at the heart of a much wider landscape of ancient sites across the open hills of southwest England. Its eventual form was the culmination of modifications over at least 1,500 years, beginning around 3000 B.C. with the creation of a circular ditch-and-bank monument 375 feet in diameter. Stone or timber posts, or a combination of the two, were then arranged in linear patterns within the circle.

At some point, probably around 2500–2200 B.C., the site was transformed by the introduction of circles made of stones from two principal sources. The larger sarsen stones were brought from the Marlborough Downs, a range of hills about 20 miles to the north. The smaller bluestones—so-called because they have a blue tinge when wet or freshly cut—were brought by land and water from the Preseli Hills more than 150 miles away in southwest Wales.

The sarsens each weigh up to 50 tons and were arranged in an inner horseshoe and outer circle. The two-to-five-ton bluestones were set up between them in a double arc, and then rearranged 200 or 300 years later into a circle and an inner oval (which were altered again later to form the current horseshoe).

The standing stones were manhandled into sloped holes and then hauled upright using ropes, weights, and timber supports. The lintel stones were probably raised gradually on timber scaffolds. The lintel and standing stones were joined using intricate mortise holes and protruding tenons, and the lintel stones were linked using sophisticated tongue-and-groove joints.

A third phase of building between 1800 and 1500 B.C. involved the digging of two concentric rings of pits, possibly for more circles or for a rearrangement of the bluestones that was never completed.

■ THE STONEHENGE SITE

While much is understood about the building of Stonehenge, less is known about the site's origins. The circles' location, like that of the many ancient sites nearby, may be a result of the open and gently undulating grassland common to the region's chalk downs. At a time when much of Britain was forested, and clearance required considerable labor, an already open site had obvious advantages.

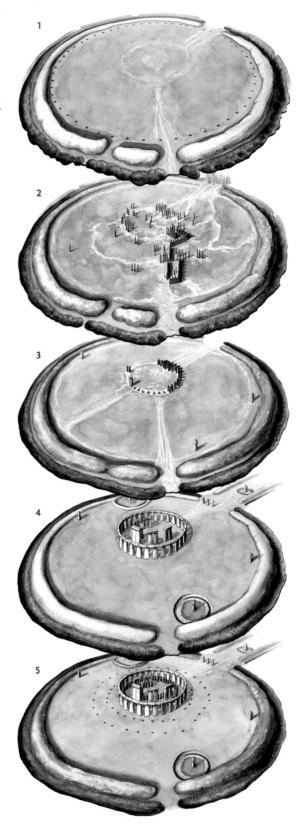

Moreover, the region was already rich in ritual significance. Surviving close to Stonehenge are at least four deep pits from 8000 B.C.—probably dug to contain timber posts from a ceremonial structure—as well as barrow tombs and earth causeway monuments from 4000 B.C.

Like most henge monuments, Stonehenge was built on natural routes across the landscape, so it was accessible to large numbers of people. In this case it was the Ridgeway, Britain's oldest "road," a route that is at least 5,000 years old and can still be traced along a line of high ground between Dorset on the southwest coast and the Wash in eastern England.

Like similar monuments, Stonehenge has yielded artifacts from outside its immediate vicinity. Many of these artifacts share certain characteristics, such as the distinctive motifs that link a vessel found near Oxford, a tomb in Orkney, and a mace head from the Boyne Valley in Ireland. Such similarities suggest that beliefs at the time were held and shared widely, and may even have been disseminated by rituals akin to pilgrimage. Research at Stonehenge, for example, suggests that as many as 4,000 people may have congregated repeatedly at the site.

■ THE MYSTERY OF THE STONES

Archaeologists know that in its earliest incarnations, from about 3000 to 2400 B.C., Stonehenge was used as a cremation cemetery. Theories as to its use thereafter proliferate. They include the ideas that it was a place of coronation for Danish kings, a Druid or Roman temple, or the site of Celtic sacrifice—all quaint but impossible ideas because they involve a later time frame. Some scholars claim the site was a cult place of healing because many burials show signs of trauma and deformity, suggesting people went to Stonehenge in a failed attempt to be cured of disease or disability. Others believe it was a place of ancestor worship or a vast astronomical device for predicting solar and lunar events.

The last theory is probably closest to the truth, for the site has clear astronomical alignments. Thus, the most widely accepted idea today is that Stonehenge was a temple linked to the movement of the sun, albeit one that was set in a much wider geographical and ultimately unknowable ritual context. ■

Story of the stones *(opposite)* The great stone circle of Stonehenge has stood on Salisbury Plain in southern England for millennia. The probable stages of its construction are illustrated opposite and described below:

1. A circular ditch-and-bank monument, approximately 375 feet across, is cut into Salisbury Plain about 3000 B.C. **2.** In the middle of the Neolithic period, timber posts are erected in linear patterns. The site is used as a cemetery. **3.** By around 2400 B.C. pairs of four-ton bluestones are brought about 150 miles from Wales. **4.** Stonehenge gains its iconic shape with the creation of the 16-foot-high sarsen circle—30 worked stones topped by lintels. **5.** Bluestones that had been cast aside are repositioned as a circle, and a double ring of pits is dug.

Mysterious meaning The purpose of Stonehenge remains unclear. Among many theories are that it was a Druid place of worship, a center of healing, or a device for predicting solar and lunar events. Most archaeologists now believe that it was a site linked to the movement of the sun.

THE IRON AGE
Home, Hearth, and Ritual in the Celtic Hill Forts

The Iron Age in Britain and Ireland ran from 800 B.C. to A.D. 43, an 800-year span that saw many variations in lifestyle and settlement, but during which tribes across the islands were often linked by trade, language, farming, and cultural exchange.

Life in the hilltop forts, whose remains still scatter the British Isles, was probably typical of the time. Individual families or social groups within the enclosures lived in huts and roundhouses constructed of wood, thatch, and a weatherproof daub of clay, straw, and animal manure. Smaller huts housed animals or provided storage. Pits were dug for additional storage, and huts were ringed with drainage ditches.

Inside, a fire burned constantly for warmth, cooking, and the smoking or drying of meat, fish, and herbs. Spelt, barley, oats, and rye were used to make beer, porridge, and bread, which were supplemented by milk, dairy, honey, nuts, berries, and other wild foods. Livestock such as pigs, cattle, and sheep were widespread, and horses were used to pull carts and chariots. Roman writers praised the abilities of Britain's domesticated working dogs, which were exported across Europe.

The same Roman writers remarked on the appearance of the Britons, in particular on the vivid colors, stripes, and checks of their clothes. Tunics of wool and linen, tied with a belt, were worn over tight breeches. Cloaks were popular, and they were fastened with a wide variety of decorative brooches and pins, many of which have survived. Men and women wore their hair long, often braided, and men sported beards, mustaches, and ceremonial bronze or gold neck rings known as torques.

Color and decoration were not limited to personal and domestic ornaments. Iron and bronze artifacts such as decorative shields and swords, along with gold, amber, glass, coral, and semiprecious stones, testify to the considerable artistic sophistication of the age, a phenomenon in part inspired by trade and cultural exchange with Celtic cultures in France and elsewhere.

Ritual and religious life underlined the importance of agriculture, with most ceremonies and festivals tied to the seasons. For example, Irish oral tradition spoke of the feasts of Imbolc—a time in February, possibly tied to the lactation of ewes and the start of a new life cycle for livestock—and Samhain, in November, which marked the end of one year and beginning of the next. Samhain was also a time when spirits could pass between worlds, a distant echo of our own Halloween. The gods of earth and water were placated with sacrifice, or with the burial of precious ritual objects that are regularly discovered to this day. ■

Neolithic defenses Maiden Castle near Dorchester in southwest England is one of the largest and most complex Iron Age forts in Europe. One of several hundred similar settlements across Britain, it attained its present size around 450 B.C. after having been a site of ritual and other importance since at least 4000 B.C. Earth and timber ramparts protected its population until the fort fell into decline around 100 B.C.

"The Iron Age Britain into which the Romans eventually crashed was a dynamic, expanding society. Protected by hillforts . . . with recognizable street patterns, places of ceremony and worship and rich with forges and workshops."

SIMON SCHAMA, *A HISTORY OF BRITAIN*, 2000

Home and hearth *(above)* Iron Age dwellings were built within enclosures shielded by earth banks and wooden palisades. Individual huts were constructed in the lee of the enclosure to provide protection from the elements.

A foreign field *(right)* This first- or second-century-B.C. bronze and enamel clasp probably came from a horse's harness. Although it is British, it was found in France, suggesting the extensive links between the Celtic cultures of the period.

ROMAN CONQUEST
England and Wales Succumb to the Power of Rome

Britain was no stranger to the burgeoning power of Rome in the last centuries of the Iron Age. Tribes in southeast England traded with Roman merchants, and Mediterranean culture had already begun to infiltrate the Celtic world. English tribes also traded with their counterparts in Gaul (modern-day France), and it was probably these links that first attracted the more belligerent attention of Rome.

This attention came in the shape of Julius Caesar (100 B.C.–44 B.C.), then fighting in Gaul, who made the first of two assaults on England in 55 B.C., possibly to forestall English interference with his French campaigns. On his first foray, he established a beachhead on England's south coast, only to be forced to withdraw after four days of storms battered his troops. The following summer he returned with 800 ships and 27,000 men, defeating various tribal chieftains before marching inland (possibly as far as the River Thames). Forced to attend to more pressing problems in Gaul, he retreated across the English Channel, never to return, having probably spent just 20 days in Britain.

Emperor Augustus (63 B.C.–A.D. 14) threatened but never carried out assaults on Britain on at least three occasions. A Roman invasion of sorts finally took place in A.D. 43, when around 50,000 men landed in southern England and defeated the English at the Battle of the Medway. Emperor Claudius (10 B.C.–A.D. 54) himself then visited Britain but stayed for less time than Caesar—just 16 days, long enough to receive the submission of 11 British kings at Colchester, the capital of the dominant Catuvellauni tribe.

Over the next four years, the Romans advanced through southern England. At first the process was less one of conquest than of assimilation, for many tribes already had so-called client kings who paid a tribute to retain power under Roman protection. More force was required in the wilds of Wales (which were not subdued until around A.D. 75) and in the face of revolts such as that of Boudicca in A.D. 60 (see sidebar).

Around A.D. 69, Emperor Vespasian instigated a campaign probably designed to bring all of mainland Britain under Roman control. One of his generals, Quintus Petillius Cerialis, reached as far north as Carlisle by A.D. 74; another, Gnaeus Julius Agricola, pushed deep into Scotland from A.D. 77 to 83, possibly as far as Inverness, where he may have defeated the Caledonii tribe at the Battle of Mons Graupius (ca A.D. 83). Scotland's remote margins would never be entirely secured, however, and fortresses there were abandoned as early as A.D. 87, by which date the "conquest" of much of the rest of Roman Britannia was complete. ∎

Boudicca's Revolt

British rulers under the Romans had to pay for the privilege of their positions, so when the king of the Iceni died in A.D. 60, he left half his inheritance to Emperor Nero and half to his wife, Boudicca. When the Romans took the entire legacy, flogged Boudicca, and raped her daughters, Boudicca and the Iceni rose in revolt. They razed Roman Colchester and slaughtered the Ninth Legion before moving to London, where burned debris below the old city and skulls hacked from their bodies testify to the ferocity of the assault. Boudicca eventually took poison rather than be captured.

Caesar in Britain Roman soldiers land on the southeast coast of England and subdue the native Celtic inhabitants. Roman general Julius Caesar was probably the first to bring troops to Britain in 55 and 54 B.C., though his precise landing points, and the course of his two short campaigns in the country, remain a mystery.

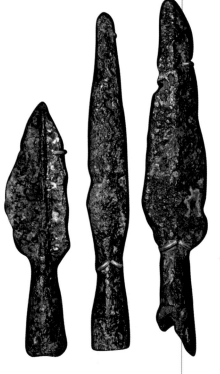

To the point Spear tips from a Roman fort at Camerton, near Bath. Such spearheads were designed to break off on impact to prevent the enemy from reusing them.

"In stature she was tall and in appearance most terrifying, her glance fierce, her voice harsh, and with a mass of tawny hair cascading to her hips."

DIO CASSIUS (DIED A.D. 235), ROMAN HISTORIAN, ON BOUDICCA

Claudius The Romans invaded Britain in A.D. 43 on the orders of Emperor Claudius (10 B.C.–A.D. 54), depicted here in an idealized contemporary marble bust.

ROMAN BRITAIN
The Rise and Fall of Rome's Northernmost Province

Some early historians saw the Britons under the Romans as a surly people enslaved by tyrannical masters. Others painted them as benighted individuals rescued by the civilizing effects of Rome. In fact, many Britons benefited from the newcomers, and many had already developed sophisticated social, cultural, and economic structures long before the arrival of Claudius in A.D. 43 (see page 28).

At the same time, Britain—Britannia to the Romans—did change under Rome, and the first motor of change was its great standing army. After A.D. 80, about 16,000 legionaries, along with a similar number of auxiliary troops, were stationed in England and Wales. All needed supplying, and as a result, small civilian towns *(vici)* soon developed around many of the new Roman forts. Larger towns *(coloniae)* such as York and Gloucester evolved to accommodate army veterans, while others *(civitas)* grew up on or close to the sites of former tribal settlements adopted by Romans as new administrative centers.

All these towns provided rich craft, agricultural, and mercantile opportunities, and all were eventually linked by new roads such as Watling Street, the Fosse Way, and Ermine Street. Many also gained access to Rome's wider markets through ports at Chichester, Dover, Richborough, and London. By A.D. 120, London had displaced Colchester as the capital of Roman Britain (Britannia), a substantial province in A.D. 300 with a population that may have been as high as five million.

Many Britons benefited from Rome's rich heritage (see sidebar), but cultural and other types of interchange were not all one-way. Tribal leaders paid tributes to Rome, and organized taxation arrived in the shapes of a much hated *tributum capitis,* or poll tax (levied per head); a sales tax; and a 5 percent inheritance tax. Rome also availed itself of British raw materials such as coal, iron, jet, lead, salt, gold, silver, and especially Cornish tin, a constituent of bronze.

Decline inevitably set in as Rome itself declined. After the third century many towns, including London, had to be walled, and after the fourth century few new villas were built. Trades and crafts stagnated, and economic activity declined as troops were withdrawn to bolster the empire's borders elsewhere. At the end of the fourth century, many Britons and their leaders, far from cheering Rome's fall, argued about how best they could prevail upon the Romans to stay. ■

Romans and Barbarians This idealized painting by English artist Henry Perronet Briggs (1793–1844) is titled "The Romans Teaching the Mechanical Arts to the Ancient Britons" (1831). Rome's main cultural legacy in Britain was often found in the many villas that dotted the more prosperous and Romanized rural areas of southern and central England. Often built on profits from farming, most of these grand houses had a level of artistic and domestic refinement—frescoed walls, under-floor heating, and tiled or mosaic flooring—then unknown in the British Isles.

Britain's Roman Towns

Urban settlements of many types proliferated across much of Britain during the Roman era. While rarely as grand as their European counterparts, English and Welsh towns had all the components of Roman towns elsewhere in the empire, such as baths, forums (public squares), amphitheaters, and basilicas (large trade buildings and social meeting places). Only classical temples were relatively few in number, possibly because Britain's Celtic deities continued to be worshipped widely, and even temples to Roman gods were built to the Celtic plan of an enclosed area around a small inner cell.

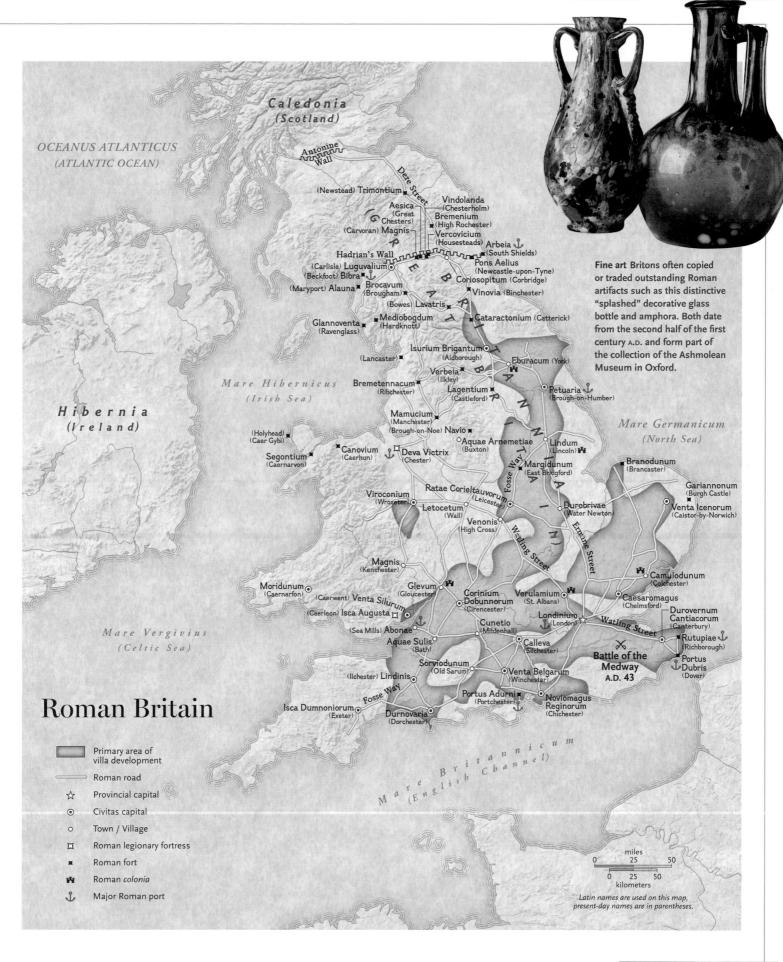

Caledonia
(Scotland)

OCEANUS ATLANTICUS
(ATLANTIC OCEAN)

Antonine Wall

Dere Street

Trimontium (Newstead)

Vindolanda
(Chesterholm)

Aesica
(Great
Chesters)

Bremenium
(High Rochester)

Magnis (Carvoran)

Vercovicium
(Housesteads)

Hadrian's Wall

Arbeia
(South Shields)

Luguvalium (Carlisle)

Pons Aelius
(Newcastle-upon-Tyne)

Bibra (Beckfoot)

Coriosopitum (Corbridge)

Alauna (Maryport)

Brocavum
(Brougham)

Vinovia (Binchester)

Lavatris (Bowes)

Cataractonium (Catterick)

Glannoventa
(Ravenglass)

Mediobogdum
(Hardknott)

Isurium Brigantum
(Aldborough)

Eburacum (York)

(Lancaster)

Verbeia
(Ilkley)

Mare Hibernicus
(Irish Sea)

Bremetennacum
(Ribchester)

Lagentium
(Castleford)

Petuaria
(Brough-on-Humber)

Hibernia
(Ireland)

Mamucium
(Manchester)

Navio
(Brough-on-Noe)

Aquae Arnemetiae
(Buxton)

Lindum
(Lincoln)

Mare Germanicum
(North Sea)

Holyhead
(Caer Gybi)

Canovium
(Caerhun)

Deva Victrix
(Chester)

Branodunum
(Brancaster)

Segontium
(Caernarvon)

Margidunum
(East Bridgford)

Gariannonum
(Burgh Castle)

Viroconium
(Wroxeter)

Ratae Corieltauvorum
(Leicester)

Durobrivae
(Water Newton)

Venta Icenorum
(Caistor-by-Norwich)

Letocetum
(Wall)

Fosse Way

Venonis
(High Cross)

Magnis
(Kenchester)

Ermine Street

Watling Street

Camulodunum
(Colchester)

Moridunum
(Caernarfon)

Glevum
(Gloucester)

Corinium
Dobunnorum
(Cirencester)

Verulamium
(St. Albans)

Caesaromagus
(Chelmsford)

Venta Silurum (Caerwent)

Isca Augusta (Caerleon)

Cunetio
(Mildenhall)

Londinium
(London)

Watling Street

Durovernum
Cantiacorum
(Canterbury)

Abonae (Sea Mills)

Aquae Sulis
(Bath)

Calleva
(Silchester)

Rutupiae
(Richborough)

Battle of the
Medway
A.D. 43

Portus
Dubris
(Dover)

Sorviodunum
(Old Sarum)

Venta Belgarum
(Winchester)

Lindinis (Ilchester)

Isca Dumnoniorum
(Exeter)

Fosse Way

Portus Adurni
(Portchester)

Noviomagus
Reginorum
(Chichester)

Durnovaria
(Dorchester)

Mare Vergivius
(Celtic Sea)

Mare Britannicum
(English Channel)

Roman Britain

Primary area of
villa development

Roman road

☆ Provincial capital

⊙ Civitas capital

○ Town / Village

⌂ Roman legionary fortress

∎ Roman fort

🏰 Roman *colonia*

⚓ Major Roman port

Fine art Britons often copied
or traded outstanding Roman
artifacts such as this distinctive
"splashed" decorative glass
bottle and amphora. Both date
from the second half of the first
century A.D. and form part of
the collection of the Ashmolean
Museum in Oxford.

miles
0   25   50

0   25   50
kilometers

Latin names are used on this map,
present-day names are in parentheses.

THE NORTHERN FRONTIER

Hadrian's Wall and the Taming of a Troubled Border

◆ KEY DATES ◆

A.D. 122 **Emperor Hadrian visits Britain with a plan for a wall that will help consolidate its troubled northern frontier.**

A.D. 128 **Work on the wall is completed in just six years. It runs for 73 miles across some of Britain's wildest terrain.**

A.D. 138 **A new emperor, Antoninus, begins a second barrier to the north of Hadrian's Wall. Within 30 years it has been abandoned.**

Emperor Hadrian (A.D. 76–138) visited Britain in A.D. 122. He was the first emperor to do so since Claudius in A.D. 43 (see page 28). Forty years earlier, Roman forces had penetrated deep into Scotland (see page 28), only to withdraw over several decades—in the face of weather, wilderness, and hostile natives—to an ill-defined frontier region of forts, fortified roads, and unruly tribes across the remote far north of present-day England.

One of Rome's wisest emperors, Hadrian was known for reining in the empire's unsustainable expansion and defending its existing frontiers. Bringing the same wisdom to Britain, he resolved not to extend but to consolidate the province's troublesome northern border. The result was Hadrian's Wall, begun in A.D. 122 and completed in just six years. Built by 15,000 legionaries with the help of British labor, it stretched for 73 miles from Britain's east to west coast.

For most of its course, Hadrian's Wall consisted of an earth (later stone) rampart up to 15 feet high and backed by a *vallum,* or fortified ditch, between two mound walls. Major forts also lined much of its route, and every mile there was a gate protected by a barracks, or milecastle. The Romans' finest frontier fortification, Hadrian's Wall remains Britain's—and one of Europe's—best preserved monuments from antiquity.

At the time, the wall was intended not as a definitive border to be defended at all costs—though it eventually helped define today's border between England and Scotland—but as a place from which to police movement across the region and to collect tolls and taxes from people crossing. It also served as a scouting base and fallback for isolated Roman forts across the intractable region to the north.

Within months of Hadrian's death in A.D. 138, his successor, Antoninus Pius (86–161), determined to reoccupy the lands beyond Hadrian's Wall. Over the next four years, he built his own earth defense, the 37-mile Antonine Wall, about 100 miles to the north of Hadrian's Wall. Within 25 years, Antoninus's successor, Marcus Aurelius (121–180), preoccupied by problems elsewhere in the empire, pulled Rome's forces back to Hadrian's original wall.

Hadrian's old frontier remained the limit of Roman expansion for 50 years, until the campaigns of Emperor Septimius Severus (ca 145–211) between A.D. 208 and 211. Severus went to Britain, where he confronted the belligerence of two tribes, the Maeatae and the Caledonii, with several powerful land and naval assaults. Crack elements of Rome's Praetorian Guard had pushed deep into Scotland when illness forced Severus to agree to peace (he would die in York shortly afterward), at which point the Romans withdrew from Scotland's far north, never to return.

By A.D. 285, new Angle and Saxon raiding parties from Europe were testing Rome's defensive capabilities, and a preoccupation with the northern frontier gave way to a line of fortifications along England's eastern and southern coasts known as the Saxon Shore. After A.D. 367, and the rise of the powerful Picts and Scotii in Scotland, Rome abandoned the troubled lands north of Hadrian's Wall once and for all. ■

Stone splendor A second-century relief from Hadrian's Wall. The area around the wall has yielded numerous carvings and inscriptions, providing valuable information about the daily lives of the Roman soldiers garrisoned in the region.

Borderline Almost 1,900 years after it was built, large sections of Hadrian's Wall still march across the beautiful but inhospitable landscapes of northern England.

"The Roman . . . frontier was usually more subtly nuanced. The empire shaded into 'foreign' territory across many kilometres that were a melting pot of cultural difference and often a hot-spot of trading and commercial activity."

MARY BEARD, *TIMES LITERARY SUPPLEMENT*, 2007

Emperor Hadrian The emperor responsible for the wall that bears his name visited Britain in A.D. 122 as part of a wider tour to assess the farthest reaches of the Roman Empire.

SAXONS TO NORMANS

A.D. 410–1066

"*Of their own free will, they invited in under the same roof the enemy they feared worse than death.*"

GILDAS (CA 475–CA 550), *THE RUIN OF BRITAIN*

Anglo-Saxon
Britain and Ireland

Anglo-Saxon kingdom, ca 700

○ Anglo-Saxon gold hoard

● Other gold hoard

N O R T H

S e a

A T L A N T I C

O C E A N

G R E A T

Bamburgh Hoard

NORTHUMBRIA

B R I T A I N

Irish Sea

West
Yorkshire
Hoard

Harkirke Hoard

LINDSEY

IRELAND

Pentney Treasure

EAST
ANGLIA

Staffordshire
Hoard

MERCIA

Ipswich Hoard

Brantham Hoard

ESSEX

Canterbury-
St. Martin's Hoard

Crondall Hoard

KENT

Celtic

WESSEX

SUSSEX

Appledore
Hoard

Sea

miles
0   50   100

0   50   100
kilometers

Trewhiddle Hoard

E n g l i s h   C h a n n e l

PAGAN INVADERS AND EARLY KINGDOMS

THE DEPARTURE OF THE ROMANS IN A.D. 410–411 WAS A WATERSHED FOR BRITAIN. AFTER almost four centuries of relative peace and prosperity, the former fragment of empire and its virtually helpless inhabitants faced an unprecedented onslaught from a medley of pagan aggressors. Resolute and relentless, the incomers swarmed across the sea from the lowlands of northern Europe. Southern England was worst hit, but Wales and Scotland were also affected. Age-old ways of life were obliterated, and beliefs, culture, and language were marginalized. Only Ireland was spared. Historians dispute the invaders' intent but agree on their identity—the Angles, the Saxons, and the Jutes—and few dispute that they came to stay.

And stay they did. Britain was no stranger to these tribes—they had long raided, traded with, and settled parts of England and Scotland—but without Rome's protective embrace, the Britons were all but powerless in the face of the incoming hordes. By the end of the fifth century, the newcomers had either assimilated many indigenous Britons or forced them west and north to join the Celtic tribes that had avoided Roman rule. In time, the incomers, along with their subjugated and reluctant hosts, formed a more or less single people who became known as the Saxons or the Anglo-Saxons.

The period is tantalizing, for while art and artifacts survive— many of them beautiful—written records are few and often unreliable. Much of what historians know comes from two writers: Gildas (ca 500–570), a British monk who wrote a vivid but dubious account of his people before and after the arrival of the Saxons; and the Venerable Bede (672/3–735), an Anglo-Saxon

monk who produced a more credible chronology from oral testimony and other sources collected long after the event.

■ SAXONS, CELTS, AND CHRISTIANITY

By the end of the fifth century, Celtic strongholds in the British Isles comprised Ireland, Wales, much of Scotland, and parts of northwest and southwest England. Saxon Britain, by contrast, embraced most of southern and eastern England. The two regions were largely separated by ethnicity and culture, but they evolved similar tribal structures. First came small fiefdoms (a throwback to pre-Roman times), followed by the emergence of larger kingdoms. These kingdoms acquired kings, but in Saxon Britain they also acknowledged a ruler of greater power—the *bretwalda* ("Britain ruler").

One of the first bretwaldas was Ethelbert (ca 560–616), the ruler of what is today Kent, the most formidable of the Saxons'

Saxon warrior *(previous pages)* Life across eastern Britain after the fall of Rome was dominated by the arrival of the Saxons, the Jutes, and the Angles, warlike and pagan peoples from the lowlands of northern Europe. Conquering or displacing many native Britons, they largely replaced Roman and earlier Celtic culture with their own beliefs, languages, and tribal kingdoms. The consequences can be felt across the British Isles to this day.

TIME LINE

563
St. Columba founds Iona Abbey

595
Canterbury becomes a focus of the mission
to convert England under Pope Gregory I

ca 600
Ethelbert becomes the first Saxon king
to convert to Christianity

604
St. Augustine founds St. Paul's Cathedral

604
St. Augustine establishes the archbishopric
at Canterbury

635
St. Aidan founds an abbey at Lindisfarne

793
Lindisfarne is desecrated by Vikings

871
Alfred the Great ascends the Wessex throne

878
Alfred prevails over the Viking army
at Battle of Edington

991
King Ethelred II starts to pay Vikings
to leave England in peace

1013
Danish king Forkbeard seizes Saxon throne;
Ethelred II flees to Normandy

1014
Forkbeard dies; Ethelred reclaims throne

1016
Ethelred dies; Cnut assumes control
of the country

1042
Edward the Confessor is crowned

1042
The Vikings leave England

1053
Godwin, Earl of Wessex, dies

1066
King Edward dies; Harold II, last Anglo-
Saxon king of England, is crowned

1066
William of Normandy defeats King Harold II
at Battle of Hastings

early kingdoms. Ethelbert is famous as the ruler who received a papal mission from Rome, and as the first Saxon king to convert to Christianity in A.D. 600 (most other Saxon rulers followed his example over the next 80 years. In Celtic Britain, men such as St. David in Wales and St. Patrick in Ireland forged a distinctive form of Celtic worship (see page 50).

Celtic Britain and Ireland also developed distinct political identities. This was especially true of Wales, where kingdoms developed that were more cohesive and owed much to the pre-Roman character of earlier Celtic tribes. Kingdoms remained smaller in Ireland, which was scattered with as many as 150 clan fiefdoms.

■ THE RISE OF THE SAXON KINGDOMS

Anglo-Saxon Britain, by contrast, consisted of just seven kingdoms around A.D. 600: Kent, Sussex, Essex, Wessex, Mercia, Northumbria, and East Anglia. The last, settled by the Angles, eventually lent its name to England. For the next 200 years, these kingdoms battled for supremacy.

Northumbria was the first to rise to prominence after Kent. Ascendancy then passed to Mercia, first under King Wulfhere (died ca 675), who probably expanded his kingdom as far as London; and then under King Offa (died 796), who was known for Offa's Dyke, an earth barrier (much of which survives) along Mercia's border with Wales. Offa's less effectual successors allowed dominance to pass to Wessex, which produced

what many historians regard as the first king of all the "English," Egbert of Wessex (died 839). Within years of coming to the throne, however, Egbert and the rest of Britain and Ireland faced a powerful threat from overseas.

■ THE VIKINGS

The Vikings came from Scandinavia—from parts of present-day Denmark, Norway, and Sweden—and initially had more or less one thing on their mind: plunder. They had no qualms about spilling Christian blood, nor any regrets about ransacking their victims' most sacred places. In Britain, this meant monasteries, which were both wealthy and virtually undefended. Better still, they were often on the coast, which made them perfect prey for the Vikings and their sublime seafaring skills.

Britain got its first taste of Viking methods in 787—a modest affair in which a royal official greeting the newcomers on a Wessex beach was summarily hacked to death. The monasteries soon followed, beginning in 793 with the raids on Lindisfarne, England's greatest religious house, and continuing in 795 and 806 with attacks on Iona, an equally precious abbey off Scotland's west coast.

Pickings were so easy that the Vikings quickly realized they need not stop at plunder: Conquest and settlement were there for the taking. They duly overwintered in Ireland for the first time in the 840s, and in Scotland they rapidly assimilated much of the northwest coast and most of the major islands. The story was the same in England, where the Saxon kingdoms tumbled one by one—East Anglia in 865, Mercia between 871 and 875, and Northumbria in 874. In time, only Wessex remained.

■ ENGLAND'S RISE AND FALL

Wessex fought back under two kings: Ethelred and his more celebrated brother, Alfred the Great (ca 849–899), whose victory over a Viking army in 878 spared Wessex and allowed it to flourish as a center of law, learning, and culture (see pages 54–55). Alfred's son, Edward the Elder (ca 870–924), consolidated his father's achievements. Alfred also persisted in war against the Vikings, who nevertheless continued to occupy, or reoccupy, large swathes of England and Scotland, areas later known as the Danelaw.

Edward was also busy on other fronts. He produced at least 18 children, a surfeit that all but guaranteed a subsequent period of dynastic uncertainty. One son, Ethelstan (ca 895–939), managed to be the first king formally to rule "all England," but affairs of state remained uncertain until the accession in 959 of King Edgar I (ca 943–975).

Edgar's reign marked the high point of Saxon power. England saw a return to peace and stability, the introduction of currency and other reforms, and the revival of the

Lost gold *(above)* This sublime filigree figure is one of more than 3,500 Anglo-Saxon artifacts from the Staffordshire Hoard, a priceless trove discovered by an amateur treasure hunter in a farmer's field in central England in 2009.

Viking attack *(opposite)* The Vikings were pagans from Scandinavia who began violent raids on most parts of the British Isles in the eighth century. Rich and undefended monasteries were among their favorite targets.

> "*They arrived with their mail shirts / Glittering, silver-shining links / Clanking an iron song as they came. / Sea-weary still, they set their broad, / Battle-hardened shields in rows / Along the wall . . . Their armor rang; / Their ash-wood spears stood in a line, / Grey-tipped and straight . . .*"

BEOWULF (CA 700–750)

HOUSES OF WESSEX AND DENMARK
802-1066

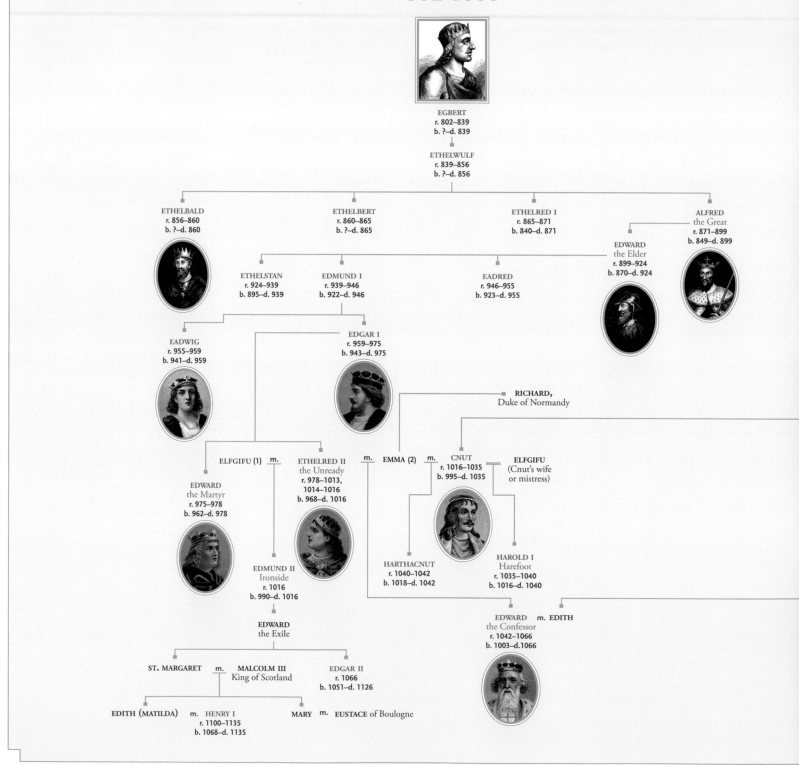

EGBERT
r. 802–839
b. ?–d. 839

ETHELWULF
r. 839–856
b. ?–d. 856

ETHELBALD
r. 856–860
b. ?–d. 860

ETHELBERT
r. 860–865
b. ?–d. 865

ETHELRED I
r. 865–871
b. 840–d. 871

ALFRED
the Great
r. 871–899
b. 849–d. 899

EDWARD
the Elder
r. 899–924
b. 870–d. 924

ETHELSTAN
r. 924–939
b. 895–d. 939

EDMUND I
r. 939–946
b. 922–d. 946

EADRED
r. 946–955
b. 923–d. 955

EADWIG
r. 955–959
b. 941–d. 959

EDGAR I
r. 959–975
b. 943–d. 975

RICHARD,
Duke of Normandy

ELFGIFU (1)   **m.**   **ETHELRED II**
the Unready
r. 978–1013,
1014–1016
b. 968–d. 1016

m.   **EMMA (2)**   **m.**   **CNUT**
r. 1016–1035
b. 995–d. 1035

ELFGIFU
(Cnut's wife
or mistress)

EDWARD
the Martyr
r. 975–978
b. 962–d. 978

EDMUND II
Ironside
r. 1016
b. 990–d. 1016

HARTHACNUT
r. 1040–1042
b. 1018–d. 1042

HAROLD I
Harefoot
r. 1035–1040
b. 1016–d. 1040

EDWARD
the Exile

EDWARD   **m. EDITH**
the Confessor
r. 1042–1066
b. 1003–d.1066

ST. MARGARET   **m.**   **MALCOLM III**
King of Scotland

EDGAR II
r. 1066
b. 1051–d. 1126

EDITH (MATILDA)   **m.**   **HENRY I**
r. 1100–1135
b. 1068–d. 1135

MARY   **m.**   **EUSTACE** of Boulogne

KINGS OF SCOTLAND

Kenneth mac Alpin r. 843–858 HOUSE OF ALPIN

Donald I r. 858–862 HOUSE OF ALPIN

Constantine I r. 862–877 HOUSE OF ALPIN

Aedh r. 877–878 HOUSE OF ALPIN

Eochaid r. 878–889 HOUSE OF ALPIN

Donald II r. 889–900 HOUSE OF ALPIN

Constantine II r. 900–943 HOUSE OF ALPIN

Malcolm I r. 943–954 HOUSE OF ALPIN

Indulf r. 954–962 HOUSE OF ALPIN

Dubh r. 962–966 HOUSE OF ALPIN

Culen r. 966–971 HOUSE OF ALPIN

Kenneth II r. 971–995 HOUSE OF ALPIN

Constantine III r. 995–997 HOUSE OF ALPIN

Kenneth III r. 997–1005 HOUSE OF ALPIN

Malcolm II r. 1005–1034 HOUSE OF ALPIN

Duncan I r. 1034–1040 HOUSE OF DUNKELD

Macbeth r. 1040–1057 HOUSE OF DUNKELD

Lulach (the Fool) r. 1057–1058 HOUSE OF DUNKELD

Malcolm III Canmore r. 1058–1093 HOUSE OF DUNKELD

Date Ranges Dates in early history are difficult to determine with certainty. The ranges given on this family tree are approximations based on the best resources available.

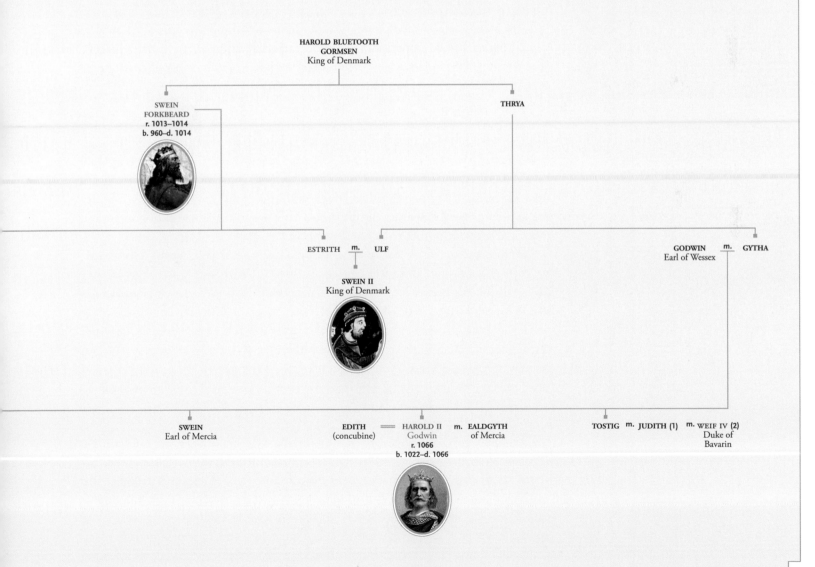

HAROLD BLUETOOTH
GORMSEN
King of Denmark

SWEIN
FORKBEARD
r. 1013–1014
b. 960–d. 1014

THRYA

ESTRITH m. ULF

GODWIN
Earl of Wessex m. GYTHA

SWEIN II
King of Denmark

SWEIN
Earl of Mercia

EDITH
(concubine) ═══ HAROLD II
Godwin
r. 1066
b. 1022–d. 1066 m. EALDGYTH
of Mercia

TOSTIG m. JUDITH (1) m. WEIF IV (2)
Duke of
Bavarin

Alfred the Great King Alfred laid the ninth-century foundations of the English state. Here, he considers the model of a ship that will form the germ of England's Royal Navy.

monastic tradition after the depredations of the Vikings. Among the reforms was the regional demarcation of shires and counties, boundaries that survived almost unchanged until as recently as 1974.

Edgar's successors were less accomplished. His son, Edward, by his first wife, died mysteriously during a visit to his second wife, Elfthryth, thus enabling Elfthryth's own son, Ethelred II (ca 968–1016), to take the throne. Posterity remembers Ethelred as "the Unready," from the Old English word *unraed*. In truth, the word means not "unprepared" but "badly advised," but whatever the precise translation, the insinuations were apposite—Ethelred's reign, while not without administrative successes, proved more or less disastrous.

Matters were not helped by a renewed spate of Viking attacks—not just any attacks, but assaults from two of the most formidable Danish kings ever to set foot in Britain: Harold Bluetooth Gormsen (ca 935–987) and his son, Swein Forkbeard (ca 960–1014).

England proved ill equipped to face the Danes. Edgar had bequeathed Ethelred a prosperous kingdom, but not one of any military standing. Ethelred therefore contrived the doomed policy of the Danegeld—effectively the paying of blackmail money to the Vikings to leave England in peace. The result was inevitable. After the first payment, in 991, the Viking armies simply came back for more, returning time and again over 20 years to drain England of both gold and powers of self-determination. In 1013, with the country on its knees, Forkbeard seized not just his habitual tribute but also the throne itself. Ethelred II, deposed and humbled, fled to exile in Normandy.

■ THE NORMAN CONNECTION

Ethelred's choice of Normandy, a French dukedom, as his place of exile was no accident. It was home to Emma, the daughter of Richard, Duke of Normandy. In 1001 or 1002 Ethelred had married Emma, with whom he had a son, future English king Edward the Confessor (ca 1003–1066). Involving the Normans was not without sense—they might prove powerful allies against the Danes—but allowing them near England's royal bloodline was to have disastrous consequences.

The Normans, or *Nortmanni,* were originally Vikings—the name means "Norse men" or "men of the north." After 911, they had settled in northern France, much as they had settled in the British Isles. And much as in the British Isles, they had proved too strong for the native kings, who had been forced to grant them the lands that would become Normandy. While the Normans eventually forged a French domain, they also retained an ancestral allegiance to their Danish cousins. As recently as the year 1000, for example, they had allowed Danish forces to spend the winter in Normandy. It was just these ancient ties of blood that Ethelred's marriage had been designed to undermine.

■ THE LAST OF THE SAXON KINGS

Events in England took an unexpected turn with the sudden death of Forkbeard in 1014. Ethelred, probably emboldened by his powerful son, Edmund II Ironside (988/93–1016), returned from Normandy with uncharacteristic vigor to reclaim his throne. Two years later, however, Ethelred II died in turn, leaving the throne to Edmund. Swein's equally forceful son, Cnut (ca 995–1035)—also known as Canute—then returned to assert the Danish claim to the throne. When a bruising series of encounters between Cnut and Edmund failed to settle the issue, the two agreed to divide England: Edmund would take Wessex and Cnut the lands north of the Thames.

A month later, however, fate intervened again. This time it was the 23-year-old Edmund who died, leaving Cnut to assume control of the whole country. Edmund's kin and supporters were exiled or killed, and Cnut—despite having a wife and two sons—married Emma of Normandy, the same Emma of Normandy who had been married to Ethelred.

Cnut—remembered for the story of his futile commands to the waves to retreat—eventually ruled well, but spent much of his time in his Scandinavian kingdoms. He delegated power to several trusted followers, including Godwin, Earl of Wessex, a man who despite obscure origins built a vast power base rooted in his lands and his marriage to Gytha, Cnut's sister-in-law (or sister).

On Cnut's death, his two marriages produced a disputed succession, resolved in part by the convenient demise of the two Danish claimants—Harold I, who was probably assassinated, and Harthacnut, who died from overindulging at a wedding. At this point of dynastic impasse, Godwin used his powers to restore England's Saxon line of kings.

The king in question, crowned in 1042, was Edward, later dubbed "the Confessor"—the son of Cnut's queen, Emma of Normandy, by her first marriage to Ethelred the Unready. Godwin's daughter, Edith, quickly became Edward's bride.

Godwin died in 1053 but left his sons—in particular, Harold Godwin—in such powerful positions that they were able to exert considerable control over England for the last ten years of Edward's reign. Edward and Edith were childless, which left open the question of the succession. And it is here, at a point when some of the most decisive events in British history took place, that dates and facts become vague.

Suffice to say that around 1050, perhaps later, Edward reputedly received a visit from Duke William of Normandy, the 23-year-old grand-nephew of Edward's mother, Emma. William later claimed that during this visit Edward promised him the English throne. He also claimed that Harold Godwin reiterated the promise while in Normandy in 1064.

Promise or no, William's claims to succeed Edward were hardly compelling. Neither were those of a Danish contender, and the rightful Saxon candidate, Edgar, the great-grandson of Ethelred the Unready, was just 14. Harold Godwin had no blood claim, but when Edward died in 1066, he was already England's de facto ruler, had popular support, controlled the levers of power, and had proved himself a military leader with victories against the Scots and the Welsh. He was also the choice of the Witan, the king's royal council. Above all, in a claim contrary to Edward's supposed promise to William, Harold decreed that Edward, on his deathbed, had made over "all the kingdom" to Harold's "protection."

Harold was crowned on January 6, 1066. Nine months later, William arrived in England to dispute the claim and to change the course of British history. ■

Monarch's music Cnut—or Canute—was a Danish king who took the English throne by force in 1016. Here, he is portrayed on the River Nene in eastern England. He is listening to the choir of Ely Cathedral, pictured on the hill above.

MIGRATION
Britons Displaced and Britain Transformed

Peoples from mainland Europe were no strangers to Britain. They had settled its pleasant, prosperous lands for thousands of years, from the earliest ancestors of *Homo sapiens* to the Celtic migrations of the Iron Age. But the influx that followed the departure of Rome in A.D. 410–411 was proportionately the largest in the island's history and shaped its destiny in ways that resonate to this day.

According to myth, the influx's unhappy beginnings lie with Vortigern, a British king who invited Germanic mercenaries from northern Europe to help defend England from the Scots. Having secured victory, the mercenaries' leaders, Horsa and Hengest, either were not paid or betrayed Vortigern and seized land in Britain for themselves.

Vortigern and his adversaries may have been actual, mythical, or composite figures—historians are unsure—but they represent something of what happened in post-Roman Britain. Historians are equally uncertain of the incomers' intent, but whether by invitation, conquest, assimilation, or a mixture of the three, several pagan peoples linked by culture and language had settled large areas of Britain by the end of the fifth century.

They included the Jutes, from Jutland on the west coast of Denmark; the Saxons, from the North Sea coast between Jutland and the

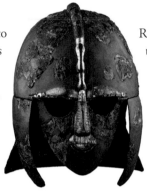

The face of power A seventh-century Anglo-Saxon helmet from the Sutton Hoo ship-burial site in Suffolk, England

River Weser; and the Angles, from the Angeln region on the Baltic coast. Each group gravitated toward a different part of England or Scotland: the Jutes to Kent, the Isle of Wight, and central southern England; the Angles to north and central England—present-day East Anglia, the Midlands, Northumbria, and the Scottish borders; and the Saxons to southern England and the surviving counties of Sussex (from South Saxon) and Essex (East Saxon), and the old kingdom of Wessex (West Saxon).

For the most part, the Romanized and Celtic Britons were confined or consigned to the regions they had occupied under the Romans—Wales, Scotland, Ireland, and northwest and southwest England. Many Celts and other Britons migrated in their own right, mainly to Armorica in France, where they established a British Celtic outpost that became present-day Brittany. Others moved between the Celtic parts of the British Isles. Among them were migrants from Ireland's east coast who settled in Wales, southwest England, the Isle of Man, and southwest Scotland.

The migrants' languages went with them and evolved into two groups in the process. One was the Brythonic—Cumbric, Cornish, Welsh, and Breton. The other was the Goidelic—Manx on the Isle of Man and the surviving forms of Scottish Gaelic *(Gàidhlig)* and Irish *Gaeilge*. ∎

Last redoubt Bamburgh Castle, on England's wild northeast coast. The fortress occupies a site that was probably once the citadel and capital of Bryneich, a British kingdom forged after the departure of the Romans from Britain in A.D. 410–411. In A.D. 547 it fell to Ida, king of the Angles, one of the Germanic races that swarmed into England in the fifth and sixth centuries.

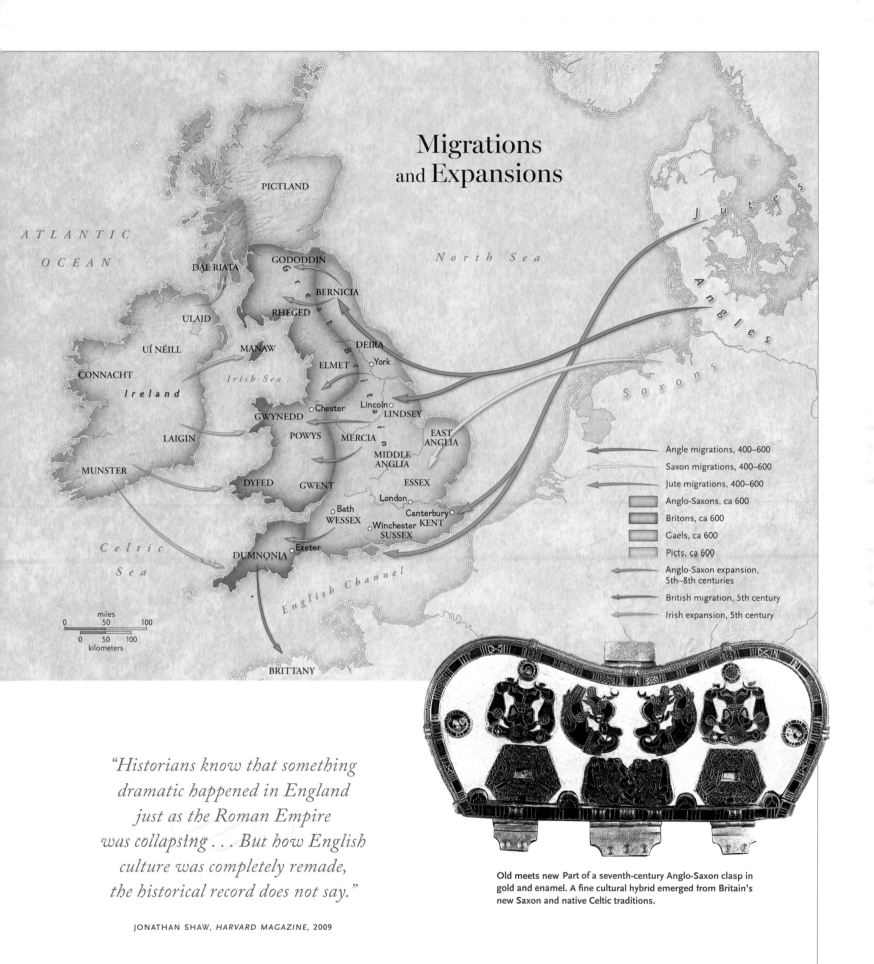

Migrations and Expansions

PICTLAND

ATLANTIC OCEAN

North Sea

Jutes

Angles

GODODDIN

DÁL RIATA

BERNICIA

ULAID

RHEGED

UÍ NÉILL

MANAW

DEIRA

York

ELMET

Irish Sea

Ireland

CONNACHT

Saxons

Lincoln

Chester

GWYNEDD

LINDSEY

LAIGIN

POWYS

MERCIA

EAST ANGLIA

MIDDLE ANGLIA

MUNSTER

DYFED

GWENT

ESSEX

London

Bath

WESSEX

Canterbury

Winchester **KENT**

SUSSEX

Celtic Sea

DUMNONIA

Exeter

English Channel

BRITTANY

miles
0   50   100

0   50   100
kilometers

→ Angle migrations, 400–600
→ Saxon migrations, 400–600
→ Jute migrations, 400–600

▢ Anglo-Saxons, ca 600
▢ Britons, ca 600
▢ Gaels, ca 600
▢ Picts, ca 600

→ Anglo-Saxon expansion, 5th–8th centuries
→ British migration, 5th century
→ Irish expansion, 5th century

"Historians know that something dramatic happened in England just as the Roman Empire was collapsing . . . But how English culture was completely remade, the historical record does not say."

JONATHAN SHAW, *HARVARD MAGAZINE*, 2009

Old meets new Part of a seventh-century Anglo-Saxon clasp in gold and enamel. A fine cultural hybrid emerged from Britain's new Saxon and native Celtic traditions.

EARLY CHRISTIANITY

Saxon Paganism and the Triumph of the Church

A lmost nothing is known of how, when, and where Britain and Ireland first adopted Christianity. The earliest documentary evidence of a Christian presence in the islands dates from A.D. 200 and the writings of Tertullian (ca 160–225), a Roman raised in North Africa, who spoke of "the haunts of Britons, inaccessible to the Romans, but subject to Christ." On the ground, however, only a small number of Christian murals, mosaics, and other artifacts survive from the Roman period. Even the dates of England's most celebrated early martyr, St. Alban, are disputed, with his death put variously at A.D. 201, 251, or 301.

■ THE RISE OF CELTIC CHRISTIANITY

The fifth and sixth centuries saw the retreat of a nascent Christianity in the face of the Saxons, the Angles, and the Jutes, all of whom were pagans. Historians dispute the degree to which the religion was compromised, but according to a broad general pattern, Christianity was largely confined to the areas of Celtic domination in the north, west, and southwest of the British Isles, while England in the south and east reverted to paganism with a Saxon stamp.

Pre-Roman pagan traditions also reasserted themselves in the Celtic areas, or mingled with Christian beliefs to create a distinct form of Celtic Christianity. This was especially true in Ireland, whose flourishing Christian tradition provided a springboard for later missionaries to return Christianity to Britain's Saxon kingdoms.

Part of Ireland's strength was its early conversion to the Christian cause. This conversion was traditionally ascribed to St. Patrick (probably active ca 460 or 490) and the evangelizing of men such as St. Brendan (ca 488–577) and St. Fionnán of Clonard (ca 470–549). Also contributing to Ireland's strength was its monastic tradition, which spread to the remotest parts of the island and provided a degree of unity in a country otherwise fragmented by clan fiefdoms. One of the tradition's most famous sons was St. Columba (ca 521–597), noted for founding the great abbey of Iona, off the west coast of Scotland, in A.D. 563.

Meeting of minds This painting shows Oswald, the second Christian ruler of Northumbria, a Saxon kingdom in northeast England, greeting St. Aidan, a monk from the great Scottish abbey of Iona. In A.D. 635, at Oswald's invitation, Aidan created an abbey at Lindisfarne, which would become one of England's most important centers of culture and scholarship.

■ SAXON CHRISTIANITY

Anglo-Saxon paganism prevailed for almost 200 years. It first yielded to Christianity under Ethelbert (reigned

A Pagan Linguistic Legacy

A nglo-Saxon paganism has survived in the English words *Tuesday*, *Thursday*, and *Friday*, named after Tiw, Thunor (later Thor), and Freya, the Germanic gods of law and order, thunder, and fertility respectively. Wednesday owes its name to Woden, the supreme Saxon deity; Saturday comes from the Roman god Saturn; and Sunday and Monday hark back to earlier pagan associations with the sun and the moon. Easter derives from Eostre, the Anglo-Saxon goddess of spring or dawn, while Yule is the modern form of the Anglo-Saxons' 12-day festival of Géol.

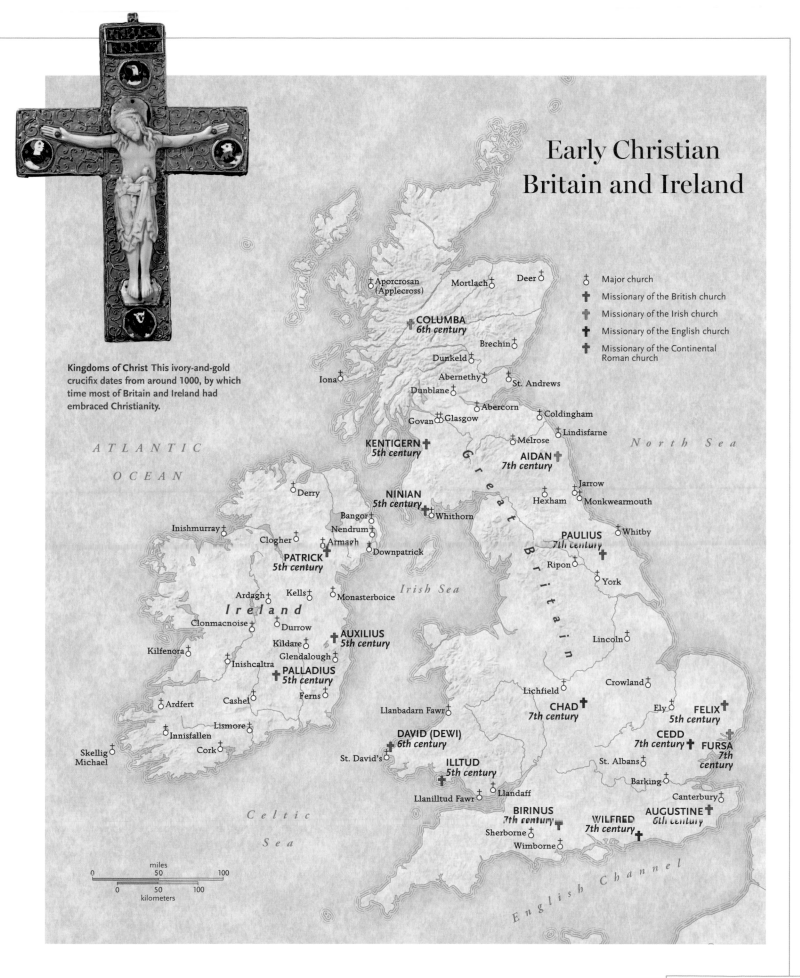

Early Christian Britain and Ireland

Kingdoms of Christ This ivory-and-gold crucifix dates from around 1000, by which time most of Britain and Ireland had embraced Christianity.

Major church
Missionary of the British church
Missionary of the Irish church
Missionary of the English church
Missionary of the Continental Roman church

ATLANTIC OCEAN

North Sea

Irish Sea

Ireland

Great Britain

Celtic Sea

English Channel

Aporcrosan (Applecross)
Mortlach
Deer
COLUMBA 6th century
Brechin
Dunkeld
Iona
Abernethy
St. Andrews
Dunblane
Abercorn
Coldingham
Govan
Glasgow
Lindisfarne
Melrose
KENTIGERN 5th century
AIDAN 7th century
Jarrow
Derry
NINIAN 5th century
Whithorn
Hexham
Monkwearmouth
Bangor
Nendrum
Armagh
Whitby
Inishmurray
Clogher
Downpatrick
PAULIUS 7th century
PATRICK 5th century
Ripon
York
Ardagh
Kells
Monasterboice
Clonmacnoise
Durrow
Lincoln
Kilfenora
Kildare
AUXILIUS 5th century
Inishcaltra
Glendalough
PALLADIUS 5th century
Ardfert
Cashel
Ferns
Crowland
Lismore
Llanbadarn Fawr
Lichfield
CHAD 7th century
Ely
FELIX 5th century
Innisfallen
Cork
DAVID (DEWI) 6th century
CEDD 7th century
FURSA 7th century
Skellig Michael
St. David's
ILLTUD 5th century
St. Albans
Llanilltud Fawr
Llandaff
Barking
Canterbury
BIRINUS 7th century
AUGUSTINE 6th century
Sherborne
WILFRED 7th century
Wimborne

miles
0   50   100
0   50   100
kilometers

ca 560–616), king of the Saxon kingdom of Kent. Ethelbert was married to Bertha, the great-granddaughter of Clovis (ca 466–511), king of the Franks, who ruled a kingdom that covered much of present-day France.

Like the Saxons, the Franks were originally a Germanic people and had similar pagan beliefs until they became Christian under Clovis in A.D. 496. Unlike the Saxons, they also adopted the art, language, and manners of the former Roman Empire. In tandem with Romano-Christianity, this Romanization created a powerful postimperial regime that yielded some of the great names of the medieval age, notably Charlemagne (ca 742–814), and gave its name, Francia, to present-day France.

Abbey interior A re-creation of the 12th-century priory church at Lindisfarne in northeast England. Lindisfarne was founded in the seventh century but rebuilt on several occasions, notably after a Viking raid in 793, and reestablished by the Normans around 1093. It was dissolved in 1537.

In 560, Ethelbert's marriage to a scion of this prestigious kingdom just across the English Channel represented a diplomatic coup that was designed to bolster Ethelbert's position as England's then preeminent Saxon king. More to the point, it brought Bertha and her Christian entourage to Canterbury, Ethelbert's Kentish capital.

Bertha's continuing Christianity was a condition of her marriage, and either she created a church or Ethelbert granted her a surviving Romano-British church outside the city walls. Either way, this Christian seed in a pagan kingdom, along with the likelihood of a safe haven, may have been the reason Pope Gregory I (ca 540–604) chose Canterbury as the focus of his famous mission to convert England in 595.

The mission arrived with its leader, Augustine, in 597. At first Ethelbert declined to be converted: He had seen the benefits the Franks had gained from Christianity—not least its ideas of kingship and supreme authority—but wanted time to reflect on a change that could have powerful political repercussions. Augustine was allowed to proceed, however, and he established an archbishopric at Canterbury—still the principal seat of the Church of England—as well as bishoprics in London and elsewhere. In the process he founded the first St. Paul's Cathedral (604).

Whitby Abbey The first abbey on this site, on England's northeast coast, was host in 664 to the Synod of Whitby, a meeting that decided the future course of Christianity in the British Isles. The present abbey dates from the 13th century and owes its ruined state to Henry VIII's suppression of the monasteries in 1536 (see pages 124–125). Bram Stoker visited the ruins in 1890, an experience that inspired his Gothic novel *Dracula*.

■ CHRISTIAN BRITAIN

Ethelbert eventually converted around 600, and over the next 80 years other Saxon kings followed: Wessex became Christian around 635; Mercia in 655; and Sussex, one of the last, in 679. In the north, Edwin, king of Northumbria, was baptized around 628 by a Roman monk, Paulinus, who then founded York Minster, still the seat of England's second great archbishopric. Northumbria received a further Christian boost in 635, when its next king, Oswald, brought a monk, Aidan, from Columba's monastery at Iona to found a great abbey at Lindisfarne off the Northumbrian coast.

Many more monasteries followed, notably Whitby (657) and Jarrow (682), the latter home to the Venerable Bede (672/3–735), whose ecclesiastical writing is one of the glories of Anglo-Saxon literature. Monasteries became centers of culture and learning, their legacy exemplified by the illuminated manuscripts of the Lindisfarne Gospels (ca 698). They also proliferated and became richly endowed, occupying a key place in the social and cultural fabric of much of Britain and Ireland until their dissolution after 1536 (see pages 124–125).

■ THE SYNOD OF WHITBY

Much of the British Isles now had two distinct and ultimately competing strands of Christianity: the grandiose version imported directly from Rome to Canterbury and York and the more austere and insular Celtic form practiced in Iona and Ireland. England chose the former at the Synod, or Council, of Whitby (664), a meeting called by King Oswald's brother and heir Oswy (612–670). While some of its decisions might now appear trivial—agreeing on how to calculate the date of Easter, for example—the decision to follow Rome, and thus to join the mainstream of European Christian thought and observance, was of immense importance. Like Ireland, while much of Britain might in the future be politically fractured or riven by rival claims to the throne, its church was now a unified body under a unified authority that ministered to the whole country. ■

Illuminated beauty A page depicts St. Matthew from the *Book of Kells* (ca 800), an illuminated Latin manuscript of the Gospels. Among the most beautiful of many such monastic manuscripts, it has long been displayed in Ireland, but was probably the work of both British and Irish monks.

CELTS AND SAXONS

Retreat, Advance, and the British Isles Divided

By the end of the fifth century, the Angles, Saxons, and Jutes who had swarmed into lowland Britain were effectively a single colonizing group known as the Saxons or the Anglo-Saxons. Britain's earlier Celtic and Romano-British peoples survived north of Hadrian's Wall, in Cumbria and Cornwall, and beyond the Valley of the Severn in present-day Wales.

Where it took place, the Saxon advance was almost total. It is estimated that as many as 200,000 illiterate, pagan, and warlike incomers joined two million indigenous Britons, the latter reduced by famine, disease, and a century of strife. Proportionately it was the largest foreign influx in British history. In central England, where the Saxon presence was strongest, DNA evidence suggests that as much as 90 percent of the native male population was killed, enslaved, or driven out.

The Celts did not give up without a fight. Later chroniclers alluded to the Battle of Mount Badon, or Bladon (ca 500), whose triumphant Celtic king may have borne the nickname "the Bear" (*artos* in Celtic), a hint of the historical realities that may have inspired the legend of King Arthur and the Knights of the Round Table.

On the whole, however, the Celts retreated or retrenched (see sidebar). Their towns and those of the Roman Britons were often laid waste, old trade routes withered, and the aristocratic landowners of the former Roman villas migrated or were replaced by Anglo-Saxon warlords. Administration continued after a fashion, but without the coherent or comprehensive reach of the Romans.

A new language, Anglo-Saxon, or Old English, the precursor of modern English, replaced Latin and the Celtic tongues. New gods and new social and political norms were established. Houses were made of wood, not stone, and arranged in scattered hamlets rather than in towns. Life revolved around a communal hall where the Anglo-Saxons ate, caroused, and elected their leaders, for early Saxon rule was by consent, with leaders chosen by their peers or answerable to them.

Saxon society later became less egalitarian as fiefdoms coalesced and elites forged kingdoms in which they strove to secure exclusive privileges. But somewhere in the early Saxon halls was the faintest echo of an elective kingship and form of government that would evolve and prevail in much of the British Isles for 1,500 years. ■

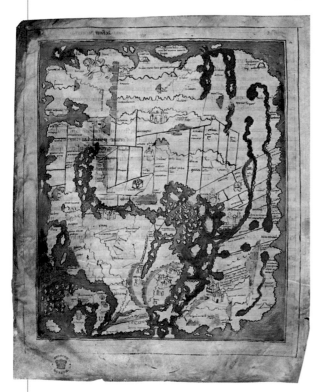

The Hereford Mappa Mundi This 11th-century Anglo-Saxon "world" map was among the first to include an accurate depiction of the British Isles, seen at bottom left.

The Celts in Wales, Scotland, and Ireland

Saxons were lowland dwellers used to the plains of northern Europe, and in Britain they tended to stop at the mountains. The uplands of Wales, therefore, provided sanctuary to native Celts, refugee Britons, and Irish settlers, and allowed the growth of tribal kingdoms (Powys, Gwent, Deheubarth, and Gwynedd) that endured until the 12th century. Much the same happened in Ireland, which was spared Saxon intervention and saw the development of perhaps 150 clan fiefdoms linked by language, culture, and the codified laws of the Celtic Gaels, who probably settled the island around 100 B.C. Despite the instability created by so many rival clans, elaborate forms of overlordship—from local kings (*truath*) to the High King (*Ard Rí*)—allowed powerful dynasties to emerge, notably the Eóganacht in the south and the Uí Néill in the north and east. Irish settlers also mingled with native Scots to become Picts, Scotland's most powerful tribe from Roman times to at least A.D. 800. The Picts and other Scottish tribes held off the Saxons, but squabbled among themselves until united by the common threat of the Vikings in the ninth century.

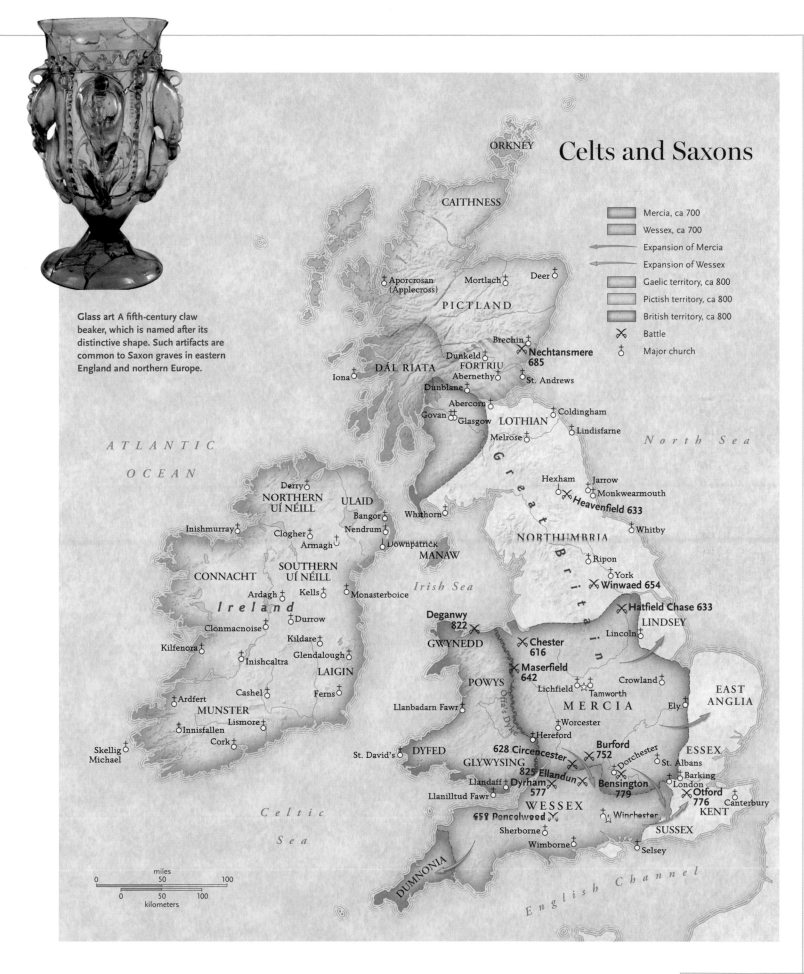

Celts and Saxons

Glass art A fifth-century claw beaker, which is named after its distinctive shape. Such artifacts are common to Saxon graves in eastern England and northern Europe.

ORKNEY

CAITHNESS

Aporcrosan
(Applecross)   Mortlach   Deer

PICTLAND

Iona   DÁL RIATA   FORTRIU
Dunkeld   Brechin   Nechtansmere
685
Abernethy   St. Andrews
Dunblane
Abercorn   Coldingham
Govan   LOTHIAN   Lindisfarne
Glasgow
Melrose

Derry   Hexham   Jarrow
NORTHERN   Monkwearmouth
UÍ NÉILL   ULAID   Heavenfield 633
Inishmurray   Bangor   Whithorn
Clogher   Nendrum   NORTHUMBRIA   Whitby
Armagh   Downpatrick
MANAW   Ripon
York
CONNACHT   SOUTHERN   Irish Sea   Winwaed 654
UÍ NÉILL
Ardagh   Kells   Hatfield Chase 633
Ireland   Monasterboice   LINDSEY
Clonmacnoise   Durrow   Deganwy   Lincoln
Kilfenora   Kildare   822
Inishcaltra   Glendalough   GWYNEDD   Chester
LAIGIN   616
Maserfield
Cashel   Ferns   POWYS   642   Crowland   EAST
Ardfert   Lichfield   ANGLIA
MUNSTER   Llanbadarn Fawr   Tamworth
Lismore   MERCIA   Ely
Innisfallen   Worcester
Cork   Hereford
Skellig   628 Circencester   Burford   ESSEX
Michael   St. David's   DYFED   752   Dorchester   St. Albans
GLYWYSING   825 Ellandun   Barking
Llandaff   Dyrham   Bensington   London
Llanilltud Fawr   577   779   Otford
WESSEX   Winchester   776   Canterbury
658 Poncolwood   KENT
Sherborne   SUSSEX
Wimborne   Selsey

DUMNONIA

Legend

- Mercia, ca 700
- Wessex, ca 700
- Expansion of Mercia
- Expansion of Wessex
- Gaelic territory, ca 800
- Pictish territory, ca 800
- British territory, ca 800
- ⚔ Battle
- ♱ Major church

ATLANTIC OCEAN

North Sea

Celtic Sea

English Channel

miles
0   50   100
0   50   100
kilometers

THE VIKINGS

Two Centuries of Blood, Conquest, and Plunder

The Vikings hailed from present-day Denmark, Norway, and Sweden, where the violent birth pangs of statehood in the eighth century produced an unruly society in which ambitious men turned to piracy as a means to wealth and power. Wide-ranging in their quest for plunder, they reached Iceland, Greenland, and North America; sailed up the Seine to Paris; spread through the Mediterranean to Constantinople (Istanbul); and penetrated the waterways of Russia and the Ukraine to Kiev and beyond.

To natural aggression they added a secret weapon, the longship, an oceangoing fighting machine that was easy to build and perfect for its predatory purpose. Strong, flexible hulls combined with oars and sails made for speed and versatility, while a shallow draft—a key reason the Vikings raided so successfully—allowed boats to navigate rivers or to be pulled onto beaches without the need for a harbor.

Wealthy monasteries provided the Vikings' first targets—the first, ransacked in 793, was Lindisfarne on England's northeast coast—but within 50 years seasonal summer raiding gave way to conquest, notably in England, where all the Saxon kingdoms except Wessex fell, and in Scotland, where much of the coast and most of the islands succumbed. Ireland proved more resistant, but even there the Vikings triumphed, especially on the coast, where their *longphorts* (fortified ports) became the germs of cities such as Dublin, Limerick, and Waterford.

The Vikings' reputation for violence was well deserved. One defeated Saxon king was thrown into a pit of venomous snakes; Viking archers used another as target practice; a third, Ella of Northumbria, reportedly suffered execution by "blood eagle"—which, according to many scholars, meant his ribs were broken and pulled out to resemble blood-stained wings before salt was poured on the wounds and his lungs were wrenched from his body.

Yet once they settled, it appears many Vikings assimilated quickly, intermarrying and often adopting Christianity and the more decorous habits of their neighbors. In much of England they remained a powerful, if sometimes intermittent, presence until 1042, while in Scotland their Norwegian descendants did not relinquish certain of their territories until 1266.

The Vikings' legacy was partly political: Without them, who knows how England's Saxon kingdoms might have developed, or whether Ireland might have been united sooner, or how the virtual disappearance of the once powerful Picts affected the history of Scotland? The incomers' legacy also included trading, shipbuilding, artistic, and other skills, as well as long-lasting linguistic memorials: *awe, anger, ball, die, egg, gun, guest, husband, happy, law, loan, plow, trust, sister, skill, sky, slaughter, steak, weak,* and *wrong* are just some of the words the Vikings bequeathed to English. ∎

All at sea *(right)* The Vikings were among the greatest seafarers of their age. They used their distinctive and superbly designed longships to sail from their Scandinavian bases deep into modern-day Russia and as far afield as North America and the eastern Mediterranean.

The Lindisfarne Stone *(below)* This fragmentary relief was probably carved to commemorate the devastating Viking raid on the great abbey at Lindisfarne in A.D. 793. Countless monks were slain by the raiders, who are shown here raising their weapons during the slaughter.

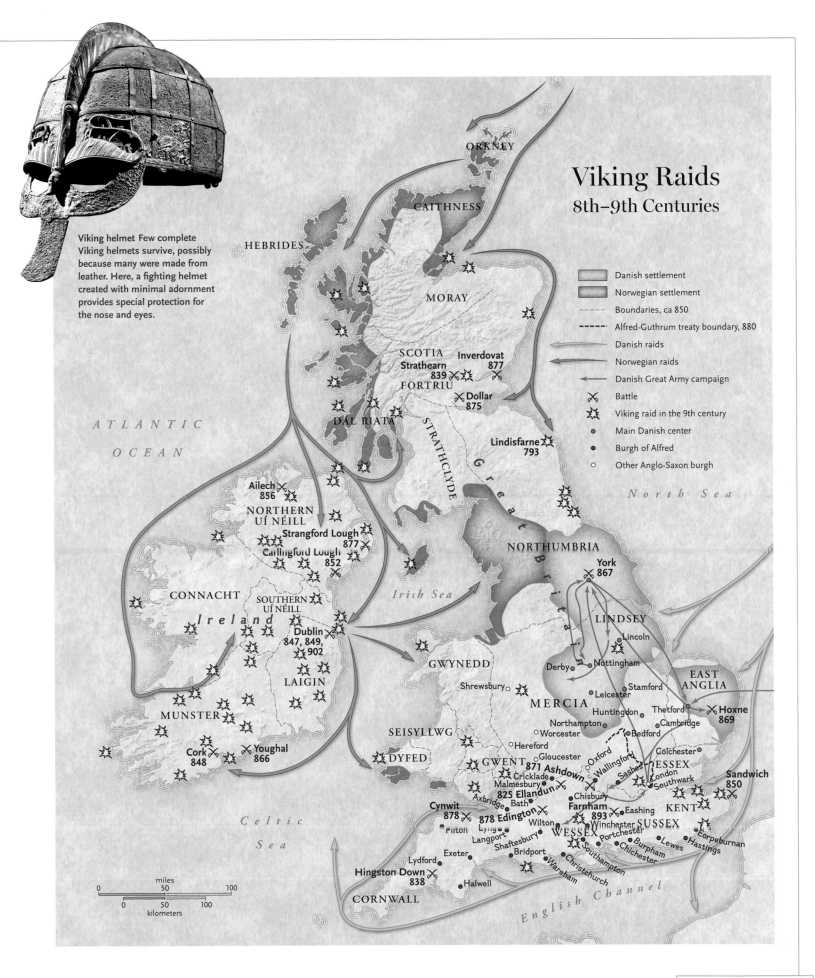

Viking helmet Few complete
Viking helmets survive, possibly
because many were made from
leather. Here, a fighting helmet
created with minimal adornment
provides special protection for
the nose and eyes.

Viking Raids
8th–9th Centuries

	Danish settlement
	Norwegian settlement
---	Boundaries, ca 850
– – –	Alfred-Guthrum treaty boundary, 880
←	Danish raids
⇐	Norwegian raids
←	Danish Great Army campaign
✕	Battle
✳	Viking raid in the 9th century
●	Main Danish center
●	Burgh of Alfred
○	Other Anglo-Saxon burgh

ORKNEY

CAITHNESS

HEBRIDES

MORAY

SCOTIA
Strathearn   Inverdovat
839   877
FORTRIU
Dollar
875

DÁL RIATA

STRATHCLYDE

Lindisfarne
793

ATLANTIC
OCEAN

North Sea

Ailech
856

NORTHERN
UÍ NÉILL

Strangford Lough
877
Carlingford Lough
852

NORTHUMBRIA

Great Britain

York
867

CONNACHT

SOUTHERN
UÍ NÉILL

Irish Sea

LINDSEY

Lincoln

Ireland

Dublin
847, 849,
902

Derby   Nottingham

EAST
ANGLIA

GWYNEDD

Stamford

LAIGIN

Shrewsbury   Leicester
MERCIA   Huntingdon   Thetford   Hoxne
Northampton   Cambridge   869

MUNSTER

SEISYLLWG   Worcester   Bedford

Hereford   Oxford   Wallingford   Colchester
Gloucester   Sashes   ESSEX

Cork   Youghal
848   866

DYFED   GWENT   871 Ashdown   London
Cricklade   Southwark
825 Ellandun   Chisbury
Malmesbury   Sandwich
Axbridge Bath   Farnham   850
Cynwit   Wilton   893   KENT
878   878 Edington   Lyng   Eashing
Filton   Winchester SUSSEX
Langport Shaftesbury WESSEX Portchester Eorpeburnan
Exeter   Southampton Burpham Hastings
Bridport   Christchurch Chichester Lewes
Lydford   Wareham
Hingston Down   Halwell
838
CORNWALL

Celtic
Sea

English Channel

miles
0   50   100

0   50   100
kilometers

ALFRED THE GREAT

The Vikings Defeated and the Seeds of English Statehood

Alfred (ca 849–899) is the only English monarch to have been given the accolade "Great," a tribute to a visionary king who defeated the Vikings, nurtured culture and learning, reformed the army, created a navy, transformed law and justice, and forged an embryonic English state that long outlived its Saxon roots.

The son of Ethelwulf, king of Wessex, Alfred came to the throne in 871. Almost immediately he was faced with invasion. The Vikings had already conquered England's other Saxon kingdoms; now they wanted Wessex. Still too weak for military heroics, the fledgling king bought the Vikings off instead. In 878, the invaders came back. This time a besieged Alfred fled to the marshes of Athelney in Somerset. It was here, according to legend, that he took refuge with a shepherd and his wife and burned the wife's cakes while lost in thought.

Alfred emerged from hiding to defeat the Vikings at the Battle of Edington (878), a victory against the odds without which Britain's last Saxon bastion would have fallen and any notion of England as a fledgling nation would have floundered. At the same time, Alfred realized he could not defeat the Vikings completely, and he formalized the division of England between Wessex and a Viking sphere of influence subsequently known as the Danelaw.

Next, Alfred created a navy, based on the invaders' own longships. Considered the germ of the British Royal Navy, it secured its first victory—against the Vikings themselves—in 882. Alfred then strengthened his kingdom's land defenses by creating a network of *burhs* or *burghs* (boroughs), fortified settlements no more than a day's march apart, each garrisoned and endowed with enough land to be self-sufficient. Most, in time, became important English towns.

Defense of the realm King Alfred the Great supervises the rebuilding of the old Roman walls of London. Alfred's capital was at Winchester, in southern England, but London was part of his campaign to reinforce towns across his kingdom in the face of Viking attacks.

Alfred also awarded a *thegnship,* or knighthood, to large landowners in return for military service one month out of three. A similar system was extended to the irregular peasant army, or *fyrd;* which guaranteed troops rest and time to tend their farms. When the Vikings attacked again in 885 and 892 to 895, the new defenses held firm.

Although Alfred revitalized London, he established his capital at Winchester, already an important royal and religious center. Rebuilt to a Roman grid plan, the city became the focus of a dazzling court and gave expression to the rich cultural, religious, and intellectual legacy for which Alfred is remembered.

Visits to Rome and the courts of Frankish (French) kings in his youth had nurtured Alfred's love of scholarship. "I know nothing worse of a man," he wrote, than "that he should not know." He endowed schools and made it his quest that "if we have the peace, all the young men of England . . . may be devoted to learning." Attempting to reverse the Vikings' assault on monasteries, the country's great seats of learning, he invited scholars from across Europe to his court. He also became a scholar in his own right and may have translated some of the earliest surviving works from Latin into English.

Around 890, Alfred commissioned the first of the *Anglo-Saxon Chronicles,* eight surviving manuscripts written over 250 years by monks across England. The finest documentary resource of the period, they are also the first history of any country in Europe in its own tongue. Alfred also drew on existing Saxon legal codes and combined them with Roman and Christian law to create his own Doom Book (from *dom,* meaning "law" or "judgment"), cementing the notion of legal precedent and creating a cornerstone of English common law. ■

England
During the Reign of Alfred the Great
871–899

Irish Sea

Celtic Sea

North Sea

English Channel

MERCIA

WESSEX

EAST ANGLIA

Torksey

Chester

Nottingham 867

Repton

Buttington

Bridgnorth

Thetford

Cambridge

Gloucester

Oxford

Sutton Courtenay

Wallingford

Mersea Island

Cricklade

Wantage

Sashes

Benfleet

Shoebury

Malmesbury

London

Southwark

Alfred the Great Born, 849

Ashdown 871

Reading

Thorney

Rochester

Isle of Sheppey

Bath

Chisbury

Englefield 870

Reading 871

Milton Regis

Isle of Thanet

Axbridge

Edington 878

Basing 871

Eashing

Canterbury

Cynwit 878

Wedmore

Kingston Deverill

Sutton Veny

Appledore

Watchet

Athelney

Aller

Wilton 871

Winchester

Eorpeburnan

Pilton

Lyng

Langport

Shaftesbury

Alfred the Great Died, 899

Lewes

Hastings

Southampton

Burpham

Exeter 893

Bridport

Wimborne Minster

Wareham 876

Portchester

Chichester

Lydford

Christchurch

Swanage

Halwell

Viking Stronghold
Battle or siege
Burgh
Roman Road

miles
0   20   40

0   20   40
kilometers

"He seems to me a very foolish man, and very wretched, who will not increase his understanding while he is in the world."

KING ALFRED THE GREAT (CA 849–899)

Coins for a king Two sides of a silver penny from the 880s, part of the coinage reformed by Alfred the Great. One face *(top)* is inscribed with ÆLFR/EDREX ("King Alfred") and a portrait of Alfred, the reverse *(bottom)* with LVNDONIA, a monogram representing London.

The Alfred Jewel The inscription on this exquisite artifact in gold, enamel, and quartz reads AELFRED MEC HEHT GEWYRCAN—Alfred Ordered Me Made— suggesting that it may have belonged to Alfred the Great.

EDWARD THE CONFESSOR

Godly Churchbuilder and Agent of England's Doom

Edward the Confessor (ca 1003–1066) was England's last Anglo-Saxon king, the great-great-great-grandson of Alfred the Great and the son of Ethelred the Unready and his wife Emma of Normandy. While he was alive his Norman connections created tensions with his Saxon nobles, and in death his childless state left the throne open to dispute between one of his distant relatives, William of Normandy—better known as William the Conqueror—and Harold Godwin, the son of the most powerful of his Saxon subjects.

Edward never expected to become king. He was one of seven sons, and in the confusion following his father's death in 1016, the throne eventually passed to the Danish king, Cnut. Young Edward and his brother Alfred took refuge as guests of their mother's family in Normandy. Here, in the absence of their mother—who married Cnut and remained in England—they grew up to be more Norman than English.

After Cnut's death in 1035, the throne was disputed by Harold I (Harefoot) and Harthacnut, Cnut's sons by his first wife, Elfgifu, and Edward's mother (Emma), respectively. Nineteen years after they had left, Edward and Alfred returned to England as pawns in a struggle for power that involved Emma, the rival Danish heirs, and England's leading nobles, of whom Godwin, Earl of Wessex was the most potent.

Edward's ships were beaten back. But when Alfred landed in England, Godwin's troops captured him and handed him over to Harold's men, who blinded and mutilated him "so carelessly . . . that he soon perished." Harold duly became king but died soon thereafter. Harthacnut took the crown in turn, but he also died prematurely (reputedly after a drinking binge), though not before appointing his half brother Edward as regent.

Being appointed to the throne was one thing, but achieving it was quite another, and the event was possible only with the support of Godwin, the man complicit in his brother's murder. Edward needed Godwin—he even married his daughter—but his natural antipathy colored the early years of his reign. The result was a surge of factional unrest, a blight exacerbated by Edward's all-too-obvious Norman sympathies. A Norman, Robert of Jumièges, was appointed Archbishop of Canterbury; French was spoken at court; and Norman nobles were favored with land and positions.

Past glory Edward the Confessor is shown seated at a banquet, from the *Decrees of Kings of Anglo-Saxon and Norman England,* an illuminated English manuscript probably created at least 300 years after the king's death.

Among the most alarming portents for the English was the goodwill Edward bestowed on one Norman in particular: William the Bastard, the son of his mother's nephew, Duke Robert of Normandy. Robert never married William's mother—hence the title Bastard—but on Robert's death, William was the only heir to his dukedom. On assuming the title, William set about turning Normandy into a formidable military force.

In 1051, Edward attempted to exert his power by forcing Godwin into exile in France. Within a year, however, factional politics brought him back, stronger than ever. Henceforth, Edward appeared to lose interest in the affairs of state. Instead, power passed to Godwin and, after Godwin's death in 1053, to his son, Harold—the same Harold who, as King Harold II, would confront William the Bastard, better known as William the Conqueror, at the Battle of Hastings in 1066 (see page 58).

Historians dispute the reasons for Edward's lapse and offer different assessments of his achievements. His sainthood (bestowed in 1161) and the title Confessor—meaning someone who was not martyred but actively testified to his faith—suggest his eventual piety; and his forceful early career, when his position was precarious, and various administrative reforms belie his later reputation as a weak king who indirectly led England to calamity. In fact, the last 15 years of his reign, albeit with Harold Godwin at the helm, were peaceful and prosperous. There were two problems, however: Edward had no children, and thus no heirs, and Harold alienated his incompetent brother, Tostig, by removing him from power in northern England. Both problems were to have fatal consequences (see page 58).

Edward meanwhile diverted a tenth of royal revenues to a great new church in the riverside fields outside London's old Roman walls. Called the west minster and dedicated to St. Peter, it provided a counterpoint to the existing east minster, or St. Paul's, which had been founded inside the walls in 604 (see page 185). Westminster Abbey, as it is now known (see opposite), became England's finest church and the place where most of England's kings and queens have been crowned for almost a thousand years. Edward also built a palace close to the church, the Palace of Westminster, a precursor of today's Houses of Parliament. In doing so, he made Westminster England's religious and political heart, a status it retains to the present day. ∎

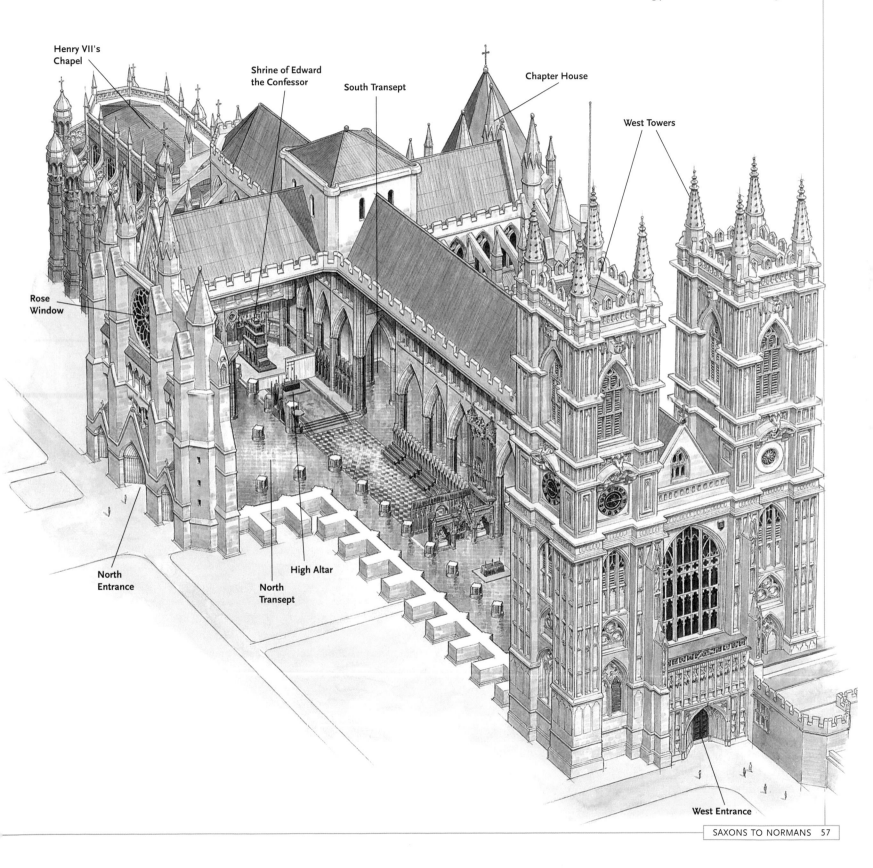

Westminster Abbey London's magnificent abbey was begun by Edward the Confessor—who is buried there—and has played host to the coronations of most English monarchs for almost a thousand years. It is also the last resting place of countless national figures.

Henry VII's Chapel

Shrine of Edward the Confessor

South Transept

Chapter House

West Towers

Rose Window

North Entrance

North Transept

High Altar

West Entrance

THE NORMAN INVASION
British and Irish History Changed Forever

E ngland had a problem in 1066. Two men claimed the throne: Harold II and William of Normandy. Neither claim bore much scrutiny. Harold was the son of a powerful noble, little more, and William was a Norman with a promise and a distant right by blood. England's previous king, Edward the Confessor, had died without an heir. Harold had effectively ruled for the last ten years of Edward's reign. When Edward died, England declared Harold king. William was related to Edward's mother and claimed—as Harold did—that Edward had promised him the crown.

England defeated William of Normandy's knights confront King Harold's English foot soldiers at the Battle of Hastings. William's force eventually won the day.

William was determined to invade, Harold to defend. Both faced difficulties. William's plans were especially fraught. Calais, the closest port to England, was out of his hands. As a result, he faced a longer crossing from his Norman domain. In addition, he fought with horses, and so he needed a fleet of heavy ships for their passage. More to the point, many of his knights, dismayed by the invasion's poor prospects, refused their oaths of loyalty: Fighting in France was one thing, foolhardy foreign adventures quite another.

Harold, knowing an invasion was planned, conscripted a peasant militia to guard England's southern coast. But then the summer of 1066 arrived. It was an English summer, full of storms and high winds. William's amphibious force, confined to port, battled the elements. Harold's peasants, held ready through the lull, fretted over their imminent harvests.

Harold had other problems. His alienated brother, Tostig, had allied with Harald Hardrada, a Norse king with his own tenuous claims to the English throne. Both men promised trouble, which duly arrived in September 1066, when an invasion force landed in the north.

Tostig and Hardrada swept all before them, defeating an English army at Fulford Gate before taking the city of York. Undeterred, Harold gathered his army and embarked on one of English history's greatest forced marches, covering some 185 miles from London to York in four days. His foes, surprised and unprepared, were crushed at the Battle of Stamford Bridge.

Even as Harold celebrated victory, however, news came that William's 500 ships had finally landed near Hastings. Harold once more responded boldly. Leading his exhausted army south, he decided to stake all on an almost immediate confrontation with William.

Battle was joined at Senlac Hill on October 14. Harold was arrayed on the slopes, William in a shallow valley below. William's force was smaller, perhaps as few as 4,000 men, and included foot soldiers, archers, and cavalry. Harold also had horses, but, like most Saxon and Viking armies, his men fought mostly on foot and in unordered hand-to-hand combat.

On the morning of battle, Harold's 7,000 troops formed a wall of shields in readiness for the Norman attack. When it came, the English axes and spears inflicted heavy damage on the Norman knights. With each successive wave, however, the English also lost men to William's archers.

What happened next is unclear, but for some reason the English shield formation broke ranks and charged down the hill. This marked a turning point, for in open combat the English became more vulnerable to the Norman cavalry. Possibly William ordered feigned retreats to lure his enemy from formation; possibly part of the Breton (non-Norman) forces on his right wing turned tail and were pursued when rumors of William's death began to circulate.

In the end, it was not William's but Harold's death that proved decisive. The English king probably died not from an arrow to the eye, as myth would have it, but after being hunted down and hacked to pieces by a special scouting party. So mutilated was his body, it is said that his mistress, Edith Swan-Neck, had to be summoned to identify its dismembered parts.

The English capitulation was not immediate. The battle, one of the longest in British medieval history, went on for six hours. Last-ditch defenses proved to no avail, however. England's principal army had been defeated and its leader slain. The Normans' initial invasion had been successful. Now all that remained was conquest. ∎

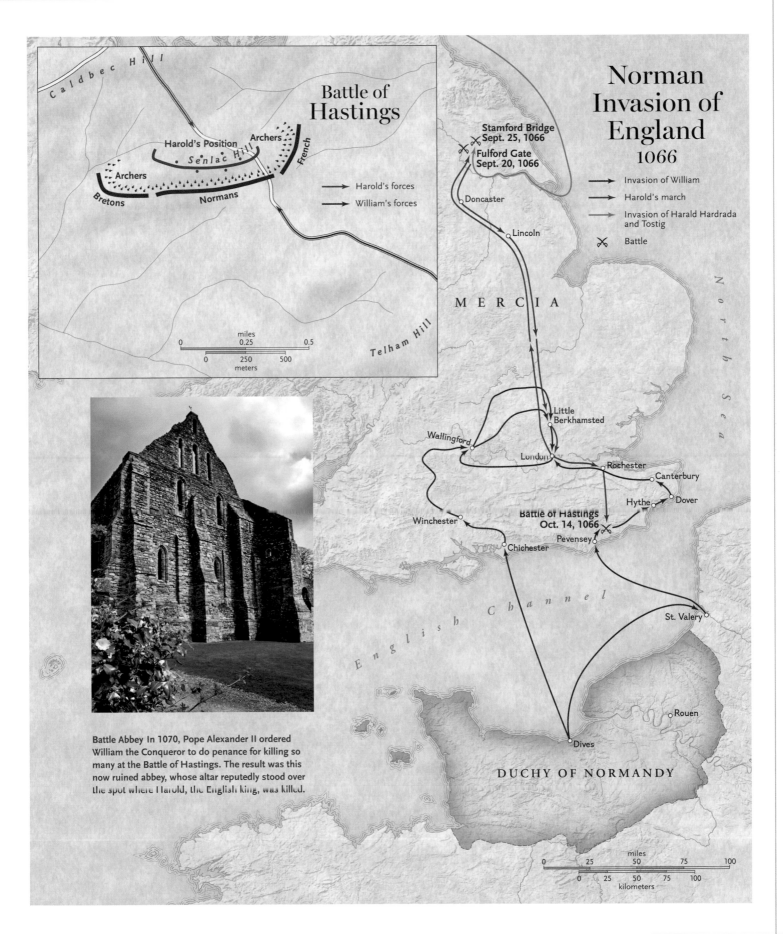

Battle of Hastings

Caldbec Hill

Harold's Position

Archers

Senlac Hill

French

Archers

Bretons

Normans

Telham Hill

→ Harold's forces

→ William's forces

miles
0   0.25   0.5

0   250   500
meters

Norman Invasion of England
1066

Stamford Bridge
Sept. 25, 1066

Fulford Gate
Sept. 20, 1066

Doncaster

Lincoln

→ Invasion of William

→ Harold's march

→ Invasion of Harald Hardrada
and Tostig

⚔ Battle

MERCIA

North Sea

Little
Berkhamsted

Wallingford

London

Rochester

Canterbury

Hythe

Dover

Battle of Hastings
Oct. 14, 1066

Winchester

Pevensey

Chichester

English Channel

St. Valery

Rouen

Dives

DUCHY OF NORMANDY

miles
0   25   50   75   100

0   25   50   75   100
kilometers

Battle Abbey In 1070, Pope Alexander II ordered William the Conqueror to do penance for killing so many at the Battle of Hastings. The result was this now ruined abbey, whose altar reputedly stood over the spot where Harold, the English king, was killed.

THE MEDIEVAL AGE
❧ 1066–1485 ❧

"A wonderful land is this, and a fickle; which has exiled, slain, destroyed or ruined so many kings."

RICHARD II, IN THE TOWER OF LONDON, 1399

The British Isles
11th–15th Centuries

Welsh kingdoms, 10th century
Irish kingdoms, circa 1000
Kingdom of England, 1066
Duchy of Normandy, 1066
Added to England by 1092
Scotland, 1139–1157
Islands controlled by the Norse

North Sea

Atlantic Ocean

Irish Sea

Celtic Sea

English Channel

KINGDOM OF THE HEBRIDES

SCOTLAND

Dornoch
Fortrose
Elgin
Aberdeen
Brechin
Dunkeld
Perth
St. Andrews
Stirling
Falkirk
Dunbar
Glasgow
Edinburgh
Berwick

GREAT BRITAIN

Derry
AILECH (AILEACH)
ULIDIA
AIRGÍALLA (ORIEL)
CONNACHT
MIDE (MEATH)
IRELAND
Dublin
LAIGHIN
Limerick
Kilkenny
MUMHA
Waterford
Cork

Wigtown
Carlisle
Durham
CUMBERLAND

York
Lincoln

Rhuddlan
Chester
Caernarvon
GWYNEDD
Lichfield
ENGLAND
Norwich
POWYS
Montgomery
Coventry
Ely
Cardigan
Hereford
DEHEUBARTH
Woodstock
St. David's
Carmarthen
BRYCHEINIOG
Oxford
Pembroke
GWENT
London
MORGANNWG
Llandaff
Windsor
Runnymede
Bath
Canterbury
Wells
Winchester
Lewes
Hastings
Salisbury
Chichester
Exeter

ARTOIS

Rouen

NORMANDY

BLOIS

BRETAGNE

miles
0   50   100

0   50   100
kilometers

THE YEARS OF BATTLE AND BLOOD

WILLIAM OF NORMANDY MOVED QUICKLY AFTER HIS VICTORY AT THE BATTLE OF HASTINGS. Within two months he had been crowned William I. Over the next few years, the invader became the conqueror. Revolts were ruthlessly suppressed, castles were built, and church and state were transformed. Vast tracts of English land were distributed to the king's accomplices, and the Great Survey—later known as the Domesday Book—was commissioned to assess the subsequent state of the kingdom. Scotland, largely untouched, received a wave of refugees from the south; Wales, wild and inviolate, remained free, save on its lowland borders. Ireland, too, remained unscathed. England, however, on William's death in 1087, was a country conquered.

William's oldest son, Robert, inherited his French territory, while his next son, also called William (ca 1056–1100), became king of his British dominions. Nicknamed Rufus from the Latin for his red hair, William II was extravagant where his father had been frugal, and he antagonized the barons and the clergy alike. In 1100, he was killed in a hunting "accident," though the fact that his brother, Henry (1068–1135), was in the king's party raised strong suspicions of his complicity in William's death.

Henry seized the throne as Henry I in the absence of William's rightful heir—his elder brother, Robert, who was fighting in the First Crusade (page 82). He then married Edith, the great-granddaughter of Edmund Ironside (king in 1016), thus bolstering his claim to the succession by forging a link with the bloodline of England's earlier Saxon kings. He also repaired relations with the church and barons, and made legal and financial reforms that further consolidated the Norman state.

Henry fathered 21 children, only two of whom were legitimate: his son William and daughter Matilda. In 1120, William drowned while returning to England from Normandy, thus leaving Matilda (1102–1167) as Henry's nominated heir. England had no tradition of female monarchy, and many of Henry's barons opposed Matilda in favor of the king's nephew, Stephen (son of Adela, William the Conqueror's daughter). Matilda's marriage to Geoffrey of Anjou further alienated Anglo-Norman opinion, for Anjou, a region in western France, was an enemy of Normandy.

On Henry I's death in 1135, it was Stephen (ca 1097–1154) who took the throne, an act that precipitated almost 20 years of civil strife between rival supporters of the king and Matilda. In 1148, Matilda's son with Geoffrey of Anjou, Henry (1133–1189), took up her cause. He succeeded to the throne as Henry II in 1154—Stephen's only heir, Eustace, having died a year earlier.

Spoils of war *(previous pages)* Pontefract Castle in northern England, portrayed in a 17th-century painting by Flemish artist Alexander Keirincx, was built around 1070 by the Norman Ilbert de Lacy on land granted to him by William I for help rendered during the Norman Conquest of 1066. Many similar grants and many other castles were built in the period, when countless English nobles lost their lands to the Norman invaders.

1072
William the Conqueror invades
eastern Scotland

1085
William commissions the Domesday Book

ca 1098
Construction of the Tower of London
is completed

1100
William II is killed in hunting "accident";
William's brother, Henry, seizes the throne

1170
Thomas Becket is murdered

1175
Henry II and barons establish control
of eastern Ireland

1189–1192
Richard the Lionheart launches the Third
Crusade

1215
Rebelling barons force King John to seal
Magna Carta

1297
William Wallace defeats English at
Battle of Stirling Bridge

1305
Wallace is captured and hanged

1314
Scots, commanded by Robert the Bruce,
defeat English army at Bannockburn

1325
Queen Isabella leaves for France; she and
Roger of Mortimer force Edward to abdicate

1330
Edward III seizes control of England

1337–1453
The Hundred Years' War

1348
An outbreak of the Black Death begins in
England

1399
Bolingbroke usurps the throne as Henry IV

1415
Henry V defeats French at Battle of Agincourt

1455–1485
The Wars of the Roses

Henry II was the first English king of the Plantagenet line, named after the broom plant *(planta genista)* that his father used in his family emblem, or perhaps wore as a sprig in his helmet or planted as cover on his land for hunting. The name was applied subsequently (but not at the time) to the line of English kings up to 1485. Henry and his two sons, Kings Richard I and John, are also sometimes known as Angevins, from their titles as Counts of Anjou.

■ MURDER TO MAGNA CARTA

Like his grandfather Henry I before him, Henry II was a forceful king who restored order to a country exhausted by civil conflict. Legal reforms included rudimentary trial by jury (1166) and royal courts with traveling judges to replace local courts run by the barons. Henry II's system survives in part to this day. A warrior king in the chivalric mold, he also won recognition as the feudal overlord of Wales and Ireland (see pages 80–81) and gained partial power over the Scots. In 1170, however, his attempts to exert control over the church led to the murder of Thomas Becket (see pages 78–79), Archbishop of Canterbury and his former friend and chancellor.

Henry married the redoubtable Eleanor of Aquitaine (1120/22–1204), previously married to the French king, and she brought the lands of Aquitaine in central-southern France to Henry's domain. Henry now ruled a vast kingdom but, like kings before him, was cursed by the problem of his succession. He preferred his younger son, John; Eleanor favored their older son and rightful heir, Richard.

Richard eventually prevailed, but not before an ailing Henry had been forced to confront both sons and his estranged wife in battle. Henry died a broken man in 1189.

Richard I or Richard the Lionheart (1157–1199) is misremembered as one of the great English kings, mainly for what were costly and often dubious exploits in the Crusades (see page 82), but he spent virtually no time in England during his ten-year reign. His brother, John (1167–1216), plotted against him during his many absences, but succeeded by right upon Richard's death in France in 1199.

John quickly proved a disaster. He lost all England's possessions in France except Aquitaine and alienated the church, the papacy, and England's leading barons. In 1215, a revolt by the barons forced him to agree to Magna Carta, a "Great Charter" that addressed the barons' grievances (see page 86). When John and the pope revoked the charter within a year, the barons revolted and forced John to flee. He died a sick and exhausted fugitive in 1216.

Norman nemesis *(above)* William the Conqueror, in an imagined portrait from the 16th century. After his successful invasion in 1066, William ruthlessly subdued England and transformed it into a Norman kingdom by his death in 1087.

High point *(opposite)* Salisbury Cathedral in Wiltshire, southern England. Many of Britain's great religious buildings have their roots in the medieval age. Salisbury was begun in 1220 and consecrated in 1258. Its spire, the tallest in England (404 feet), was completed in 1320.

■ CULTURE AND WAR

John's son, Henry III (1207–1272), was just nine years old at his father's death in 1216. Normally an infant king should have been a recipe for further disaster, but two effective regents, William Marshal and Hubert de Burgh, nursed the kingdom back to order before Henry took power in his own right in 1227.

Henry was pious and cultured, and his 56-year reign was one of art, culture, and learning. The first colleges were founded at Oxford, along with many of the first great Gothic cathedrals, notably Salisbury, dedicated in 1258. But Henry's extravagance—as well as that of his French wife, Eleanor—provoked baronial revolt, in particular that of the powerful Simon de Montfort, who captured both Henry and his son and heir, Edward I (1239–1307), before being defeated by Edward at the Battle of Evesham in 1265.

Edward's prowess in battle was a sign of things to come. As king from 1272, "Long-shanks," as he was known—he was six feet two inches tall—defeated the Welsh in 1277 before turning to the Scots (see page 88). Castles were built to subdue the Welsh, and one of them, Caernarfon, was the birthplace of Edward's son and heir, the future Edward II, who for the first time took the title Prince of Wales, still the title of the monarch's first-born son.

Edward II (1284–1327) inherited a secure kingdom that he squandered through self-indulgence, poor judgment, and military catastrophe. His probably homosexual relationship with first Piers Gaveston and then Hugh Despenser, and the favors he lavished on both, scandalized the court, outraged his nobles, and alienated his queen, Isabella (1292/5–1358), the daughter of the French king. The nobles forced Gaveston's exile in 1311 and executed him when he returned to England a year later. Isabella was briefly reconciled to Edward II and bore a son, Edward, in 1312.

In 1314, the king led an English army and suffered a shattering defeat against the Scots under Robert the Bruce at Bannockburn (see page 90), remembered to this day as a high point in Scotland's struggle for independence. Isabella meanwhile had left her

> *"It is the dominion of foreigners, with no Englishman who is earl, abbot, or bishop. The newcomers devour the riches of England, with no hope of the misery coming to an end."*
>
> WILLIAM OF MALMESBURY (1095–1143), ON NORMAN ENGLAND

husband for France, along with her son, Edward, where in 1325, she met and started living openly with an English exile, Roger of Mortimer. Raising an army, the pair found willing supporters among England's disenchanted barons and quickly captured Edward II and Despenser.

Despenser was executed in Isabella's presence—he was strung up, castrated, forced to watch his genitals being burned, hanged, and, while still conscious, disemboweled, beheaded, and quartered. Not for nothing did Isabella become known as the She-Wolf of France. However, even she balked at killing an anointed king, who, legal opinion suggested, could be removed only by abdication. Edward was duly forced to renounce the throne before being imprisoned in Berkeley Castle, Gloucestershire, where he died—almost certainly murdered on Isabella's orders—in 1327.

If Isabella and Mortimer had thought to rule indefinitely on behalf of Isabella's son, Edward, they discounted Edward himself, who as Edward III (1312–1377) would become one of England's greatest medieval kings. In 1330, while just 17, he moved against his mother and her lover by secretly organizing a raid on their home in Nottingham Castle as they prepared for bed. Mortimer was executed and Isabella banished to quiet retirement.

■ A HUNDRED YEARS OF CONFLICTS

Edward III's reign (1327–1377) was one of chivalry and extravagance—feasts, jousts, and courtly high fashion—as well as military victories that saw the king declared one of Europe's greatest medieval generals. It was also the period of the Black Death (see page 92), a Europe-wide plague pandemic (1348–early 1350s), and saw the emergence of an English literary tradition led by writers such as Geoffrey Chaucer (ca 1343–1400), author of *The Canterbury Tales* (see page 94).

Edward also played a pivotal role in a confused series of conflicts with France that later would be known as the Hundred Years' War (1337–1453). France had long been central to English (and often Scottish) affairs, not least because of the ambiguous position of Anglo-Norman and later English kings, and their claims to French territories through birth, marriage, and ancestral kinship.

A year into Edward's reign, in 1328, with his mother, Isabella, still in power, the French king, Charles IV, had died without an heir. Isabella pressed Edward's claim to the throne through birth, on the basis that the French king was her brother. The French *parlement* disagreed, and the throne passed to Charles's cousin, Philip IV. In

The rewards of war *(above)* This richly embellished liturgical manuscript dates from the ninth century. It was stolen from Constantinople (now Istanbul) in 1204, one of many artifacts looted by European armies during the Crusades.

Done to death *(opposite)* William II, the son of William I, is killed in a hunting "accident." The fact that his brother, Henry, was in the king's hunting party and later seized the throne raised the suspicion that William's death was deliberate.

HOUSES OF NORMANDY AND PLANTAGENET
1066–1485

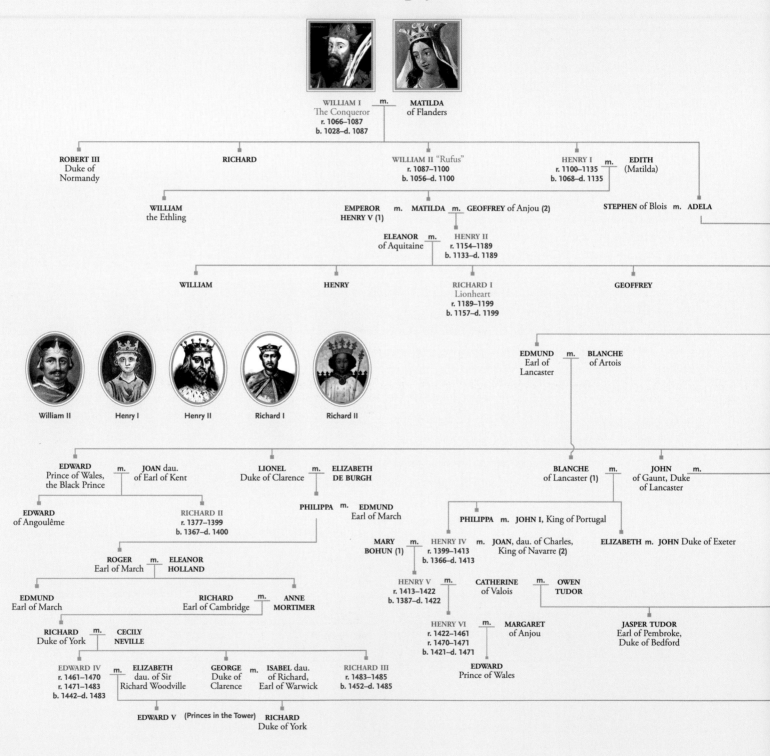

WILLIAM I
The Conqueror
r. 1066–1087
b. 1028–d. 1087

m.

MATILDA
of Flanders

ROBERT III
Duke of
Normandy

RICHARD

WILLIAM II "Rufus"
r. 1087–1100
b. 1056–d. 1100

HENRY I
r. 1100–1135
b. 1068–d. 1135

m.

EDITH
(Matilda)

WILLIAM
the Ethling

EMPEROR
HENRY V (1)

m. **MATILDA** **m.** **GEOFFREY** of Anjou (2)

STEPHEN of Blois **m.** **ADELA**

ELEANOR
of Aquitaine

m.

HENRY II
r. 1154–1189
b. 1133–d. 1189

WILLIAM

HENRY

RICHARD I
Lionheart
r. 1189–1199
b. 1157–d. 1199

GEOFFREY

EDMUND
Earl of
Lancaster

m.

BLANCHE
of Artois

William II

Henry I

Henry II

Richard I

Richard II

EDWARD
Prince of Wales,
the Black Prince

m. **JOAN dau.**
of Earl of Kent

LIONEL
Duke of Clarence

m. **ELIZABETH**
DE BURGH

BLANCHE
of Lancaster (1)

m. **JOHN**
of Gaunt, Duke
of Lancaster

m.

EDWARD
of Angoulême

RICHARD II
r. 1377–1399
b. 1367–d. 1400

PHILIPPA **m.** **EDMUND**
Earl of March

PHILIPPA **m.** **JOHN I,** King of Portugal

ELIZABETH **m.** **JOHN** Duke of Exeter

ROGER **m.** **ELEANOR**
Earl of March   **HOLLAND**

MARY **m.** **HENRY IV** **m.** **JOAN, dau. of Charles,**
BOHUN (1)   r. 1399–1413   King of Navarre (2)
               b. 1366–d. 1413

EDMUND
Earl of March

RICHARD
Earl of Cambridge

m. **ANNE**
MORTIMER

HENRY V **m.** **CATHERINE** **m.** **OWEN**
r. 1413–1422   of Valois   **TUDOR**
b. 1387–d. 1422

RICHARD
Duke of York

m. **CECILY**
NEVILLE

HENRY VI **m.** **MARGARET**
r. 1422–1461   of Anjou
r. 1470–1471
b. 1421–d. 1471

JASPER TUDOR
Earl of Pembroke,
Duke of Bedford

EDWARD IV
r. 1461–1470
r. 1471–1483
b. 1442–d. 1483

m. **ELIZABETH**
dau. of Sir
Richard Woodville

GEORGE
Duke of
Clarence

m. **ISABEL dau.**
of Richard,
Earl of Warwick

RICHARD III
r. 1483–1485
b. 1452–d. 1485

EDWARD
Prince of Wales

EDWARD V (Princes in the Tower) **RICHARD**
Duke of York

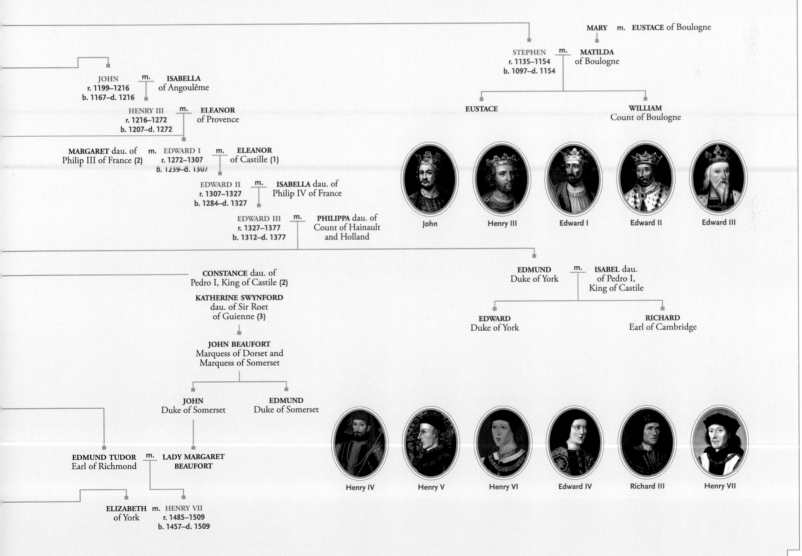

KINGS AND QUEENS OF SCOTLAND

Malcolm III Canmore r. 1058–1093 HOUSE OF CANMORE
Donald III (Donald Bane) r. 1093–1094 HOUSE OF CANMORE
Duncan II r. 1094 HOUSE OF CANMORE
Donald III (Donald Bane) r. 1094–1097 HOUSE OF CANMORE
Edgar r. 1097–1107 HOUSE OF CANMORE
Alexander I r. 1107–1124 HOUSE OF CANMORE
David I r. 1124–1153 HOUSE OF CANMORE
Malcolm IV r. 1153–1165 HOUSE OF CANMORE
William I r. 1165–1214 HOUSE OF CANMORE
Alexander II r. 1214–1249 HOUSE OF CANMORE
Alexander III r. 1249–1286 HOUSE OF CANMORE
Margaret (Maid of Norway) r. 1286–1290 HOUSE OF CANMORE

1290–1292 **Interregnum**
John Balliol r. 1292–1296 HOUSE OF BALLIOL
1296–1306 **Interregnum**
Robert I (The Bruce) r. 1306–1329 HOUSE OF BRUCE
David II r. 1329–1371 HOUSE OF BRUCE
Edward Balliol r. Aug.–Dec. 1332 (also for periods 1333–1346) HOUSE OF BALLIOL
Robert II r. 1371–1390 HOUSE OF STUART
Robert III r. 1390–1406 HOUSE OF STUART
James I r. 1406–1437 HOUSE OF STUART
James II r. 1437–1460 HOUSE OF STUART
James III r. 1460–1488 HOUSE OF STUART

Date Ranges Dates in early history are difficult to determine with certainty. The ranges given on this family tree are approximations based on the best resources available.

MARY m. **EUSTACE** of Boulogne

STEPHEN m. **MATILDA**
r. 1135–1154 of Boulogne
b. 1097–d. 1154

JOHN m. **ISABELLA**
r. 1199–1216 of Angoulême
b. 1167–d. 1216

EUSTACE

WILLIAM
Count of Boulogne

HENRY III m. **ELEANOR**
r. 1216–1272 of Provence
b. 1207–d. 1272

MARGARET dau. of m. **EDWARD I** m. **ELEANOR**
Philip III of France (2) r. 1272–1307 of Castille (1)
b. 1239–d. 1307

EDWARD II m. **ISABELLA** dau. of
r. 1307–1327 Philip IV of France
b. 1284–d. 1327

John

Henry III

Edward I

Edward II

Edward III

EDWARD III m. **PHILIPPA** dau. of
r. 1327–1377 Count of Hainault
b. 1312–d. 1377 and Holland

EDMUND m. **ISABEL** dau.
Duke of York of Pedro I,
King of Castile

CONSTANCE dau. of
Pedro I, King of Castile (2)

KATHERINE SWYNFORD
dau. of Sir Roet
of Guienne (3)

EDWARD
Duke of York

RICHARD
Earl of Cambridge

JOHN BEAUFORT
Marquess of Dorset and
Marquess of Somerset

JOHN
Duke of Somerset

EDMUND
Duke of Somerset

Henry IV

Henry V

Henry VI

Edward IV

Richard III

Henry VII

EDMUND TUDOR m. **LADY MARGARET**
Earl of Richmond **BEAUFORT**

ELIZABETH m. **HENRY VII**
of York r. 1485–1509
b. 1457–d. 1509

1340, Edward reasserted his claim and led an invasion that culminated in the Battle of Crécy (1346), one of England's greatest medieval triumphs.

Among those on the battlefield was Edward's 16-year-old son and heir, Edward the Black Prince (1330–1376), so-called because of his black armor. A gifted soldier, he led an English army to an another resounding victory at the Battle of Poitiers, where he captured the French king, Jean II, in 1356.

From there, Edward III's fortunes in France waned for the same reasons those of his successors waned over the centuries. Battles were fought on French soil, which meant long lines of communication, and relied largely on the promise of plunder and ransom for finance. The latter soon dried up, so that victory in individual battles, however crushing, could not be followed up by conquest.

In 1376, Edward III's heir, Edward the Black Prince, died suddenly, followed a year later by Edward III himself. The next in line to the throne was the Black Prince's son,

England triumphant King Edward III and his son, the Black Prince, depicted at the Battle of Crécy (1346), one of the most resounding victories for the English during the period of Anglo-French conflicts known as the Hundred Years' War. The painting, by Benjamin West, is dated 1788.

Richard, just ten years old. Watching at his coronation was John of Gaunt, Duke of Lancaster (1340–1399), younger brother of the Black Prince and the third and next surviving son of Edward III (a second, Lionel, had died in 1368).

Gaunt was a shadowy figure, but his many offspring and several marriages—the first to Blanche of Lancaster, hence his title—meant that all English kings after Richard II, and all the conflicts that came to be known as the Wars of the Roses (see pages 98–99), would stem from this pivotal hereditary moment.

Richard II (1367–1400) initially seemed to be made of the right stuff. He personally faced down Wat Tyler and other leaders of the Peasants' Revolt in 1381, an uprising provoked largely by increased taxes. Richard was also a patron of the arts and triumphed in Ireland (in 1394 and 1395), but like Edward II before him he antagonized court and country alike by indulging favorites and alienating his leading nobles.

Among the latter was his cousin Henry Bolingbroke (1367–1413), son of John of Gaunt through his first wife, Blanche. In 1399, Bolingbroke and a small army joined the powerful Percy nobles in the northeast, usurped the throne (Bolingbroke became Henry IV), and imprisoned Richard, who, like Edward II, would die mysteriously in captivity.

Henry IV was the first of the three monarchs of the House of Lancaster, but he was king for less than 13 years—a reign dominated by challenges to his throne—before his son, Henry V (1387–1422), succeeded him in 1413. Capable and forceful, Henry V reignited English claims to the French crown. Victories at Agincourt in 1415 (see pages 96–97) and elsewhere, and marriage to Catherine, the French king's daughter, established him widely as France's rightful ruler. He died suddenly from dysentery (contracted on the battlefield) at the age of 34.

Henry's death brought his son by Catherine to the throne as Henry VI (1421–1471), aged just nine months, then (and still) a record for the youngest English king. His regents proved unequal to the task of retaining France, where English influence waned until the Hundred Years' War effectively petered out in 1453. When Henry reached adulthood, he proved no more capable than his regents. He was hamstrung by diffidence and bouts of mental illness that made for a weak monarchy and allowed the open conflict among rival noble factions that would be known as the Wars of the Roses (1455–1485).

This 30-year period was among Britain's bloodiest: Kings and princes were murdered, and thousands were slain in battle (see page 98). At the period's end, one battle, Bosworth, in 1485, between Henry Tudor and Richard III, would decide the country's fate and usher in a new royal dynasty (see pages 100–145). ■

Richard III This painting from 1520, after a lost original, represents the earliest known portrait from an original rendering of an English king. A controversial figure, Richard III usurped the throne during the Wars of the Roses and was eventually defeated in battle by Henry Tudor, the future Henry VII.

"England hath long been mad, and scarr'd herself, / The brother blindly shed the brother's blood, / The father rashly slaughter'd his own son, / The son, compell'd, been butcher to the sire: All this divided York and Lancaster."

WILLIAM SHAKESPEARE, *RICHARD III*, CA 1592–1593

CONQUEST

Starvation and the Sword Secure Norman Power

William the Conqueror's victory at the Battle of Hastings in 1066 was merely the beginning. In its wake came a merciless campaign of subjugation that by William's death in 1087 had established Norman rule and changed the face of England and parts of Wales forever.

The English did not go quietly. Even as William was being crowned in Westminster Abbey on Christmas Day 1066, fires raged and riots flared in the streets outside. Discontent quickly spread and erupted with particular violence in northern England, where rebellion invited William's most brutal repression, the so-called Harrying of the North (1069–1070), in which the countryside was laid waste and many thousands died of starvation.

William and his followers also built more than 70 castles, not, as in the time of King Alfred's burghs, to protect towns and villages, but as fortresses designed to subdue the resident populations. Many castles were raised near the wild border with Wales, where William granted large estates to his most trusted followers in return for their subjugation of a lawless land.

Such grants were repeated across the country. Medieval warfare required the support of nobles and their armies, who in return served in expectation of reward. William met this expectation after 1066 by seizing the estates of English landowners and distributing them to his Norman followers. An estimated 4,000 English nobles lost their lands to fewer than 200 Normans, until less than 5 percent of England was in its original hands. It is believed that 200,000 Normans settled in England, and about the same number of Britons—around a tenth of the population—succumbed to the sword or starvation.

Where England fell, parts of Scotland followed. William invaded the east of the country in 1072 and forced the Scottish king, Malcolm III, into a treaty that recognized William as his overlord. The church was next, as Norman abbots and bishops replaced most of their English counterparts. A spate of churchbuilding ensued, a testament to the wealth of 11th-century England and to a pious streak in William's complex character: In 1087, around a quarter of all land in England was in church hands.

Other institutions also changed: The country's old shire courts, for example, were replaced by manorial courts in which justice was dispensed by the new Norman lords or their lesser knights, rather than local nobles and the king's representatives.

William returned to Normandy in 1072, just six years after the Battle of Hastings, and largely remained there until his death, underlining the swift and comprehensive nature of his conquest. An everyday Anglo-Saxon way of life survived the transformation, but the new ruling elite, in church and state, was French, as were the country's ruling language and culture. The newcomers had not only conquered England, but also transformed it, in less than a generation. ■

March to power William of Normandy being crowned king of England in an 18th-century painting by Benjamin West. William lost many men in his victory at the Battle of Hastings, fought on October 14, 1066, and waited for reinforcements before moving to subdue London. After he secured the city, his coronation took place in Westminster Abbey on Christmas Day in 1066, just ten weeks after the Normans first set foot in Britain.

The Death of William

William I died as he lived—fighting. He succumbed to wounds sustained in a fall from his horse while battling to regain territory from Philip I of France. William suffered a lingering death during which he had time to repent: "I am stained with the rivers of blood I have spilled." Chroniclers of his burial at St. Stephen's Abbey in Caen, where his tomb can still be seen, recount how his corpse's "swollen bowels burst and an intolerable stench assailed the nostrils of bystanders."

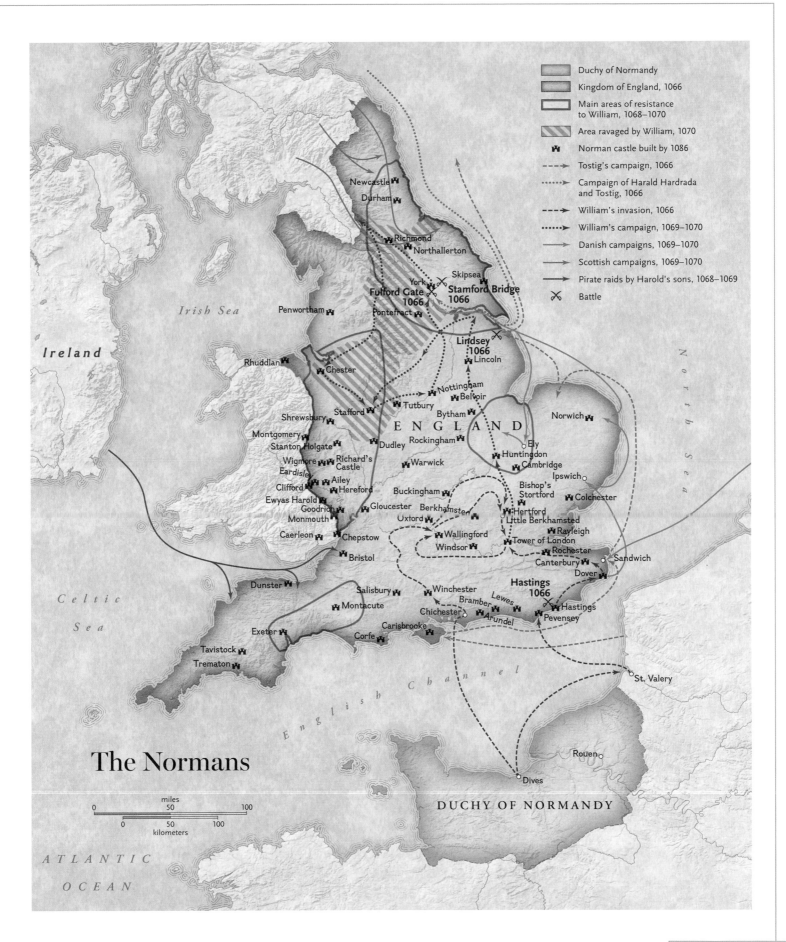

The Normans

Legend:
- Duchy of Normandy
- Kingdom of England, 1066
- Main areas of resistance to William, 1068–1070
- Area ravaged by William, 1070
- Norman castle built by 1086
- Tostig's campaign, 1066
- Campaign of Harald Hardrada and Tostig, 1066
- William's invasion, 1066
- William's campaign, 1069–1070
- Danish campaigns, 1069–1070
- Scottish campaigns, 1069–1070
- Pirate raids by Harold's sons, 1068–1069
- Battle

Irish Sea

Ireland

Newcastle
Durham
Richmond
Northallerton
Penwortham
Skipsea
York
Fulford Gate 1066
Pontefract
Stamford Bridge 1066
Rhuddlan
Chester
Lindsey 1066
Lincoln
Nottingham
Belvoir
Shrewsbury
Stafford
Tutbury
Bytham
Norwich
Montgomery
Stanton Holgate
Dudley
Rockingham
Wigmore
Richard's Castle
Warwick
Ely
Huntingdon
Eardisley
Cambridge
Clifford
Ailey
Hereford
Buckingham
Ipswich
Ewyas Harold
Goodrich
Gloucester
Berkhamsted
Bishop's Stortford
Colchester
Monmouth
Uxford
Hertford
Little Berkhamsted
Caerleon
Chepstow
Wallingford
Rayleigh
Tower of London
Bristol
Windsor
Rochester
Canterbury
Sandwich
Dover
Dunster
Salisbury
Winchester
Hastings 1066
Montacute
Bramber
Lewes
Hastings
Chichester
Arundel
Pevensey
Exeter
Corfe
Carisbrooke
Tavistock
Trematon

ENGLAND

North Sea

Celtic Sea

English Channel

ATLANTIC OCEAN

St. Valery
Rouen
Dives

DUCHY OF NORMANDY

miles
0   50   100
0   50   100
kilometers

THE TOWER OF LONDON

Fortress, Prison, Palace, and Place of Execution

William the Conqueror used several weapons to subdue the English: terror, force of arms, starvation, and the laying waste of the countryside. Once his enemies were subdued, however, he needed to ensure they remained subdued. The most efficient method of doing so was the construction of castles, of which William and his newly enriched nobles built more than 70 in England and Wales. One of the most important was in London, which, while not yet the capital (then Winchester), was already the country's largest and most prosperous city.

The White Tower The keep at the heart of the Tower of London is the oldest part of the fortress. After 1070 William the Conqueror began it on the site of an earlier wooden stockade. It takes its name from the fact that it was whitewashed in 1240.

After his coronation at Westminster Abbey in 1066, William withdrew to Essex, outside London, while, in the words of a chronicler, "several strongholds were made ready to safeguard against the fickleness of the city's huge and fierce population." One of these strongholds was on the south bank of the River Thames, on a site already protected on two sides by the city's surviving Roman walls.

Like many Norman castles, this early fortress consisted of a simple motte, or earth mound, and bailey (enclosure), on top of which stood a tower. Speed was of the essence after the conquest (many of the Normans' castles were begun in the two years after 1066), so towers were usually built from wood and later replaced with stone. This was the case in London, where work began on a later stone tower in the mid-1070s and was completed around 1100.

For centuries afterward it remained one of Europe's largest castles, 118 feet long by 106 feet wide and, at 90 feet high, London's tallest point until the building of Old St. Paul's Cathedral around 1310. This original structure survives to this day as the Tower of London's central keep, along with the original St. John's Chapel (ca 1080), London's oldest church.

The tower's first major additions, notably a wall around the site, came during the 1220s. They included the Salt Tower, whose slit windows allowed archers to fire on those attacking from the river below, and the Bloody Tower, so-called because it witnessed the disappearance of the young "princes in the tower," presumed murdered on the orders of Richard III in 1483 (see page 98). In 1240, the original central keep gained its current name, the White Tower, after Henry III had it whitewashed.

From 1275 to 1279, Edward I built St. Thomas's Tower and the water gate known as Traitors' Gate, so-called because it was the route by which many prisoners entered the tower. Tudor times saw the rebuilding of the Chapel Royal of St. Peter ad Vincula, now a place of worship for the tower's resident community, but once the burial place of many of those executed privately in the tower (as opposed to those executed in public nearby); Queens Anne Boleyn, Catherine Howard, and Jane Grey are among the chapel's occupants. In 1485, Henry VII created the Yeoman Warders, or Beefeaters, where, in 1605, Guy Fawkes was tortured for his part in the Gunpowder Plot (see pages 160–161). For 200 years after 1669, the Martin Tower housed the Crown Jewels (they now reside in the Waterloo Barracks, begun in 1845). As late as 1952, the Tower of London was home to some of the nation's more notorious prisoners—namely the Kray twins, Britain's most infamous 20th-century gangsters. ■

"I hear I shall not die before noon, and I am very sorry therefore, for I thought to be dead by this time and past my pain . . . I heard say the executioner is very good, and I have a little neck."

ANNE BOLEYN, BEFORE HER EXECUTION, 1536

Royal crest *(right)* This stained glass dates from the 15th century and is among the oldest in the Tower of London. It comes from a room in the Byward Tower that may once have been a royal apartment.

The Tower of London *(below)* From a small fort begun in the 11th century on the Thames near London's old Roman walls, the Tower grew over the centuries to become one of Europe's greatest citadels.

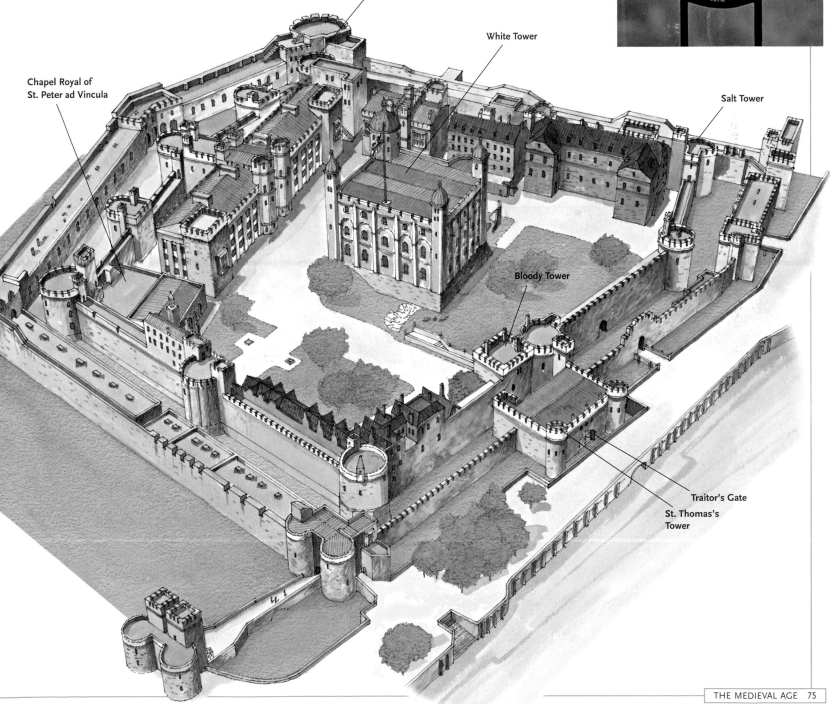

Martin Tower

White Tower

Chapel Royal of St. Peter ad Vincula

Salt Tower

Bloody Tower

Traitor's Gate

St. Thomas's Tower

THE DOMESDAY BOOK

A Unique Medieval Record for the Ages

The Domesday Book of 1086 is the oldest and most important medieval record of the social and economic life of England and Wales. Nothing comparable was produced elsewhere in Europe, and nothing like it would be produced in Britain until the first population census of 1801. It survives to this day, in the National Archives of the United Kingdom in Kew.

The project, an immense national survey, was commissioned by William the Conqueror in 1085 and completed in less than a year. The Norman takeover had resulted in a confused transfer of territory as estates were taken from the English and given to William's followers. Twenty years on, William wanted a record of who now owned the land, an appraisal of the nation's assets, and—vitally—an assessment of the revenues due to him as king.

The undertaking was enormous, but it was not comprehensive. Records are missing for Scotland, parts of northwest England, and much of Wales. The Norman capital of Winchester was not appraised, possibly because it was exempt from many taxes; nor was London, already Britain's largest city, perhaps on similar grounds or because a recent fire hampered the assessors' task.

Nevertheless, the reach of the king's men was remarkable. Detailed questions were posed to juries of new Norman and existing English inhabitants summoned from the country's manors, shires, and hundreds. These were Saxon administrative divisions that had survived the Norman Conquest, and without which the vast bureaucratic project would have been impossible. That the information could be compiled at all underlined the extent to which William had consolidated and centralized Norman power.

The Domesday Book's level of detail is extraordinary. In all, 13,418 places and 268,984 people are mentioned in the 475-page Little Domesday, which contains detailed accounts of eastern England, and the two-volume, 413-page Great Domesday, an edited version of assessments from the rest of the country. (The latter had fewer pages but was called "great" because it was bound in larger covers.) Among many other details, we learn that the county of Essex had 13,171 pigs, while Suffolk had 4,343 goats but only two donkeys. At the other extreme, it emerged that the king and his family directly owned 17 percent of England, and 54 percent belonged to his tenants-in-chief, or nobles.

Today, these and other details paint an incomparable picture of life before and after 1066, for William's men asked questions about land and resources at, after, and prior to the conquest. The information also highlights the fate of much of England and Wales down the centuries—many Domesday villages survive, for example, and about 80 percent of the agricultural land recorded in 1086 was still being farmed more than 800 years later at the outbreak of World War I.

So powerful was the survey's writ that within a hundred years, its original names, the King's Rolls or the Winchester Book, had been replaced by its present nickname, coined because its absolute nature left a hapless population as powerless to resist its decree as they would be on doomsday, God's day of final judgment. ■

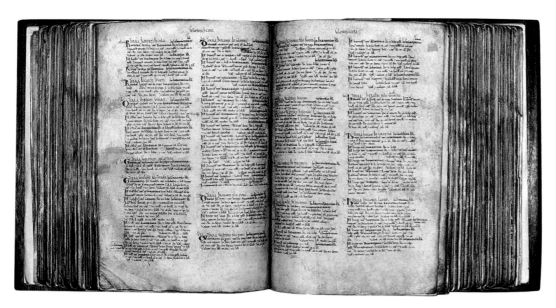

The Great Domesday One of the original Domesday documents, created after 1085 on the orders of William the Conqueror. A vast national survey, the Domesday project was designed to assess land ownership and the revenues due to William after the Norman invasion. Completed in less than a year, it took its name from the idea that its findings were as immutable as those of God on the Day of Judgment.

Full disclosure Scribes collating Domesday data. According to a chronicle of 1085, "The king sent his men all over England to ascertain how many 'hides' of land there were in each shire, and how much land and livestock the king owned in the country, and what annual dues were lawfully his . . . So very thoroughly did he have the inquiry carried out that not one ox, nor one cow, nor one pig escaped notice in his survey."

THOMAS BECKET

Murder in the Cathedral

Henry II Thomas Becket and Henry were friends but fell out after Becket became Archbishop of Canterbury and refused to implement the king's religious reforms.

Henry II (1133–1189) was one of the most dynamic of medieval kings, but in the eyes of his contemporaries, and in the judgment of posterity, his reign was stained by the murder of Thomas Becket (ca 1118–1170), his former friend, chancellor, and Archbishop of Canterbury.

The son of a London merchant, Becket was already a highly regarded royal secretary on Henry's accession in 1154. The two became close, hunting, gaming, and drinking together. "Never were two men more of a mind," wrote Becket's friend William FitzStephen.

Henry had brought order to the country, but the church, with its separate laws and courts, remained a power apart. When the old Archbishop of Canterbury died in 1162, Henry saw a chance to extend his control over the clergy by appointing Becket to the highest religious office in the land.

For reasons unknown, however, Becket's character changed after he became archbishop. From a high-living court official he became a pious ascetic, donning a hair shirt and resisting the changes Henry had appointed him to make. "It will be God I serve before you," he told the king.

Relations between the former friends quickly broke down, and in 1164 Becket was forced to flee to France. He remained there for six years until Henry, under pressure from the pope, allowed his return. No sooner was he back, however, than Becket excommunicated several bishops who had conspired with the king in his absence.

An enraged Henry, then in France, responded with a famous outburst: "What miserable drones and traitors have I nurtured within my household that they let their lord be treated with such shameful contempt by a low-born cleric?"

Four knights took the outburst at face value and crossed to Canterbury, where, on December 29, 1170, they murdered Becket before the high altar of his cathedral. Shock at the death reverberated around Europe. Henry insisted that he had been misunderstood, but to widespread disbelief. Pope Alexander III declared Thomas a saint—his shine at Canterbury became one of Christendom's major points of pilgrimage—and ordered a mortified Henry to do penance. The king donned a hair shirt and walked barefoot to the cathedral, where he spent a day and night fasting by Thomas's tomb. He then invited five strokes of the rod from every bishop present and three from each of the cathedral's 80 monks.

The blow to Henry's royal authority was even greater, and he was forced to back off in his battle with the clergy, which largely retained its authority and judicial independence. Becket's murder altered the balance of power between church and state for centuries, a situation that would be reversed only by a king even more forceful than Henry II: Henry VIII. ∎

◆ KEY DATES ◆

JUNE 2, 1162 Thomas Becket, Henry II's former chancellor, is ordained a priest. The following day he is made Archbishop of Canterbury.

DECEMBER 29, 1170 Four of Henry's knights, believing they act with the king's approval, murder Becket in Canterbury Cathedral.

FEBRUARY 21, 1173 Pope Alexander III makes Becket a saint. Becket's shrine becomes one of the most venerated in Christendom.

JULY 12, 1174 Henry goes to Canterbury to do penance for Becket's death. He is whipped by each of the 80 monks present.

1538 Henry VIII orders the destruction of Becket's shrine, and 21 carts are required to remove its ornaments. The saint's bones are burned and cast to the winds. A candle now burns permanently at the shrine's site.

Saint's reliquary A casket created to contain relics belonging to Thomas Becket after his canonization in 1173. Becket became one of the most revered martyrs of the medieval age.

Murder most foul Several monks witnessed Becket's death in Canterbury Cathedral. "He received a blow," wrote one, Edward Grim, "but still stood firm. At the third blow he fell to his knees, offering himself a living victim and saying in a low voice, 'For the name of Jesus, I am ready to embrace death.' " A fourth blow rent Becket's skull, spilling "blood white with the brain, and the brain red with the blood."

THE CONQUEST OF IRELAND

A Norman Invasion and a Country Divided

Ireland in the 12th century was a country of small kingdoms ruled by a handful of royal families. For precisely a hundred years it had remained largely untroubled by the Normans' invasion of England. This happy state of affairs changed in 1166, when a ruler from one of the royal dynasties, Diarmait Mac

Invitation to invasion Henry II presents a papal bull to the Archbishop of Cashel in Ireland after Henry's belated invasion of the country in 1171. England's only pope, Adrian IV, reportedly granted Henry the bull, which sanctioned his intervention in Ireland, in 1155. The pope hoped Henry would force changes on the Irish church to bring it in line with Roman worship and governance.

Murchada (ca 1101–1171), king of Leinster, sought help against his rivals from Henry II of England.

Henry already had his eyes on Ireland; reputedly he had secured a papal bull in 1155 from Adrian IV (the only English pope), who sanctioned any future invasion of the country in the hope that Henry would reform the Irish church along Roman lines. When Murchada made his request in 1166, however, Henry was preoccupied with the problem of Thomas Becket (see pages 78–79). With Henry's approval, Murchada turned instead to a powerful Anglo-Norman baron, Richard FitzGilbert, better known by his subsequent sobriquet, Strongbow.

In 1169 and 1170, FitzGilbert crossed to Ireland, quickly captured Waterford and other key cities, defeated Murchada's Irish rivals, and married Murchada's daughter, Aoife. The ease with which a small army had made such large gains (a lack of armor and cavalry were factors in the Irish defeats) now piqued the interest of Henry and other Welsh and Anglo-Norman barons.

Within a year, Henry—the first English king to set foot in Ireland—had taken Dublin. Soon after, he made gains at Cork, Limerick, and elsewhere. In 1171, he secured the fealty of the Irish kings. A year later, he convened the Synod of Cashel to impose the papacy's long-demanded reforms on the Irish church. In 1175, when it became clear that the English could not be dislodged, a treaty recognized the control of Henry and his barons in much of eastern Ireland. The wilder and less prosperous west remained with the Irish kings. English monarchs also now inherited a new title, the Lordship of Ireland, and delegated a Lord-Lieutenant of Ireland to rule on their behalf.

Strongbow and his allies were by no means the last Britons to cross to Ireland. Countless Anglo-Normans followed in their wake, and over the centuries they became assimilated into Irish culture and into what came to be known as the Pale (An Pháil in Irish)—the Anglo-Irish dominated north and east of the island (from the Latin *palus* ("stake"), suggesting a fenced boundary within which certain local laws prevailed).

Subsequent English royal control waxed and waned, however, and though much of the Pale and beyond bowed on a theoretical feudal knee to the English king, in practice, the distractions of the Hundred Years' War and the Wars of the Roses, among other things, meant that for more than 300 years, Irish chieftains and the assimilated English incomers were able to forge a largely independent existence. Only under Henry VIII and the Tudors would England return to Ireland with renewed intent (see pages 142–143). ∎

Kilkenny Castle This fortress in southeast Ireland, though altered since its construction, dates from around 1173–1195. It was among the first of many built by Norman nobles from England who conquered territory in Ireland after 1170. Anglo-Irish landowners would play a significant role in the island's subsequent history.

On the move This effigy, which resides in Christ Church Cathedral, Dublin, may represent Richard FitzGilbert (Strongbow), known for his role in the early Anglo-Norman invasions of Ireland. FitzGilbert may once have been interred in the cathedral but probably was reburied later in Ferns Cathedral in County Wexford.

> "*The kings of England have for a long period kept down the people of Ireland in a state of intolerable bondage, accompanied with unheard-of hardships and grievances. Nor was there found during that time, any person to redress their grievances.*"
>
> POPE CLEMENT V, LETTER TO EDWARD II, 1311

RICHARD I AND THE CRUSADES

England Abandoned for Foreign Fields

Royal seal Richard I is portrayed here as a chivalric knight. In truth, the English king was responsible for ordering the massacre of 2,700 Muslim prisoners at Acre, in the Holy Land, during the Third Crusade.

Richard I (1157–1199) is remembered as one of England's warrior kings, a courageous knight whose deeds earned him the name Coeur de Lion, or Lionheart. Yet a less English king would be hard to imagine. He did not speak the language, had only one English ancestor—his great-grandmother, Matilda—and during his ten-year reign spent just six months in his kingdom. The French territories of his parents, Henry II and Eleanor of Aquitaine, provided one distraction; an obsession to join the Crusades, or holy wars, provided another.

Crusades were nothing new. As early as the eighth century of the Christian era, the followers of the Prophet Muhammad, founder of Islam, had conquered much of the southern Mediterranean. For the most part, the resulting caliphates had little impact on western Europe. Around 1071, however, a later Muslim people, the Seljuks, took Jerusalem and threatened Constantinople (present-day Istanbul). If Constantinople fell, Italy and the Christian West might be next.

In 1095 the danger led Pope Urban II to summon the First Crusade, an expedition of European armies that in 1099 recaptured Jerusalem and established crusader states in the Holy Land. Muslim forces triumphed during the Second Crusade of 1147 and again in 1187, when the greatest of the Muslim generals, Saladin (ca 1137/38–1193), retook Jerusalem. The Third Crusade—Richard's crusade—was called two years later.

Richard was decisive and organized. For example, before leaving for Palestine, he arranged for the delivery of 60,000 horseshoes and 14,000 sides of pork. Money was no object. Of the taxes needed for his campaigns, Richard was unrepentant: "I would sell London," he said, "if I could find a buyer." His men were therefore well led and well equipped when they landed in the Holy Land in 1191. After a five-week siege, they took Acre, a city that had held out against other crusader armies for more than two years.

Sixteen months of further campaigning proved fruitless, however, and Richard was forced to settle with Saladin without capturing Jerusalem, his main goal. He also squabbled with his fellow crusaders, and after he was shipwrecked in the Adriatic in 1192, he was captured and ransomed by one of them, Duke Leopold of Austria. The ransom, equivalent to three years' worth of total taxes in England, was raised and paid.

Richard returned briefly to his English kingdom and quickly settled a plot by his brother, the future King John (whom he pardoned), before traveling to France, where he died at age 41 while fighting near Bordeaux. On his deathbed, he ordered that his disemboweled and salted body be buried next to his parents at Fontevraud Abbey in Anjou, and that his heart be sent not to England but to Normandy. ∎

Christian plunder An 11th-century gold and enamel reliquary depicting the Annunciation. This artifact was one of many looted and taken to Europe by crusader armies during their campaigns in the Middle East.

Face-to-face Richard I in the Holy Land in battle with Saladin, leader of the Muslim forces, during the Third Crusade (1188–1192). Richard was an accomplished soldier but was unable to defeat Saladin. The two eventually made peace, and Richard was forced to abandon his main aim, the retaking of Jerusalem.

"The Crusaders forsook God before God forsook them. Every one was eager for blood . . . and massacred both men and women . . . so that such a slaughter had never been seen."

AN EYEWITNESS TO THE CAPTURE OF JERUSALEM, 1099

French funeral Richard the Lionheart was buried in France. During his ten-year reign, he spent just six months in his English kingdom.

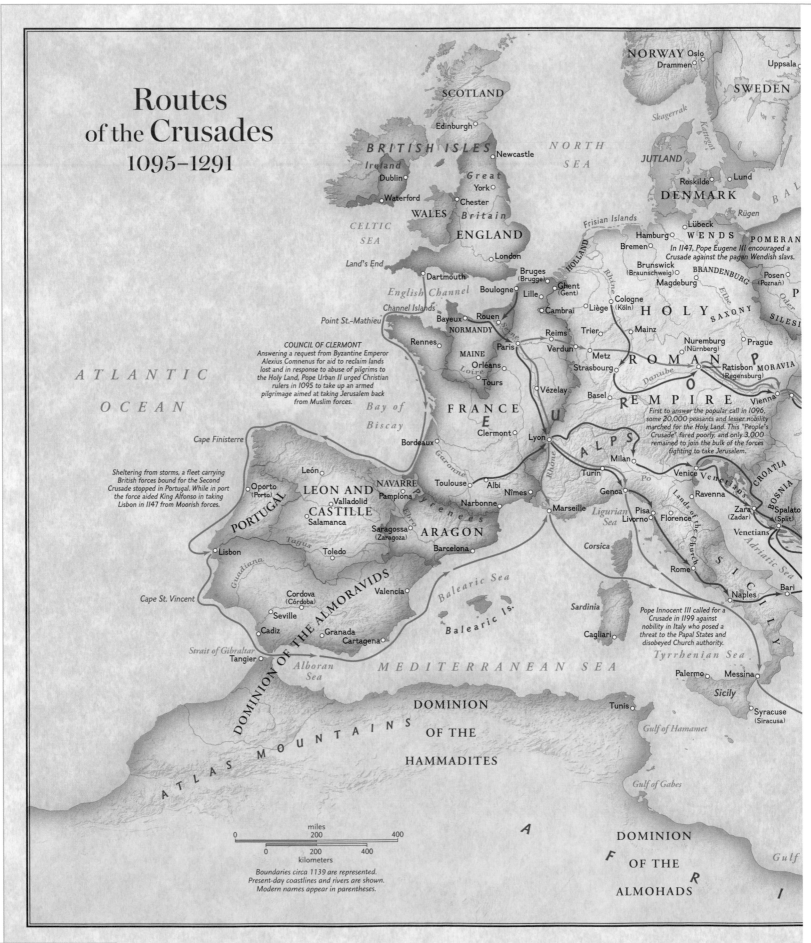

Routes
of the Crusades
1095–1291

NORWAY ○ Oslo
○ Drammen

○ Uppsala

SWEDEN

Skagerrak

SCOTLAND

○ Edinburgh

*NORTH
SEA*

JUTLAND

○ Roskilde   ○ Lund

DENMARK

Rügen

BRITISH ISLES

Ireland   ○ Newcastle

○ Dublin   *Great*   York ○
○ Waterford   ○ Chester

WALES   *Britain*

ENGLAND

Frisian Islands

○ Lübeck   **POMERAN**

Hamburg ○   **WENDS**
Bremen ○

*In 1147, Pope Eugene III encouraged a
Crusade against the pagan Wendish slavs.*

Brunswick ○   **BRANDENBURG**
(Braunschweig)   Magdeburg ○   Posen ○
(Poznań)

*CELTIC
SEA*

○ London

○ Dartmouth

English Channel

Bruges ○
(Brugge)   Ghent ○
(Gent)

Boulogne ○
Lille ○

Cambraï ○   Liège ○

Cologne ○
(Köln)

HOLY   **SAXONY**   **SILESI**

○ Mainz

Nuremburg ○
(Nürnberg)   ○ Prague

P

Channel Islands

Bayeux ○   Rouen ○
NORMANDY

Reims ○   Trier ○

Verdun ○   Metz ○

ROMAN   ○ Ratisbon   **MORAVIA**
(Regensburg)

Point St.-Mathieu

○ Rennes

MAINE

○ Paris

Orléans ○

Loire

○ Tours

Strasbourg ○   **P**

○ Vézelay   Basel ○   *Danube*   **O**

EMPIRE   *Vienna*

*COUNCIL OF CLERMONT
Answering a request from Byzantine Emperor
Alexius Comnenus for aid to reclaim lands
lost and in response to abuse of pilgrims to
the Holy Land, Pope Urban II urged Christian
rulers in 1095 to take up an armed
pilgrimage aimed at taking Jerusalem back
from Muslim forces.*

*Bay of
Biscay*

FRANCE   **E**

○ Clermont   ○ Lyon

*First to answer the popular call in 1096,
some 20,000 peasants and lesser nobility
marched for the Holy Land. This "People's
Crusade" fared poorly, and only 3,000
remained to join the bulk of the forces
fighting to take Jerusalem.*

A L P S

○ Milan

U

*ATLANTIC

OCEAN*

Cape Finisterre

Venice   **Venetians**

CROATIA

○ Bordeaux

Garonne

Turin ○   *Po*

Ravenna ○

BOSNIA

○ León

NAVARRE
Pamplona ○

○ Toulouse   ○ Albi

Nîmes ○

Genoa ○

Zara ○
(Zadar)   Spalato ○
(Split)

*Sheltering from storms, a fleet carrying
British forces bound for the Second
Crusade stopped in Portugal. While in port
the force aided King Alfonso in taking
Lisbon in 1147 from Moorish forces.*

○ Oporto
(Porto)

Valladolid ○

**LEON AND

CASTILE**

Salamanca ○

Narbonne ○

Marseille ○

*Ligurian
Sea*

Pisa ○   ○ Livorno
Florence ○

Lands of the Church

Venetians

Adriatic Sea

Tagus

○ Saragossa
(Zaragoza)

ARAGON

○ Toledo

Barcelona ○

Corsica

Rome ○

S

Guadiana

Cape St. Vincent

○ Lisbon

DOMINION OF THE ALMORAVIDS

Cordova ○
(Córdoba)

○ Valencia

Balearic Sea

Balearic Is.

Sardinia

*Pope Innocent III called for a
Crusade in 1199 against
nobility in Italy who posed a
threat to the Papal States and
disobeyed Church authority.*

Naples ○   ○ Bari

I

C

I

L

Y

○ Seville

○ Cadiz

○ Granada
Cartagena ○

Cagliari ○

Tyrrhenian Sea

Strait of Gibraltar
Tangier ○

*Alboran
Sea*

M E D I T E R R A N E A N   S E A

Palermo ○   ○ Messina

Sicily

Syracuse ○
(Siracusa)

**DOMINION OF THE

HAMMADITES**

A T L A S   M O U N T A I N S

Tunis ○

Gulf of Hamamet

Gulf of Gabes

Gulf

miles
0   200   400

0   200   400
kilometers

*Boundaries circa 1139 are represented.
Present-day coastlines and rivers are shown.
Modern names appear in parentheses.*

**DOMINION

OF THE

ALMOHADS**

**A

F

R

I**

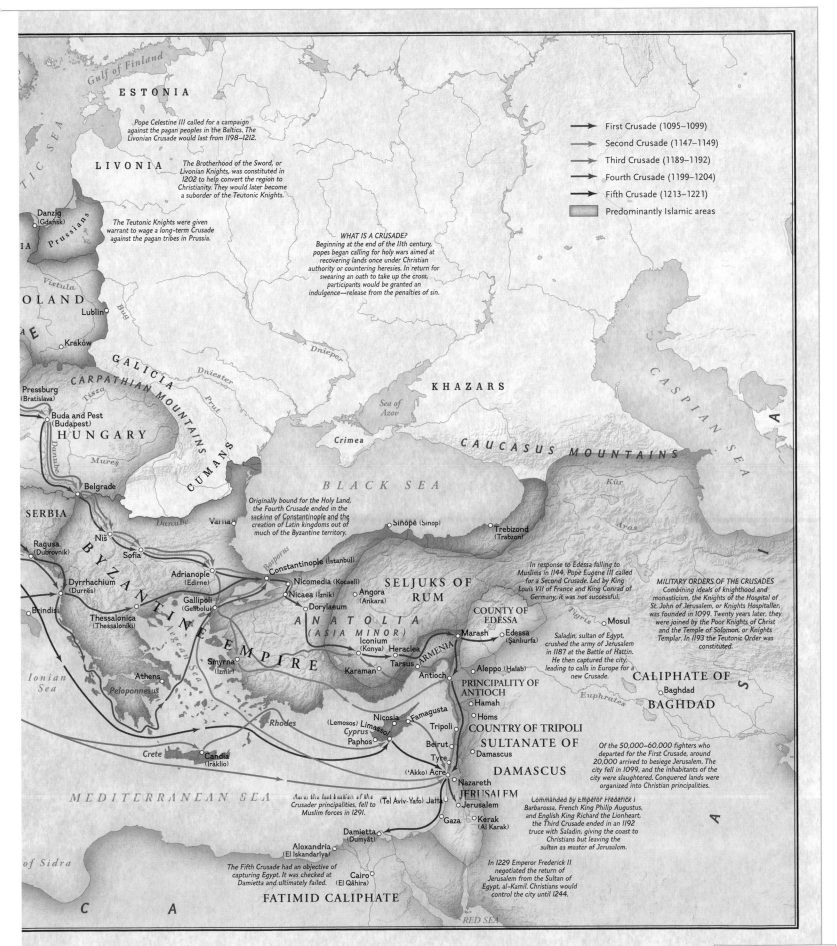

ESTONIA

Pope Celestine III called for a campaign against the pagan peoples in the Baltics. The Livonian Crusade would last from 1198–1212.

LIVONIA

The Brotherhood of the Sword, or Livonian Knights, was constituted in 1202 to help convert the region to Christianity. They would later become a suborder of the Teutonic Knights.

Danzig (Gdańsk)

Prussians

The Teutonic Knights were given warrant to wage a long-term Crusade against the pagan tribes in Prussia.

WHAT IS A CRUSADE?
Beginning at the end of the 11th century, popes began calling for holy wars aimed at recovering lands once under Christian authority or countering heresies. In return for swearing an oath to take up the cross, participants would be granted an indulgence—release from the penalties of sin.

First Crusade (1095–1099)
Second Crusade (1147–1149)
Third Crusade (1189–1192)
Fourth Crusade (1199–1204)
Fifth Crusade (1213–1221)
Predominantly Islamic areas

POLAND

Vistula

Lublin

Bug

Kraków

GALICIA

CARPATHIAN MOUNTAINS

Dniester

Prut

Tisza

KHAZARS

CASPIAN SEA

Pressburg (Bratislava)

Buda and Pest (Budapest)

HUNGARY

Mures

Danube

CUMANS

Sea of Azov

Crimea

CAUCASUS MOUNTAINS

Kür

Aras

Belgrade

SERBIA

Ragusa (Dubrovnik)

Niš

Sofia

BLACK SEA

Originally bound for the Holy Land, the Fourth Crusade ended in the sacking of Constantinople and the creation of Latin kingdoms out of much of the Byzantine territory.

Sinope (Sinop)

Trebizond (Trabzon)

Varna

Dyrrhachium (Durrës)

Adrianople (Edirne)

Constantinople (Istanbul)

Nicomedia (Kocaeli)

Nicaea (İznik)

SELJUKS OF RUM

In response to Edessa falling to Muslims in 1144, Pope Eugene III called for a Second Crusade. Led by King Louis VII of France and King Conrad of Germany, it was not successful.

MILITARY ORDERS OF THE CRUSADES
Combining ideals of knighthood and monasticism, the Knights of the Hospital of St. John of Jerusalem, or Knights Hospitaller, was founded in 1099. Twenty years later, they were joined by the Poor Knights of Christ and the Temple of Solomon, or Knights Templar. In 1193 the Teutonic Order was constituted.

BYZANTINE

Gallipoli (Gelibolu)

Angora (Ankara)

Dorylaeum

COUNTY OF EDESSA

Tigris

Mosul

Brindisi

Thessalonica (Thessaloníki)

EMPIRE

ANATOLIA (ASIA MINOR)

Iconium (Konya)

Heraclea

Marash

Edessa (Şanlıurfa)

Saladin, sultan of Egypt, crushed the army of Jerusalem in 1187 at the Battle of Hattin. He then captured the city, leading to calls in Europe for a new Crusade.

CALIPHATE OF

Ionian Sea

Smyrna (İzmir)

Tarsus

ARMENIA

Aleppo (Halab)

Baghdad

BAGHDAD

Athens

Peloponnesus

Karaman

Antioch

PRINCIPALITY OF ANTIOCH

Euphrates

Hamah

Homs

Rhodes

Nicosia

Famagusta

Tripoli

COUNTRY OF TRIPOLI

(Lemosos) Limassol
Cyprus Paphos

SULTANATE OF

Of the 50,000–60,000 fighters who departed for the First Crusade, around 20,000 arrived to besiege Jerusalem. The city fell in 1099, and the inhabitants of the city were slaughtered. Conquered lands were organized into Christian principalities.

Crete

Candia (Iráklio)

Beirut

Tyre

Damascus

DAMASCUS

('Akko) Acre

Nazareth

MEDITERRANEAN SEA

Acre, the last bastion of the Crusader principalities, fell to Muslim forces in 1291.

(Tel Aviv-Yafo) Jaffa

JERUSALEM

Jerusalem

Commanded by Emperor Frederick I Barbarossa, French King Philip Augustus, and English King Richard the Lionheart, the Third Crusade ended in an 1192 truce with Saladin, giving the coast to Christians but leaving the sultan as master of Jerusalem.

Gaza

Kerak (Al Karak)

Damietta (Dumyât)

Aloxandria (El Iskandariya)

of Sidra

The Fifth Crusade had an objective of capturing Egypt. It was checked at Damietta and ultimately failed.

Cairo (El Qâhira)

In 1229 Emperor Frederick II negotiated the return of Jerusalem from the Sultan of Egypt, al-Kamil. Christians would control the city until 1244.

FATIMID CALIPHATE

RED SEA

MAGNA CARTA

A Constitutional Touchstone for the Ages

Among English monarchs, only Richard III is more reviled than King John (1167–1216). Within a few years of succeeding Richard I in 1199, John had plunged the country into chaos: Military setbacks in France brought humiliation; tax demands became unrelenting; a papal dispute caused uproar in the church; and John's own character, for all his intelligence and attention to administrative detail, suggested he could not be trusted.

By 1215, many of John's nobles were bent on revolt. Marching on London, they forced the king to address their grievances in a charter—later known as Magna Carta—to which John, attempting to buy time, gave his royal assent on June 15, 1215.

For those present, the document was a practical solution to an immediate problem. Within weeks, however, both sides had broken its terms, and John successfully asked Pope Innocent III to annul it as "shameful, illegal, and unjust." Magna Carta was not intended as permanent declaration of principle, theory, or legal rights. Many of its 63 clauses dealt with lesser grievances, such as fishing rights, death duties, and the standardization of weights and measures. Nor was it a bill of rights that guaranteed liberty to all free men, a modern concept that did not exist at the time—the "free men" it cited (see below) referred merely to "free" landholders, who amounted to less than 40 percent of the population.

Rather, Magna Carta was a reiteration of the ancient customs of justice and feudalism, a device used by the elite of medieval society to rein in the power of the king, whose perversion of a monarch's feudal privileges and arbitrary dispensation of justice were seen as increasingly despotic.

Yet the terms of Magna Carta could not be undone. Even at the time, they were widely disseminated in copies read aloud around the kingdom. And though often subsequently ineffectual in the face of more powerful kings, and originally drafted to protect only a small elite, the charter was gradually co-opted by a wider constituency and its clauses more freely interpreted.

Magna Carta's prose now echoes in documents the world over, not least in the U.S. Constitution and the Universal Declaration of Human Rights. "To no one will we sell, to no one deny or delay right or justice," reads Magna Carta Clause 40. Clause 39, the basis of both habeas corpus and trial by jury, asserts, "No free man shall be seized or imprisoned, or stripped of his rights or possessions, or outlawed or exiled . . . except by the lawful judgment of his equals or by the law of the land."

In codifying the powers of nobles in relation to kings, Magna Carta marked a pivotal point in the shift from monarchical authority. It was an attempt to bind kings, in the same manner as subjects, to the rule of law and to the country's established customs. As such it was a landmark in the history of liberty under the law and a constitutional touchstone for England and other nations for centuries to come. ■

In the round This memorial was inaugurated in 1957 at Runnymede, on the River Thames, close to the spot where King John agreed to the terms of Magna Carta in 1215. Runnymede was a short distance from Windsor Castle, King John's fortress retreat outside London.

◆ KEY FACTS ◆

CURSED KING "Foul as it is," wrote 13th-century chronicler Matthew Paris, "Hell itself is defiled by the fouler presence of John."

ON THE DAY John and his leading barons agreed upon the 63 clauses making up Magna Carta on June 19, 1215.

MISSING LINKS Only four copies of Magna Carta survive of the many distributed to be read around the kingdom. Only one has survived with its seal intact.

PARCHMENT Magna Carta is written on parchment—sheepskin that is soaked, dried, stretched, and scraped to produce a smooth surface.

IN SHORT Magna Carta is hard to read because it is in old Latin, because the medieval script is unfamiliar, and because parchment was expensive and words were abbreviated to save space.

Final text *(left)* When Magna Carta was first written, many copies were prepared and distributed to be read as proclamations in towns and cities around the kingdom. Today, only four of these original documents survive. The charter was reissued several times in the 13th century, and 17 of these later copies survive, including the document pictured here. Issued in 1225, during the reign of Henry III, it was the final version of the charter.

Seal on the deal *(below)* King John signs Magna Carta under duress in the presence of his leading barons on June 19, 1215. It is believed John did not actually sign a document, and may not even have been able to write. Instead, scribes wrote up the verbal terms of the agreements made at the time in the days following the event. They then authenticated copies of the Charter of Liberties, as it was then known, with a wax seal.

"The democratic aspiration is no mere recent phase in human history. It is human history . . . It blazed a new in the Middle Ages. It was written in Magna Carta."

FRANKLIN D. ROOSEVELT, INAUGURAL ADDRESS, 1941

THE RISE OF SCOTLAND
A Struggle for Nationhood and Independence

Geography set Scotland apart from the earliest times, its islands and mountains a fortress home to scattered Celtic tribes before the advent of the Romans. The Romans, when they came, ventured into the lowland south of the region, but little farther, leaving Britain's northernmost lands to the Picts and a patchwork of other tribal kingdoms.

As Saxon tribes poured into England in the sixth century, so Irish tribes poured into western Scotland, and it is the latinized name for an Irish people—the *Scotti*—that would give the Scots their name. Angles also came to the region and founded Bernicia, a kingdom that straddled today's Scottish border. The Vikings followed in the ninth century and secured territory on Scotland's islands and northwest mainland.

■ THE ROOTS OF CONFLICT

It was Scotland's founding monarch, Kenneth mac Alpin (Cináed mac Ailpín) (died 858), who challenged the Vikings' presence, much as one of England's founding monarchs, Alfred the Great, challenged their presence in the south. Kenneth, like Alfred, forged a kingdom that would be enlarged and consolidated by his successors, but while England's eventual foes were the Normans, Scotland's were their own near neighbors: the English.

In this the Scots were partly to blame. For almost 200 years, until the reign of Duncan I in 1034, the Scottish kings followed a form of succession known as tanistry. Rather than passing from father to son, the throne alternated between branches of the mac Alpin family, passing from cousin to cousin or nephew to uncle. The result was a weak monarchy, which is one reason why Edward the Elder (870–924), Alfred the Great's son, was able to force the Scottish king, Constantine II (died 952), to submit to his rule in 918.

It was the beginning of English claims to overlordship of Scotland. In 1072, for example, after the Norman Conquest, Malcolm III of Scotland (ca 1031–1093) was forced to submit to the might of William I. English influence also increased as Anglo-Normans moved north during the 12th century and intermarried with the Scottish nobility. Among them were families that later would shape Scottish history, such as the Bruces, the Comyns, and the Stewards (see page 116).

Bridge too far The Battle of Stirling Bridge in 1297, a stirring victory for William Wallace over the English. The narrow bridge, which hampered the English, contributed to the defeat.

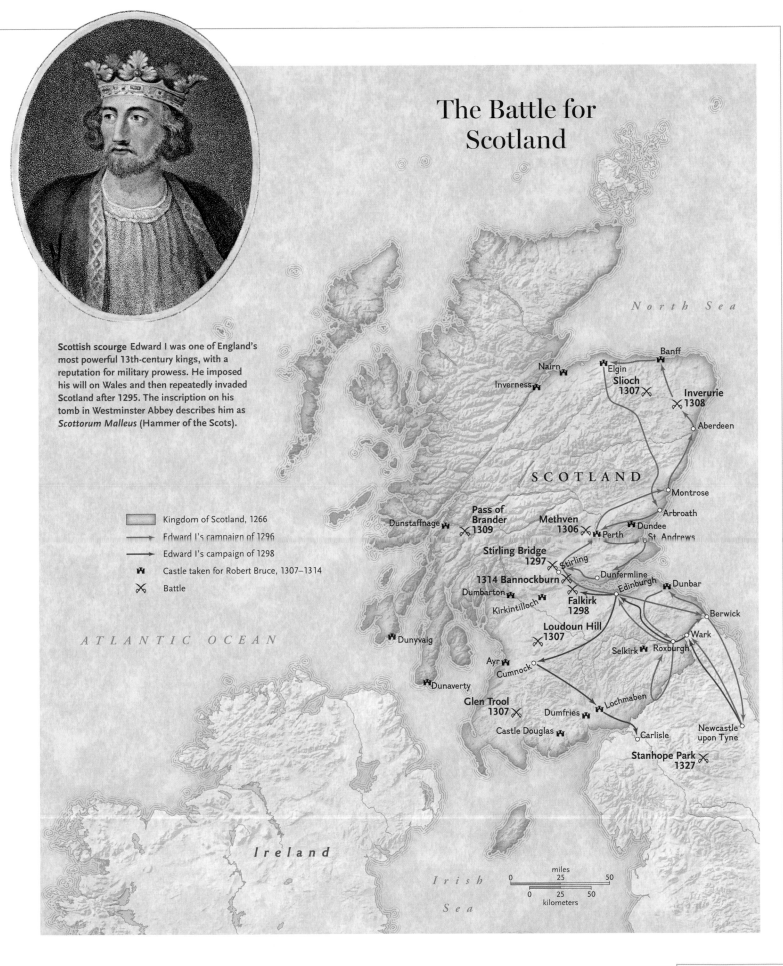

The Battle for Scotland

Scottish scourge Edward I was one of England's most powerful 13th-century kings, with a reputation for military prowess. He imposed his will on Wales and then repeatedly invaded Scotland after 1295. The inscription on his tomb in Westminster Abbey describes him as *Scottorum Malleus* (Hammer of the Scots).

North Sea

SCOTLAND

Kingdom of Scotland, 1266

Edward I's campaign of 1296

Edward I's campaign of 1298

Castle taken for Robert Bruce, 1307–1314

Battle

ATLANTIC OCEAN

Banff
Elgin
Nairn
Slioch
1307
Inverurie
1308
Inverness
Aberdeen

Montrose
Arbroath
Pass of
Brander
1309
Methven
1306
Perth
Dundee
Dunstaffnage
St. Andrews

Stirling Bridge
1297
Stirling
1314 Bannockburn
Dunfermline
Dumbarton
Edinburgh
Dunbar
Kirkintilloch
Falkirk
1298
Berwick
Loudoun Hill
1307
Wark
Ayr
Selkirk
Roxburgh
Cumnock
Dunyvaig
Lochmaben
Glen Trool
1307
Dumfries
Newcastle
upon Tyne
Dunaverty
Castle Douglas
Carlisle
Stanhope Park
1327

Ireland

Irish

Sea

miles
0   25   50
0   25   50
kilometers

THE CRISIS OF SUCCESSION

The English did not have it all their own way. Scotland enjoyed powerful leadership under Kings David I (ca 1080/5–1153) and William I, the Lion (ca 1142/3–1214). The latter reigned for 49 years, the longest of any Scottish medieval monarch, and introduced the surviving red lion rampant to the Scottish royal standard.

In time, however, the weakness of the Scottish succession again drew the English north. The death of Alexander III in 1286 left his three-year-old granddaughter, Margaret, as heir. The infant Margaret had been promised in marriage to the future Edward II of England (son of Edward I), a match that would have united the English and Scottish crowns. Edward I was one of the most forceful of English kings, and he was in the process of subduing Wales and its native princes. When Margaret died in 1290, the ensuing succession crisis allowed him to turn to Scotland as well.

SCOTLAND SUBDUED

Such was the turmoil—there were 13 claimants to the throne—that Edward was effectively invited to choose the Scottish king. An Anglo-Scottish parliament was called, and in November 1292, a commission of 24 jurors, with Edward at its head, chose John Balliol (ca 1240/50–1313/14) as monarch.

Balliol, who was descended from a daughter of David I, pleased no one. As Edward's puppet, he proved unpopular among the Scots, and when he attempted to assert his independence by seeking a French alliance, he antagonized Edward. In 1296, Edward marched north, defeated the Scots at the Battle of Dunbar, and replaced Balliol with an English administration backed by an occupying army.

For ten years the Scottish throne remained vacant, with resistance to Edward confined largely to the guerrilla warfare of William Wallace (see sidebar, page 88). Two events, however, marked a turning point in Scottish fortunes. The first was the rise of Robert I the Bruce (1274–1329).

Like Balliol, Bruce had claims to the throne, and in February 1306, he (or his followers) reinforced those claims by murdering his chief rival, John Comyn. He then declared himself king, only to be forced into exile in the same year after defeats by the English.

Bruce was not gone long. The following year, the death of Edward I—killed by dysentery as he marched north to take on the Scots again—brought Edward II to the English throne. Edward II lacked his father's military and administrative prowess, and Bruce scored an almost uninterrupted string of victories that began at Loudon Hill in 1307 and culminated in Bannockburn in 1314. The latter was Scotland's finest hour on the battlefield, a rout against the odds that saw Edward and his shattered army flee.

TO INDEPENDENCE AND BEYOND

In 1320, Bruce had his nobles draw up the Declaration of Arbroath, partly aimed at securing papal approval for his reign, but also a resounding assertion of Scottish independence. The assertion became fact in 1328, when the chaos around the accession of the young Edward III to the English throne led to the Treaty of Edinburgh, whereby Edward renounced his claims to lordship of Scotland, marking an effective truce and tacit recognition of Scottish independence.

Further Scottish dynastic feuding followed Bruce's death a year later, and English and Scottish conflicts continued for centuries, but Bruce and Wallace's work was largely done. Better still for the Scots, in one of history's sweeter ironies, one of Bruce's descendants would ascend to the English throne some 300 years later as James I of England. ∎

Royal review Scottish king Robert the Bruce surveys his troops before the Battle of Bannockburn in 1314. The Scots carried spears, used en masse in battle to form an impenetrable phalanx. Bruce would lead his men to a resounding victory over a larger English army led by Edward II. Unlike most battles, which lasted a few hours, Bannockburn was fought over two days. Edward fled the field in panic, helping turn defeat into a rout, with the death of perhaps 11,000 of his 18,000 soldiers.

Lucky charm The eighth-century Monymusk Reliquary, which may have belonged to St. Columba (died 597), was carried into battle by the victorious Scots at Bannockburn in 1314.

Set in stone A royal seal from 1326 depicting Robert the Bruce enthroned and, on the reverse, as a warrior and knight. Bruce was the king of Scotland between 1306 and his death in 1329.

THE BLACK DEATH

The Disease That Helped Change History

The Black Death was a plague pandemic that struck Britain and Ireland in the middle of the 14th century. It killed a large proportion of the population and precipitated far-reaching social and economic consequences.

The disease had its origins in the Far East and was initially transmitted by bites from infected fleas, which in turn were carried by black rats aboard merchant ships. Its first outbreak in England was in the port of Weymouth, in June 1348, on the country's south coast. By the fall it had reached London, which, with its filthy streets and close-packed population, was a perfect breeding ground for disease. In 1349 it spread to most parts of Britain and Ireland and killed indiscriminately, regardless of age or class. Edward III's own daughter, Joan, who was 13, was among those who died.

At the time, the pandemic was known as the Pestilence or the Great Mortality. The term Black Death, which came later, was a reference to the dark swellings (buboes) and livid marks on the body that developed in the disease's most common bubonic form. Death in such cases usually arrived within a week, after a high fever and a lapse into coma, but was not inevitable.

Second and third forms of the disease, possibly mutations of the first, caused death by blood poisoning and, in the pneumonic form, through attacks on the lungs. This last version, possibly the most prevalent in 1348, was the deadliest: Death could occur in hours, and airborne transmittal was rapid.

Fourteenth-century records are unreliable (or nonexistent), but research suggests a mortality rate in Britain and Ireland of about 45 percent in a population of between five and six million. It was the largest proportionate population decline in the islands' history. Entire villages disappeared, identifiable today only as grassy mounds in empty fields; crops rotted for want of laborers; and livestock wandered the countryside untended. So many people died that church graveyards became full and led to the creation of hurriedly dug mass graves, or "plague pits," with corpses stacked more than five deep.

The disease petered out by the winter of 1350, but the pestilence would return to both Britain and Ireland several times, most famously in the Great Plague that struck London in 1665 (see page 182).

None of the subsequent outbreaks, however, had the lasting effects of the 1348 pandemic, which, in wiping out swathes of rural laborers, had profound economic repercussions. Wages increased, as fewer workers meant a greater demand for their services. Feudal or hired farmhands previously tied to a single master could now migrate and offer their services to the highest bidder. Other rural laborers, deprived of work on the land, turned to more skilled artisan trades. As land became plentiful and demand for food lower, prices fell, forcing some landowners to sell their holdings. This, in turn, created a larger class of landowning yeomen. Finally came the changes that laid the foundations for England's lucrative wool industry, as the shortage of workers accelerated a move away from labor-intensive arable farming to grazing and sheep rearing. ■

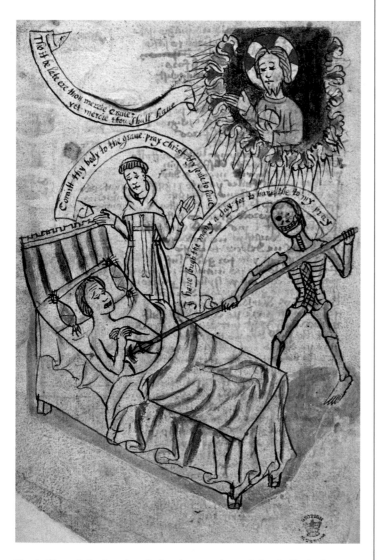

The devil's work A priest gives the last rites to a plague victim. God looks down from above while Satan wounds the victim on the right. At least two million Britons died during the Back Death plague pandemic of 1348 to 1350.

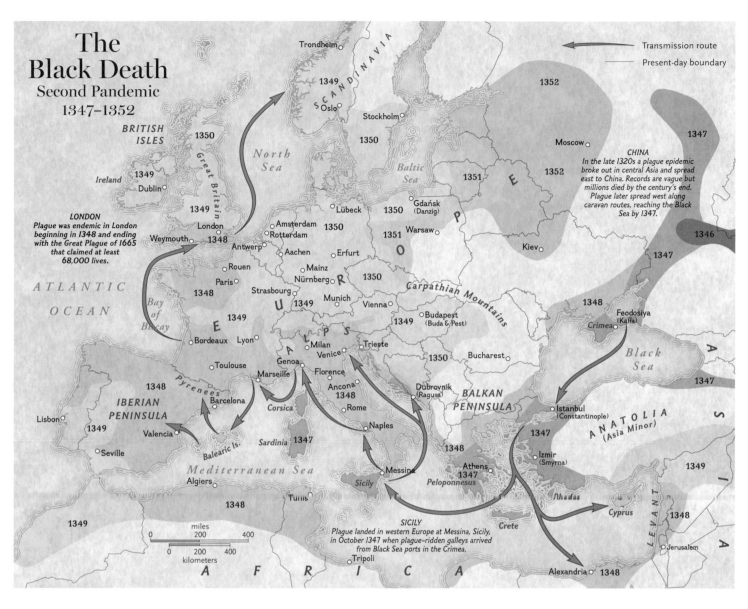

The Black Death
Second Pandemic
1347–1352

Transmission route

Present-day boundary

BRITISH ISLES

1350

North Sea

1349

1352

1347

SCANDINAVIA

Trondheim

Oslo

Stockholm

Baltic Sea

1350

Moscow

CHINA
In the late 1320s a plague epidemic broke out in central Asia and spread east to China. Records are vague but millions died by the century's end. Plague later spread west along caravan routes, reaching the Black Sea by 1347.

Ireland

1349

Dublin

1350

1349

Lübeck

1350

Gdańsk (Danzig)

1351

1352

1347

LONDON
Plague was endemic in London beginning in 1348 and ending with the Great Plague of 1665 that claimed at least 68,000 lives.

Weymouth

London

1348

Amsterdam

Rotterdam

1350

Warsaw

1351

Kiev

1346

Antwerp

Aachen

Erfurt

1347

ATLANTIC OCEAN

Rouen

Paris

Mainz

Nürnberg

1350

Carpathian Mountains

1348

Bay of Biscay

1348

Strasbourg

1349

Munich

Vienna

Budapest (Buda & Pest)

Feodosiya (Kaffa)

Crimea

1349

Bordeaux

Lyon

ALPS

Milan

Venice

Trieste

1349

1350

Bucharest

Black Sea

1347

Toulouse

Marseille

Genoa

Florence

Ancona

1348

Dubrovnik (Ragusa)

BALKAN PENINSULA

Istanbul (Constantinople)

1348

IBERIAN PENINSULA

Barcelona

Corsica

Rome

ANATOLIA (Asia Minor)

1347

Lisbon

Pyrenees

Valencia

1349

Naples

1348

Izmir (Smyrna)

1349

Seville

Balearic Is.

Sardinia

1347

Messina

Athens

1347

Peloponnesus

Rhodes

Cyprus

1348

Algiers

Mediterranean Sea

Sicily

1348

Crete

Jerusalem

1348

Tunis

SICILY
Plague landed in western Europe at Messina, Sicily, in October 1347 when plague-ridden galleys arrived from Black Sea ports in the Crimea.

Alexandria

1348

1349

Tripoli

A F R I C A

miles
0   200   400

0   200   400
kilometers

LEVANT

ASIA

"The Triumph of Death" This painting by Pieter Bruegel the Elder, dated around 1562, powerfully evokes a medieval society ravaged by plague. The 1348 outbreak in Britain had many long-term consequences, especially in the countryside. Shortage of labor meant rural workers were able to demand new freedoms and higher wages. Other laborers were forced to leave the land as demand for food fell and farms were sold. Measures to restrict laborers' freedoms and to control wages and inflation led to revolt and unrest.

GEOFFREY CHAUCER
The Medieval Father of English Literature

Geoffrey Chaucer (ca 1343–1400) was the son of a London wine merchant. He enjoyed a varied career as a royal page, a customs official, a soldier, a diplomat, a lawyer, and a clerk of the king's works, but it is his for his literary accomplishments, and *The Canterbury Tales* (ca 1387–1400) in particular, that he is best remembered.

The Canterbury Tales is written in the vernacular—that is, in the common spoken language of the day. English had a long tradition as a literary language, beginning with works in Old English, or Anglo-Saxon, which evolved largely from the Germanic and Nordic languages of the Angles, the Saxons, and the Vikings. Latin also was widely used as a written language, especially after the spread of Roman Christianity from A.D. 600, while French became the dominant idiom of court and the elite after the Norman Conquest of 1066.

English continued to evolve, however, and by Chaucer's day, a form of so-called Middle English, enriched with French and Latin, was on the rise, at least in the households of ordinary people. Chaucer was not the first to use this language in literature, but *The Canterbury Tales* was its first masterpiece.

The work concerns a group of "wel nyne and twenty" pilgrims bound for Thomas Becket's shrine at Canterbury (see pages 78–79). It is a motley gathering drawn from several ranks of English society: a miller, a prioress, a plowman, a friar, a dyer, a carpenter, a knight, and many more. Prior to their departure, they meet at the Tabard Inn in London, where the innkeeper suggests that each tell a story to enliven the journey. In the end, only 24 are told, of the 120 Chaucer probably planned before his death. The poet includes himself among the pilgrims, but no sooner has he started his tale than his host cuts him short, using the kind of earthy language that has endeared the poem to generations of schoolchildren: "By God, quod he, 'for pleynly, at a word' / Thy drasty [worthless] ryming is nat worth a toord."

Although *The Canterbury Tales* has plenty of bawdy humor, it contains much more than that. Blending a dazzling variety of styles, it mixes the traditions of Chaucer's native tongue with those of French romances and Italian writers such as Dante, Petrarch, and Boccaccio, whose work the poet encountered on diplomatic visits to Italy. It also mixes the coarse with the courtly, the poetic with the prosaic. Ideas and asides tumble forth, sly satire is never far away,

and a wealth of detail and description brings a whole medieval world to life: the poor knight, fallen on hard times, whose tunic is smudged by his rusting chain mail; the "humble" monk who dines on roast swan; the social-climbing prioress, feeding her lapdog tidbits and affecting a French accent. ∎

Poet of the past Geoffrey Chaucer is remembered as the author of *The Canterbury Tales* (ca 1387–1400), one of the first and finest works written in the vernacular English of the day. But as a witness to events such as the Black Death and the Peasants' Revolt, Chaucer also created a vivid chronicle of everyday life in 14th-century England. He is depicted here in a panel from around 1590, painted 190 years after his death.

Chaucer's Contemporaries

The age of Chaucer and the rise of vernacular literature included William Langland (ca 1330–ca 1400), who wrote *The Vision of Piers Plowman* (1360–1387), a visionary and allegorical work concerned with the search for religious truth *(left)*. The age is also remembered for Chaucer's friend John Gower (ca 1340–1408), who is known for *Confessio Amantis* (1386–1390), a series of narrative tales built around the confession of an aging lover. An author known only as the Pearl Poet wrote *Sir Gawain and the Green Knight*, a courtly poetic tale that drew on the legend of Arthur and the Round Table.

Travelers' tales Pilgrims en route to the shrine of Thomas Becket at Canterbury. The pilgrimage—one of the most popular in the medieval world—was the same one followed by the disparate characters of Chaucer's *Canterbury Tales*. The poet has most of his 29 pilgrims tell a story to help pass the time on their journey.

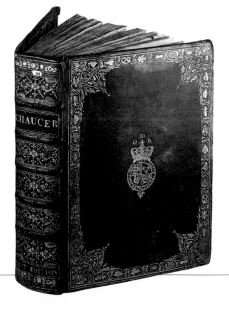

First edition This rebound copy of *The Canterbury Tales*, now in the British Library, was probably the first book produced on Britain's earliest printing press, established by William Caxton in Westminster in 1476.

"Love will not be constrain'd by mastery. / When mast'ry comes, the god of love anon / Beateth his wings, and, farewell, he is gone. / Love is a thing as any spirit free."

GEOFFREY CHAUCER, "THE FRANKLIN'S TALE," 1387–1400

THE BATTLE OF AGINCOURT

A Warrior King and Victory Against the Odds

The quarter of a century beginning in 1390 had seen a lull in the Hundred Years' War (1337–1453) between England and France. But when the 25-year-old Henry V (1387–1422) came to the English throne in 1413, France was in the throes of a civil war that had left it weak and vulnerable. Able and ambitious, and with claims to the French throne, Henry needed no further prompting. In 1415, he crossed the English Channel and besieged the French port of Harfleur. During the siege, he lost a third of his 10,000 men to dysentery, a curse of the medieval battlefield that eventually claimed Henry himself when he was just 34 years old.

The losses forced Henry to abandon a planned march on Paris. Instead, he turned north toward Calais. En route, near the village of Agincourt, he met a French force led by Charles d'Albret, deputizing for the French king, Charles VI. The two armies comprised perhaps 6,000 English and Welshmen against 20,000 or more Frenchmen. On the morning of battle, October 25, 1415, they faced each other across a plowed field flanked by thick woods. Henry headed a central division of archers and lightly armored foot soldiers. Forces under Lord Camoys and the Duke of Norfolk guarded his flanks. To either side, additional ranks of archers stood protected by rows of sharpened stakes, or palings, angled into the ground. The French, by contrast, prepared for a frontal assault using waves of heavily armored knights.

Three hours of fighting left up to 1,500 English and Welsh troops dead (some estimates claim just 150) against 10,000 or more French casualties. Henry had won an overwhelming victory for several reasons. The first was that the young king seized the initiative and moved his men into position swiftly, which allowed his archers to fire into the unformed mass of the French army. Then there were the woods, which funneled the French toward the English and then, when they came up against the palings, hemmed them in with no means of escape. In addition, two weeks of rain had left the battlefield thick with mud, which slowed and then exhausted the French knights, who were burdened by armor that weighed up to 110 pounds.

The French advance was chaotic, made up of relentless waves of men and horses. As more troops advanced, the sea of mud worsened. And as the front ranks fell and floundered in the mire, they were cut down by the archers or impaled on the English stakes. Thousands of knights behind them continued to press forward, creating a solid mass of men and horses. Many of the French drowned in the mud or were suffocated and trampled to death by their own troops. The rest, so tightly packed they could barely wield their swords, were easily picked off. ∎

Finest hour England's victory at the Battle of Agincourt in 1415 is one of the most celebrated in the nation's history. A weary army, beset by hunger and illness, defeated a French force three times its size, thanks in part to the English archers and the mud that engulfed the French knights.

"Once more unto the breach, dear friends, once more; / Or close the wall up with our English dead . . . / The game's afoot: Follow your spirit, and upon this charge / Cry 'God for Harry, England, and Saint George!'"

WILLIAM SHAKESPEARE, *HENRY V*, 1598

The Longbow

England's archers did more than anyone to secure victory at Agincourt. Their famous longbows—often more than six feet long—required extraordinary strength and ability to fire, so the troops using them were highly trained. Yew, ash, and elm were favored woods. Longbows also had greater range, penetrating power, and firing speed than the French crossbows. Such was the weight of the English volleys that a French chronicler, reporting the white of the arrows' goose-feather flights filling the air, observed that snow seemed to be falling over the battlefield.

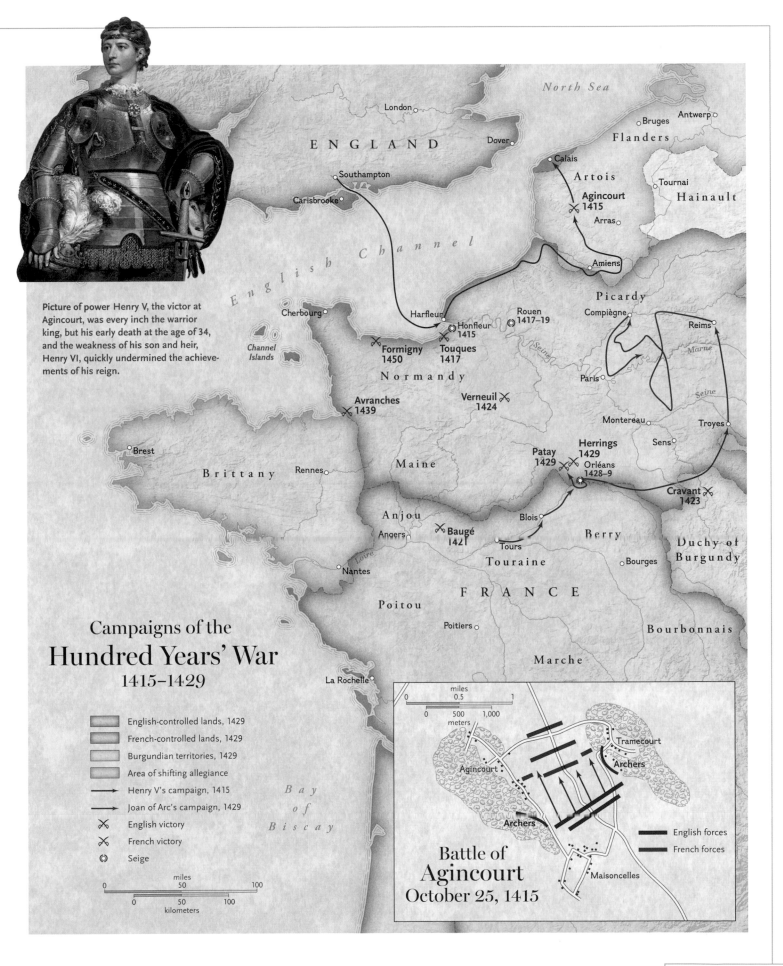

Picture of power Henry V, the victor at Agincourt, was every inch the warrior king, but his early death at the age of 34, and the weakness of his son and heir, Henry VI, quickly undermined the achievements of his reign.

North Sea

London

ENGLAND

Dover

Bruges   Antwerp

Flanders

Calais

Artois   Tournai   Hainault

Agincourt
1415

Southampton

Arras

Carisbrooke

Amiens

English Channel

Picardy

Cherbourg

Compiègne   Reims

Harfleur   Rouen
1417–19

Honfleur
1415

Marne

Channel
Islands

Formigny   Touques
1450   1417

Seine

Normandy

Paris   Seine

Avranches
1439

Verneuil
1424

Montereau   Troyes

Sens

Brest

Patay   Herrings
1429   1429

Orléans
1428–9

Cravant
1423

Maine

Rennes

Brittany

Blois

Anjou

Baugé
1421

Angers

Tours

Berry

Duchy of
Burgundy

Bourges

Nantes

Loire

Touraine

FRANCE

Bourbonnais

Poitou

Poitiers

Marche

Campaigns of the
Hundred Years' War
1415–1429

La Rochelle

Bay
of
Biscay

	English-controlled lands, 1429
	French-controlled lands, 1429
	Burgundian territories, 1429
	Area of shifting allegiance
→	Henry V's campaign, 1415
→	Joan of Arc's campaign, 1429
✕	English victory
✕	French victory
۞	Seige

miles
0   50   100

0   50   100
kilometers

Battle of
Agincourt
October 25, 1415

miles
0   0.5   1

0   500   1,000
meters

Tramecourt

Archers

Agincourt

Archers

English forces
French forces

Maisoncelles

THE WARS OF THE ROSES

A Blood-Soaked Fight for the English Throne

The Wars of the Roses were a dynastic feud fought between rival claimants for the throne backed by England's most powerful noble families. On one side was the House of Lancaster, descended from Edward III's third son, John of Gaunt. This house had obtained the throne through Henry IV's usurpation and kept it through the reigns of Henry V and Henry VI. On the other side was the House of York, whose claim derived partly from Philippa, daughter of Lionel, Edward III's second son, who died before John but was senior to him. This claim was stronger in that it was untainted by usurpation but weaker because it came through the female line. Both claims, in the words of one historian, "were weak enough to warrant a fight."

In 1454, Henry VI's mental instability and losses in France the previous year led Parliament to declare Richard Plantagenet, Duke of York (1411–1460), Protector and Defender of the Realm. Henry then recovered his faculties, and his wife, Margaret of Anjou (1430–1482), gave birth to a Lancastrian heir, Edward, Prince of Wales. York then defeated Henry and the Lancastrian forces at St. Albans (1455) and again at Northampton (July 1460) with an army led by Richard Neville, Earl of Warwick (1428–1471), a cousin and key noble backer. With him was York's charismatic son, the future Edward IV.

Henry VI was captured, but what appeared to be a decisive victory was undone first at Wakefield (December 1460), when Lancastrian forces marshaled by Margaret, Henry's wife and queen, killed York, and then at the Second Battle of St. Albans (February 1461), where Warwick, too, was defeated. But York's son, Edward, gathered a vast army and marched on London. There, on March 4, 1461, he declared himself King Edward IV. He then defeated a Lancastrian army at Towton (March 29, 1461) in one of Britain's bloodiest battles. As many as 75,000 men, or a tenth of all males of fighting age, were involved, and perhaps 28,000 of them were killed.

After the defeat, Margaret fled to France with her son; Edward was crowned king, and the conflict appeared over. But in 1464, Edward married Elizabeth Woodville, a great beauty but also a commoner and the widow of a rival Lancastrian killed in battle. Many begrudged her lack of status and the favors lavished on her family, while the secret marriage outraged Warwick, who had planned a different wife for Edward.

In one of the great betrayals of British history, Warwick changed sides and joined forces with the exiled Margaret in France. He ordered the

Mark of a monarch The royal seal of Edward IV, a king from the House of York, one of the two main opposing factions during the Wars of the Roses. Edward's controversial marriage and early death undermined his triumph in the conflict.

marriage of his daughter, Anne Neville, and Margaret's son, Edward, the Lancastrian heir to the throne. Then, with French support, he landed in England in 1470 and forced Edward IV to flee to Burgundy. Henry VI was restored to the throne under Warwick's control. Warwick's duplicity and power are why posterity remembers him as "the Kingmaker."

The Lancastrian interlude lasted just six months. Edward IV returned to England, defeated and killed Warwick at the Battle of Barnet (April 14, 1471), and then extinguished the Lancastrian flame at Tewkesbury (May 4, 1471), where Margaret was captured and her son, Edward, was killed. Henry VI was imprisoned and died in mysterious circumstances 18 days later, possibly murdered by Edward IV's 18-year-old brother, Richard, Duke of Gloucester (1452–1485), the future Richard III.

Edward IV's reign and the Yorkist succession seemed set, but after 12 years, in 1483, Edward died suddenly at the age of just 40. His heir, Edward V (1470–ca 1483), one of his sons with Elizabeth Woodville, was just 12. The only candidate for guardian was his uncle, Richard, Duke of Gloucester, the same man who may have murdered Henry VI 12 years earlier.

Richard was ambitious, and after his brother Edward IV's death, he moved on the throne and forced Parliament to recognize him as Richard III (crowned July 6, 1483) on the grounds that his brother's secret marriage to Elizabeth Woodville was invalid. As such, the young prince, Edward, along with his younger brother Richard, was illegitimate and disbarred from the succession.

Sometime around September 1483, the two princes, then in the Tower of London, disappeared, never to be seen again (two small skeletons were unearthed in the tower in 1674 during the reign of Charles II). Since then the mystery of the "princes in the tower" has tantalized historians, the balance of opinion being that Richard III had them murdered to prevent them from becoming figureheads for rebellion.

If this was Richard's intention, however, he failed, for rebellion flared anyway. His presumed guilt and murderous ambition split the Yorkist camp. Then Richard III's only son and heir, an 11-year-old named Edward, borne with Anne Neville, who had been widowed at Tewkesbury—the same daughter Warwick had married to Henry VI's son, Edward (see above)—died a year later. The succession was wide-open. A last flicker of the Lancastrian line, a man named Henry Tudor, stepped into the breech. A showdown loomed (see pages 112–113). ∎

No quarter Edward IV defeated Margaret and her son, Edward, Prince of Wales, the Lancastrian heir to the throne, at a decisive battle at Tewkesbury in 1471. In the scene portrayed above, Edward IV's troops pursue and massacre their defeated enemy inside Tewkesbury Abbey.

Wars of the Roses
1455–1487

🏰 Lancastrian castle
⚔ Lancastrian victory
🏰 Yorkist castle
⚔ Yorkist victory

North Sea

Irish Sea

Dunstanburgh
Hedgely Moor ⚔🏰 **1464**
Hexham 1464 ⚔

Pickering 🏰
Knaresborough 🏰
Lancaster 🏰
Leeds 🏰 **Towton 1461**
Wakefield ⚔🏰 Pontefract 🏰
1460 Conisborough 🏰
Sandal 🏰
Bolingbroke 🏰

Blore Heath ⚔
1459 Tutbury 🏰 🏰 Grantham
Leicester 🏰 Stamford 🏰
1459 Ludford Bridge Fotheringhay 🏰
Kenilworth 🏰 **Bosworth 1485** ⚔
Mortimer's Cross ⚔ ⚔ **Northampton 1460**
1461 **Second St. Albans 1461** ⚔
1471 Tewkesbury ⚔ Edgecote **First St. Albans 1455** ⚔
Skenfrith 🏰 **Moor**
Kidwelly 🏰 Monmouth 🏰 **1469** ⚔ **Barnet 1471**
Ogmore 🏰

miles
0   50   100

0   50   100
kilometers

English Channel

"Now is the winter of our discontent / Made glorious summer by this sun of York; / And all the clouds that lour'd upon our house / In the deep bosom of the ocean buried."

WILLIAM SHAKESPEARE, *RICHARD III*, 1592

TUDOR BRITAIN
1485–1603

"We are, by the sufferance of God, King of England; and the Kings of England in times past never had any superior but God."

HENRY VIII, 1515

Counties of Tudor England and Wales
1485–1603

SCOTLAND

NORTH SEA

IRELAND

IRISH SEA

CELTIC SEA

ENGLISH CHANNEL

FRANCE

Durham
Alnwick
Newcastle-upon-Tyne
Carlisle
Cumberland
Durham
Durham
Appleby
Westmorland
MAN
Lancaster
York
York
Lancashire
ENGLAND
Anglesey
Beaumaris
Flint
Cheshire
Derby
Lincoln
Denbigh
Flint
Chester
Lincoln
Carnarvon
Denbigh
Nottingham
Carnarvon
Stafford
Derby
Nottingham
Walsingham
Merioneth
Dolgellau
Shrewsbury
Stafford
Leicester
Rutland
Oakham
Norfolk
Montgomery
Shropshire
Leicester
Norwich
WALES
Montgomery
Warwick
Northampton
Huntingdon
Cambridge
Radnor
Worcester
Warwick
Northampton
Huntingdon
Cambridge
Suffolk
Cardigan
New
Radnor
Worcester
Northampton
Bedford
Cambridge
Ipswich
Cardigan
Breeknockshire
Hereford
Worcester
Bedford
Colchester
Pembroke
Carmarthen
Brecon
Hereford
Gloucester
Buckingham
Hertford
Essex
Pembroke
Carmarthen
Monmouth
Gloucester
Oxford
Aylesbury
Hertford
Chelmsford
Glamorgan
Monmouth
Gloucester
Oxford
Buckingham
Middlesex
London
Pembroke
Monmouth
Abingdon
Cardiff
Wiltshire
Berkshire
Surrey
Maidstone
Trowbridge
Hampshire
Surrey
Guildford
Kent
Somerset
Winchester
Sussex
Dover
Taunton
Southampton
Chichester
Shoreham
Lewes
Devon
Dorset
Exeter
Dorchester
Launceston
Cornwall
Plymouth
Truro
Dartmouth

miles
0 · 25 · 50

kilometers
0 · 25 · 50

A REVOLUTION IN CHURCH AND STATE

THE CLAIM OF THE FUTURE HENRY VII TO THE ENGLISH THRONE WAS WEAK. HIS FATHER, Edmund Tudor, was the son of Henry V's widow, Catherine of Valois, by her second marriage to Owen Tudor, a Welsh squire in her service. On his mother's side, he descended from the Lancastrian John of Gaunt, and thus Edward III, by Gaunt's third (and legally doubtful) wife, Katherine Swynford. But then destiny began to call. First, other Lancastrian claimants fell by the wayside. Henry VI was murdered in 1471, and his son and heir, Edward, died at the Battle of Tewkesbury in the same year. On the Yorkist side, the Duke of Gloucester, the brother of Edward IV (who himself died in 1483), probably murdered Edward's heirs—the "princes in the tower"—and made himself King Richard III in 1483.

Two determined women tipped the scales further: Lady Margaret Beaufort (Henry Tudor's mother) and Elizabeth Woodville (Edward IV's widowed queen and the mother of the murdered princes). The pair secretly arranged for Elizabeth's daughter, also named Elizabeth, to marry Henry. The Woodvilles and Tudors would be united, the Yorkist and Lancastrian bloodlines would converge, and a dynastically credible contender for the throne, Henry Tudor, would be pitched against the usurping Richard III.

■ HENRY VII AND THE TUDOR SUCCESSION

The plan worked. Henry landed in Wales from exile in France and defeated and killed Richard III at the Battle of Bosworth in 1485 (see pages 112–113). After his coronation in 1485, Henry married Elizabeth, as arranged, on January 18, 1486. But while the marriage united York and Lancaster, it did nothing to prevent challenges to the throne. The first came in 1487, when the Yorkist faction tried to pass off the son of an Oxford joiner, Lambert Simnel, as one of the "princes in the tower." The revolt was put down, and Simnel was sent to work in the royal kitchens. Another challenge, in 1491, centered on Perkin Warbeck, who appeared in Ireland in 1491 claiming to be Richard, the second of the "princes in the tower." Warbeck gained the support of both the French and the Scottish kings before being captured and thrown in the Tower of London, where he was executed in 1499.

War and peace *(previous pages)* The ships of the Spanish Armada engage in battle with the English fleet in 1588 in a painting by Nicholas Hilliard (1547–1619). England's victory in the battle was one of the high points of the Tudor age. The Lady Chapel of Henry VII *(page 105)* in London's Westminster Abbey, looking toward the tombs of Henry VII (1457–1509), England's first Tudor king, and his wife, Elizabeth of York (1466–1503).

TIME LINE

1471
Henry VI is murdered

1483
Richard III names himself king

1485
Henry Tudor becomes king after defeating
and killing Richard III at Battle of Bosworth

1503
Margaret Tudor and James IV
of Scotland marry

1509
Henry VII dies; Henry VIII
assumes the throne

1509
Henry VIII marries Catherine of Aragon

1513
Battle of Flodden Field

1533
Henry VIII marries Anne Boleyn

1536–1540
The Dissolution of the Monasteries

1536
Anne Boleyn is executed

1547
Henry VIII dies; his son Edward VI
is named king

1553
Edward VI dies of consumption at age 15

1553
Lady Jane Grey proclaimed queen for nine
days; Mary I forces Grey to renounce her
claim and takes the throne

1554
Mary I marries Philip II of Spain

1558
Mary dies; Elizabeth I succeeds her

1564
William Shakespeare is born

1587
Mary, Queen of Scots is executed

1588
The English fleet defeats Spanish Armada

1603
Queen Elizabeth dies childless; James VI of
Scotland is crowned James I of England

Securing the throne also meant securing the succession, and in 1486, Elizabeth gave birth to a son named Arthur. It also meant seeking foreign alliances, and in 1488, when Arthur was 18 months old, he was promised to Catherine of Aragon, the three-year-old daughter of Ferdinand II and Isabella I of Spain (the marriage took place in 1501). Elizabeth also had a daughter, Margaret, who would marry James IV of Scotland, and another, Mary, whose descendants included the doomed Lady Jane Grey (see page 129).

More important than either daughter was another son, also named Henry, who was born in 1491. His significance became clear in 1502, when the 15-year-old Arthur died. The young Henry now became heir not only to the throne, but also to his dead brother's wife, who was promised to him in 1503. In 1509, before the wedding could take place, Henry VII died.

■ HENRY VIII

The reign of Henry VIII (1491–1547) began with rejoicing and high hopes. The new king was more than six feet tall, youthful, and extroverted, and he was a fine hunter, archer, and tennis player. He wrote poetry and songs, took an interest in theology, and spoke French, Latin, Spanish, and Italian. Unlike his miserly father, he was also prepared to be extravagant: "Avarice is fled the country," wrote one courtier, Lord Mountjoy.

Two months after his accession on April 21, 1509, Henry married his brother's widow, Catherine of Aragon, who in 1511 gave birth to a son. The baby died less than two months later, but for now the succession could wait. Instead, the first 20 years of Henry's reign were given over largely to foreign affairs, and to France in particular.

Where Henry VII had been cautious and had avoided costly wars, the young Henry VIII was hungry for military glory. His campaigns in France became part of a wider struggle for mastery in Europe involving Francis I of France and Charles V (1500–1558), Catherine of Aragon's powerful nephew, who ruled Spain and parts of Italy, the New World, Austria, Burgundy, and the Netherlands.

Henry won modest victories against the French, such as the Battle of Spurs in 1513, and in the same year his generals crushed the Scots at Flodden Field (see pages 116–117). He also secured diplomatic triumphs, such as the Field of the Cloth of Gold, a magnificent summit with Francis I, in 1520. While Henry fought, he largely left the affairs of state to his assured first minister, Thomas Wolsey (ca 1475–1530).

■ THE BREAK WITH ROME

Henry's wife, Catherine, gave birth to a daughter, Mary, in 1516, but by 1526 the marriage had not produced the male heir Henry craved. In that year, Henry began wooing a court beauty, Anne Boleyn, and in time he determined to marry her. Wolsey was charged with securing a papal annulment of his marriage to Catherine, on the doctrinally debatable basis that the papacy should not have sanctioned the union with his dead

"For one bishop of your opinion, I have a hundred saints of mine; and for one Parliament of yours, and God knows of what kind, I have all the general councils of the church for a thousand years."

SIR THOMAS MORE AT HIS TRIAL FOR DENYING HENRY VIII'S ROYAL SUPREMACY, 1535

HOUSE OF TUDOR
1485-1603

HENRY VII
r. 1485–1509
b. 1457–d. 1509

m.

ELIZABETH
of York

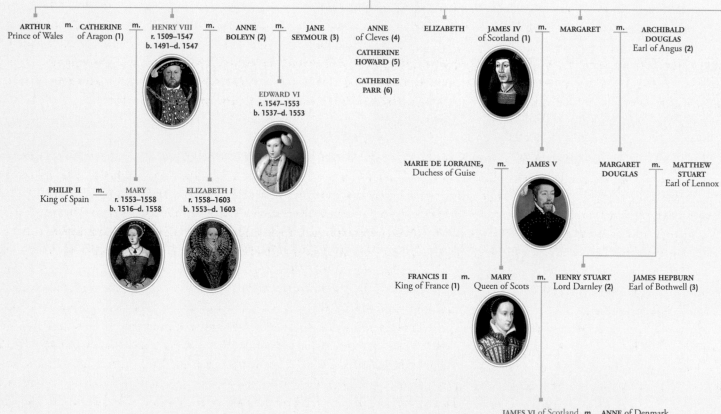

ARTHUR
Prince of Wales

m.

CATHERINE
of Aragon (1)

m.

HENRY VIII
r. 1509–1547
b. 1491–d. 1547

m.

ANNE
BOLEYN (2)

m.

JANE
SEYMOUR (3)

ANNE
of Cleves (4)

CATHERINE
HOWARD (5)

CATHERINE
PARR (6)

ELIZABETH

JAMES IV
of Scotland (1)

m.

MARGARET

m.

ARCHIBALD
DOUGLAS
Earl of Angus (2)

EDWARD VI
r. 1547–1553
b. 1537–d. 1553

MARIE DE LORRAINE,
Duchess of Guise

m.

JAMES V

MARGARET
DOUGLAS

m.

MATTHEW
STUART
Earl of Lennox

PHILIP II
King of Spain

m.

MARY
r. 1553–1558
b. 1516–d. 1558

ELIZABETH I
r. 1558–1603
b. 1553–d. 1603

FRANCIS II
King of France (1)

m.

MARY
Queen of Scots

m.

HENRY STUART
Lord Darnley (2)

JAMES HEPBURN
Earl of Bothwell (3)

JAMES VI of Scotland m. **ANNE** of Denmark
r. 1567–1625
b. 1566–d. 1625

JAMES I of England
r. 1603–1625
b. 1566–d. 1625

KINGS AND QUEENS OF SCOTLAND

James III r. 1460–1488 HOUSE OF STUART

James IV r. 1488–1513 HOUSE OF STUART

James V r. 1513–1542 HOUSE OF STUART

Mary, Queen of Scots r. 1542–1567 HOUSE OF STUART

James VI (James I of England 1603–1625) r. 1567–1625 HOUSE OF STUART

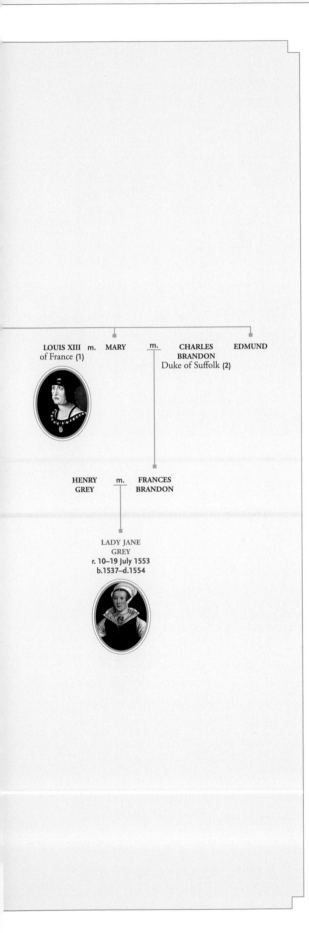

LOUIS XIII m. MARY m. CHARLES EDMUND
of France (1)   BRANDON
                           Duke of Suffolk (2)

HENRY m. FRANCES
GREY   BRANDON

LADY JANE
GREY
r. 10–19 July 1553
b.1537–d.1554

brother's wife. Annulment on any basis became impossible in 1527 when Charles V sacked Rome and took Pope Clement VII prisoner. In thrall to Charles, Clement was powerless to make a decision that went against Catherine, his captor's aunt.

Wolsey died in 1530 and was replaced first by humanist and scholar Sir Thomas More (1478–1535) and then by Thomas Cromwell (1485–1540). Both men became key in unraveling what became known as Henry's Great Matter (see pages 122–123)—how to escape his marriage and to marry Anne Boleyn without the assent of the papacy.

In the end, the answer was simple: Henry was a king ordained by God, he claimed, so he, not the pope, had ultimate authority over his kingdom; as such, he could adjudicate in church affairs and grant his own annulment. The legal and doctrinal measures required to implement the decision led to England's break with the Roman Catholic Church and forced Henry to borrow ideas from the Protestant religious reforms then sweeping Europe (see pages 126–127).

In 1531, the clergy was cowed into accepting Henry, not the pope, as the "sole head and protector of the Church of England." In 1533, the Archbishops' Court declared Henry's marriage to Catherine void. (Anne became queen and gave birth to the future Elizabeth I in the same year.) The First Act of Succession (1534) declared Princess Mary illegitimate and required all adult males to take the Oath to the Succession or be charged with treason. Next was the Act of Supremacy (1534), declaring the king "the only supreme head in earth of the Church of England." Those who refused to take the oaths—notably Sir Thomas More—were imprisoned or executed.

■ HENRY'S LAST YEARS

All these changes came within a legal framework, passed by the so-called Reformation Parliament (1529–1536), whose last act was to approve the closure of England's lesser religious houses. Initially presented as a means to root out decadence, the Dissolution of the Monasteries (see page 124) was in reality a device to obtain the monasteries' immense wealth.

Cromwell, an able first minister in the mold of Wolsey, pushed through the dissolution, along with most matters of state from 1534 to 1540. As with Wolsey, however, no amount of success could prevent his fall. Henry had already tired of Anne Boleyn, executed in 1536, and been delivered of the son he craved, the future Edward VI, by Jane Seymour in 1537. After Jane's death, Cromwell organized Henry's disastrous fourth marriage to Anne of Cleves, a debacle that led to Cromwell's execution in 1540.

With England and Rome dealt with, Henry moved against Ireland, where in 1541 he forced the Irish parliament to recognize him as King of Ireland and Head of the Irish Church. In 1543 Wales followed, and this country would, as the relevant act of parliament put it, remain "incorporated, annexed, united, and subject to and under the Imperial Crown of the realm."

Scotland proved harder to subdue. By now, Henry was overweight and crippled with gout and edema. Nonetheless, he still had a taste for battle, and in 1543 he attempted to cajole the Scots with a treaty promising a marriage between his heir, the seven-year-old Edward, and the Scottish heir, Mary, Queen of Scots, then less than a year old. When Mary's regent changed his mind, Henry attempted to force the match in an invasion dubbed the Rough Wooing (1544).

Three years later Henry was dead. He had overseen some of the most momentous events in British history, yet for all the marriages and upheavals in church and state, he ended up squandering his riches and bringing a divisive Protestantism to England

Royal display The Field of the Cloth of Gold, a meeting in France between Henry VIII and the French king Francis I in 1520, portrayed in a 16th-century painting in the style of Hans Holbein the Elder. The event took its name from the magnificence of the occasion.

and Wales by the back door. More to the point, the maneuvering over nearly 40 years to secure the succession had produced just three surviving children and only one male heir: the sickly, nine-year-old Edward.

■ EDWARD VI AND LADY JANE GREY

Edward VI (1537–1553) ascended the throne on January 28, 1547. His father's will stipulated that the country be ruled by a council of 16 regents until Edward was 18, but Edward's uncle Edward Seymour (the brother of Henry's third wife, Jane Seymour) delayed the announcement of Henry's death until he could maneuver himself into power as the sole ruling regent.

Seymour then joined with other religious radicals such as Archbishop Thomas Cranmer to push through more sweeping Protestant reforms. The 1549 Act of Uniformity outlawed the Catholic Mass; the clergy were allowed to marry; and statues, frescoes, and stained glass in churches were destroyed. Cranmer produced his first Book of Common Prayer in English in 1549 and another, more radical version in 1552.

Seymour also continued Henry's expensive wars in Scotland and France. But he debased the coinage to help pay for them and then attempted to fix prices when inflation soared. Revolts against his religious reforms and administrative incompetence led the council to appoint John Dudley, Earl of Warwick, in his place. Seymour was executed in 1552, and Warwick was made Duke of Northumberland.

A year later, 15-year-old Edward VI died of consumption. On his deathbed, with Northumberland's persuasion, he named 16-year-old Lady Jane Grey as his successor. Henry VIII's will had stipulated that Mary, his daughter with Catherine of Aragon, was next in line, but Mary was staunchly Catholic. By promoting the Protestant Jane

> *"We thought that the clergy had been our subjects wholly, but now we have well perceived that they be but half our subjects . . . for all the prelates make an oath to the pope, clean contrary to the oath that they make to us."*

HENRY VIII, 1532

as a puppet, Edward, Northumberland, and the religious reformers wished to preclude any chance of Mary's succession and a return to Catholicism.

Grey had been married (against her wishes) to Northumberland's son. Northumberland was also her uncle. Her claim to the throne was tenuous: She was Henry VIII's great-niece, her mother Frances having been the daughter of Henry VIII's sister, Mary. Grey herself had no desire to be queen; she is said to have fainted on being told of her accession.

■ MARY I

Northumberland's plans quickly unraveled. Mary made a counterclaim to the throne and gathered an army of 10,000 men to march on London. Legality and legitimacy won the day. Catholics supported Mary's claim, but many Protestants rebelled against the upstart Northumberland, the flouting of Henry VIII's will, and the denial of succession by right and bloodline. Faced with overwhelming force, Northumberland surrendered and was executed. Mary was popularly approved of and in 1553 became the first crowned queen of England. Lady Jane Grey, "queen" for nine days but never crowned, was imprisoned.

Mary's early religious reforms returned the country to the position it had occupied at Henry VIII's death. But soon after, it appeared she was set on a return to obedience to the pope, something that after 20 years of reform a more nationalistic England, including many of its Catholics, resisted.

Mary dissipated further goodwill with her marriage to Philip II of Spain, a Catholic, in 1554. At age 38, Mary quickly needed a Catholic heir to prevent her Protestant half sister, Elizabeth, from ascending the throne. But to the country at large, the marriage suggested England might become subservient to a foreign power.

A 1554 revolt against the marriage and the Catholic reforms by Sir Thomas Wyatt was defeated. This led to the execution of Lady Jane Grey, who was blameless except for the fact that her continued existence provided a focus for Protestant hopes. Legal moves to undo the work of Henry VIII, Edward VI, Cranmer, and the Protestant reformers then proceeded in tandem with the burning of almost 300 Protestant "heretics" (see pages 128–129). People who held the mainstream opinion were alienated by such ferocity and even further outraged in 1558, when an alliance with Spain at Philip's prompting saw the humiliating loss of Calais, England's last possession in France. By now, Mary's marriage had produced no children, and when she died in November 1558, it was with the knowledge that despite all her efforts, Elizabeth would succeed to the throne.

Marked men This anti-Catholic allegory (1556) dates from the reign of Mary I. Victims of Mary's persecution, such as Bishops Ridley and Latimer, are depicted as lambs. The wolves represent Stephen Gardiner, Mary's Catholic Lord Chancellor, and Bishops Bonner and Tunstall, who took part in the persecutions.

Elizabeth I

Elizabeth I (1533–1603) was Henry VIII's second daughter, the only child of his marriage to the mother she barely knew, Anne Boleyn. Widespread acclamation greeted her accession, but the religious convulsions of the previous 35 years—from Catholic to Protestant and back again—presented the new queen with an immediate dilemma. Her subjects now embraced a wide range of religious beliefs. But where, precisely, on a wide range of doctrinal and other issues did Elizabeth's sympathies lie?

Realizing it would be impossible to satisfy all parties, the queen was clever and equivocal, and she deliberately left open the precise nature of her religious settlement. While the 1559 Acts of Supremacy and Uniformity restored Protestantism and made it clear there would be no return to Rome, the queen observed that she would not "open windows into men's souls." In other words, while doctrine was set by law (in the Thirty-Nine Articles of Religion, 1562), there would also be tolerance in return for outward, if not inward, obedience.

Elizabeth's next dilemma was marriage. The securing of an heir and the succession were fraught, as the experiences of her mother, father, and half sister Mary had shown.

Elizabeth I Panels behind Elizabeth in George Gower's "Armada Portrait" (ca 1588) show the defeat and destruction of the Spanish Armada on Britain's rocky coast. The queen's fingers, resting on a globe, point to the Americas as a sign of England's colonial ambition and her mastery of the seas.

Elizabeth realized that to marry a foreigner invited overseas entanglements and alliances; to marry an Englishman risked domestic factions and jealousies that could spill over into revolt.

Elizabeth's solution was further equivocation: Instead of marrying she would remain single indefinitely as the Virgin Queen, wedded to her country and her subjects. She briefly considered and rejected suitors, and male dalliance was restricted to court favorites such as Lord Robert Dudley (see page 130). "England," said Elizabeth, "would have but one mistress and no master."

As her reign progressed, however, circumstance inevitably forced Elizabeth to change. Nowhere was this truer than in relations with Scotland, which by 1560 had experienced a reformation of its own, propelled into an austere Protestant position by hard-liners such as Calvinist John Knox. As in England, Scotland's religious upheavals pitched Protestant against Catholic, and one Catholic in particular: Scotland's monarch, Mary, Queen of Scots (see pages 132–133).

Holding court The Elizabethan era saw a flowering of literary talent. Here Shakespeare and fellow writers are portrayed at the Mermaid Tavern. The inn, a popular meeting place, was destroyed in the Great Fire of London of 1666.

By 1567, Mary's calamitous life, and the civil strife surrounding Scotland's embrace of Protestantism, led her to flee to England. Mary was Elizabeth's cousin, once removed, and, while Elizabeth remained childless, Mary was next in line to the English throne. Mary appealed to Elizabeth for sanctuary, but her Catholicism made her a figurehead for unrepentant English Catholics, and thus Mary was a danger. Sure enough, plot followed plot. Elizabeth's advisers pleaded in vain for Mary's execution.

In 1570, Elizabeth was excommunicated, throwing even greater suspicion on Catholics, who were now freed from allegiance to her. In 1571, an Italian banker hatched the Ridolfi Plot, designed to place Mary on the throne after a Spanish invasion. Still Mary survived. Not until 1586, after 19 years' captivity, did Elizabeth (reluctantly) order Mary's execution, this time in the wake of a plot by a nobleman, Anthony Babington.

■ SPAIN AND THE ARMADA

Foreign affairs also forced change on Elizabeth. For the most part England had stayed out of direct interference in the affairs of France and Spain—wars were costly and damaging—though England had given covert aid to French Protestants (Huguenots) and to Dutch Protestants rebelling against the rule of Spain. Elizabeth also intervened in Ireland and effectively sanctioned acts of piracy—or privateering—against Spain and its colonial possessions by championing Sir Francis Drake, Sir John Hawkins, and other seafarers who made their names in this period (see pages 136–139).

In 1588, however, England was left with no choice but to confront Spain, defeating the Spanish Armada (see pages 140–141), a vast invasion fleet, in a battle that occupies a special place in the hearts of the English.

After 1588, the flavor of Elizabeth's reign began to change as death deprived an aging queen of friends and advisers. There were also military setbacks against Spain and in Ireland, along with higher taxes, failed harvests, and widespread unemployment in England. Yet Elizabeth's carefully cultivated personality cult, along with her redoubtable will, survived to the end. She died a virgin queen, as promised, and thus brought an end to the Tudor dynasty: Her successor, the son of Mary, Queen of Scots, was a Stuart, James VI of Scotland. ■

THE BATTLE OF BOSWORTH

England's Destiny Decided in a Clash of Arms

Henry Tudor's defeat of Richard III to become Henry VII at the Battle of Bosworth in 1485 was one of the most momentous in British history. Without it there would have been no Tudor dynasty, no Henry VIII, and perhaps no English Reformation. Things had begun badly for Richard, who like kings before him required the support of his nobles and the private armies they brought to the fray. But the enmities nurtured by the Wars of the Roses meant that old loyalties could no longer be trusted. Worse, the assumption that Richard had ordered the murder of the "princes in the tower" (see page 98) had alienated many of his own Yorkist supporters.

As a result, of the three key men from whom Richard sought help—Lord Stanley, the Earl of Northumberland, and the Duke of Norfolk—only Norfolk was entirely reliable. Stanley, who was married to Margaret Beaufort, was especially suspect. Margaret had been married before, to none other than Edmund Tudor. Their son, Henry, was the same Henry who now stood opposite Richard. To guarantee Stanley's loyalty, Richard took his young son hostage: Should Stanley prove disloyal, his son would be killed.

On the opposing side, Henry gathered some 3,000–5,000 supporters after sailing from exile in France. Having no experience of war, he entrusted their command to the Earl of Oxford, a veteran supporter of the Lancastrian cause. Richard, by contrast, probably had 10,000 troops, though 6,000 of them belonged to the unreliable Stanley. Sure enough, when battle was joined on August 22, Stanley positioned his men at a distance.

Intending to overwhelm Henry's smaller army, Richard's troops began their attack by surging from their hilltop position. Henry's troops stood firm. As the fighting intensified, Richard urged Stanley to the fray. When Stanley prevaricated, Richard ordered his son's execution, but to no avail: Richard's henchmen stayed their hands and, like many on the day, waited to see how events turned out.

Oxford's troops now began to gain the upper hand. As Norfolk's men started to flee, Richard ordered Northumberland into battle. Northumberland, like Stanley, demurred. Then Stanley seemed to declare for Henry. It was a critical moment. Sensing all was lost, Richard staked everything on a fight to the death with Henry. It is said that he reached within a sword's length of his foe before being hacked down, and that Stanley himself placed Richard's fallen crown on Henry's head. Richard's corpse, reported one chronicler, was slung over a horse and "trussed as a hog or other vile beast and all besplattered with mire and filth." The Tudor age had begun. ∎

Battle of Bosworth 1485

SCOTLAND
IRELAND
ENGLAND
WALES
London

◆ KEY DATES ◆

JANUARY 28, 1457 Henry Tudor, the future Henry VII, is born at Pembroke Castle in Wales to Edmund Tudor and Margaret Beaufort.

JULY 6, 1483 Richard III, regent for his nephew, Edward V, is crowned king after Parliament declares Edward illegitimate.

AUGUST 7, 1485 After 15 years in exile, Henry Tudor, the Lancastrian heir to the throne, lands near Milford Haven in West Wales.

AUGUST 22, 1485 Henry and Richard meet at the Battle of Bosworth, where Henry is victorious and Richard is slain.

OCTOBER 30, 1485 Henry is crowned Henry VII at Westminster Abbey in London and becomes the first Tudor monarch.

JANUARY 18, 1486 The recently crowned Henry VII marries Elizabeth of York, thus uniting the Houses of York and Lancaster.

The Tudor Rose: Dynasties United

The Wars of the Roses that convulsed England in the 15th century take their name from the red rose symbol of the House of Lancaster and the white rose of the House of York. But at the time the term was not used, and the symbols belong largely to a later branding exercise. When Henry VII, the Lancastrian victor of Bosworth, attempted to link the factions by marrying Elizabeth of York, the daughter of the Yorkist Edward IV, he forged a so-called Tudor rose *(left)* that combined the white and red roses. The symbol is still part of the United Kingdom's royal coat of arms.

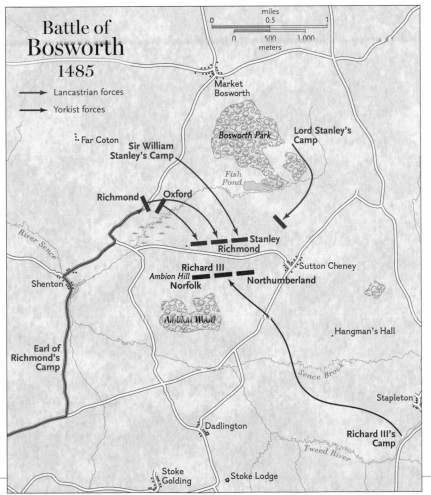

Battle of Bosworth 1485

→ Lancastrian forces

→ Yorkist forces

Battle of Bosworth After Richard III's supporters deserted him, Richard *(above, on a white horse)* was killed after seeking single combat with his adversary, Henry Tudor. Richard's skeleton, found in 2013, showed wounds to the head. One blow had hacked away the rear of the skull; another would have penetrated deep into the brain.

"Richard probably got within yards of Henry before his horse . . . became stuck in marshy ground or was killed from underneath him. At some point he loses his helmet and then the violent blows start raining down on his head . . . From becoming unhorsed, it probably took only a few minutes before he was dead."

ROBERT WOOSNAM-SAVAGE, ROYAL ARMOURIES (NATIONAL MUSEUM OF ARMS AND ARMOUR), 2013

HENRY VII: MAN AND MONEY

The Books Balanced and a Dynasty Established

Monarchs come and go. Some leave a mark on history through personality or force of arms. Others are shadowy figures, their achievements unsung. Henry VII is among the latter, his character elusive, his 24 years on the throne little noted. Yet few kings began with so little and ended with so much. A reign forged in the aftermath of battle, after 30 years of civil strife, with the throne disputed and its authority threadbare, ended with the Tudor dynasty secure, stability restored, and the royal coffers overflowing.

Henry's early life barely hinted at such an outcome. His mother, Margaret, was just 13 when she bore him. His father, Edmund Tudor, was already dead. When Margaret remarried, Henry's care was entrusted to an uncle. At age 14, when his Lancastrian lineage and the accession of the Yorkist Edward IV put him in danger, he was cast off again, this time to exile in France.

Uprooted, living in peril, and reliant on his hosts, Henry became reserved, shrewd, and secretive—but also ambitious, courageous, and politically adept, qualities borne out by his triumph at Bosworth, his dynastic marriage, and the consolidation of his position as king. His marriage in particular reveals a more human

A head for figures A testoon, or shilling coin, bears a portrait from the life of Henry VII. One of Henry's greatest achievements was restoring the royal finances.

side, for despite its political imperative (the union of York and Lancaster) it seems to have been a match informed by love.

His bride, Elizabeth, was 19, tall, and gentle. Henry was slender but well built, and with an aspect, in the words of a chronicler, that was "cheerful and courageous." His teeth, though, were "few, poor, and black-stained" and his hair thin. The writer Sir Francis Bacon later described him as a "prince, sad, serious, full of thoughts . . . For his pleasures, there is no news of them."

In fact, Henry liked to hunt and pursued all the other courtly essentials of music, dancing, and gaming. But Bacon's description reflected a prevailing view. Posterity likes color in its heroes, and Henry has been criticized for his bland commitment to money and administration. But who can blame him? Administration was what a war-ravaged country needed. And a monarch without money was barely a monarch at all.

Henry became rich in many ways—from customs duties, increased by 25 percent by stimulating English exports and promoting the merchant fleet; from the reassertion of old feudal rights; from chasing lapsed rents from crown lands, where revenues rose tenfold; and from fines levied for infractions large and small: The Duke of Buckingham, for example, was fined £2,000 ($3,245), a vast sum at the time, for failing to seek royal permission for his widowed mother to remarry.

Yet for all his accumulation, when a show of majesty was required, Henry reached into his pocket. A royal palace was built on the Thames at Sheen, and at the wedding of Arthur, his son, to Catherine of Aragon, the jewels alone cost the equivalent of $13 million in today's terms. Vast sums were also lavished on the chapel that would accommodate Henry's tomb in Westminster Abbey (see page 57).

Even so, Henry's spending made little impression on the estimated $985 million by modern reckoning that he bequeathed to his son, Henry VIII. It was an inheritance Henry set about spending with a gusto that would have had his father turning in his well-appointed tomb. ∎

Made to last *(left)* Henry VII receives Books of Indentures, or agreements, from the monks of Westminster Abbey. The books, still bound in red, survive to this day.

Tudor capital *(opposite)* A Flemish illumination from the poems of Charles d'Orléans shows the Tower of London and Old London Bridge during the reign of Henry VII.

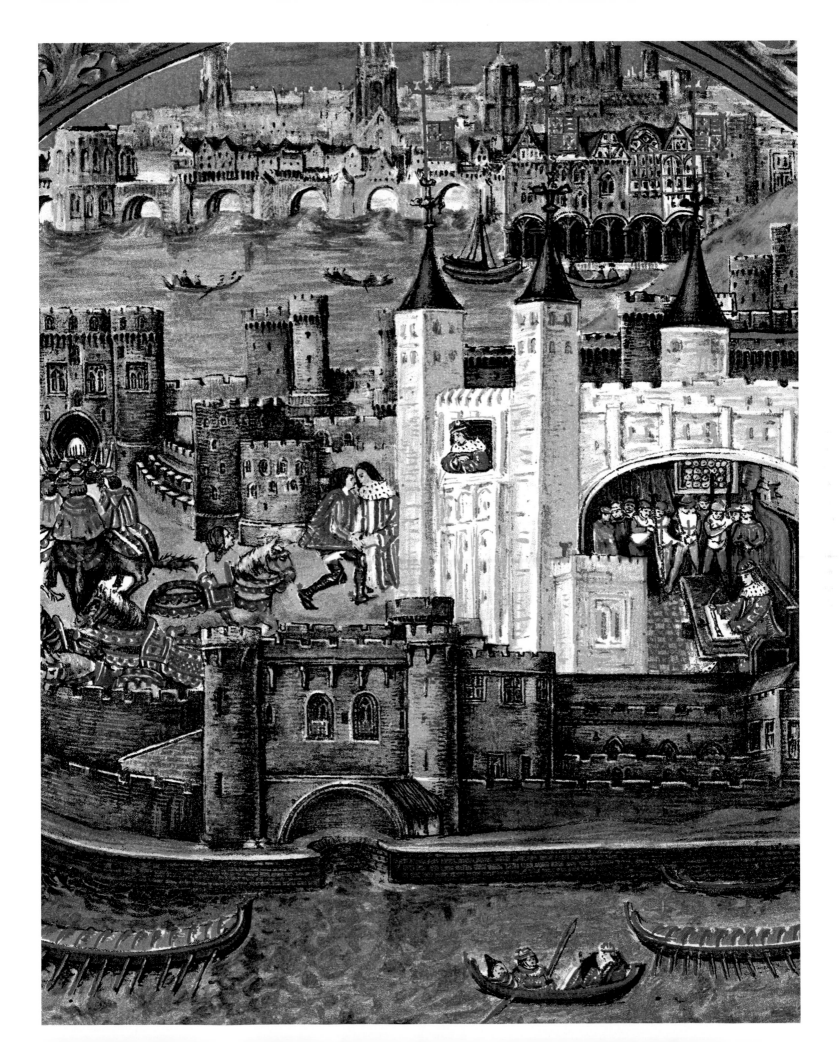

THE BATTLE OF FLODDEN FIELD

An English Triumph Amid the Mud and the Blood

It's a battle that never should have been. England and Scotland were old foes, but in 1502, Henry VII and the Scottish king, James IV, had signed the Treaty of Perpetual Peace. In 1503, Henry had sought to lend weight to the accord by marrying his 14-year-old daughter, Margaret Tudor, to James. Ten years later, however, with Henry VIII on the throne and fighting in France, James used Henry's absence, the demands of Scotland's older alliance with the French, and the fact that Margaret's long-promised dowry was still to be paid as reasons to attack England.

In Henry's absence, his wife, Catherine of Aragon, took charge and proved a more than capable deputy. The general responsible for defending England's border, Thomas Howard, Earl of Surrey, was ordered north. En route, he stopped at Durham Cathedral to collect the banner of St. Cuthbert. No English army that had marched into Scotland had ever lost a battle under its protection.

Meanwhile, James led a Scottish army south. His force probably numbered around 30,000 men, more than Surrey could muster, a factor that should have proved decisive in the coming battle. So, too, should the Scots' starting position, high on Branxton Hill, close to Flodden Edge in the county of Northumberland. But the Scots had been forced to hurry to Branxton, and their guns were not properly trained on the English. The English guns, by contrast, raked the Scots to deadly effect when battle was joined. The Scots were forced to descend, formation broken and knee-deep in mud, and quickly floundered in the marshy valley that separated them from the English.

The result was carnage. The Scots' modern pikes—which resembled long spears—were designed to combat cavalry and proved unwieldy at close quarters. The traditional shorter bills (hooked blades) of the English, by contrast, proved murderously efficient at short range. James and his commanders led from the front, in the accepted manner of medieval battles; Surrey and his generals, in the new fashion of the day, commanded safely from the rear. Within two hours James was dead—the last monarch from the British Isles to die in battle.

Estimates of the total number of dead vary, but the Scots probably lost at least 15,000 men, including most of their social, political, and military elite. The consequences echoed down the centuries, both in Scotland—where James's heir, James V, was just 17 months old—and in England, where the infant king's eventual daughter, Mary, would return to haunt history as Mary, Queen of Scots. ■

SCOTLAND
River Tweed — Battle of Flodden Field, 1513
Durham Cathedral
IRELAND
ENGLAND
WALES
London

◆ KEY DATES ◆

AUGUST 8, 1503 Margaret Tudor, the daughter of Henry VII, marries James IV of Scotland, linking the English and Scottish thrones.

AUGUST 22, 1513 James IV, in support of France, crosses the River Tweed and enters England with a force of 30,000 or more troops.

SEPTEMBER 9, 1513 The English inflict a crushing defeat on the Scots at Flodden Field in one of the bloodiest battles of the age.

SEPTEMBER 21, 1513 James V, son of James IV, slain at Flodden Field, is crowned king of Scotland.

DECEMBER 14, 1542 James V dies at age 30 and is succeeded by his six-day-old daughter, Mary, Queen of Scots.

FEBRUARY 8, 1587 Mary, Queen of Scots, is executed on the orders of her cousin, Elizabeth I, after being imprisoned in England for 19 years.

JULY 25, 1603 James VI of Scotland, son of Mary, Queen of Scots, is crowned James I of England as the closest kin to the deceased Elizabeth I.

Steward, Stewart, Stuart: The Origins of a Dynasty

When David II of Scotland died childless in 1371, he named his nephew, Robert Stewart, his successor. Stewart's family had come to Scotland via France as the FitzAlans after 1066. They became hereditary High Stewards of Scotland and, in the 13th century, took the name Steward, later Stewart, after the title. The marriage of a later Stewart, James IV, to Margaret Tudor joined the royal houses of England and Scotland. Their son, James V, was father to Mary Stuart (a Gaelic version of the name Stewart), who was mother to James VI of Scotland, later James I of England.

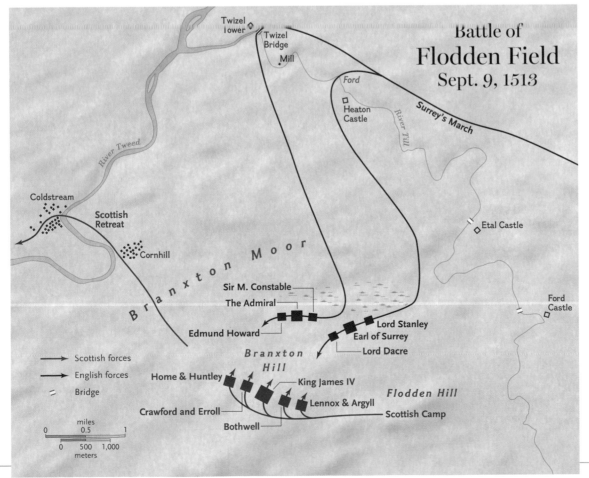

Battle of

Flodden Field
Sept. 9, 1513

Twizel Tower

Twizel Bridge

Mill

Ford

Heaton Castle

River Till

Surrey's March

River Tweed

Coldstream

Scottish Retreat

Cornhill

Branxton Moor

Etal Castle

Ford Castle

Sir M. Constable

The Admiral

Edmund Howard

Lord Stanley

Earl of Surrey

Lord Dacre

Branxton Hill

Home & Huntley

King James IV

Flodden Hill

Crawford and Erroll

Lennox & Argyll

Scottish Camp

Bothwell

→ Scottish forces

→ English forces

⚬ Bridge

miles
0   0.5   1

0   500   1,000
meters

Battle of Flodden Field
Henry VIII was recently crowned and fighting in France when James IV of Scotland invaded England in 1513. Henry's wife, Catherine of Aragon, took charge and dispatched an English army north. The two sides met on Branxton Hill, near Flodden Edge, where the English guns forced the Scots to leave their superior position high on the hill. When they descended into the marshy valley, the English arms proved more suitable to combat at close quarters. In the rout that followed, James IV was killed, along with as many as half his 30,000-strong army.

THE *MARY ROSE*

A Great Tudor Ship Past and Present

In 1485, despite its island status, Britain had gone for centuries without a significant maritime presence. The great battles of the medieval world—Hastings, Agincourt, Crécy—were fought on land, and the island's watery defenses had proved no barrier against the Romans, Saxons, Vikings, or Normans. England had no standing navy—in time of war monarchs simply requisitioned private ships that were often unsuitable for combat—and even the nation's merchant fleet played second fiddle to the seafarers of Italy and Portugal.

Henry VII took the first steps toward creating a navy by commissioning a handful of ships that could be used for either war or trade. His son, Henry VIII, added many more, spurred by conflicts with France and Scotland, both of which boasted superior fleets. By Henry's death, England's dockyards were booming and the country's navy numbered 53 ships.

Today, the most famous vessel of the Tudor age is the 600-ton *Mary Rose,* not because she was the biggest—that honor went to *Henri Grace à Dieu,* or *Great Harry,* which at about 1,500 tons was the world's largest battleship at her launch in 1514—but because of her dramatic demise and the stirring tale of her recovery 472 years later.

Plans for the *Mary Rose* may have been drawn up under Henry VII, but she was not built until 1510, at Portsmouth on England's south coast, immediately after Henry VIII's accession. Her name probably came from the Virgin Mary or from Henry VIII's sister, Mary Tudor. The ship first saw action in 1512 against the French. A year later, she was used to carry troops to northeast England to fight at Flodden Field (see pages 116–117). Further minor engagements against the French followed. Between 1522 and 1535, she was kept in reserve and saw little action. Around 1536, she was probably refitted, perhaps as a result of the funds flowing into royal coffers from the Dissolution of the Monasteries (see pages 124–125).

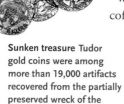

Sunken treasure Tudor gold coins were among more than 19,000 artifacts recovered from the partially preserved wreck of the *Mary Rose.*

In 1545, *Mary Rose* was called into what would be her last action, as part of an English fleet of 60 to 80 vessels that faced a larger French force at the Battle of the Solent. The wider battle's course remains unclear, but it is known that on July 19, the *Mary Rose* sailed from Portsmouth in full view of a watching Henry VIII and his entourage. Within minutes, barely a mile from shore, she had listed heavily to starboard. Water flooded into her gun ports, her heavy guns crashed across the suddenly slanting decks, and in a few seconds—with "a long drawn out wail," in the words of one eyewitness—she disappeared beneath the waves.

Modern efforts to recover the *Mary Rose* began in 1965 and culminated in the rediscovery of her timbers, preserved by clay and silt, in May 1971. In 1978, work began to raise the wreck from the seabed, a task that included the removal of more than 19,000 artifacts and required more than 28,000 dives. By 1982, the ship and its immense supporting cradle were ready to be lifted.

Successfully raised, the wreck was taken to a nearby naval base, where it was wrapped in protective foam and polyethylene. Water was sprayed on the timbers to prevent shrinking and the formation of bacteria that would lead to rot. When the water was turned off, a special wax was added to the timbers to prevent their decay. Today *Mary Rose*'s home is in Portsmouth Historic Dockyard, not far from another famous vessel, Admiral Lord Nelson's flagship, H.M.S. *Victory* (see pages 232–233). ∎

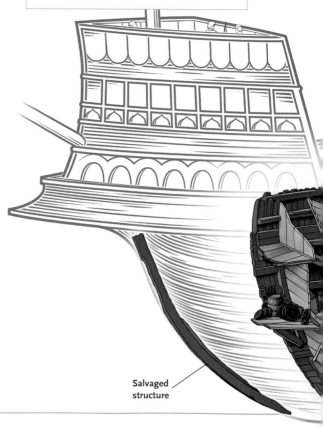

Salvaged structure

◆ KEY DATES ◆

JULY 19, 1545 Bound for battle with the French, the Mary Rose sinks in less than a minute and claims the lives of hundreds of men.

JUNE 16, 1836 The ship is rediscovered when fishing nets catch on the wreck. Divers John and Charles Deane explore the site.

OCTOBER 11, 1982 After 11 years of work, the ship's hull is finally raised, in an operation watched on television by 60 million people worldwide.

Fatal flaw Eyewitnesses agreed the *Mary Rose* was executing a sharp turn before she sank—too sharp, perhaps, especially since a gust of wind blew up at the moment of the maneuver *(illustrated at left)*. She was also heavier than usual: 285 soldiers supplemented the normal crew of 415, and she was laden with weightier guns than she had been designed to carry. Top-heavy, turning too fast, gun ports flooding— one, all, or factors unknown proved fatal.

Former glory This illustration *(below)* reveals much of what was learned of the *Mary Rose* when she was raised in 1982. At her launch in 1511, she was one of the largest and most modern ships afloat.

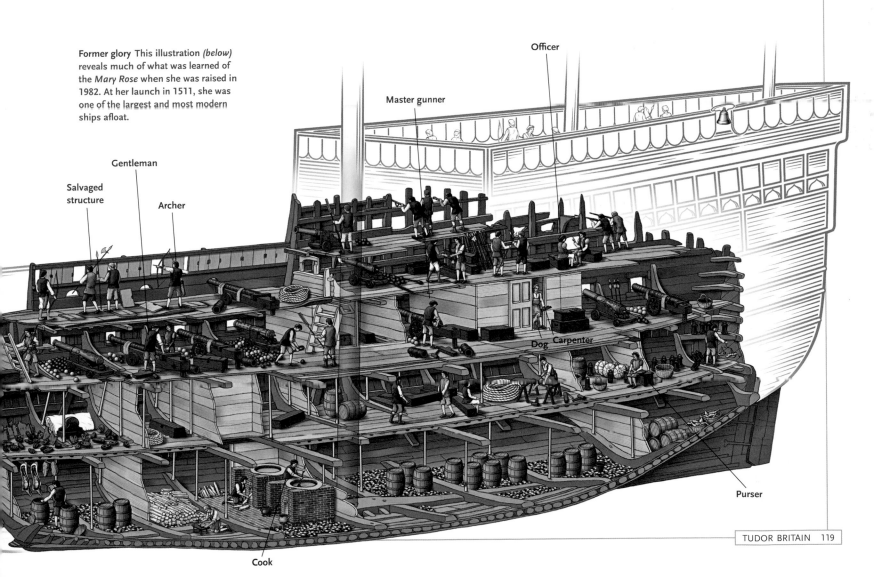

Officer

Master gunner

Gentleman

Salvaged structure

Archer

Dog   Carpenter

Purser

Cook

THE WIVES OF HENRY VIII

Divorced, Beheaded, Died . . . Divorced, Beheaded, Survived

Henry's married life started well. Catherine of Aragon (1485–1536) was 23 years old to Henry's 18 when they wed in 1509. She was beautiful and fluent in French, Spanish, and Latin (but not English), and she had dynastic connections to Charles V of Spain, Europe's most powerful ruler. In 1516, she gave birth to the future Mary I. After at least five miscarriages and stillbirths, however, she could not produce Henry's much-desired male heir.

Nor could the most famous of Henry's wives, Anne Boleyn (ca 1501–1536), a bright and spirited court beauty who probably first caught Henry's attention in 1526 but refused him her bed until she was queen in 1533. She gave birth to the future Elizabeth I in the same year, but after less than three years of turbulent marriage and no sign of a male heir, she, too, was cast aside.

Henry's wandering eye had already stumbled on the demure Jane Seymour (1508–1537), one of Anne's ladies-in-waiting. Anne was convicted on (almost certainly false) charges of incest and adultery and was beheaded on May 19, 1536. Henry proposed to Jane the following day. On October 12, 1537, Jane succeeded where her predecessors had failed and gave birth to the long-awaited male heir, the future Edward VI.

Complications at the birth, however, led to Jane's death 12 days later. Henry was distraught: "Divine Providence," he wrote, "hath mingled joy with the bitterness of the death who bought me this happiness." Alone among Henry's wives, Jane was given the honor of lying in state for three weeks and was buried with great pomp in Windsor Castle.

There would be no more children. Henry's 1540 marriage to Anne of Cleves, the daughter of a German duke, was a diplomatic match settled sight unseen. Henry was horrified when he finally met his bride—the "Flanders mare" was his reputed description—and the marriage was unconsummated. Anne willingly agreed to an annulment six months later.

Three weeks after the annulment, on July 28, 1540, Henry, then 49, married another court beauty, the ill-fated Catherine Howard (ca 1521–1542), a cousin of Anne Boleyn and just 19 or 20 years old. Whereas Anne had almost certainly not been adulterous, Catherine almost certainly was, and she paid the price in 1542, when she lost her head in the Tower of London.

Henry's last marriage in 1543, to the twice-widowed Catherine Parr (1512–1548), brought him contented companionship in old age. Intelligent and well balanced, Catherine reconciled Henry to his three children, to whom she was a model stepmother, and oversaw their education. She outlived Henry and took a fourth husband, making her England's most-married queen. ∎

Larger than life Henry VIII cut a dashing figure in his youth, but in his fifties his waistline expanded to an estimated 60 inches. By 1545, he was so ill and overweight that he could no longer walk and had to be carried by four servants.

Catherine of Aragon Henry married his first wife, the daughter of Spanish king Ferdinand II, in 1509. She gave birth to the future Queen Mary I in 1516 but failed to produce Henry's hoped-for male heir.

Anne Boleyn England's tumultuous split from Rome was required before Henry could marry Anne, mother of Elizabeth I, in 1533. After she failed to produce a son, Henry had her executed in 1536.

Jane Seymour Henry proposed to Jane the day after Anne Boleyn's execution, and they were married a month later. She bore a son, the future Edward VI, in 1537 but died within 12 days of the birth.

Anne of Cleves Henry did not meet Anne, the daughter of a German duke, until they married in 1540. The marriage, arranged for diplomatic reasons, was annulled by mutual consent after six months.

Catherine Howard Henry was 49, Catherine 19 or 20, when the pair married in 1540, three weeks after his separation from Anne. Accused of premarital liaisons, Catherine was executed in 1542.

Catherine Parr Twice married and twice widowed, the down-to-earth Catherine offered comfort to Henry in his old age after their marriage in 1543. She outlived him and married a fourth time.

HENRY'S GREAT MATTER

Church and State Turned Upside Down

Henry VIII's problem in 1526 was simple: Seventeen years of marriage to his first wife, Catherine of Aragon, had produced no male heir, and Catherine's advanced age—41—suggested that none was likely. In addition, Henry had become besotted with a court beauty, Anne Boleyn. Only a drastic solution would satisfy both his lust and the demands of a safe succession.

For any children with Anne to be legitimate, Henry needed to leave Catherine and marry Anne. Catherine refused to cooperate, however, and the only person with the authority to annul the marriage was the pope. This conundrum—what became known as "Henry's Great Matter"—turned England upside down.

Henry began his search for a solution in the Bible, in which Leviticus suggests that no man should marry his dead brother's wife. Henry had done just that, and had required a special papal dispensation to do so. He therefore argued that Rome had exceeded its authority, and that his marriage to Catherine was invalid and should be annulled.

In 1527, the job of presenting this argument to the pope was entrusted to Thomas Wolsey. But no sooner had Wolsey begun the task than Emperor Charles V, Europe's most formidable ruler and Catherine of Aragon's nephew, sacked Rome and captured Pope Clement VII, who was left powerless to grant an annulment.

Henry was a Catholic who abhorred the Lutheran notions that had taken much of Europe by storm since 1517 (see pages 126–127), but finding himself blocked by Rome, he now turned a pragmatic eye to Protestant ideas that might help solve his problem. In this he was prompted by Anne Boleyn—who did have Lutheran sympathies—and by a previously obscure Cambridge theologian, Thomas Cranmer (1489–1556). Anne plied Henry with books, not the least William Tyndale's *The Obedience of a Christian Man* (1528), which reiterated the fact that according to the Bible (Kings and Romans) God ordained kings, not priests, with his power. "This is a book," said Henry, "for me and all kings to read."

Cranmer also urged Henry to turn to the Bible. He stressed that Henry's problem was moral, not legal, and that Cranmer and his fellow theologians could use the Bible's absolutes to argue in Henry's favor. For a start, Cranmer pointed out, there was no pope in the Bible. There were, however, princes, and it was God who anointed them to rule both the state and God's church on Earth.

Henry was transfixed. Here was a solution that solved his problem and addressed the ambiguities of authority between popes and kings that the dispute exposed. In the end, the solution to the Great Matter was simple. Henry's power exceeded that of the pope: He could authorize his own divorce. ∎

A queen's trial Catherine of Aragon pleads her case before Henry VIII and Thomas Cranmer in a painting by Henry Nelson O'Neil (1817–1880). Catherine acted with dignity throughout Henry and his officials' protracted attempts to annul her marriage. She refused to agree to a divorce or to renounce the title of queen. Kept under house arrest after 1531, she was protected in part by the fact that her nephew, Emperor Charles V, was Europe's most powerful ruler and a man with whom Henry could not risk war.

Royal reward This plan of Hampton Court Palace and its gardens dates from circa 1713. Built on a bend of the River Thames, just west of London, the magnificent palace, begun in 1514, was the work of Thomas Wolsey *(below)*, who rose to fame and fortune through his role as Henry VIII's chief minister. Wolsey's failure to secure an annulment of Henry's marriage to Catherine of Aragon led to his downfall. The palace, which survives to this day, passed to Henry upon Wolsey's death.

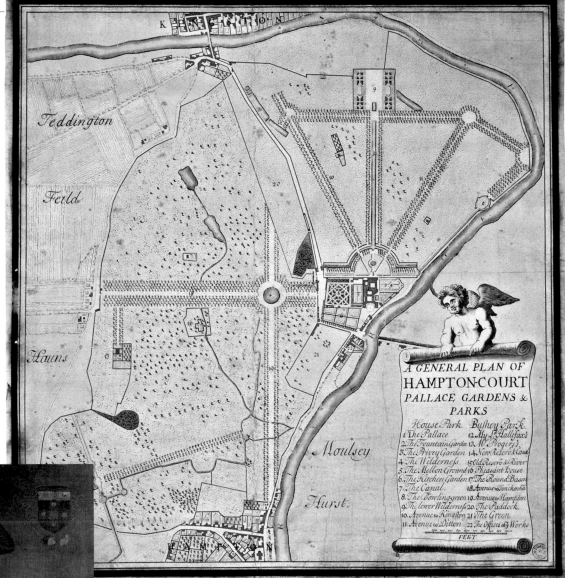

A GENERAL PLAN OF
HAMPTON-COURT
PALLACE, GARDENS &
PARKS

House Park.   Bushey Park.
1. The Pallace   12. My L.ᵈ Hallifax's
2. The Fountain Garden 13. Mʳ Roger's
3. The Privy Garden   14. New Reserv.ᵗ & Canal
4. The Wildernefs   15. Old Reserv.ᵗ & River
5. The Mellon Ground 16. Pheasant house
6. The Kitchen Garden 17. The Round Bason
7. The Canal   18. Avenue to Twickenha
8. The Bowling-green 19. Avenue to Hampton
9. The lower Wildernefs 20. The Paddock
10. Avenue to Kingston 21. The Green
11. Avenue to Ditton 22. The Offices of Works

FEET

Thomas Wolsey From lowly origins as a butcher's son, Wolsey (ca 1475–1530) rose to become a cardinal in 1515 and Henry VIII's Lord Chancellor in the same year. One of the most powerful ministers in British history, he died shortly before the trial that would have led to his execution.

"He is sure a prince of a royal courage, and hath a princely heart; and rather than he will either miss or want any part of his will or appetite, he will put the loss of one half of his realm in danger . . . and set private whim against Christendom."

THOMAS WOLSEY ON HENRY VIII, 1530

THE DISSOLUTION OF THE MONASTERIES

A King's Greed and a Nation's Loss

Religious houses in many forms—monasteries, convents, abbeys, priories—had been a feature of Britain and Ireland since the sixth century. After Henry VIII's break with Rome, these institutions presented the king with both a challenge and a temptation. They were a challenge because their Catholic monks, with their long papal allegiance, might oppose his will, and a temptation because many religious houses were immeasurably rich. And by the 1530s, the crown needed money, the royal coffers having been drained by Henry's youthful profligacy and wars with France and Scotland.

Gone for good The ruins of Lindisfarne Priory, pictured in ca 1837. Some 800 religious houses were dissolved after 1535. Their land and possessions were sold, and the buildings were ransacked, leaving countless ruins that dot the British landscape to this day.

The monasteries' precise wealth is disputed, but only as regards degree, for by any measure they were the country's richest landowners after the crown. Innumerable bequests over the centuries had endowed them with up to a third of all land in England, along with associated rents, tithes, and other sources of income.

Many monasteries were also centers of learning, and most were woven deep in the tapestry of national life, providing employment, schools, hospitals, alms, homes, and charity for the old and infirm. Others, decadent and diminished after centuries of comfortable living, were less worthwhile.

Dissolving monasteries was nothing new. Henry V, for example, had appropriated monastic wealth to help pay for the Battle of Agincourt. Nor were accusations of spiritual bankruptcy: John Morton, Henry VII's archbishop, had complained of the "incurable uselessness" of smaller houses and the ignorance and laziness of their monks.

It was such accusations that Thomas Cromwell set about exploiting as a money-spinning idea in 1535, when his agents began the *Valor Ecclesiasticus (Church Valuation),* an investigation into the state of the monasteries across England. Its findings were predictable and largely biased, and in 1535–1536, an act of Parliament legislated for the dissolution of the 200 or so smallest monasteries. Over the next five years, the larger houses followed, making 800 or more in total.

Abbots were encouraged to surrender their properties "voluntarily," with the sole option of execution for those who refused. While compliant monks and nuns often received pensions, the consequences for the monasteries, their adherents, and their dependents were generally catastrophic. A few of the ancient buildings survived and were turned into churches and cathedrals, but most were ransacked, leaving the poignant ruins that dot the English, Welsh, and Irish landscapes to this day.

The monasteries' immense cultural riches were similarly dispersed. Gold and silver plate was sold and melted down, and jewels and paintings scattered. Priceless monastic libraries were destroyed. At the time of the dissolution Worcester Priory, for example, had 600 books, of which only six survive, and all but three of the 646 books from the Augustinian Friary in York were destroyed. Chronicler John Bale, writing in 1549, recorded their fate: "A great nombre of them whych purchased those . . . mansyons resrved of those lybrarye bokes, some to serve theyr jakes [toilets], some to scoure candelstyckes, and some to rubbe their bootes . . ."

The wider consequences of the dissolution were even more profound. The sale of monastic land to anyone who could afford it marked the largest transfer of wealth, and the largest change in the English landscape and its ownership, since the Norman Conquest. This economic revolution created a broader class of merchant and other landowners, where previously land had largely been confined to the nobility. More to the point, this new and influential class had a powerful vested interest in supporting the status quo. Either during or after Henry's reign, few would have sanctioned a return to Catholicism or any other change that required them to surrender their newly acquired lands.

And what of all the money and all the land, which, had it remained in royal hands, might have bankrolled the crown forever and a day? Gone in the blink of an eye, squandered by Henry on war and vainglorious ambition. ∎

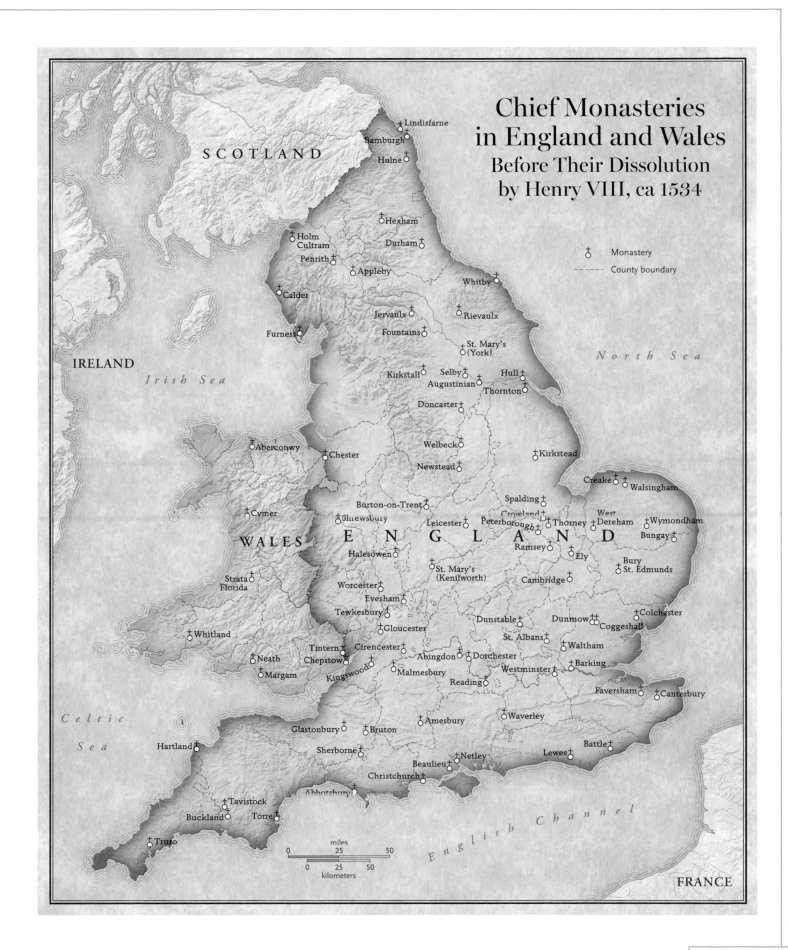

Chief Monasteries
in England and Wales
Before Their Dissolution
by Henry VIII, ca 1534

✝ Monastery
--- County boundary

SCOTLAND

IRELAND

ENGLAND

WALES

Lindisfarne
Bamburgh
Hulne
Hexham
Holm Cultram
Durham
Penrith
Appleby
Whitby
Calder
Jervaulx
Rievaulx
Furness
Fountains
St. Mary's (York)
Kirkstall
Selby
Hull
Augustinian
Thornton
Doncaster
Welbeck
Newstead
Kirkstead
Aberconwy
Chester
Creake
Walsingham
Cymer
Burton-on-Trent
Spalding
Crowland
West Dereham
Wymondham
Shrewsbury
Leicester
Peterborough
Thorney
Bungay
Ramsey
Halesowen
Ely
Strata Florida
St. Mary's (Kenilworth)
Bury St. Edmunds
Worcester
Cambridge
Evesham
Whitland
Tewkesbury
Dunstable
Dunmow
Colchester
Neath
Gloucester
St. Albans
Coggeshall
Margam
Tintern
Cirencester
Waltham
Chepstow
Abingdon
Dorchester
Barking
Kingswood
Malmesbury
Westminster
Reading
Faversham
Canterbury
Amesbury
Waverley
Glastonbury
Bruton
Battle
Hartland
Sherborne
Lewes
Beaulieu
Netley
Christchurch
Abbotsbury
Tavistock
Buckland
Torre
Truro

North Sea

Irish Sea

Celtic Sea

English Channel

FRANCE

miles
0   25   50
0   25   50
kilometers

THE ENGLISH REFORMATION

A Roller Coaster of Dogma and Doctrine

The English Reformation—the move to Protestantism from Catholicism and religious subservience to Rome—took place against a wider movement across much of Europe. Its pivotal moments came during the Tudor period, but dissatisfaction with the papacy had deeper roots both at home and abroad. In Italy, St. Francis (ca 1181–1226), among others, had reacted against the wealth of the church, and in England, John Wycliffe (ca 1330–1384) and the Lollards—from the Middle Dutch for "Mutterers," after the sound of their murmured prayers—had challenged Rome's authority and translated the first Bible from Latin to English (ca 1382).

The spark that lit the Protestant fire came in 1517, when a German theologian, Martin Luther (1483–1546), is said to have nailed his 95 theses, or complaints, to a church door in Wittenberg. Luther and those like him sought religious authority in the Bible, not in Rome, and wished to return to a simpler Christianity stripped of what they viewed as Catholic accretions such as altars, vestments, confession, clerical celibacy, the sale of indulgences, and prayers for the dead. A corollary of such ideas was that royal authority derived from God, not from Rome, which is why by 1526 German princes were disseminating the idea that monarchs should determine the religion of the states they ruled.

In England, Henry VIII abhorred Lutheranism to the extent that Pope Leo X awarded him the title Defender of the Faith in 1521 for Henry's work *Assertion of the Seven Sacraments*, which attacked Luther's ideas and defended papal authority. By 1530, however, the doctrinal maneuvers Henry needed to marry Anne Boleyn (see pages 122–123) required him to adopt certain aspects of Protestant thought. Once unleashed, Protestantism in England took on a momentum of its own.

Henry VIII remained a religious conservative, but the chief architects of his divorce, notably Archbishop Thomas Cranmer, were more inclined toward reform. Thus, in 1539, Miles Coverdale's English translation of the Bible appeared with royal acceptance, but in the same year Henry also sanctioned the more reactionary Act of the Six Articles, which among other things made it heresy to deny the fundamental Catholic doctrine of the Eucharist.

Reformers regained the upper hand under the more Protestant Edward VI, with an English prayer book in 1549 and a second, more radical version three years later. Mary I's accession wrenched England back toward Catholicism, while Elizabeth I was clear in her desire to rule a Protestant country. Elizabeth's otherwise vague religious settlement, however, steered a middle course that survives to this day: a church that was Protestant in doctrine but—with its vestments and traditional rituals—occasionally Catholic in appearance. ■

Triumph of the faith This "Allegory of the English Reformation" (ca 1570) shows Edward VI and the defeated figure of the pope *(center)*, with monks exiting left; Henry VIII *(left)* on his deathbed; the Protestants' destruction of holy images *(top right)*; and figures that include Thomas Cranmer, Archbishop of Canterbury *(in white)*; Edward's uncle and protector, Edward Seymour; and John Dudley, Duke of Northumberland.

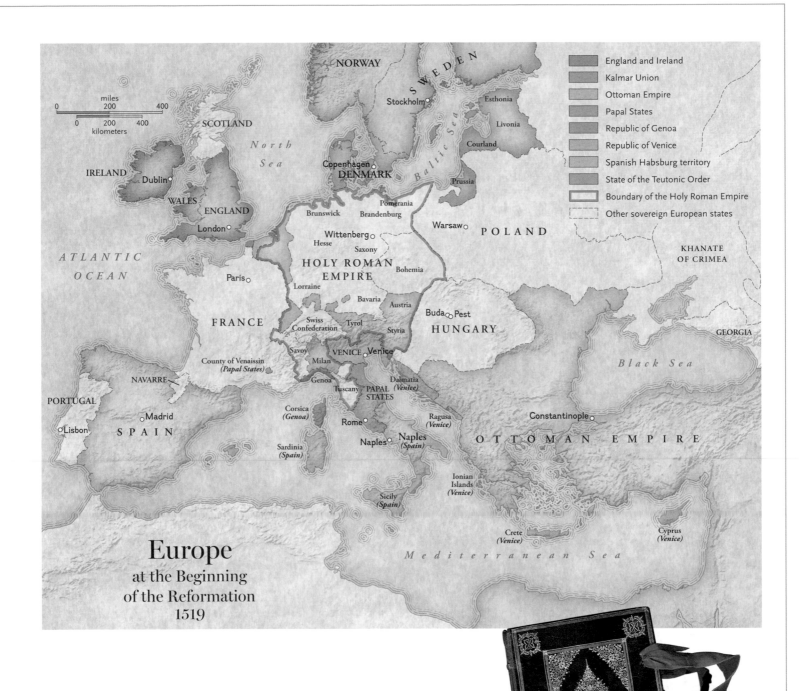

Europe
at the Beginning
of the Reformation
1519

Legend:
- England and Ireland
- Kalmar Union
- Ottoman Empire
- Papal States
- Republic of Genoa
- Republic of Venice
- Spanish Habsburg territory
- State of the Teutonic Order
- Boundary of the Holy Roman Empire
- Other sovereign European states

"Unless I am convinced by the testimony of the Scriptures or by clear reason (for I do not trust either in the pope or councils alone, since it is well known that they have often erred), I am bound by the Scriptures I have quoted and my conscience is captive to the word of God."

MARTIN LUTHER, AT THE DIET OF WORMS, 1521

Holy book The first Protestant Book of Common Prayer in English was created in 1549 during the reign of Edward VI. It was revised in 1552 and then several more times until 1662. This copy is dated 1632.

THE YEARS OF TERROR

Repression, Vengeance, and the Flames of Persecution

The reign of Mary I (1516–1558) began quietly. After the death of her half brother, Edward VI, in 1553, and the failed attempt to place Lady Jane Grey on the throne, the new queen enjoyed widespread goodwill. Although she was Catholic, and inherited an ostensibly Protestant kingdom, her legal right to the throne as Henry VIII's daughter had proved compelling. Better still, she seemed ready to reach a gentle consensus on the vexed question of religion.

Early appearances proved deceptive, however, for below the surface Mary was consumed with a ruthless desire to return her kingdom to Rome and the "true" faith. She was, she said, "a virgin sent of God to ride and tame the people of England." And "if God be for us," she asked, "who can be against us?" Mary had two main ways to secure a Catholic future. One was to produce an heir, and another was to instill terror. The first failed after her marriage to Philip II of Spain in 1554 produced only phantom pregnancies and the subsequent knowledge that at 38 her chances of producing a child were gone.

The terror started in February 1555. Its main instrument was the burning of "heretics," a punishment that Mary had included among the legal reforms she introduced to unpick the religious changes of the last 20 years. Such punishment was not new—one of the first recorded instances in England had occurred in 1401. The difference now was that Protestantism was not a fanatical creed, but an accepted religious observance that had taken hold across the country.

Nevertheless, at least 283 Protestants from all classes—227 men and 56 women—were burned alive in the 45 months from February 1555 to November 1558. Among the first was John Hooper, former Bishop of Gloucester, whose executioners, unused to this rarely invoked punishment, bungled his killing. They not only failed to provide enough sticks for the task, but also used green wood that burned slowly. With only the lower half of his body consumed, Hooper hugged bundles of reeds to his chest to hasten his death and cried out, "For God's love, good people, let me have more fire."

After Hooper, the most infamous killings were those of Hugh Latimer and Nicholas Ridley, burned together at the stake in Oxford in 1555. Latimer was a preacher respected for his work with the poor, Ridley a former Bishop of London who helped draft the Book of Common Prayer in 1549. Latimer suffocated quickly, but Ridley endured agonies: "I cannot burn," he screamed. By now, victims' families had learned to bribe executioners to tie pouches of gunpowder to the necks of condemned men. A guard pulled away the damp sticks, and flames leaped to ignite the charge and put Ridley out of his misery.

Mary had already alienated everyday opinion across the religious divide with her marriage to Philip II of Spain, which seemed to threaten foreign interference in English affairs. In time, the cruelty and number of Mary's killings dissipated her remaining stores of goodwill. Most Catholics might not have been avid supporters of Latimer and Ridley, but they could see the beliefs of the two martyrs were sincerely held. A third Oxford burning, that of Thomas Cranmer, proved the most damaging to Mary (see sidebar). It was telling that by June 1558, the previously public executions were being held behind closed doors.

Months later Bloody Mary (her widespread sobriquet) was dead, succeeded by her Protestant half sister Elizabeth. Far from making England Catholic, Mary ended up ensuring the opposite, and it is partly due to her actions that Catholics remain disbarred from the British throne to this day. ∎

The Death of Cranmer

Mary I reserved a special loathing for Thomas Cranmer (1489–1556), Henry VIII's Archbishop of Canterbury and one of the great spiritual and theological architects of the English Reformation. It was Cranmer who had helped build a case against—and then annul the marriage of—her mother, Catherine of Aragon, to Henry VIII. And it was Cranmer who had then proclaimed Mary a bastard, effectively taking away her ability to marry. Within weeks of her accession in 1553, Mary had Cranmer arrested, and in time he was forced to watch the burning of Latimer and Ridley to terrify him into recanting his Protestant faith. Recant he did, six times, and though church law suggested those who recanted should be saved, Mary's personal grudge saw to it that he would burn. On the day of his execution, instead of repeating his recantation as expected, he repudiated his confession in a dramatic coup de théâtre and declared the pope an Antichrist. As flustered guards hurried him to the pyre, he reached toward the flames first with the "unworthy hand" that had signed his confession.

Page 845
The Burning of W. Seaman, T. Carman, & T. Hudson at Norwich.

Modest martyrs Not all those burned at the stake during Mary's persecutions were prominent clergymen. This engraving shows the 1558 execution in Norfolk of Thomas Carman, Thomas Hudson, and William Seaman. Hudson was a glovemaker, and Seaman, 26, was a modest landowner who left a wife and three small children.

"As they waited to die at the stake, Hugh Latimer turned to Nicholas Ridley and said: 'Be of good comfort Master Ridley, and play the man; we shall this day, by God's grace, light such a candle in England as I trust shall never be put out.'"

FOXE'S BOOK OF MARTYRS, 1563

Death of an innocent The 16-year-old Lady Jane Grey was one of the first victims of Mary I's reign. Powerful relatives exploited Jane's distant claim to the throne, but when their coup failed, the blameless Jane, having reigned for nine days, was executed in the Tower of London.

ELIZABETH I

A Golden Queen in a Golden Age

The 44-year reign of England's greatest monarch was largely one of peace and prosperity. This period saw Britain's first steps onto the world stage: Spain was repelled, the New World explored, and colonies established; court and cultural life flourished.

Just two when her mother, Anne Boleyn, was executed, Elizabeth grew up largely at Hatfield House, a stately home north of London, in a household of 120 people. Serious and intelligent, she blossomed under a series of excellent tutors but experienced only a semblance of normal family life as part of the household of Catherine Parr, Henry VIII's last wife.

Brought up a Protestant, she found favor during the short reign of her half brother, Edward, but at the age of 20 was also at the side of her Catholic half sister, Mary, when she rode into London to her coronation in 1553. As next in line to the throne, however, she was a focus for Protestant hopes and was imprisoned in the Tower of London in 1554. Mary's advisers argued for her execution, but she survived—barely—and kept a low profile throughout the remainder of her sister's reign.

This and the many other dangers and uncertainties of her youth shaped Elizabeth's later life by sharpening her political skills and showing her that caution, ambiguity, and femininity were tools that she could use to her advantage. She was also shrewd enough to appoint capable and fiercely loyal advisers such as William Cecil (1520–1598), who was at her side for 40 years. She also knew to keep the frivolities of court, including the antics of her male favorites, largely separate from the affairs of state.

Elizabeth was also aware of the potency of myth and majesty. Then and now, she basked in a golden glow as a mixture of goddess and mother figure—Gloriana, Good Queen Bess, the Virgin Queen. Such myths were carefully cultivated. She was always depicted in fine clothes and jewels—her jewelry collection was said to be Europe's finest—and all portraits of her were carefully scrutinized and had to follow an approved prototype. It took two hours to prepare for her daily appearance at court.

Elizabeth projected the same larger-than-life figure in the flesh. Most summers, she embarked on a "progress" around the country, often on horseback or in an open litter, for the benefit of her people, and always in the company of a glittering entourage. Even in frail old age, at 68, addressing the fractious Parliament in 1601, she maintained the myth and the magic: "Though you have had and may have mightier and wiser princes," she told the assembled dignitaries in what became known as her "Golden Speech," "yet you never had nor shall have any that will love you better." ■

Lord Robert Dudley, Royal Favorite

Robert Dudley (ca 1532/3–1588) was the leading man in Elizabeth's romantic life. He was the son of John Dudley, executed by Mary I for placing Lady Jane Grey on the throne. Robert may have met Elizabeth when both were imprisoned in the Tower of London. His wife's mysterious death in 1560, a year after Elizabeth's coronation—which Dudley helped organize—caused much gossip. Thereafter, he enjoyed considerable power and favor. When he remarried after 18 years, the queen banned his new spouse from court. Were Elizabeth to have married, Dudley would probably have been the man.

Royal display *(above)* Elizabeth I, surrounded by courtiers, on one of her regular summer "progresses" around her kingdom. This small box *(left)*, made as a New Year's gift, once belonged to Elizabeth.

Golden age A rare English gold coin bears the portrait of Elizabeth I. The coin probably dates from 1594 to 1596, late in Elizabeth's reign, when the queen was in her early 60s. She died in 1603, at age 69.

MARY, QUEEN OF SCOTS

Royal, Rootless, Romantic . . . Beheaded

In 1503, Margaret Tudor, the daughter of Henry VII, married James IV, king of Scotland. In 1542, James's son, James V, had a daughter, Mary. Six days after her birth, James V died and the newborn Mary became Mary, Queen of Scots. After 1559, while Elizabeth I of England remained childless, this made the Catholic Mary—Elizabeth's cousin and closest relative—next in line to England's Protestant throne.

Mary's life was one of the most eventful in British history. As an infant she was briefly betrothed to Henry VIII's son, the future Edward VI, and was brought up in France on the orders of her French mother, Mary of Guise. At 15, she married the French king, Francis II, thus becoming queen of France and Scotland. Three years later, already widowed at 18, she returned from Paris on Francis's death.

In 1565, aged 22 and increasingly willful and romantic, she married her cousin, the dissolute Henry Stuart, Lord Darnley, with whom she had a child, James, the future James VI of Scotland and James I of England. In 1566, the jealous Darnley murdered Mary's friend and secretary, David Rizzio. A year later, Darnley was blown

Aberdeen Jewel This 16th-century pendant contains a lock of hair said to have belonged to Mary, Queen of Scots.

up in his bed, and Mary—widely believed to be complicit in his death—married his presumed murderer, the Earl of Bothwell. Soon afterward, in July 1567, the exasperated Scottish court forced Mary to abdicate in favor of her 13-month-old son with Darnley. In May of the following year, Mary, still only 25, fled south to seek sanctuary from her cousin, Elizabeth I.

The two queens had never met and never would meet, and while Elizabeth, to her court's dismay, did not refuse her royal relative, Mary presented a dilemma: Should Elizabeth die or be killed, Mary was next in line to the throne. This made her an obvious focus of plots, particularly those of the Catholic kind. As a result, Mary remained under house arrest for 19 years. She was monitored and constantly moved, but spared by Elizabeth.

The end came in 1586, when Elizabeth's spymaster, Sir Francis Walsingham, intercepted coded letters from Mary to a group of Catholic conspirators. Although the evidence was incontrovertible, Elizabeth still prevaricated: She signed Mary's death warrant but refused to send it for execution. In the end, the queen's council took matters into their own hands and Mary was beheaded at Fotheringhay Castle in 1587. ∎

Final deliverance Mary, Queen of Scots, in a painting by John Callcott Horsley from 1871. Mary remained under house arrest in England for 19 years after seeking sanctuary from her cousin, Elizabeth I. Doves from the outside world at the open window symbolize her captivity. At the center, her jailer, Bess of Hardwick, enters the room with the warrant for Mary's execution.

Mary, Queen of Scots

⚔ Castle or manor house

⚲ Cathedral, abbey, or priory

SCOTLAND

ATLANTIC OCEAN

Stirling Castle Chapel
Crowned, Sep. 9, 1543

Loch Leven Castle
Imprisoned, June 16, 1567
Abdication in favor of her
son James VI, June 24, 1567

Inchmahome Priory
Moved for safety, Sept. 1547

Dumbarton Castle
Moved, Feb. 1548

Holyrood Palace, Edinburgh
Married Lord Darnley, July 29, 1565
Married Earl of Bothwell, May 15, 1567

Linlithgow Palace
Born Dec. 8, 1542

North Sea

Bolton Castle
Imprisoned, July 1568

Irish Sea

IRELAND

Moved and confined to
several palaces in England,
1568–1587

Sheffield Castle
Chatsworth House
Wingfield Manor
Tutbury Castle

Fotheringhay Castle
Executed, Feb. 8, 1587

Peterborough Cathedral
Buried, July 1587

WALES

ENGLAND

Celtic Sea

Westminster Abbey,
London
Reinterred, 1612

miles
0   50   100
0   50   100
kilometers

English Channel

Notre Dame Cathedral, Paris
Married Dauphin Francis,
Apr. 24, 1558

FRANCE

Château d'Amboise
Moved, Aug. 1548

Devout danger A prayer book belonging to Mary, Queen of Scots. Mary was brought up a Catholic, which alienated the strictly Protestant church in Scotland and made her a dangerous focus of Catholic hopes when she fled her homeland for England in 1568. Elizabeth I, her cousin, protected Mary until proof of her involvement in a Catholic plot led to her execution in 1587.

James I While Elizabeth I remained childless, Mary, Queen of Scots, was next in line to the English throne. After Mary's execution in 1587 and Elizabeth's death in 1603, the succession passed to Mary's son, James VI of Scotland, James I of England.

"I came into this kingdom under promise of aid, against my enemies and not as subject, instead of which I have been imprisoned. I do not deny that I have earnestly wished for liberty . . . but can I be responsible for the criminal projects of a few desperate men?"

MARY, QUEEN OF SCOTS, AT HER TRIAL, 1586

TOWN AND COUNTRY

Money and Trade, Land and Houses

Many of the changes that swept Britain in the 18th century had their roots in the Tudor period. The English and Scottish Reformations transformed religious and cultural experience, while an early drift from the countryside to towns and cities, and to London in particular, helped precipitate social and economic changes that would underpin the nation's later increase in mercantile activity and greater imperial reach.

Rural life in England and beyond had remained largely unchanged for centuries after the upheavals of the Norman Conquest. Britain and Ireland were almost entirely agrarian and lagged behind more advanced economies such as Flanders in northern Europe and the great city-states of Italy. Most Britons were peasant farmers, often bonded to feudal masters. They produced hides and grain and mined small quantities of lead, iron, and coal. Wool, though, was the nation's staple, accounting for 90 percent of all English exports under Henry VII.

Wool and its production therefore became powerful instruments of change. After the Black Death of 1348 to 1350, for example, a reduced workforce led to an increase of "enclosed" land to support sheep farming (which required fewer workers than cultivation). Peasants who were evicted or rendered landless by enclosure (see sidebar) were often forced to towns and cities. There, they could turn to more skilled crafts, creating a virtuous circle of trade and economic diversity—though some also turned to crime and vagrancy.

Growing urban populations increased demand for food and goods, while trade reforms under Henry VII, among others (aimed at increasing customs duties), began to stimulate more sophisticated mercantile activity overseas. Guilds and livery companies, designed to foster trade, crafts, and professions, also proliferated.

People also increasingly came to understand the benefits of a sound currency, and during the reigns of Henry VII and Henry VIII, England benefited from a coinage that was only rarely debased. It was no coincidence that under Henry VII England moved toward a cash economy, away from the long-standing medieval barter of the rural market or fair.

The most radical rural change in the period was the emergence of a new landed class. Previously, the country's great landowners probably numbered fewer than a hundred families. After the Dissolution of the Monasteries (see pages 124–125), when an enormous amount of monastic land was sold, many hundreds more joined their ranks.

The landed gentry old and new set their estates to work. In their prosperous wake came a slew of great houses, often distinguished by their brick towers, pilasters, and black-and-white half-timbered frames. Many survive to this day, notably at Burghley, Knole, Longleat, and Hardwick, among the finest architectural treasures of the age.

London, too, bloomed with great Tudor houses and palaces, chiefly at Hampton Court. By the Elizabethan era, the city was the largest in Britain and Ireland. Westminster, near its heart, was the seat of power, and the old "square mile" of the Roman settlement its commercial focus. Goods from across the country were brought by river or along the old Roman roads and exported from the city's flourishing port. By 1600, London's population was around 200,000, making it one of Europe's five greatest cities. ■

Enclosure: The Good and the Bad

The practice of enclosure—fencing and consolidating parcels of land—might seem trivial today, but for hundreds of years it was a fundamental process that reshaped much of rural Britain. The concept of exclusive private ownership of land would have been alien to much of a medieval population. A lord of the manor might own an estate, but others would have ancient shared rights on its "common" land to draw water, to cut wood, to graze stock, or to grow crops. As wool became England's staple export, however, and sheep needed to be fenced, owners sought to enclose the open field systems of much of lowland Britain. Many peasants lost their livelihoods.

Critics railed against enclosure's iniquities (see quote, opposite), and officials passed measures to prevent the practice. After about 1630, however, enclosure by mutual consent became more common, and after 1750, Parliament encouraged it by passing some 4,000 Acts of Enclosure. By then farming practices had changed, and enclosed land allowed increased efficiency and investment in roads, drainage, and buildings that common rights often precluded.

Time of change A fair in the 1560s at Bermondsey, now part of London but then in the English countryside. While most of Britain remained rural, the Tudor period saw an increase in urban populations, as well as greater prosperity and a proliferation of crafts, guilds, and mercantile activity.

"*Your shepe that were so meke and tame, and so smal eaters, now become so great devowerers that they eate up the very men them selfes. They consume whole fields, howses and cities . . . Noble men leave no ground for tillage, thei inclose all into pastures; they pluck down townes, and leave nothing standynge but the churche to be made a shepehowse.*"

SIR THOMAS MORE, *UTOPIA*, 1516

Made to measure An earthenware watering can from the Tudor era. An almost identical watering device can be seen at the cottage that belonged to Anne Hathaway, Shakespeare's wife, in Stratford, suggesting that many items in the period had started to be mass-produced.

TUDOR SEAMEN

Explorers and Navigators, Pirates and Slavers

First attempts An engraving dated 1590 depicts English ships arriving off the coast of present-day North Carolina in 1585, during the first of two failed attempts to found a colony—England's first in America—on Roanoke Island.

Britain and Ireland always had sailors, but until the Tudor period they were often anonymous figures—fishermen, modest merchants, or reluctant seafarers pressed into action when the king's agents requisitioned their ships in time of war. During the 16th century, however, a different breed of sailor was born, fostered by the creation of the Tudor navy and the rich opportunities offered by the colonies of the New World.

The first of the new breed was a foreigner from Italy: Zuan Chabotto, or John Cabot, who set sail for Newfoundland in 1497 on a voyage sanctioned by Henry VII. The timing and the destination were no coincidence. Five years earlier, in 1492, another Italian, Christopher Columbus, in the pay of another foreign power, Spain, also had set sail and stumbled on the New World.

Spain and Portugal were the maritime superpowers of the day, and England feared being left behind in the scramble for the New World. This fear was increasingly realized during the 16th century, but in the meantime a raft of explorers began to extend England's maritime reach in other directions. During the reign of Mary I, they included Sir Hugh Willoughby and Richard Chancellor, who sailed to Russia from 1553 to 1555 as part of an attempt to find a passage to the East via the Arctic. From 1557 to 1560, Anthony Jenkinson traveled down the Volga River and across the Caspian Sea to reach Persia. Mary's reign also saw some of England's first ventures in Africa, with expeditions by John Lok and Thomas Wyndham to modern-day Guinea. Africa also provided the stage for Sir John Hawkins, who made some of the first British slaving voyages to the region beginning in 1562.

Hawkins was a so-called privateer—an individual adventurer—but one who often conducted his "business" with the overt or, more usually, covert support of the monarch. Privateers and their investors kept the profits, while the state was able to defray the costs of what, when foreign vessels were plundered, was war (or piracy) by any other name.

Another such privateer was Sir Martin Frobisher, who after 1576 made three voyages to plunder French ships and to seek a "northwest passage" to the Far East. He made landfall in northeast Canada but failed, like many after him, to find the fabled passage. Another explorer, Sir Humphrey Gilbert, armed with a patent from Elizabeth I "to inhabit and fortify any barbarous lands" not taken by a "Christian prince," claimed Newfoundland in 1583.

Gilbert today is little known, unlike his more famous half brother, Sir Walter Raleigh, who in the mid-1580s was the driving force behind England's first colony at Roanoke Island in present-day North Carolina. After the colony's failure, Sir Richard Grenville, Raleigh's distant cousin, set sail again in 1587 to the same area with 90 men, 17 women, and 9 children. By 1590, this effort too had failed; the colonists' fate is unknown to this day.

Sir Francis Drake, by contrast, tasted triumph as a navigator and privateering scourge of the Spanish. In 1572, he sailed to the Gulf of Panama and became the first Englishman to see the Pacific Ocean. In 1577, he set off in his ship, the *Golden Hind,* to harry Spain's Pacific colonies and traveled farther up the Pacific coast of the Americas than any European before him. En route, Drake wintered in a region he called New Albion, close to the site of present-day San Francisco. He then crossed the Pacific. In 1580, he arrived home laden with booty and became the first Englishman to circumnavigate the globe. Further triumphs followed: ventures to Florida and the West Indies in 1585, and a role in the defeat of the Spanish Armada (see page 140). Drake died of dysentery while fighting the Spanish off Panama and was buried at sea on January 28, 1596. ■

WEAPEMEOC

Trinety harbor

Early habit This tobacco pouch inscribed in Latin, with clay pipes and a bone tobacco stopper, may once have belonged to Sir Walter Raleigh, who was partly responsible for popularizing tobacco at the English court.

"Disturb us, Lord, to dare more boldly, to venture on wider seas, where storms will show your mastery, where losing sight of land, we shall find the stars."

ATTRIBUTED TO SIR FRANCIS DRAKE, 1577

Sir Walter Raleigh A portrait from life painted in 1598. Raleigh was known as an explorer, a writer, a spy, a courtier, and a soldier. He was favored by Elizabeth I but executed during the reign of James I.

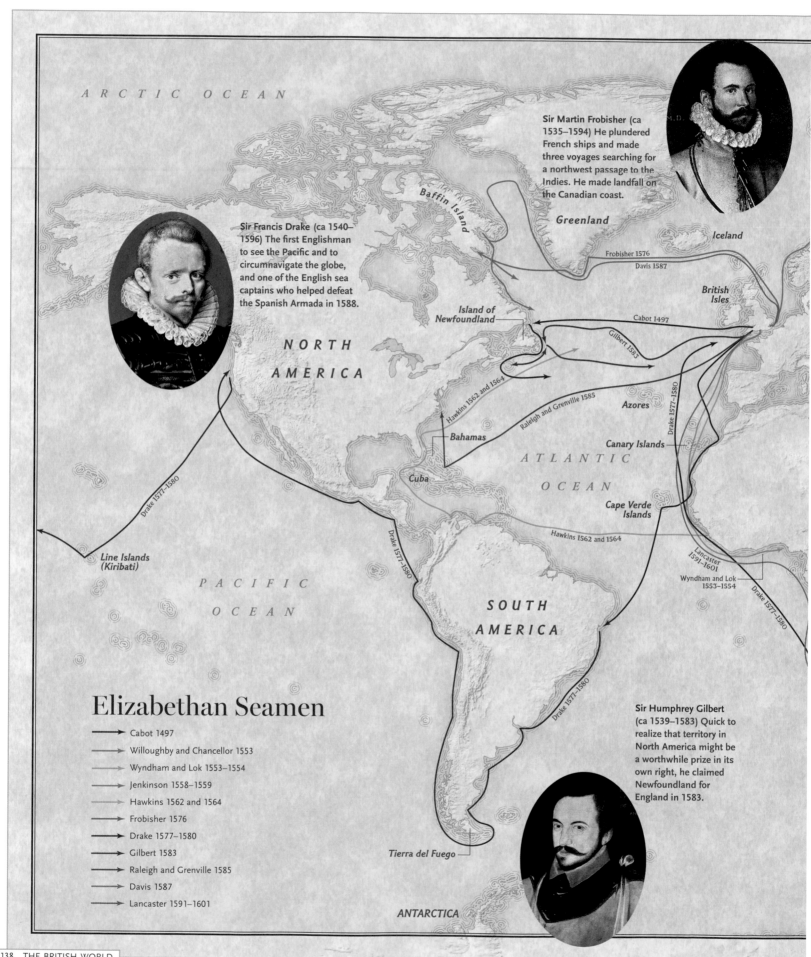

Sir Martin Frobisher (ca 1535–1594) He plundered French ships and made three voyages searching for a northwest passage to the Indies. He made landfall on the Canadian coast.

Sir Francis Drake (ca 1540–1596) The first Englishman to see the Pacific and to circumnavigate the globe, and one of the English sea captains who helped defeat the Spanish Armada in 1588.

Sir Humphrey Gilbert (ca 1539–1583) Quick to realize that territory in North America might be a worthwhile prize in its own right, he claimed Newfoundland for England in 1583.

ARCTIC OCEAN

Baffin Island

Greenland

Iceland

British Isles

Island of Newfoundland

Cabot 1497

Frobisher 1576

Davis 1587

Gilbert 1583

NORTH AMERICA

Hawkins 1562 and 1564

Raleigh and Grenville 1585

Azores

Drake 1577–1580

Bahamas

Canary Islands

ATLANTIC OCEAN

Cuba

Cape Verde Islands

Drake 1577–1580

Line Islands (Kiribati)

PACIFIC OCEAN

Hawkins 1562 and 1564

Lancaster 1591–1601

Wyndham and Lok 1553–1554

Drake 1577–1580

SOUTH AMERICA

Drake 1577–1580

Elizabethan Seamen

→ Cabot 1497
→ Willoughby and Chancellor 1553
→ Wyndham and Lok 1553–1554
→ Jenkinson 1558–1559
→ Hawkins 1562 and 1564
→ Frobisher 1576
→ Drake 1577–1580
→ Gilbert 1583
→ Raleigh and Grenville 1585
→ Davis 1587
→ Lancaster 1591–1601

Tierra del Fuego

ANTARCTICA

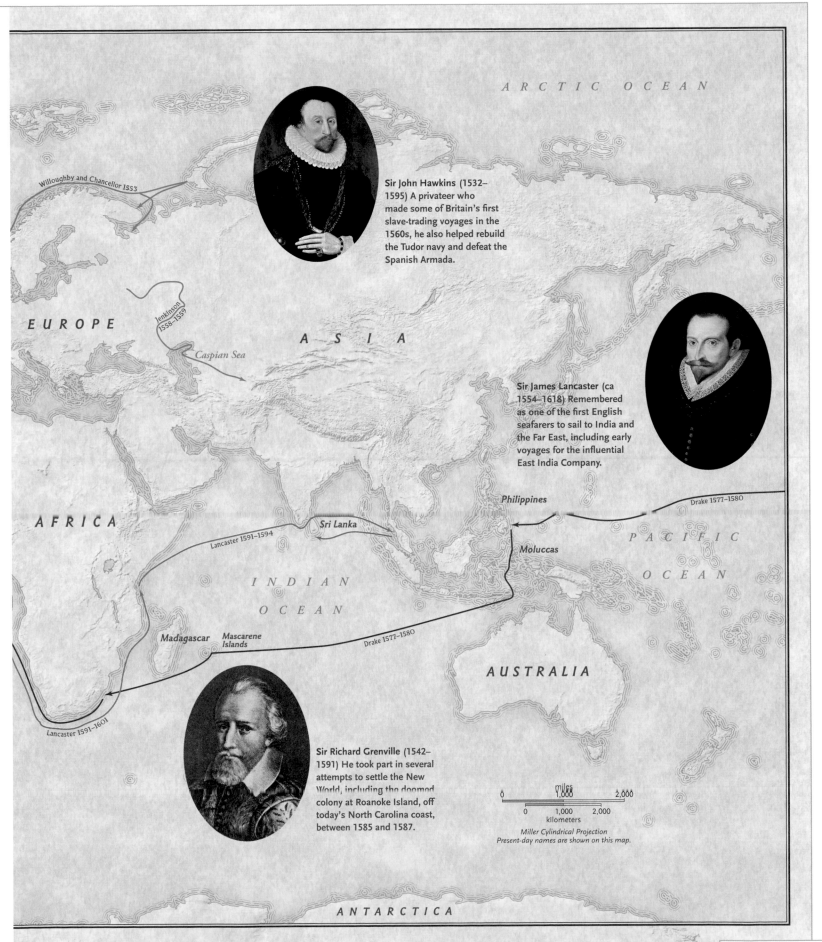

ARCTIC OCEAN

Willoughby and Chancellor 1553

EUROPE

Jenkinson 1558–1559

Caspian Sea

ASIA

Sir John Hawkins (1532–1595) A privateer who made some of Britain's first slave-trading voyages in the 1560s, he also helped rebuild the Tudor navy and defeat the Spanish Armada.

Sir James Lancaster (ca 1554–1618) Remembered as one of the first English seafarers to sail to India and the Far East, including early voyages for the influential East India Company.

AFRICA

Lancaster 1591–1594

Sri Lanka

Philippines

Drake 1577–1580

Moluccas

PACIFIC OCEAN

INDIAN OCEAN

Madagascar   Mascarene Islands

Drake 1577–1580

Lancaster 1591–1601

AUSTRALIA

Sir Richard Grenville (1542–1591) He took part in several attempts to settle the New World, including the doomed colony at Roanoke Island, off today's North Carolina coast, between 1585 and 1587.

miles
0   1,000   2,000

0   1,000   2,000
kilometers

Miller Cylindrical Projection
Present-day names are shown on this map.

ANTARCTICA

THE SPANISH ARMADA

Victory at Sea and England Triumphant

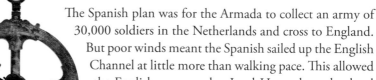

When the Spanish Armada, or great fleet, entered the English Channel in late July 1588, its 150 ships, 8,000 sailors, and 18,000 or more troops was the largest force launched against the British Isles since the Vikings. Protestant England had tried the patience of Spain for 30 years by plundering the ships and colonies of her Catholic king, Philip II, and giving succor to his rebellious Protestant subjects in the Spanish Netherlands. Now, with the Spanish Armada and the invasion of England, Spain would have vengeance.

England's destiny rested with the 24 ships of war and around 50 merchant vessels awaiting Philip's fleet. The battleships on both sides were probably the same size—around 1,000 tons—but the English guns were superior. The English vessels were also sleeker, designed for plundering and maneuvering in coastal waters; the Spanish ships, by contrast, were lumbering and broad beamed, made for stability as they carried the spoils of the New World across the Atlantic. English crews and commanders—men such as Drake, Hawkins, and Frobisher—were also more experienced.

Lost at sea A Spanish astrolabe, found off Ireland in 1845, close to where three ships of the Armada were wrecked in 1588

The Spanish plan was for the Armada to collect an army of 30,000 soldiers in the Netherlands and cross to England. But poor winds meant the Spanish sailed up the English Channel at little more than walking pace. This allowed the English commander, Lord Howard, to shepherd and harass them at will: "We pluck their feathers by little and little," he reported.

Elizabeth herself donned a breastplate and addressed a force of 17,000 men waiting on the Thames to defend England's shores. "I am come," she said, "in the midst and heat of the battle, to live or die among you all . . . I know I have the body of a weak and feeble woman, but I have the heart and stomach of a king."

Even as she spoke, the battle was almost done. Howard's fireships (see below) had started the rout; English broadsides and the so-called Protestant wind, which forced the Spanish to take a long and calamitous return voyage north, did the rest. Half the vast Spanish fleet perished, along with thousands of men. The English lost around 100 sailors and not a single ship. ■

Trial by fire The English sent fireships laden with gunpowder into the heart of the Spanish Armada. Although few enemy vessels were destroyed, the Spanish fleet broke and fled in panic. The English pursued and hunted down their foe at the Battle of Gravelines. Storms and treacherous seas completed the Spanish rout.

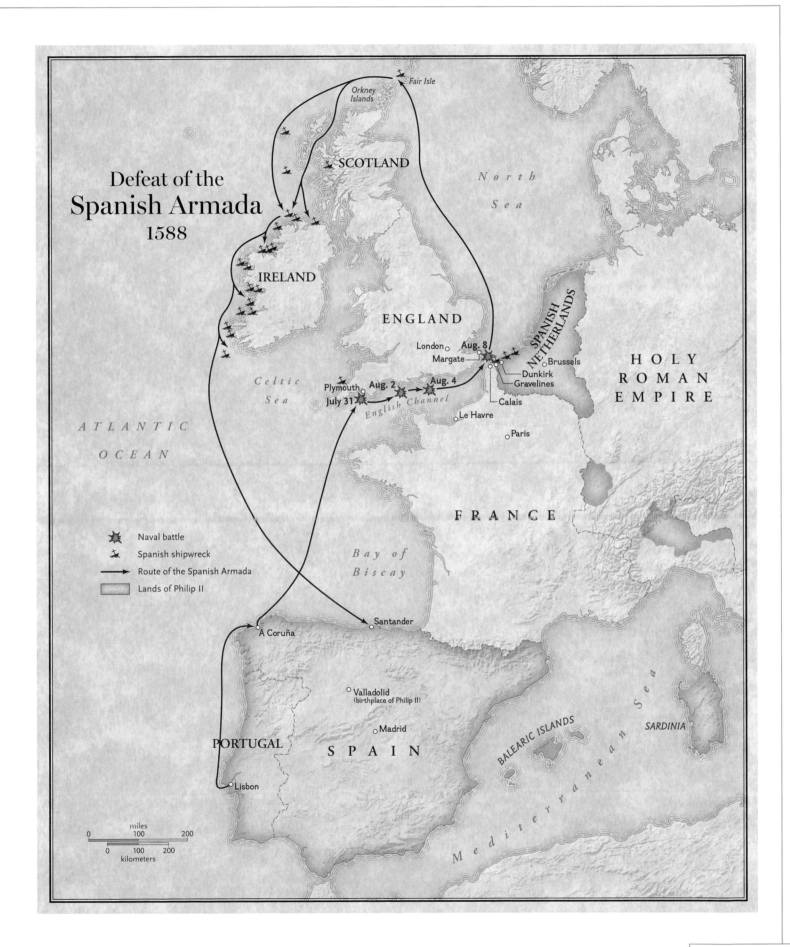

Defeat of the
Spanish Armada
1588

North Sea

SCOTLAND

Fair Isle

Orkney Islands

IRELAND

ENGLAND

London ○   Aug. 8

Margate

Celtic Sea

Plymouth   Aug. 2   Aug. 4

July 31   *English Channel*

SPANISH NETHERLANDS

Brussels ○

Dunkirk

Gravelines

Calais

Le Havre ○

Paris ○

HOLY ROMAN EMPIRE

ATLANTIC OCEAN

FRANCE

Bay of Biscay

Naval battle

Spanish shipwreck

Route of the Spanish Armada

Lands of Philip II

Santander ○

A Coruña ○

Mediterranean Sea

BALEARIC ISLANDS

SARDINIA

○ Valladolid
(birthplace of Philip II)

○ Madrid

PORTUGAL

S P A I N

○ Lisbon

miles
0   100   200

0   100   200
kilometers

IRELAND AND THE TUDORS

Revolt, Conquest, and the Seeds of Conflict

Much of Ireland had been nominally English since the days of Henry II (1133–1189), but by Tudor times the old colonizing Anglo-Norman lords of the 12th century had become as Irish as their indigenous counterparts. Both groups enjoyed an existence relatively independent of England, and the area of the Pale, the easterly region of more coherent English settlement, had shrunk to a small arc around Dublin. After 1485, however, the demands of the Tudor state brought Irish matters to a head.

First, Henry VII, fearful that Ireland would harbor pretenders to his throne, encouraged the Irish to reiterate their subordination to England. Next, Henry VIII, with the Catholic Irish posing an ideological challenge after the English Reformation, attempted to subdue and anglicize Ireland. In a policy known as surrender and regrant, Irish chieftains were forced so surrender their authority in return for the granting of an English title. One of the most powerful, Conn Ó Neill, became Earl of Tyrone; others were bribed with the riches of dissolved Irish monasteries. Henry also took the title King of Ireland, where previously English monarchs had merely been Lords of Ireland (a title the papacy had bestowed on Henry II).

Elizabeth I continued Henry's policy and attempted to impose Protestantism on Ireland's Catholic majority. The result was a succession of revolts after 1560, often aided by Catholic Spain. Conn Ó Neill's successor, Hugh Ó Neill, with Hugh Roe Ó Donnell, won significant victories at Clontibret (1595), Yellow Ford (1598), and Curlew Pass (1599), the last a triumph that helped seal the fate of Elizabeth's favorite, the Earl of Essex (see sidebar).

In 1601, however, the rebels suffered a heavy defeat at Kinsale, and in 1607, Ó Neill and Ó Donnell fled Ireland as part of the so-called Flight of the Earls. After 1610, an earlier English policy of plantation—the import of Protestant settlers from England and Scotland—was intensified, especially in the north, with consequences that would reverberate for centuries. ■

A Failed Favorite

Elizabeth I's lifelong favorite, Robert Dudley, Earl of Leicester, died in 1588, to be replaced in the queen's affections by his stepson, Robert Devereux (1566–1601), 2nd Earl of Essex *(pictured below)*. At Dudley's death Elizabeth was in her 50s, and Essex—handsome, hotheaded, and foolish—was in his 20s. Military campaigns involving Essex had already ended in disarray, yet in 1599, Elizabeth succumbed to his entreaties that he be allowed to confront Hugh Ó Neill and his Irish rebels (see left). Essex crossed to Ireland with a force of 16,000 men—the largest army sent to Ireland up to that time—and after a series of minor setbacks negotiated a truce with Ó Neill. Essex compounded his failure by returning to England, against Elizabeth's orders, to plead his case with a furious queen. He was dismissed and moved, as one observer said, "from sorrow and repentance to rage and rebellion." To his earlier folly he now added a series of far-fetched plots and intrigues that left Elizabeth with no choice but to order his execution in 1601.

Fight or flight The departure of Hugh Ó Neill from Ireland. Defeats at the hands of the English, and the subsequent restriction of freedoms, led to the Flight of the Earls in 1607, when leading Irish aristocratic figures such as Ó Neill decided to leave Ireland to continue their struggle from mainland Europe.

Ireland
1488–1603

SCOTLAND

Antrim

Ballyshannon
1597 ✕

Ford of the
Biscuits
1594 ✕

Yellow Ford
1598 ✕

Siege of
Collooney
1599 ✕

Monaghan
✕ Clontibret, 1595

Curlew Pass
1599 ✕

Moyry Pass
1600 ✕

Irish Sea

I R E L A N D

The
Pale

○ Tullamore ○ Philipstown   ○ Dublin

ATLANTIC

OCEAN

Maryborough ○
Stradbally ○   ○ Athy

○ Ballyragget

○ Limerick
Askeaton ○
Adare ○

○ Kilkenny

Gorey ○   ○ Arklow

○ Tipperary

Cahir ○   ○ Clonmel
Castle
○ Waterford   ○ Wexford

Conna ○

○ Cork

Siege of ✕
Dunboy
1602

✕ Siege of Kinsale
1601–1602

Celtic

Sea

WALES

ENGLAND

miles
0   25   50

0   25   50
kilometers

The Pale (area ruled by the King of England, 1488)

Plantation, 1553–1558

Raids by O'Donnell

Ó Donnell's march

Ó Neill's march

March of the Earl of Essex, 1598

March of the Earl of Essex, 1599

✕ Battle or Siege

English Channel

THE AGE OF SHAKESPEARE

Poets, Playwrights, and Individual Genius

William Shakespeare A purported portrait of the writer from around 1610, six years before his death. Many details of Shakespeare's life remain disputed or unknown.

A man "not of an age but for all time," said fellow playwright Ben Jonson of William Shakespeare (1564–1616), the greatest of the many writers, painters, and musicians who flourished in the last three decades of Elizabeth I's reign. Before Shakespeare and his contemporaries, however, there was Sir Philip Sidney (1554–1586), the archetype of the dashing Renaissance man. Courtier, politician, soldier, and poet, Sidney is best known for *Astrophel and Stella* (ca 1582), one of the first and finest sonnet sequences in English. His death at age 31 (while fighting the Spanish) inspired an elegy *(Astrophel)* by another outstanding name of the period, Edmund Spenser (ca 1552–1599). Spenser is remembered for *The Faerie Queene* (1590–1596), a courtly epic and extended allegory in which the central figure, Gloriana—"that greatest Queene of Faeryland"—is a thinly disguised Elizabeth I.

Away from the highbrow poetry of court, English drama of the period began to take a new direction, building on the traditions of England's miracle and mystery plays (old folk and religious dramas performed to everyday audiences). Dramatists such as George Peele, Robert Greene, and Thomas Nashe adopted the plays' rough humor and earthy approach—also seen in Shakespeare—but wove them into dramas of a nonreligious character. So, too, did Christopher Marlowe (1564–1593), whose key works, *Tamburlaine the Great* (1590) and *Doctor Faustus* (ca 1590), also influenced Shakespeare.

Shakespeare himself probably began to write around 1590, though the chronology of his life and works is much disputed. He was born in Stratford-upon-Avon, probably to provincial, middle-class parents. He received a good education; married Anne Hathaway at the age of 18; and had three children, one of whom died in childhood. A 1592 pamphlet confirms his presence in London as an actor-dramatist, and around 1594 he joined a theater company known as the Lord Chamberlain's Men as a writer and actor. By 1596, his fame was probably already widespread, for his father, John, an artisan, was awarded a coat of arms, probably in honor of his son's achievements; and by 1597, Shakespeare himself had acquired the means to buy New Place, a grand house in his hometown of Stratford.

After 1599, most of Shakespeare's plays were staged at the Globe Theatre, built in that year (see sidebar). In 1603, on the death of Elizabeth, the Lord Chamberlain's Men became the King's Men under the patronage of the new king, James I. Shakespeare's death came in 1616—possibly as a result of a fever brought on by a heavy night's carousing—and he was buried in Stratford's Holy Trinity Church. ■

The Globe Past and Present

Elizabethan plays were often performed in the courtyards of inns, open to the elements. Wealthier patrons might watch from an inn's upper wooden galleries while others stood in the pit—the yard itself. The authorities viewed theaters as potentially troublesome places for unruly gatherings, however, so they were often built on the fringes of towns and cities. This is one of the reasons the famous Globe Theatre was constructed in Southwark, on the south side of the River Thames, away from the heart of the City of London. Built of wood in 1599, the first theater with the Globe name burned down in two hours in 1613 when a cannon being used as a prop ignited the structure's thatch roof. It was rebuilt, and it opened a year later. Flags outside the theater advertised the type of play being performed: red for a history, white for a comedy, black for a tragedy. Actors were all men, whatever the performance, and scenery was virtually nonexistent; a written sign often served to describe a setting. A victim of the English Civil War, the Globe closed in 1642. A third incarnation, built to resemble the original as far as can be known, opened close to the old site in 1997.

> *"Our revels now are ended. These our actors, As I foretold you, were all spirits, and / Are melted into air, into thin air: / And like the baseless fabric of this vision . . . shall dissolve."*

WILLIAM SHAKESPEARE, *THE TEMPEST*, CA 1610–1611

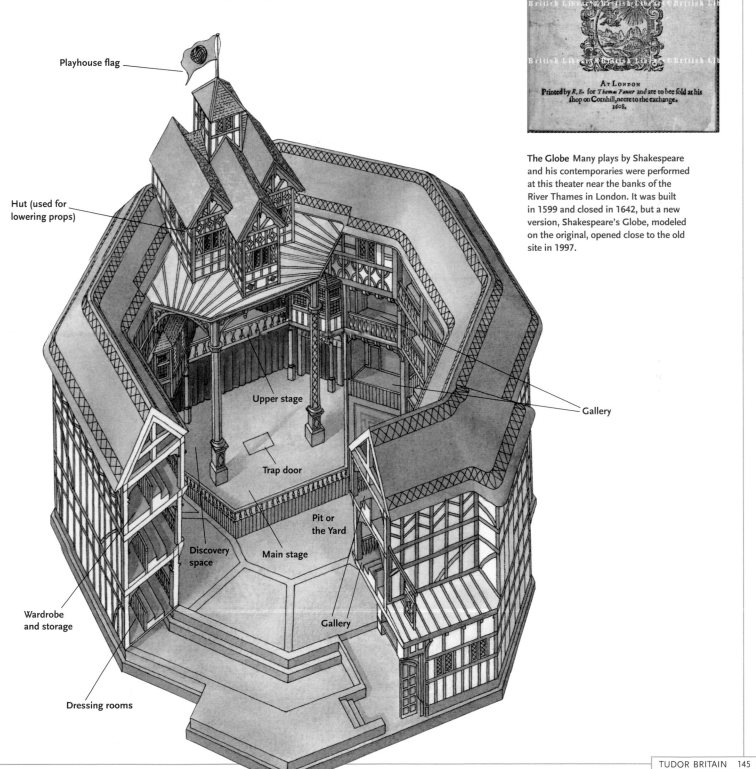

Playhouse flag

Hut (used for lowering props)

Upper stage

Trap door

Discovery space

Main stage

Pit or the Yard

Gallery

Wardrobe and storage

Gallery

Dressing rooms

The Globe Many plays by Shakespeare and his contemporaries were performed at this theater near the banks of the River Thames in London. It was built in 1599 and closed in 1642, but a new version, Shakespeare's Globe, modeled on the original, opened close to the old site in 1997.

THE STUARTS

1603—1714

*"How I came here, I know not—there's no law for it,
to make your King your prisoner."*

Restoration of the Stuarts
and the
Act of Union

✗ Battle

✸ Naval battle

○ Conspiracy or plot

→ The duke of Monmouth's route to Sedgemoor, 1685

→ William of Orange's invasion, 1688

→ Williamite campaigns, 1690–1691

⊙ Siege

▨ Scottish county submitting an address against the Union

∘ Scottish town submitting an address against the Union

ATLANTIC

OCEAN

Cromdale
1690 ✗

S C O T L A N D

Killiecrankie
1689 ✗

Massacre of Glencoe
1692 ✗

Dunkeld
1689 ✗

Archbishop of St. Andrews murdered by Covenanters
1679

G

R

E

A

Bothwell Bridge
1679 ✗

Edinburgh

Rullion Green, 1666

1679 Drumclog ✗

1680 Airds Moss ✗

Covenanters'
Sanquhar Declaration
1680

North

Sea

⊙ **Londonderry**
(Derry)
1689

Bangor

Derwentdale republican plot
1663

Enniskillen ⊙
1689

Armagh

✗ **Dromore**
1689

Newtownbutler
1689

Dundalk

Boyne
1690 ✗

Irish Sea

T

Yorkshire republican plot
1663

Aughrim
1691 ✗

I R E L A N D

⊙ **Athlone**
1690, 1691

Galway

Dublin

B

Carlow

R

I

Limerick
1690, 1691

T

E N G L A N D

Solebay
1672 ✸

Cork
1690

Kinsale
1690 ⊙

A

WALES

Lowestoft
1665 ✸

Bantry Bay
1689 ✸

I

Rye House plot
1683 ○

N

Abingdon

Popish Plot
1678 ○

London

Four Days'
Battle
1666 ✸

Celtic

Bath

Newbury

Chatham
1667 ✸

Sea

1685 Sedgemoor ✗

Wells

Frome

Shepton Mallet

Secret Treaty of Dover
1670

Bridgwater

Taunton

Sherborne

Ilminster

Exeter

Lyme Regis

Brixham

English Channel

miles
0   50   100

0   50   100
kilometers

F R A N C E

CIVIL WAR AND
THE RULE OF KINGS

THE TUDOR DYNASTY DIED WITH ELIZABETH I IN 1603. THE OLD QUEEN HAD STEADFASTLY refused to name her successor, but the ancient logic of hereditary right pointed to one man: James VI of Scotland, scion of the House of Stuart, which had ruled Scotland for 232 years and would now rule England—with Wales, Ireland, and a growing overseas empire—until 1714. James I was crowned on July 25, 1603, and though both the English and the Scottish parliaments resisted his attempt to create a formal union of the two kingdoms, James introduced a new flag that combined the red cross of St. George (England) with the white-on-blue cross of St. Andrew (Scotland). It was called the Grand Union, the Union Flag, or—when used at sea—the Union Jack, from Jacques, or James.

James quickly concluded peace with Spain, which desired an end to years of costly war as urgently as Britain did. He then addressed the issue of religion by calling a conference at Hampton Court Palace in 1604. The outcome broadly embraced the "middle way" of Elizabeth, a solution that alienated radical Catholics and Protestants alike. Catholic anger was expressed in the Gunpowder Plot of 1605, when conspirators attempted to blow up the king and Parliament. Disenchanted Puritans (more extreme Protestants)—most famously the Pilgrim Fathers, who left England aboard the *Mayflower* in 1620—began to look to emigration.

Shakespeare died in James's reign, in 1616, but the arts continued to flourish as they had under Elizabeth. Court life became more colorful, but also more corrupt, as James raised favorites such as George Villiers, Duke of Buckingham, to positions of power. It also became more expensive, as the antiquated Tudor machinery for financing the crown proved ill suited to a new age. This led to tensions with Parliament, which bridled at granting new taxes to the king. James, in turn, asserted old royal prerogatives by raising money on his own account through increased import duties and the sale of titles and monopolies.

■ MONEY, POWER, AND RELIGION

Money also dominated the reign of Charles I (1600–1649), who became king after the death of James in 1625. So, too, did religion: The new monarch's marriage in the same year to a Catholic, Henrietta Maria, the daughter of the French king, immediately alienated mainstream opinion. Protestants were further outraged after 1633, when a new Archbishop of Canterbury, William Laud, insisted on the reintroduction of ornament, fine music, and other aspects of worship that to many appeared indistinguishable from Catholicism.

Monarchy restored (*previous pages*) Charles II dances amid the pomp of his court. The painting dates from around 1660, the year Charles came to the throne after the period of dour military and parliamentary rule that followed the execution of his father, Charles I, in 1649. Charles II's accession brought stability and a more relaxed style of monarchy to Britain after the bloodshed of the English Civil War and its repressive and chaotic aftermath.

| TIME LINE |

1603
Elizabeth I dies; James I is crowned

1605
Catholics conspire to kill King James I and blow up House of Lords in Gunpowder Plot

1620
Puritans leave England on the *Mayflower*

1625
James I dies; Charles I becomes king

1641
Parliament issues Grand Remonstrance to air grievances against the king

1642–1646
Civil war between parliamentary and royal forces; Parliament is victorious

1649
Charles I is executed; Parliament abolishes the monarchy

1649
Parliamentary army, led by Oliver Cromwell, defeats the Irish at Battle of Rathmines

1650
Cromwell defeats the Scots at Battle of Dunbar

1653
Cromwell is given the title Lord Protector

1660
Charles II restored to the throne

1666
The Great Fire of London

1685
Charles II dies; his brother James II assumes the throne

1687
Sir Isaac Newton publishes his findings on motion and gravity

1688
Group of Whigs invites William of Orange to invade Britain and jointly rule with Mary

1689
Parliament passes the English Bill of Rights

1694
Mary dies; William of Orange rules alone

1707
The Act of Union unites England and Scotland under one Parliament

Charles also embroiled himself in European wars and soon antagonized Parliament with requests for money. Rebuffed, he imposed a forced loan on London merchants. When he asked for money again in 1628, Parliament agreed on condition that Charles accept the Petition of Right of 1628—a list of grievances that aimed to shackle the king, especially as regarded arbitrary taxation and imprisonment.

Charles reluctantly accepted the petition, but in March 1629 he dissolved Parliament with the remark that the House of Commons (the lower house) had attempted to "exert a universal, overswaying power, which belongs only to me, not to them." Henceforth, he vowed to rule alone. Like his father, James, this meant raising money on his own account. One source of royal income, ship tax, which previously was levied on ports for the upkeep of the navy, was now arbitrarily extended to inland areas. Another source, levying fines on those who encroached on royal forests, was extended to land that had been cleared for decades. Tensions among king, country, and Parliament increased.

In 1638, Charles blundered again. With the support of Laud, he attempted to force an English-style liturgy on Scotland. The austere Church of Scotland, informally known as the Kirk, rebelled, and with it all of Scotland. Thousands signed the Scottish National Covenant, a declaration protesting the king's acts, and raised an army against England. Charles marched north, only to lose the so-called First Bishops' War (1639), in which the size of his opponents' forces cowed him into submission without a fight.

■ THE PATH TO CIVIL WAR

Short of money, Charles had no choice but to recall Parliament in April 1640. No sooner had the body met—and issued another list of grievances—than Charles dissolved it in exasperation. The session had lasted less than three weeks—hence its later name, the Short Parliament.

In August 1640, the Scots invaded again. Once more Charles capitulated, this time by paying the Scots to retreat. In November, without money or an army worthy of the name, Charles summoned the Long Parliament, so-called because it effectively sat until 1660. Over the next year, Charles was forced to agree to most of Parliament's demands, including the abolition of the ship tax and other levies.

It was not enough. Civil war came closer in October 1641, when rebellion flared in Ireland. Again, Charles asked for money to raise an army. This time, accepting that the Irish revolt had to be crushed, Parliament agreed, but legislators feared any army might eventually be turned against itself and determined to curtail Charles's power

"The country had done something terrible. It had gone to war with itself and decapitated its king. Two decades had seen theocratic tyranny, parliamentary government, republican commonwealth and military dictatorship, as if England were trying on constitutions for size. Now after this monumental experiment in trial and error, it decided it wanted the monarch back . . ."

SIMON JENKINS, *A SHORT HISTORY OF ENGLAND,* 2011

further. In November 1641, Parliament duly issued the Grand Remonstrance, a list of 201 grievances and demands for the future.

Charles dismissed the remonstrance: "If I granted your demands," he said, "I should be no more than a mere phantom of a king." The situation began to unravel. Charles knew he had supporters in Parliament, whose demands for control of church and state had begun to alarm even its own Members. He also had many courtiers urging action against "treasonable" Members of Parliament (MPs) believed—probably rightly—to have been in contact with the Scots during the recent wars.

The final spark flew in January 1642. On the prompting of his queen, Henrietta Maria ("go you coward . . . or never see my face again"), Charles marched to Parliament to arrest five of its Members. With him were 400 heavily armed men. Having been forewarned, the five MPs escaped. In a famous exchange, Charles observed that his "birds had flown" and asked the speaker, William Lenthall, where they were. "I have neither eyes to see," replied Lenthall, "nor tongue to speak in this place, but as this House shall direct me."

Charles's failed armed intervention both confirmed Parliament's fears about his "tyrannical" intentions and underlined his ultimate impotence. It also tipped London

Royal welcome James I receives diplomats at court after his accession in 1603. James's introduction of male favorites and former Scottish aides to royal circles alienated Parliament and English courtiers alike.

against him, and the capital was vital as home to the wealthy merchants who paid and had borne the brunt of Charles's taxes. At that moment, London was also home to a mob seething with anti-Catholic ferment, intrigue, and the threat of violence.

■ THE DEATH OF A KING AND THE CHAOS OF COMMONWEALTH

Charles fled, and a long and bloody civil war ensued (see pages 170–173). Fortunes fluctuated on both sides before Parliament's ultimate victory. Several factors decided the outcome: Parliament's New Model Army was larger and better trained; a 1643 treaty brought a Scottish army to Parliament's side; and London and the south, with their greater wealth and resources, by and large supported Parliament.

At the war's end in spring 1646, Charles surrendered, escaped, and began negotiations with the Scots, who now threatened to change sides. For Parliament's army and its leaders, such as Oliver Cromwell (see pages 176–177), Charles's negotiations with the Scots were the last straw. In November 1648, after quelling a second Royalist uprising, the army issued a remonstrance demanding that the king, who had been recaptured,

Poet and politician John Milton (1608–1674), pictured here, is best known as a poet—and for his epic poem, *Paradise Lost* (1667), in particular—but he also worked for the Puritan and parliamentary cause, and then for Oliver Cromwell and the Commonwealth, whose republican ideals he supported.

be tried for treason. Parliament, now increasingly at loggerheads with the army, hoped to reach a compromise and rejected the demand. In response, an army colonel, Thomas Pride, with backing from on high, marched into Parliament and purged it of those suspected of Royalist sympathies.

After this coup, the so-called Rump Parliament (after the "rump" of Members left by Pride's Purge) set in motion the events that led to one of the most extraordinary events in British history: Charles I's execution on January 30, 1649 (see pages 174–175). On March 17, the Rump Parliament abolished the monarchy and created a "Commonwealth and free state" with Parliament as it "supreme authority."

In September 1649, Cromwell quelled revolts in Ireland with a ferocity that is remembered to this day (see pages 178–179). A year later, he did the same in Scotland, and in September 1651 he defeated Charles's son, also named Charles, at the Battle of Worcester. The son, the self-proclaimed Charles II, fled into exile.

Deprived of a king, Britain proved difficult to govern. In April 1653, Cromwell, exasperated at the Rump Parliament's indecision, dissolved the body. "You have sat here too long for the good you do," he railed. "In the name of God, go!" The army then approved a new parliament of 140 selected Puritans. This body was named the Barebones Parliament after one of its members, an Anabaptist called Praise-God Barbon. After five months, the Barebones Parliament dissolved itself and asked Cromwell to rule directly.

Cromwell, who was given the title Lord Protector, was now king in all but name (though he carefully avoided the trappings of monarchy). He dissolved Parliament again in 1654, and in 1655 he organized England into 12 regions ruled by army generals. Martial law and dour Puritan rule ensued.

King or not, on Cromwell's death in 1658, his son, Richard, was named his "heir" as Lord Protector. Weaker than his father, Richard soon lost control of the army and a restored Parliament, both of which had become weak and divided. Civil war once again threatened but was avoided thanks to the sagacity of General George Monck, commander of Britain's still powerful army in Scotland. Monck realized that the situation was hopeless and that only the old political institutions could restore stability. Having

HOUSE OF STUART
1603–1714

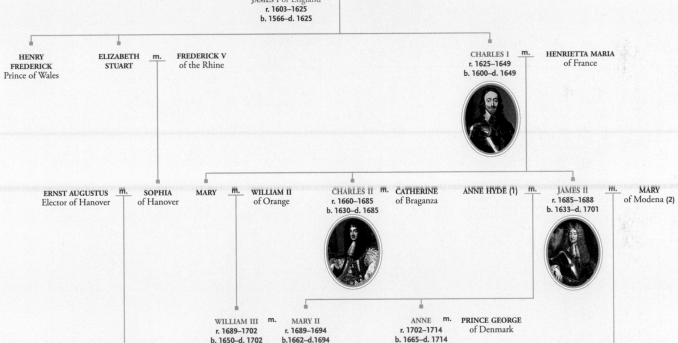

JAMES VI of Scotland
r. 1567–1625
b. 1566–d. 1625
JAMES I of England
r. 1603–1625
b. 1566–d. 1625

m.

ANNE
of Denmark

**HENRY
FREDERICK**
Prince of Wales

**ELIZABETH
STUART**

m.

FREDERICK V
of the Rhine

CHARLES I
r. 1625–1649
b. 1600–d. 1649

m.

HENRIETTA MARIA
of France

ERNST AUGUSTUS
Elector of Hanover

m.

SOPHIA
of Hanover

MARY

m.

WILLIAM II
of Orange

CHARLES II
r. 1660–1685
b. 1630–d. 1685

m.

CATHERINE
of Braganza

ANNE HYDE (1)

m.

JAMES II
r. 1685–1688
b. 1633–d. 1701

m.

MARY
of Modena (2)

WILLIAM III
r. 1689–1702
b. 1650–d. 1702

m.

MARY II
r. 1689–1694
b.1662–d.1694

ANNE
r. 1702–1714
b. 1665–d. 1714

m.

PRINCE GEORGE
of Denmark

MARIA SOBIESKI

m.

**JAMES FRANCIS
EDWARD STUART**
the Old Pretender

**SOPHIA
DOROTHEA**
of Celle

m.

GEORGE I
r. 1714–1727
b. 1660–d. 1727

**CHARLES
EDWARD STUART**
the Young Pretender
(aka Bonnie Prince
Charlie)

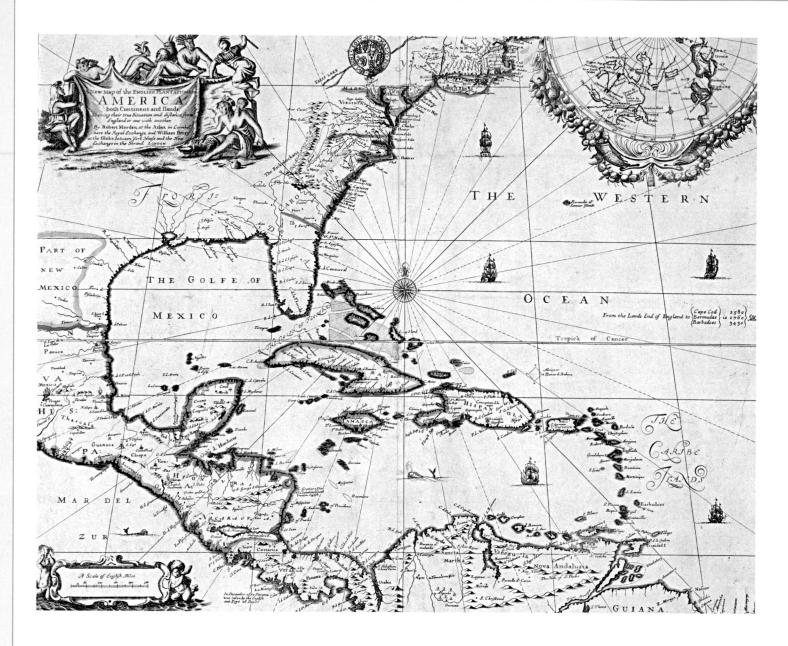

Charting success An archival map from 1673 showing England's new plantations in the Caribbean and the Americas. The Stuart period saw a marked increase in Britain's colonial possessions, along with the first mass movement of emigrants to the New World.

Final voyage *(opposite)* This 1881 painting by John Collier portrays explorer Henry Hudson, cast adrift with his son and others by Hudson's mutinous crew in 1611, shortly after the discovery of the bay in northeast Canada that bears his name. The explorer and his companions were never seen again.

fought for the Royalists in the English Civil War, he was able to broker the negotiations with all sides, which brought the Restoration—the return of the monarchy, beginning in 1660 with the reign of Charles II (1630–1685).

■ CHARLES II

Retribution for the events of the previous 20 years was surprisingly light. The army was paid off and a general pardon issued for all but the regicides—the men who had signed Charles I's death warrant in 1649. Even then, of the 41 still alive, only nine were executed. A special fate, though, was reserved for Oliver Cromwell, whose embalmed corpse was exhumed from Westminster Abbey. The head was cut off, the body dangled from a gallows at Tyburn (London's principal place of execution), and the skull stuck on a pole at Westminster Hall (the scene of Charles's trial), where it remained for 20 years.

Charles's reign was otherwise generally positive. Fun and gaiety returned to court—and to the king's bedchamber, where Charles sired at least 14 illegitimate children with

a string of mistresses. The arts and sciences were patronized, a succession of colonies was established in the Caribbean and the Americas, and a port renamed New York became English territory in 1664. Brief trade wars were fought against the Dutch, and a devastating fire and plague struck London (see pages 182–183). But at Charles's death in 1685, the only real political cloud was the lack of a Protestant heir.

■ JAMES, WILLIAM, ANNE, AND MARY

For all Charles's illegitimate children, he had no legitimate son or daughter. This brought his brother, James, to the throne. James II (1633–1701) was dull, formal, and ineffectual—"Dismal Jimmy," the Scots called him. He was also Catholic, and though two of his children through a first marriage had been raised as Protestants (Anne and Mary), the birth in 1688 to his second wife of a son, also called James, brought the prospect of an eventual Catholic succession. This on its own was intolerable, but James also alienated public opinion with his unrepentant promotion of Catholics and Catholicism.

By this time, Parliament had developed the first stirrings of political parties, broadly divided into Whigs and Tories. Whigs were avowedly Protestant, and they were strong parliamentarians: Their nickname came from a group of Scottish Presbyterians at the time of the English Civil War. Tories were more broadly royalist and sympathetic to the king and to the idea of hereditary right. Their name came from a group of Irish Catholic outlaws.

In 1688, a group of Whig grandees, with widespread popular English support, invited the Dutch ruler, the Protestant William of Orange (1650–1702), to become

Man and myth A statue of Oliver Cromwell stands outside the Houses of Parliament in London. An outstanding general, Cromwell fought for the Parliamentary cause against Charles I in the English Civil War, but as Lord Protector during the era of the Commonwealth, his rule was as autocratic as that of any king.

First footsteps This canvas by George Henry Boughton (1833–1905) portrays a group of the Pilgrim Fathers, some of the first Puritan exiles to emigrate to the New World. The settlers progress through a recently cleared woodland to worship at the small settlement in the distance.

joint ruler by marrying Mary (1662–1694), one of James II's two Protestant children. William was related to Charles I (his mother was the king's sister) and was Mary's first cousin. In the Glorious Revolution that followed, James was deposed and William III and Mary II were installed (see pages 188–189). Revolts in Scotland and Ireland in support of James were put down, though agitation in his favor of the former king and his Stuart heirs continued until 1746.

Mary proved popular, William less so, but the queen died young (at 32) in 1694. A distraught William reigned alone, becoming increasingly embroiled in wars with France. At his death in 1702, his only heir was James II's second Protestant daughter, Anne (1665–1714).

During Anne's solid but uninspiring reign, Scotland's dire economic situation, as well as its dangerous sympathies for the deposed James, hastened politicians into the Act of Union (1707). This united England and Scotland under one parliament (Scotland reluctantly), with a single currency and a joint flag, but with separate legal, religious, and education systems.

Anne's reign also saw an intensification of the wars in France, with a string of victories that included Blenheim (1704), won by John Churchill, Duke of Marlborough. A grateful nation granted Marlborough land near Oxford, where he built a great house, Blenheim Palace. One of Churchill's descendants, a boy named Winston, would be born there in 1874.

Anne suffered six miscarriages and 11 stillbirths or infant mortalities, and her one healthy child, William, died in 1700. This left the succession open again. By now, the Act of Settlement of 1701 had made it illegal for any Catholic to accede to the British throne. The next Protestant in a now distant line was the obscure 83-year-old Sophia of Hanover, a granddaughter of James I. Sophia died in June 1714, followed by Anne two months later. Sophia's son, George—a German—was next in line. ∎

JAMES I

Money and Patronage, Failure and Favoritism

Sir Anthony Weldon, a courtier to James I (1566–1625), had it about right: James, he declared in an unguarded moment, was the "wisest fool in Christendom." Weldon's assessment deftly summarized the character of a king who at first ruled effectively, but whose misjudgments and lofty view of kingship helped sow the seeds of civil war less than 20 years after his death.

James was the son of Mary, Queen of Scots (see pages 132–133), whose misadventures guaranteed him an extraordinary childhood. His father was murdered—probably blown up on his mother's orders—when he was eight months old. Five months later he became king, when the mother he barely knew, nor would know again, fled to England. Governors saw to his upbringing, with authority over Scotland delegated to regents, four of whom were murdered in quick succession. As a pawn in Scottish squabbles, James was lucky to escape with his life.

When he assumed power in 1585, however, he brought a degree of order to Scotland. His reign in England after 1603 also began well, with an end to war with Spain and moderation in the difficult area of religion (see pages 162–163). But the signs of future financial problems were already there. In 1603, James had only reached York, halfway on his progress south from Scotland to be crowned in Westminster, when he ran out of money and had to send to London for more. Extravagance would be one his failings.

In other areas, James was more accomplished. He was a capable scholar, for example, but was overly concerned with minutiae—too fond of "unbuttoning his royal store of wisdom" for the benefit of his subjects, in the words of one courtier. Among his writings he is remembered for "A Counterblaste to Tobacco" (1604), a pamphlet in which he describes the new habit of smoking as "loathsome to the eye, hateful to the nose, harmful to the brain, dangerous to the lungs."

James also revitalized court life after the doldrums of Elizabeth's last years. But while he patronized writers such as Shakespeare, John Donne, and Ben Jonson, he also had an eye for young men, and he overpromoted and lavished riches on favorites such as George Villiers, Duke of Buckingham. Life at court ultimately became coarser and more corrupt.

The fact that James allowed his favorites to interfere in politics antagonized English courtiers and parliamentarians, many of whom were already uneasy at having a "Scottish" king and a surfeit of new Scottish courtiers in their midst. Even allowing for the natural prejudice this aroused, contemporary accounts of James's character were far from flattering. Many could barely understand his broad Scottish accent, and when they could, what they heard was not always edifying: "I give not a turd for your preaching," he allegedly told one minister.

Few monarchs could have hoped to emulate Elizabeth I, but James lacked the charisma, bearing, and political acumen of his predecessor to a marked degree. His son and heir, Charles I, would be even worse. ■

King's gift The Queen's House, Greenwich, commissioned from architect Inigo Jones by Queen Anne, wife of James I, in 1616. England's first wholly classical-style building, the palace was inspired by Jones's recent visits to Italy. Legend has it James awarded Anne the land for the building in 1614 as an apology for swearing at her after she accidentally shot his favorite dog during a hunting party.

The wisest fool James I is portrayed as an idealized king in this painting by 19th-century artist John Whitehead Walton, but his failings of character and a lack of political skill in the latter part of his reign antagonized Parliament and undermined the achievements of his predecessor, Elizabeth I. A contemporary painted a different physical picture of the king: "His eyes were ever rolling . . . his beard very thin . . . his tongue too large for his mouth," and his legs "scarcely strong enough to carry his body."

Royal consorts A circa 1611 portrait miniature of Queen Anne (1574–1619), wife of James I, and its reverse side. Despite his marriage, James was known to have—and to promote—male favorites, which outraged many in the king's court.

THE GUNPOWDER PLOT

A Catholic Conspiracy and a Calamity Foiled

England's minority Catholics had high hopes of James I in 1603. When the new king relaxed the rules on recusants—those who refused to renounce their Catholic faith—their hopes appeared justified. When an unexpected number of Catholics emerged, however, the policy was reversed and their hopes were dashed. Catholics were further frustrated when Spain, Europe's leading Catholic power, failed to insert in its peace treaty with Britain clauses requesting that James ease religious persecution. It was at this point that a group of Catholic conspirators decided to take matters into their own hands.

The architects of what became known as the Gunpowder Plot aimed to blow up the House of Lords on the opening day of James's second parliamentary session—November 5, 1605—when the king, his court, and England's parliamentarians would all be in attendance. With the country's ruling class eliminated, the plotters intended to install James's nine-year-old daughter, Elizabeth, as a puppet queen under Catholic control.

The plan might have worked but for a letter intercepted on October 26, 1605. Its sender is unknown, but the finger points at Francis Tresham, for it was addressed to his brother-in-law, William Parker, Lord Monteagle. Parker was a Catholic, but he had declared himself "done with all plots" and was due to attend the opening of Parliament. He handed the letter to the authorities.

The document, which survives in the U.K. National Archives, was a warning to stay away: "My lord, out of the love I bear to some of your friends, I have care of your preservation . . . I would advise you to devise some excuse to shift of your attendance at this Parliament."

The authorities decided to wait until the eve of the opening session to catch the conspirators red-handed. The plan worked. Parliament's opening had been delayed by a plague outbreak, allowing the plotters time to gather and to place vast quantities of gunpowder in cellars rented beneath the House of Lords. When guards swept the cellars at 11 p.m. on November 4, they found 36 barrels, or 5,500 pounds, of explosives. With the barrels was one of the conspirators, Guy Fawkes, who was waiting to set fuses to a charge that modern experts calculate would have destroyed not only the House of Lords, but also Westminster Abbey, Whitehall, and everything else within a 550-yard radius.

Fawkes was taken away and tortured into revealing his co-conspirators. Like the letter that betrayed him, his confessions can still be viewed in the National Archives. (His handwriting in one confession, completed after his torture, is markedly more strained.) His name is given to the annual Guy Fawkes Night, also called Bonfire Night, on November 5. The firework celebrations held on and around this day are a tradition carried over from the bonfires lit by Londoners to celebrate the thwarting of the plot.

The punishment for the conspirators was the most extreme possible, though at the time it was described as "ordinary . . . and much inferior to their Offence." It involved each being dragged from prison backward by a horse, then hanged, cut down while still conscious, and having "his Privy Parts cut off and burnt before his face, as being unworthily begotten and unfit to leave any generation behind him . . . after to have his Head cut off." Guy Fawkes jumped from the executioner's scaffold, thus breaking his neck as he was being hanged to escape this still grimmer fate. ■

Caught in the act *(above)* This 1823 painting by Henry Perronet Briggs depicts the moment guards arrested Guy Fawkes, one of the Catholic conspirators who attempted to blow up James I and Parliament in 1605. Fawkes had been given the job of detonating the gunpowder.

A dark deed *(left)* This lantern belonged to Guy Fawkes, who hid in the cellars beneath the House of Lords for 24 hours prior to the planned culmination of the Gunpowder Plot. An intercepted letter betrayed him to the authorities.

RELIGIOUS DISSENTERS

Plots, Puritans, and New World Pilgrims

When James I came to the throne, he faced the same dilemma that had confronted Elizabeth I: England was a Protestant country, but it still contained Catholics, many of whom felt persecuted by the state and wanted restrictions on their freedoms lifted. Many Protestants, by contrast, felt that the Church of England had not been sufficiently purged of its Catholic associations and sought a purer form of Protestantism. Both sides viewed the accession of a new king as an opportunity to address the status quo.

James had the same view, and one of his first acts on coming to power was to call a religious conference at Hampton Court in 1604. The more extreme Puritans—an initially derogatory term that had been in use since the 1560s—had high hopes of James, who had been brought up in the strictly Protestant Kirk (Church) of Scotland. Even before he was crowned, 1,000 Puritans had signed a petition of demands and presented it to him as he traveled south from Scotland to London in 1603.

But they misjudged the new king, whose strict Protestant upbringing had an effect precisely opposite to that intended. Instead of following the Presbyterian example of Scotland, which insisted on church government by elders rather than bishops, the adult James preferred the existing English model. His reasons were the same ones that had appealed to Henry VIII 70 years earlier: First, kings appointed, and so controlled, the bishops; and second, if God ordained kings to rule, then kings were answerable only to God, not to Parliament, to groups of elders, or to anyone else. "If you aim at a Scottish Presbytery," James told the Puritans, "it agreeth with monarchy as God with-devil . . . Then Jack, and Tom and Will and Dick shall meet and censure me and my council." So James retained the religious "middle way" of Elizabeth I: He allowed toleration within limits while insisting more forcefully on his "divine right" to rule as he saw fit.

The solution pleased neither extreme Puritans nor the more outspoken Catholics. Although the numbers of both groups were small, Catholic dissent was expressed in the Gunpowder Plot (see page 160), and Puritan dissatisfaction revealed itself in a drift to overseas exile, in particular to the New World.

Among the earliest to flee what they saw as religious persecution was a group from Scrooby, a village in central England. They emigrated first to Leiden, in the Netherlands (in 1607), but even there they found it difficult to sustain their culture. In 1619, they approached the Virginia Company of London, which in 1607 had established the first sustainable British outpost in America at James Fort, later Jamestown (see page 164). After many mishaps, some of the group gathered at Plymouth, in Devon, and on September 16, 1620, set sail with other settlers aboard a ship called the *Mayflower*. The settlers made landfall at Cape Cod on November 21, 1620.

Eight years later, in 1628, a larger group of Puritans formed the Massachusetts Bay Company and, in 1630, crossed the Atlantic to found Massachusetts. Their numbers were swollen over the next ten years by some 20,000 refugees from the religious intolerance of Britain's new king, Charles I, and his divisive archbishop, William Laud. Ironically, it was the Puritans' intolerance, in turn, that drove Roger Williams from Massachusetts to found Rhode Island in 1636. Dissent, in different forms, found different ways to create the stirrings of a new England overseas. ■

The King James Bible

The King James Bible is one of the glories of the English language. Used for generations in English-speaking countries worldwide, it is widely praised for the simple but noble beauty of its prose. A result of the religious conference at Hampton Court chaired by James I in 1604, it was partly an appeasement to more Puritan Protestants—who had reservations about existing translations—and partly an acknowledgment that there were too many conflicting English versions of the Bible.

John Wycliffe's first complete Bible in English had appeared around 1382, and William Tyndale's Bible joined it after 1526. Miles Coverdale's first "authorized" Bible, published as the Great Bible, followed in 1539. English Protestant refugees produced the Calvinist Geneva Bible in 1560, and the rival Bishops' Bible appeared in 1568.

For the King James Bible, 47 translators were set to work in six teams. Among them were some of the greatest scholars of the day, notably Lancelot Andrewes (1555–1626), whose mastery of several languages included Greek, Latin, and Hebrew. The result, published in 1611, has been called the finest work produced by a committee.

"Being thus arrived in a good harbor, and brought safe to land, they fell upon their knees and blessed the God of Heaven who had brought them over the vast and furious ocean, and delivered them from all the perils and miseries thereof, again to set their feet on the firm and stable earth, their proper element."

WILLIAM BRADFORD, *OF PLIMOTH PLANTATION*, 1620–1647

First hand Among these signatures of the Pilgrim Fathers is the name of William Bradford *(top left)*, who served as the governor of the Pilgrims' Plymouth Colony. His journal, *Of Plimoth Plantation*, provides an important record of early American colonial life.

A new life The departure of the Pilgrim Fathers aboard the *Mayflower* in 1620, an illustration from *The Outline of History* by H. G. Wells (1920). Many religious dissenters, Protestant and Catholic alike, left England in the early part of the 17th century.

SETTLEMENT AND EXPLORATION

The First Steps Toward a British Empire

England's early colonial adventures were distinctly underwhelming. Roanoke Colony—the country's first settlement in the Americas (1584–1590), in present-day North Carolina—failed miserably (see page 136). Sir Francis Drake's first toehold on America's west coast, New Albion (1579), fared little better, though its supposed location has prospered since—as California. As a result, British "colonies" at the end of Elizabeth I's reign amounted to one: Ireland.

Things began to change under James I. In 1607, a group of settlers founded James Fort, later Jamestown, named after the king. In doing so they established Britain's first permanent settlement in North America. Its earliest steps were faltering—all but 60 of around 500 inhabitants died in the Starving Time of 1609–1610—but eventually the cultivation of tobacco helped consolidate the colony and set the pattern for many of the American outposts that followed. Twelve of the original 13 Colonies were established during the Stuart era; Georgia, the 13th, was founded in 1733.

Where trade was largely Jamestown's inspiration, many of the other American colonies were informed by religion. Protestant exiles founded most of them, notably the four Puritan colonies of Massachusetts, Rhode Island, Connecticut, and New Hampshire. Some, though, had Catholic roots—for example, Maryland (1634), largely founded by Lord Baltimore and his son, Cecilius.

Maryland was not Baltimore's first colonial adventure. He also had tried to create a settlement in Newfoundland, which had been claimed for England in 1583. The choice of Newfoundland was no accident, for Canada, rich in furs, had begun to interest Britain's new colonists and explorers. In 1610, for example, an Englishman, Henry Hudson, discovered the vast bay that bears his name, and he brought British traders and others to the region. Equally important—though its importance was not appreciated at the time—was Hudson's exploration of the river that bears his name in modern-day New York State.

For much of the time before his death, around 1611, Hudson worked for the Dutch, who founded their own American colony, New Netherland (1614), between New England in the north and Maryland and Virginia to the south. In time, the British would acquire the Dutch territories, along with their major port, New Amsterdam, renamed New York (1664) after the Duke of York, the future James II.

Faith in the future This crucifix is believed to have belonged to a Catholic settler in Jamestown, Britain's first successful colony in the Americas. The settlement, in present-day Virginia, was permanently inhabited after 1607.

Britain and the Netherlands were not alone in their colonial ambitions. France, too, sought to forge an empire in North America, starting with Acadie (Nova Scotia) after 1534 and culminating with Quebec in 1608.

The close proximity of British and French possessions promised future discord, but for now British attention in North America switched south to the settlement of the Caribbean. Tobacco from the American colonies was lucrative, but sugar from the West Indies promised—and delivered—riches beyond compare. Barbados, claimed in 1625, would become the jewel in Britain's Caribbean crown, but the Bahamas (1648) and six other colonies by 1700 were to prove almost as valuable.

Early settlers in the Americas were often indentured servants who mortgaged their labor for a number of years in return for their passage. Many were virtually slaves in all but name. Now, with the advent of labor-intensive Caribbean sugar (and American tobacco) plantations, Britain embarked on the slave trade proper. Slaves had been brought from Africa since at least the 1560s, but henceforth the trade exploded, with Britain at its heart (see pages 210–213).

The Stuart period also saw Britain make the first steps in what would soon become other vital areas of empire. In 1600, for example, Britain's East India Company was founded to secure a share of the lucrative spice trade in the Far East. In time, it had to surrender much of the region to better-financed Dutch companies. Rather than retreating, however, the company looked elsewhere and established trading relations with the great Mogul rulers of India. The result was a trading post at Surat (ca 1612), the first of many Indian footholds that eventually included (among others) Cochin (1635), now Kochi; Fort St. George (1644), present-day Chennai; and Calcutta (1690), now Kolkata. India would eventually become Britain's most prized imperial possession (see pages 220–221).

The Dutch, for their part, also looked farther afield, notably to the southern tip of Africa, where their Cape Colony (1652) and the Boer descendants of its first settlers would create another point of colonial conflict (see pages 280–281). The Dutch also made the first steps into other areas of future British interest, notably New Zealand, named after a Dutch province, and Australia, where one of the most famous navigators of the Netherlands, Abel Tasman, gave his name to Tasmania. It was left to a Briton, however—James Cook—to make the most of both discoveries in the following century. ■

Name change New York, from the water, is depicted in a hand-colored 1702 engraving by Pieter Schenk. The city, originally known as Nieuw Amsterdam, served as the capital of a Dutch colony, Nieuw-Nederland. Captured by the British in 1664, it was renamed after the Duke of York, the brother of Charles II and the future James II.

First settlement An imagined aerial view of Britain's Jamestown Colony as it might have appeared shortly after its foundation in the early 17th century. The painting is by U.S. National Park Service artist Sydney King (1906–2002).

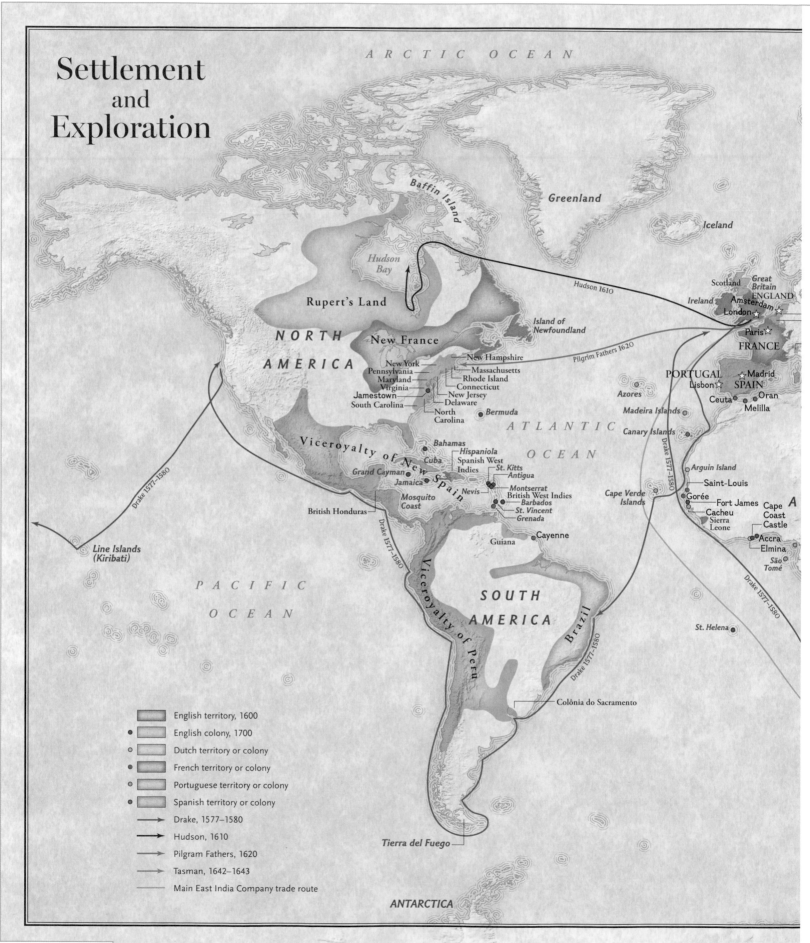

Settlement
and
Exploration

ARCTIC OCEAN

Baffin Island

Greenland

Iceland

Hudson Bay

Hudson 1610

Scotland · Great Britain · ENGLAND
Ireland · Amsterdam · London ☆ ☆
Paris ☆
FRANCE

Rupert's Land

NORTH
AMERICA

New France

Island of Newfoundland

Pilgrim Fathers 1620

New Hampshire
New York · Massachusetts
Pennsylvania · Rhode Island
Maryland · Connecticut
Virginia · New Jersey
Jamestown · Delaware
South Carolina · North Carolina
Bermuda

PORTUGAL
Lisbon ☆ · Madrid ☆ Madrid
SPAIN
Ceuta · Oran
Melilla

Azores

Madeira Islands

ATLANTIC

Canary Islands

OCEAN

Viceroyalty of New Spain

Bahamas
Cuba · Hispaniola
Spanish West Indies · St. Kitts
Grand Cayman · Antigua
Jamaica · Nevis · Montserrat
Mosquito · British West Indies
Coast · Barbados
St. Vincent
British Honduras · Grenada

Arguin Island
Saint-Louis
Gorée · Fort James · Cape
Cacheu · Coast
Sierra · Castle
Leone · Accra
Elmina
São Tomé

Cape Verde
Islands

Drake 1577–1580

Drake 1577–1580

Drake 1577–1580

Line Islands
(Kiribati)

PACIFIC

OCEAN

Cayenne
Guiana

SOUTH
AMERICA

Brazil

St. Helena

Viceroyalty of Peru

Colônia do Sacramento

Tierra del Fuego

ANTARCTICA

English territory, 1600
English colony, 1700
Dutch territory or colony
French territory or colony
Portuguese territory or colony
Spanish territory or colony
→ Drake, 1577–1580
→ Hudson, 1610
→ Pilgram Fathers, 1620
→ Tasman, 1642–1643
→ Main East India Company trade route

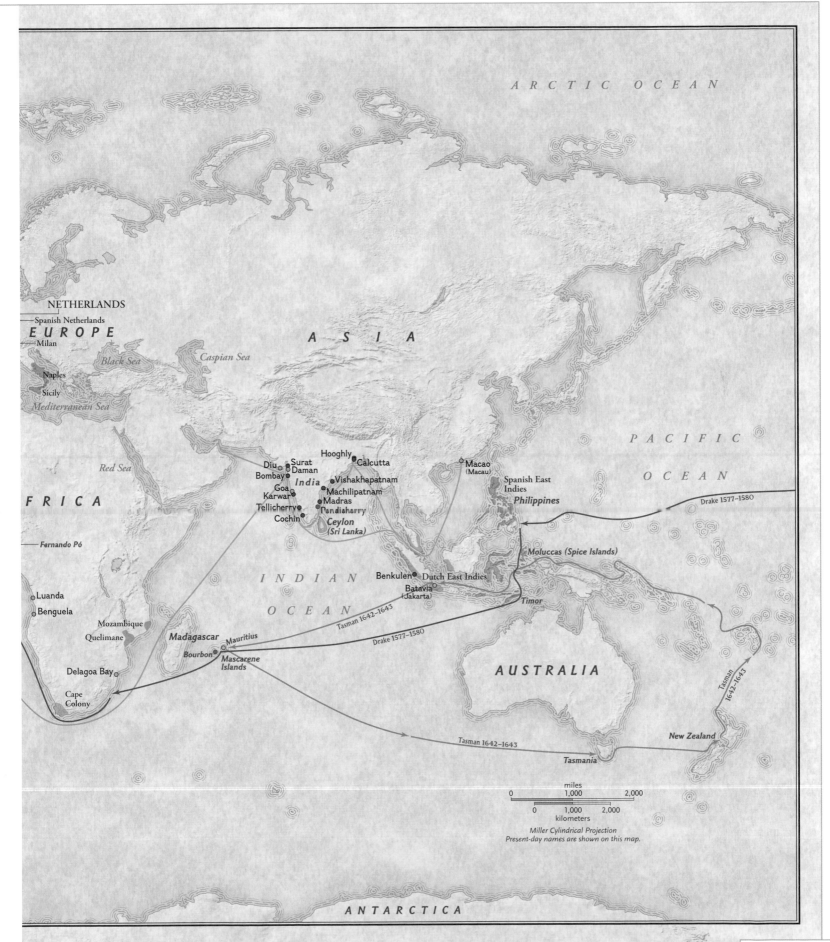

ARCTIC OCEAN

ASIA

PACIFIC

OCEAN

EUROPE

NETHERLANDS
Spanish Netherlands
Milan

Caspian Sea

Black Sea

Naples

Sicily

Mediterranean Sea

Red Sea

FRICA

Fernando Pó

Luanda

Benguela

Mozambique
Quelimane

Madagascar
Bourbon
Mascarene
Islands

Mauritius

Delagoa Bay

Cape
Colony

Diu
Bombay
Goa
Karwar
Tellicherry
Cochin

Surat
Daman
India

Hooghly
Calcutta

Vishakhapatnam
Machilipatnam
Madras
Pondicherry
Ceylon
(Sri Lanka)

Macao
(Macau)

Spanish East
Indies
Philippines

Moluccas (Spice Islands)

Benkulen
Batavia
(Jakarta)

Dutch East Indies

Timor

INDIAN

OCEAN

Tasman 1642–1643

Drake 1577–1580

Drake 1577–1580

AUSTRALIA

Tasman 1642–1643

Tasmania

Tasman
1642–1643

New Zealand

miles
0   1,000   2,000
0   1,000   2,000
kilometers
Miller Cylindrical Projection
Present-day names are shown on this map.

ANTARCTICA

CHARLES I

Solitary Child, Difficult Reign, Doomed King

Britain and Ireland have known more venal and ineffectual kings than Charles I (1600–1649), and kings with greater flaws and fewer redeeming qualities, but they have never known a king whose actions pitched his country into the bloodiest of civil wars and brought about his own trial and execution for treason.

Yet Charles's reign began well. He was 24 when he inherited the throne from his father, James I. He proved cultured and a generous patron of the arts. He also curbed the corrupt decadence of his father's court. "King Charles was temperate, chaste and serious," wrote one courtier, "so that the fools and bawds, mimics and catamites of the former court grew out of fashion."

But Charles had faults, many of them rooted in his dismal upbringing. As a young child, he was wrenched from his Scottish home after his father became king. Unable to walk until he was seven, he grew up slowly and sickly. He was frail—never taller than five feet four inches—and developed a lifelong stammer. Shy and solitary, he languished in the shadow of his elder brother, Henry, whom he idolized, and who left Charles bereft when he died in 1612.

In adulthood, Charles attached himself to mentors. The first, disastrously, was the "most despised man in the country," George Villiers, his father's old favorite. Villiers's reckless foreign escapades and extravagant behavior endeared him to few, and certainly not to the increasingly powerful Puritan element in Charles's Parliament.

The second mentor was Charles's French wife, Henrietta Maria, who after a cool early relationship—the marriage was arranged, and she burst into tears on first seeing her husband—became a steely power behind the throne. She was also Catholic, and not shy of showing it, something else calculated to antagonize both Puritans and the country at large.

Charles's father, James, lacked personal mettle and political acumen, but he was still better than his son in both regards. James was at the least garrulous and had a human touch. Charles was aloof and had a chill aestheticism. He appeared indifferent to his subjects. Charisma and humor passed him by. He placed faith in his "rights" and was unbending when they were challenged. He had little understanding of others and, fatally, failed to appreciate the changing tenor of the times.

On their own, such flaws might have counted for little, but at a time of rising religious and political tensions, when cool heads and compromise were called for, Charles could manage neither. Instead, he was duplicitous and confrontational. The result was disaster. ∎

Family and friend *(left)* This 1637 portrait of Charles I's five youngest children is by Flemish artist Sir Anthony Van Dyck. The central figure is the future Charles II, who eventually would sit for 292 known paintings. Van Dyck, one of the leading artists of his day, was responsible for more than a thousand portraits.

Man of the arts *(opposite)* Charles, seen here in another portrait by Van Dyck, "Charles I at the Hunt" (1635), was a patron of the arts who accumulated one of Europe's greatest collections of paintings. Many were sold after his execution but later were recovered to form the basis of the British royal family's current art collection.

CIVIL WAR

King, Parliament, and a People Divided

T he war that engulfed Britain between 1642 and 1646 was the most traumatic in the nation's history. Neighbor was pitched against neighbor, brother against brother. Up to a tenth of the male population is thought to have died, proportionately the highest of any British conflict before or since. Initial skirmishes, during which many people remained aloof, became bloodier. New armies with new leaders emerged. Attitudes hardened; positions became more desperate. Alliances shifted, and principles were compromised. At the conflict's end, a king stood trial for treason and Parliament, for all its high ideals, had been reduced to a rump in thrall to military might.

Most wars need a spark. In this case, it was Charles's armed march on Parliament in January 1642. For many, this was the final straw and a folly that largely tipped London against the king. Elsewhere in the country, opinion was more nuanced, and Charles enjoyed support from many who feared conflict or were simply loyal to the "natural" order of monarchy. Many were also uneasy at the implications of a victory for Parliament, especially one showing the same signs of autocracy and intolerance that had turned so many against the king.

Turning point *(top)* The Battle of Marston Moor in 1644, illustrated here in a 19th-century painting by John Barker, changed the course of the English Civil War when Scottish troops helped secure a parliamentary victory that deprived Charles I of his northern power base. The battle also marked a hardening of attitudes, and no mercy was given. "God made them as stubble to our swords," said Oliver Cromwell of at least 3,000 Royalists slaughtered on the battlefield.

Time of need *(above)* Coinage was often produced inside towns under siege to pay soldiers and to allow for everyday transactions. This silver token is from Newark, one of three Royalist towns to produce such "money of necessity" during the English Civil War.

Battle of Marston Moor
July 2, 1644

Prince Rupert
Newcastle
Byron
Porter
Cromwell
Goring
Manchester
Leven
Tockwith
Fairfax
Sike Beck
Marston Hill
Hamilton
Long Marston
Marston Fields

miles
0   0.25   0.5
0   250   500
meters

Royalist forces
Parliamentary forces

English Civil War
1642–1651

Held by Parliament, late 1643
Held by the king, late 1643
Scotland, late 1643
Confederation of Kilkenny, late 1643
Covenanter campaigns, 1642–1644
Rupert's campaign, 1644
Irish reinforcements for Charles I
Montrose's campaigns, 1644–1645
Parliamentarian campaign, 1645–1646
Battle
Siege

ATLANTIC OCEAN

North Sea

SCOTLAND

Auldearn May 9, 1645
Alford July 2, 1645
Inverlochy Feb. 2, 1645
Inverary
Dundee
Tippermuir Sept. 1, 1644
Stirling
Kilsyth Aug. 15, 1645
Berwick
Philiphaugh Sept. 13, 1645
Newburn Aug. 28, 1640
Annan Moor Oct. 21, 1645
Coleraine
Carlisle
Newcastle
Londonderry
Corbridge Feb. 16, 1644
Belfast
Dungannon
Benburb June 5, 1646
Enniskillen
Manorhamilton
Clones June 13, 1643
Scarborough
Boyle
Jamestown
Irish Sea
Marston Moor, July 2, 1644
York
Hull
Roscommon
Drogheda
Athboy
Julianstown Nov. 29, 1641
Liverpool
Bolton
Adwalton Moor June 30, 1643
Winceby Oct. 11, 1643
Galway
IRELAND
Dublin
Loughrea
Portumna
Chester
Newark
Maryborough
Kilrush Apr. 15, 1642
Jan. 25, 1644 Nantwich
Nottingham
Bunratty
Carlow
Harlech
Hopton Heath Mar. 19, 1643
Lichfield
Limerick
Shrewsbury
ENGLAND
Liscarroll Sept. 3, 1642
Naseby June 14, 1645
Duncannon
WALES
Edgehill Oct. 23, 1642
Cropredy Bridge June 29, 1644
Cork
Ardmore
Gloucester
Oxford
Turnham Green Nov. 13, 1642
Lansdown July 5, 1643
Donnington Castle
London
Bristol
Newbury Sept. 20, 1643 and Oct. 27, 1644
Brentford Nov. 12, 1642
July 13, 1643 Roundway Down
Cheriton Mar. 29, 1644
Celtic Sea
Barnstaple
Bridgwater
Langport July 10, 1645
Arundel
Stratton May 16, 1643
Exeter
Lostwithiel Aug. 13–Sept. 2, 1644
Braddock Down Jan. 19, 1643
English Channel
FRANCE

> *"Armed Soldier, terrible as Death, relentless as Doom; doing God's judgement on the Enemies of God. It is a phenomenon not of joyful nature; no, but of awful, to be looked at with pious terror and awe."*

THOMAS CARLYLE, ON OLIVER CROMWELL, 1845

Total war, in any event, seemed unlikely in early 1642. Many people remained neutral, and while most expected skirmishes of some sort, the belief was that they would bring the two sides to the negotiating table.

Charles waited until August to raise his banner at Nottingham to give many in his largely ragtag army time to bring in their harvest. Principal command of his forces was entrusted to Prince Rupert, the king's dashing 22-year-old nephew, head of a mounted troop that would become known as the Cavaliers, possibly from the French *chevalier* (knight or horseman).

Parliament's army was commanded by the Earl of Essex, the son of Elizabeth I's old favorite (see page 130). Like the Royalist forces, it had officers with experience of recent wars in Europe. In most other respects, however, it was as ramshackle as its foe. Parliament's forces became known as the Roundheads, after the close-cropped hair of the London apprentice boys who first flocked to its cause.

Charles marched south from Nottingham to engage the Parliamentarians at Edgehill (October 23, 1642), the war's first major battle. Prince Rupert won the day but then aimlessly pursued the Roundheads until all advantage was lost. Charles continued south toward London, where the Roundheads had retreated in good order. One standoff outside the city, at Brentford (November 11), went to the Royalists; a second, and more decisive, encounter at Turnham Green (November 13) went to the Roundheads. Charles's best chance of taking London, and with it total victory, was gone. The king retreated to Oxford, his base for the rest of the war, and never again threatened the capital.

Even at this early stage, patterns had emerged that would prove decisive in the conflict. Parliament's control of London and the wealthier parts of southeast England gave it access to a larger and more profitable revenue-raising base. Parliament also controlled the navy, which in turn gave it control of lucrative customs duties and prevented Charles from bringing money and supplies from abroad. Instead, the king had to seek donations from wealthy benefactors. These same men also helped raise his armies, and often insisted the troops be used to defend their own regions, thus compromising broader Royalist strategy.

In 1643, however, things were still going the king's way. The first factor to turn the tide was the arrival of the Scots on the parliamentarian side. They had been bribed with cash and the promise that in the event of a parliamentary victory, a strict, Scottish-style Presbyterian church would be established in England.

Final flourish This ornate pikeman's armor was finer than that worn by most soldiers during the English Civil War. The rapid improvement in firearm technology after the war soon rendered such armor almost redundant.

The New Model Army

The New Model Army was a professional fighting force that helped win the English Civil War for the parliamentary cause. Forged in the image of its founders, Oliver Cromwell and Thomas Fairfax *(left)*, its troops were disciplined—no swearing, gambling, drinking, or plunder were allowed. More to the point, they were well trained, well equipped—their light armor gave the troops the nickname "Ironsides"—and most important of all, regularly and properly paid from central funds. In 1644, they numbered 22,000 men, about a quarter of Parliament's forces.

Some 18,000 Scottish infantry and 3,000 cavalry duly helped win the day at Marston Moor (July 2, 1644), one of the most decisive battles of the war. Fought outside York, it deprived Charles of his northern power base. It also introduced the figure of Oliver Cromwell (see pages 176–177), an East Anglian politician turned cavalry commander.

In August of the same year, however, Charles defeated the Earl of Essex at Lostwithiel, in Cornwall. In October, another parliamentary army under the Earl of Manchester, with Cromwell in support, failed to impress at the Second Battle of Newbury, largely because of Manchester's incompetence. An increasingly influential Cromwell lambasted the failings of the army's "aristocratic" generals. Parliament listened, and sacked Essex and Manchester before agreeing to Cromwell's demands for the creation of a professional fighting force.

The resulting New Model Army (see opposite) was the second factor to turn the war Parliament's way. Once trained, the army powered to a series of victories. The most important was at Naseby (June 14, 1645), which secured central England. It was followed by the Battle of Langport (July 10), in which the Royalists lost their last major army. In May 1646, with his enemies closing in, Charles fled his Oxford base and surrendered to the Scots.

After months of wrangling, the Scots returned Charles to Parliament in January 1647, only for Charles to escape in November 1647. The king then precipitated a "second" civil war in 1648 by inciting revolts across his old power bases in north and west England. Cromwell quashed the revolts, along with a Scottish army sent south in the Royalist cause. After 1648, Cromwell and the army, which had been disposed to spare Charles, had had enough. The king's second war was his ultimate undoing. His enemies now wanted vengeance. ∎

Final walk Charles I on the way to his execution in 1649. The king's death was not inevitable, even in defeat, but his desperate actions toward the end of the English Civil War exhausted the patience of many on the opposing parliamentary side.

REGICIDE

A Trial of Strength and the Killing of a King

The trial of Charles I began on January 20, 1649, in front of a "high court of justice" at the Palace of Westminster. It was like no trial before or since, as it pitched a king who believed himself divinely ordained to rule—and thus subject to no earthly jurisdiction—against an army-backed parliament that asserted that "the people are, under God, the original of all just power" and acted on their own authority.

The charge against Charles was that he had "endeavored to subvert the ancient and fundamental laws and liberties of this nation, and in their place to introduce an arbitrary and tyrannical government." According to the indictment, he was a traitor, a murderer, and a "public and implacable enemy." But many worried that the trial and the court themselves subverted the "ancient and fundamental laws," for neither had a legal basis, and there was no precedent for trying a king for treason or any other "crime."

When the time came, Charles refused to defend himself or to enter a plea on the simple grounds that monarchs answered only to God and the "court" had no authority. "I would know by what power I am called hither," he told the court. "Remember I am your king, your lawful king . . . I have a trust committed to me by God, by old and lawful descent . . . I will not betray it to answer a new unlawful authority."

The trial lasted eight days, but its outcome was a foregone conclusion. At its climax, on January 27, Charles was condemned to death, the sentence to be carried out on January 30.

The morning of the execution was bitterly cold. The king called for two shirts, for fear that if he shivered the waiting crowds would take it as a sign of fear. His death had been timed for early in the day but was delayed while Parliament hurriedly repealed a law stating that a new monarch had to be declared immediately when another died. Thus, it was not until 2 p.m. that Charles stepped onto the platform raised against the wall of the Banqueting House in Whitehall.

Charles had taken Communion, had drunk a small glass of wine, and had distributed his most intimate possessions—including his Bible and his watch—among his children. He told his young daughter that he was "dying for the laws and liberties of this land."

Several executioners had refused the job of killing their king, another reason for the earlier delay. In the end, the one who agreed to the task (on the condition of strict anonymity) did his job well: Charles's head was removed at a single blow and held up to the waiting crowd, who greeted the scene not with the habitual cheer of a public execution but with a deep groan. It was as if, said many onlookers, the crowd realized the horror of what had been done. Chaos then ensued as hundreds fought to dip scraps of cloth in the king's blood.

The authorities hurried Charles's corpse from the scene. The head was roughly stitched back into place and the body embalmed before being buried not in Westminster Abbey—for fear it would become a focus for discontent—but in distant Windsor, in the vault of the tomb of Henry VIII in St. George's Chapel. ∎

Safety in numbers Charles I's death warrant had 59 signatories. Cromwell, whose name is third on the list, reputedly guided the pens of those reluctant to sign.

Death of a king Charles I's public execution took place outside the Banqueting House in Whitehall. The king walked confidently to the executioner's block and delivered his final words (see quote at right) with no trace of his lifelong stutter. Because the block was low, he was forced to lie rather than to kneel. He spread his arms wide, a prearranged signal that he had prayed and was ready for death. In a single flash of the executioner's blade he was gone.

"Death is not terrible to me; I bless my God I am prepared. I go from a corruptible to an incorruptible crown, where no disturbance can be, no disturbance in the world."

CHARLES I, AS HE AWAITED EXECUTION, JANUARY 30, 1649

OLIVER CROMWELL

Politician, General, and King in All but Name

It is one of the ironies of British and Irish history that of all the rulers who flitted across its pages, the most powerful was not a king, a queen, or a tribal chieftain, but a simple country squire, Oliver Cromwell (1599–1658). It was Cromwell, not any monarch, who was the first man to rule a unified state of Britain and Ireland, and to rule not at the whim of others, but with a dictatorial authority and ruthlessly applied military might.

Cromwell was born in Huntingdon, near Cambridge, to parents of the landed gentry. "I was by birth a gentleman," he would later say, "living neither in considerable height, nor yet in obscurity." In 1428, at age 29, he became a Member of Parliament for Huntingdon. During the English Civil War, he emerged as a brilliant general, with a career tally of 30 battles won, none lost. At the war's end, he was among those who insisted on Charles I's execution—a "cruel necessity," in his own words. In the ensuing constitutional chaos of the Commonwealth, he emerged first as a dominant figure and then, after 1653, as Lord Protector—a king in all but name.

Cromwell was humble, austere, and without vanity. Rank and position were of no consequence. Only merit received favor: "I would rather have a plain russet-coated captain who knows what he fights for and loves what he knows," he wrote, "than that which you call a gentleman and is nothing else." He was also a man who believed he was doing God's work—the "force of angry heaven's flame," in the words of poet Andrew Marvell.

Such conviction brooked no opposition, but to his enemies it looked like arrogance. It also looked like tyranny. When Cromwell dissolved Parliament at the point of a sword in 1653—"Go, get out, make haste, ye venal slaves, be gone"—it brought to mind Charles I's equally intemperate raid just 11 years earlier.

Cromwell was also brutal in repressing dissent, not least in Ireland (see pages 178–179) and among the many religious groups—Diggers, Quakers, Baptists, Anabaptists, Levellers, Ranters—whose radical views tried even his toleration. He also imposed military rule on Britain and Ireland. Government, he decreed, "should be for the people's good, not what pleases them." Thus, taverns, theaters, and brothels were closed; censorship was introduced; blasphemy was forbidden; and churches and ornaments were stripped and smashed. Children under 12 were flogged for swearing; fornicators were imprisoned; adulterers became subject to the death penalty; and dancing, wrestling, shooting, horse racing, and other types of entertainment were forbidden.

In the end, Parliament's hard-fought battle for freedoms produced not a brave new world, but a regime more oppressive than any monarchy. No wonder that Cromwell's legacy has divided opinion ever since. And no wonder that Britain was glad to see him go: When he died in 1658, diarist John Evelyn wrote, "it was the joyfullest funeral that I ever saw, for there was none that cried but dogs." ■

High office *(left)* Oliver Cromwell refuses to accept the crown, one of several occasions in which he declined the role of king, despite the requests of army officers and parliamentarians. After 1656, however, he was addressed as "Your Highness," and as Lord Protector he enjoyed powers and patronage as great as any monarch. Cromwell *(opposite)* was a reluctant subject, and he famously ordered artists to portray him as he was, "warts and all"—the origin of the phrase.

SCOTLAND AND IRELAND

Siege, Massacre, and the Legacy of Conquest

Ireland presented a special problem—and suffered a special and bloody solution—during the English Civil War. In 1641, partly in response to the rule of Thomas Wentworth, one of Charles I's most ruthless lieutenants, the country's Catholic majority rebelled against its largely Anglo-Protestant overlords. This in itself helped precipitate the Civil War in England, for none disputed that an army needed to be sent to quell the rebellion: The fear on Parliament's part was that if it paid for Charles to raise this army, he would use it against Parliament and its supporters.

Ireland was divided during the Civil War itself—which the Irish refer to as the Wars of the Three Kingdoms—but essentially came down in favor of the king. For a time Parliament left Ireland alone, as it was more preoccupied with the situation in England. In August 1649, however, a parliamentary army all but defeated the Irish at the Battle of Rathmines. After the battle came a campaign of consolidation, led by none other than Oliver Cromwell.

Like many English contemporaries, Cromwell shared a disdain bordering on contempt for Ireland's Catholics. When he spoke of them, it was to describe the "great work" he would do "against the barbarous and bloodthirsty Irish." He was as good as his word. During his nine months in the country, two events achieved particular infamy: In September 1649, at the Siege of Drogheda, some 3,500 Royalist soldiers, civilians, priests, and prisoners were killed; a month later, while capturing Wexford, Cromwell's troops massacred perhaps 2,000 Irish soldiers and as many as 1,500 civilians.

After Cromwell's campaigns, the 1652 Act for the Settlement of Ireland awarded Catholic lands to Protestant settlers, thus repeating a pattern established under Elizabeth I (see pages 130–131). The displaced Irish were forced to poorer land in Connacht, in western Ireland. Perhaps another 50,000 were transported to England's new Caribbean colonies. Historians dispute some of the facts, but few deny that Cromwell's time in Ireland, and his conquest, were the most repressive in the country's history. He has remained a hated figure to many ever since. ∎

Cromwell and Scotland

Scotland played a vital role in the English Civil War. The country's strict Presbyterian Protestants had a natural kinship with Parliament's Puritans. And it was Charles I's clumsy attempt to impose a religious settlement on the land of his forefathers that provided a catalyst for the conflict. Finally, some Scottish Royalists and Highland Catholics fought for the king.

After the conflict, the majority of Scots played off Parliament and king in an attempt to win a promise of a Presbyterian church in Scotland. By 1650, they had switched sides and showed allegiance to Charles's son by proclaiming him Charles II. As in Ireland, Cromwell could not allow such open revolt, and in 1650 he defeated the Scots at the Battle of Dunbar. Cromwell was more magnanimous in Scotland than in Ireland, and defeat was dressed up for Scottish benefit as consensual union—Scots were even invited into the English Parliament. But no one was fooled: The country was conquered, and the resentment this caused festered and erupted again after the union of the two countries in 1707.

Civilian casualties The Siege of Drogheda, Ireland, which was attacked first in 1641 and then in 1649, when Oliver Cromwell's troops massacred many of the town's inhabitants

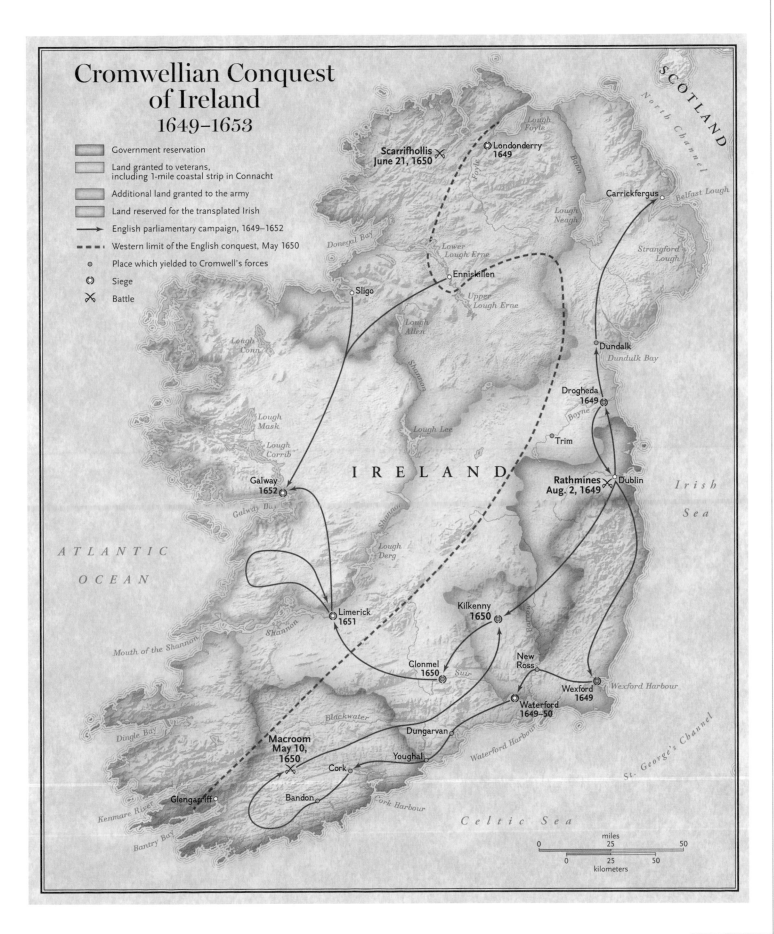

Cromwellian Conquest
of Ireland
1649–1653

Government reservation

Land granted to veterans,
including 1-mile coastal strip in Connacht

Additional land granted to the army

Land reserved for the transplanted Irish

→ English parliamentary campaign, 1649–1652

- - - Western limit of the English conquest, May 1650

○ Place which yielded to Cromwell's forces

◉ Siege

✕ Battle

SCOTLAND

Scarrifhollis
June 21, 1650

Londonderry
1649

Carrickfergus

Belfast Lough

North Channel

Lough Foyle

Lough Neagh

Strangford Lough

Foyle

Bann

Donegal Bay

Lower Lough Erne

Enniskillen

Upper Lough Erne

Sligo

Lough Conn

Lough Allen

Shannon

Dundalk

Dundalk Bay

Drogheda
1649

Boyne

Trim

Lough Mask

Lough Corrib

Lough Lee

Rathmines
Aug. 2, 1649

Dublin

Irish Sea

I R E L A N D

Galway
1652

Galway Bay

Shannon

Lough Derg

ATLANTIC
OCEAN

Limerick
1651

Kilkenny
1650

Nore

New
Ross

Wexford
1649

Wexford Harbour

Mouth of the Shannon

Shannon

Clonmel
1650

Sur

Waterford
1649–50

St. George's Channel

Macroom
May 10,
1650

Dungarvan

Blackwater

Youghal

Waterford Harbour

Dingle Bay

Cork

Cork Harbour

Glengarriff

Bandon

Celtic Sea

Kenmare River

Bantry Bay

miles
0   25   50

0   25   50
kilometers

RESTORATION

Rakes and Dandies, Kings and Mistresses

Whichever way you looked at it—unless you were a Puritan of the dourest kind—the 11 years of the Interregnum (1649–1660), the period between the execution of Charles I and the restoration of his son, Charles II, were a miserable time. Even Christmas was canceled. No wonder, then, that Charles II's return brought almost universal rejoicing.

The mechanics were easy enough. Cromwell had ruled through fear. When he died, his son and "heir," the ineffectual Richard, inspired more pity than terror. Richard's "reign" was done in eight months. As Parliament and the army bickered, it soon became clear that a return to monarchy was the only solution.

To say that Charles was welcomed home is an understatement. He landed from exile at Dover and made progress to London, where diarist John Evelyn recorded the scene. The king's retinue of 20,000 men, he wrote, took seven hours to pass through the city; they were "brandishing their swords and shouting with unexpressable joy: the ways strewn with flowers, the bells ringing, the streets hung with tapestry . . . the windows and balconies all set with ladies, trumpets, music . . ."

Installed and with the politics done, Charles settled down to enjoy himself. At heart, he may have harbored the same absolutist ideas as his father and grandfather, and he may also have had dangerous Catholic sympathies—Parliament suspected him of both—but while politics did not take a backseat to pleasure, there was no doubt which Charles preferred. Not for nothing was he known as the Merry Monarch. Affable and amoral, he accumulated 14 children from at least seven mistresses and earned the nickname "Old Rowley" after a prize stallion in the royal stud.

When not cavorting with mistresses, Charles was sailing (he bought Britain's first royal yacht), attending the races, or patronizing the arts and sciences (see pages 186–187). His relaxed style was mirrored in the world at large, both at court—home to rakes and dandies galore—and in a sense of cultural liberation that found expression in the bawdy Restoration comedies of William Congreve; the music of Henry Purcell; the satire of John Dryden; and the free-thinking genius of Sir Isaac Newton, Sir Christopher Wren, and many others. ■

"*Here lies a great and mighty King, / Whose promise none rely'd on, / He never said a foolish thing / Nor ever did a wise one.*"

JOHN WILMOT, EARL OF ROCHESTER (1647–1680),
MOCK EPITHET FOR CHARLES II

Fit for a king Armor made for the future Charles II around 1638. Charles fought in the English Civil War until 1642 and spent 14 years in exile in France and the Netherlands between 1646 and 1660. He also intrigued with the Scots and, in 1651, came to England in a failed attempt to claim his throne.

Nell Gwynn "Pretty, witty Nell" was the most popular of Charles II's many mistresses, most of whom were foreign and disliked. She might be a whore, she admitted, but at least she was "an English whore."

Crowning glory The coronation procession of Charles II to Westminster Abbey from the Tower of London, April 23, 1661. After the dour and repressive years without a king from 1649 to 1660, the splendor of Charles's coronation set the tone for the color and gaiety of the Restoration period.

THE GREAT FIRE

From a Single Spark to a City in Flames

I n the early hours of Sunday, September 2, 1666, Thomas Farynor woke to the smell of burning. Farynor was a London baker, who among other things made biscuits to feed sailors in the king's navy. His small bakery occupied premises in Pudding Lane, close to London Bridge and the River Thames. The burning he smelled was from downstairs, from a fire in his shop sparked by embers from his bread oven. The blaze was already so intense that he was beaten back to his bedchamber. After rousing his family, he clambered across the rooftops with his wife and children to an adjoining building. His maidservant, too frightened to move, became the first victim of what became known as the Great Fire of London.

No sooner had Farynor escaped than barrels of tar in his cellar exploded. Next door stood a tavern, the Star Inn, whose stables were filled with straw for its coach horses. Within minutes, both the stables and the tavern had become an inferno. An hour later, the city's rudimentary fire service arrived. In attendance was the city's Lord Mayor, Sir Thomas Bloodworth, who took one look at the blaze and declared it was so feeble "a woman might piss it out."

He was wrong. The summer of 1666 had been long and hot. Several fires had already broken out. The wooden frames and straw thatch roofs of the buildings were tinder dry. The city's streets were narrow, the buildings tightly packed. The Thames was low, and a hot, dry wind was blowing from the east. London was ripe for conflagration.

The fire spread to the wooden wharves along the Thames. It then moved to the river's warehouses, many of which were packed with timber, coal, pitch, tallow, brandy, and other materials almost designed for combustion. By lunchtime on Sunday the fire was out of control.

Mayor Bloodworth's earlier sangfroid evaporated. Now panicked, he belatedly attempted to create firebreaks by destroying buildings in the blaze's path. The city's wealthier property owners, however, refused to sacrifice their homes and businesses. Only direct orders from the king, Charles II, forced them to relent. Charles himself took to the streets to help fight the blaze, along with his brother James.

On Tuesday, the day of greatest destruction, the great old St. Paul's was consumed. Its immense lead roof, in the words of diarist John Evelyn, melted "down the streets in a stream." In the four days the fire took to burn out, 87 churches, 13,200 homes, and 44 merchant guildhalls, among other buildings, were destroyed. About 85 percent of the city's Roman and medieval heart was obliterated, and up to 100,000 Londoners were made homeless. Casualty figures are disputed, with only six deaths registered, but the demise of many poor inhabitants, and those incinerated by the blaze, almost certainly went unrecorded. ■

The Great Plague

I f the Great Fire of 1666 had a benefit, it was that it helped eradicate the Great Plague that had struck London the previous year. The fleas and rats that largely had spread the disease were consumed, and the rebuilding that followed the fire removed many of the fetid streets that had helped the epidemic proliferate. Between 1603, when 33,347 bills of mortality were issued for plague deaths, and 1665, only a handful of years in London were free of recorded deaths from the disease. The 1665 outbreak, however, was exceptional. The number of deaths is disputed, but it may have been as high 100,000—20 percent of the city's population.

Inferno The artist responsible for this depiction of the Great Fire is unknown, but the level of detail suggests the painter was an eyewitness to the event. The fire rages from the Tower of London *(right)* to London Bridge *(left)*, with Old St. Paul's Cathedral *(center)* already ablaze.

"We saw the fire as only one entire arch of fire from this to the other side the bridge, and in a bow up the hill for an arch of above a mile long: it made me weep to see it. The churches, houses, and all on fire and flaming at once; and a horrid noise the flames made, and the cracking of houses at their ruin."

SAMUEL PEPYS, DIARY ENTRY, SEPTEMBER 2, 1666

WREN'S LONDON

The Masterpiece and the City That Never Was

Within days of the Great Fire of London, Charles II had been presented with three plans to rebuild the city's ancient heart. One came from philosopher and architect Robert Hooke (1635–1703), another from writer and courtier John Evelyn (1620–1706), and a third from a scientist who had dabbled in architecture, Christopher Wren (1632–1723).

London at the time was among Europe's largest cities, containing perhaps 350,000 to 500,000 people, or a tenth of Britain's population. It was probably 17 times larger than the nation's next-largest city, Bristol. Yet until the Great Fire its appearance and infrastructure remained that of a medieval town. It retained much of its ancient Roman wall, and its houses were closely packed and mostly made of wood. Sanitation of almost any sort was absent. The narrow streets ran with filth, and the busiest thoroughfare, the Oxford Road—present-day Oxford Street—was still lined with hedges. The Thames flowed thick with sewage.

The plans presented to Charles offered the prospect of transformation. The ideas of Wren and Hooke in particular promised a city of broad boulevards modeled on those being prepared in Paris, designs that Wren had admired on a visit to the city a year before the fire. Large, linked piazzas would be created on a geometric plan, replacing the old city's tangled warren of paths, alleys, and dead ends. The north bank of the Thames would become a vast open quay, bringing valuable dock space to the heart of the capital. Sites were earmarked for landmark buildings such as the Mint, the Post Office, and the Customs House.

None of it came to pass. City landlords either refused to give up their freeholds or demanded their properties be rebuilt quickly in their original locations. Even had it wanted, Parliament lacked the funds to buy out the freeholds or to finance so vast a project. As a result, Wren was commissioned simply to rebuild St. Paul's Cathedral and to replace some of the churches lost to the fire. In the end, he or his office was responsible for 51 new churches (of which only 12 survive fully intact).

But if London lost the chance of modernity, it at least gained a masterpiece. Another great architect of the age, Inigo Jones (1573–1652), had begun restoration work on Old St. Paul's (work interrupted by the English Civil War), and Wren's plan to place a dome on the old church had been accepted just six days before the fire. Work on the new St. Paul's, built to a classical Renaissance plan—the third proposal Wren had submitted—began in 1675. It was completed in 1708 and eventually was joined by other Wren masterpieces across the city, notably Greenwich's Royal Observatory and the Royal Hospital Chelsea. ■

Mythical city This artist's impression illustrates how London might have looked had Sir Christopher Wren's plans for the capital been adopted after the Great Fire of London. St. Paul's Cathedral *(top left)* and some of Wren's proposed churches were built, but a lack of money and the resistance of property owners dashed Wren's hopes for a city of wide piazzas, broad boulevards, and spacious riverside quays.

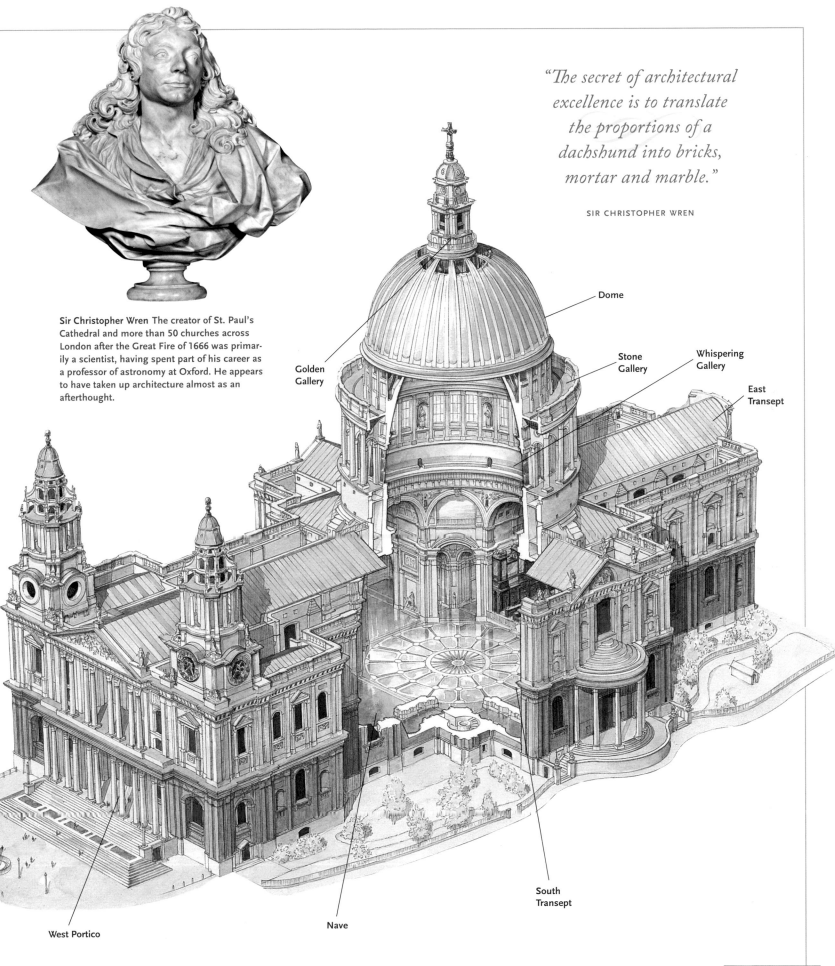

Sir Christopher Wren The creator of St. Paul's Cathedral and more than 50 churches across London after the Great Fire of 1666 was primarily a scientist, having spent part of his career as a professor of astronomy at Oxford. He appears to have taken up architecture almost as an afterthought.

"The secret of architectural excellence is to translate the proportions of a dachshund into bricks, mortar and marble."

SIR CHRISTOPHER WREN

Dome

Stone Gallery

Whispering Gallery

East Transept

Golden Gallery

South Transept

Nave

West Portico

SCIENCE AND LEARNING

Ideas and Discovery in the Age of Rationalism

In the Stuart age, science and learning blossomed, building on changes in thinking begun in the previous century and on the work of like-minded men across Europe. The new ideas of the European Renaissance led the way, undermining a medieval worldview infused with magic and superstition, and in which religion was the absolute source of knowledge and learning. In their wake came rationalism, in part pioneered by Sir Francis Bacon of Britain (1561–1626), who helped champion an empirical approach to scientific research—that is, an approach that involved reaching conclusions based on rational method, observation, and experiment rather than by deduction through assumption or blind faith.

This approach was shared by Galileo Galilei of Italy (1564–1642), who studied astronomy and the science of falling bodies; Johannes Kepler of Germany (1571–1630), who formulated laws of planetary motion; and two great French mathematicians and scientists, René Descartes (1596–1650) and Blaise Pascal (1623–1662).

In Britain and Ireland, the introduction of logarithms by John Napier (1550–1617) made astronomical calculation easier; William Gascoigne (1612–1644) invented the micrometer, revolutionizing the science of measurement; William Harvey (1578–1657) discovered that blood circulates around the body; Edmond Halley (1656–1742) produced pioneering work in astronomy (and comets in particular); and Robert Boyle (1627–1691) explored the relationship between the volume and pressure of gases, as well as formulating a particular theory of matter that anticipated atomic theory.

Britain's greatest mind of the age, however, was Sir Isaac Newton (1643–1727), whose laws of motion and gravitation, published in *Philosophiæ Naturalis Principia Mathematica* (1687), were among the most fundamental in the history of science. Newton was multitalented—he even became Master of the Mint, supervising the replacement of hammered coins with milled-edge ones—but with typical modesty wrote that if he had seen farther than other men, it was simply because he "stood on the shoulders" of the "giants" who had gone before him.

Newton and others relished the feverish atmosphere of the day. London, with its coffeehouses, gentlemen's clubs, and burgeoning press, was a hotbed of ideas and intellectual exchange. The sense of liberation that followed Charles II's restoration also encouraged new thinking: Charles himself backed the foundation of the Royal Society, founded in 1660 to improve "Natural Knowledge." The society, which numbered Newton and Boyle among its illustrious members, survives to this day. In 1675 Charles also founded the Royal Observatory in Greenwich, built to improve navigation at sea but eventually the focus of much wider research. ∎

Voice of reason An etching from 1640 showing Sir Francis Bacon (1561–1626) writing at his desk. Bacon was a philosopher, a statesman, and an essayist, but he is best remembered as a champion of an empirical, or rational, approach to science. His ideas were influential throughout the Stuart age. He died of pneumonia, contracted while conducting experiments on the effects of freezing on meat.

John Locke: On Life and Liberty

Improvements to knowledge in the Stuart age were not confined to science. Great thinkers also came to the fore, notably Englishman John Locke (1632–1704) *(left)*, a philosopher and political thinker who is often described as the founding father of democracy and classical liberal thought. It was Locke's words, contained in *An Essay Concerning Human Understanding* (1689), that inspired Thomas Jefferson's stirring cry for "Life, Liberty and the pursuit of Happiness" in the Declaration of Independence of the United States almost a century later.

Work of genius *(above)* Sir Isaac Newton (1643–1727), pictured here in a 20th-century lithograph by Jean-Leon Huens, with the prism used to prove his discovery that white light is made up of a spectrum of colors

Farsighted After experimenting with light, Sir Isaac Newton invented this reflecting telescope, a revolutionary device that used mirrors instead of a conventional lens.

"I seem to have been only like a boy playing on the seashore, and diverting myself in now and then finding a smoother pebble or a prettier shell than ordinary, whilst the great ocean of truth lay all undiscovered before me."

ATTRIBUTED TO SIR ISAAC NEWTON

THE GLORIOUS REVOLUTION

Britain Invaded for the Protestant Good

Fathering children was not Charles II's problem: He sired at least 14 illegitimate offspring. But because his wife, Catherine, was unable to bear children, fathering a legitimate heir proved impossible. Thus, when Charles died in 1685, his brother, James II (1633–1701), inherited the throne. But James was Catholic. Worse, in the eyes of many, he was avowedly Catholic, and he began indulging Catholics and promoting them at court, in the judiciary, and among the universities. A return to Catholicism, which much of Britain had resisted since Tudor times, seemed imminent.

The situation was constitutionally tolerable—though barely—while James's second wife, Mary of Modena (a Catholic princess), remained childless. With no heir, this meant that James's earlier, Protestant daughter, Mary, would eventually inherit the throne. When Mary of Modena produced a son, however, the situation changed: Calamity, perhaps even civil war, threatened.

The solution lay in the shape of Protestant Mary's husband, William of Orange (1650–1702). William was the ruler of the Dutch Republic. More to the point, he was a Protestant. After frantic behind-the-scenes diplomacy, a bishop and six other grandees (afterward known as the Immortal Seven) drafted a letter effectively inviting William to invade Britain.

William duly arrived, with a force three times larger than the Spanish Armada of exactly a century earlier. James's armies and support melted away, at least in England, and William was crowned as a joint monarch with Mary. James was encouraged to flee, his flight taken as an indication that he had "abdicated."

The events were momentous. For the first time, Britain had monarchs who had partly bypassed the concept of hereditary right not through usurpation, but at the prompting of Parliament. It was the birth of a constitutional monarchy, a system of government that survives in Britain to this day. Parliament enshrined the changes, and its ultimate authority, in the English Bill of Rights of 1689.

Naturally this was not the end of the matter. James II found support in Catholic Ireland, but a Protestant army led by William crushed James's rebellion at the Battle of the Boyne in 1690. "King Billy's" victory is still cherished by some of Northern Ireland's Protestants and the province's Orangemen. Others among Billy's supporters found their way to the American colonies. According to one theory, those who drifted into the Appalachians eventually attained a nickname of their own: hillbillies.

James also found support in Scotland, especially in the Catholic Highlands, where the Jacobite Rebellions—from the Latin *Jacobus,* or James, in favor of his son, James Stuart, and grandson, Bonnie Prince Charlie—would foster dissent for more than half a century (see pages 208–209). ■

Bound for glory William III, Prince of Orange, and his invasion force prepare to leave Holland for England. The Protestant William was formally invited to invade England in 1688 to depose the Catholic king, James II. William, who hoped to secure English support against France, was married to James's Protestant daughter, Mary, his first cousin, with whom he ruled jointly until her death in 1694.

White knight William III at the Battle of the Boyne (1690), in Ireland, where he defeated Catholic forces fighting for the former James II. James had been forced from the British throne two years earlier. The victory helped secure the joint reign of William and his wife, Mary. James and his Catholic heirs continued their attempts to reclaim the throne for more than 50 years in both Britain and Ireland.

Face-to-face A silver medal commemorating the joint coronation of William III and Mary II in 1689 as king and queen of England, Scotland, and Ireland. It is inscribed "A Noble Pair Greater Than Their Sceptres."

"It hath been found by experience that it is inconsistent with the safety and welfare of this Protestant kingdom to be governed by a popish prince."

FROM THE ENGLISH BILL OF RIGHTS, 1689

THE GEORGIAN ERA
1714–1815

"*Happy Britannia! . . . Thy country teems with wealth . . . Full are*
thy cities with the sons of Art; and trade and joy, in every busy street . . ."

JAMES THOMSON, *THE SEASONS*, 1730

Britain's Empire

- **●** English territory, 1707
- **○** Territory added to the British Empire, 1707–1815
- Portuguese territory, 1815
- Spanish territory, 1815
- French territory, 1815
- Dutch territory, 1815

PACIFIC OCEAN

AUSTRALIA

New South Wales

Van Diemen's Land

Timor

Spice Islands

Philippines

Benkulen

Dutch East Indies

Penang

NORTH AMERICA

Rupert's Land

Canada

Spanish-American Empire

British Honduras

Mosquito Coast

Grand Cayman

Bahamas

North American Colonies

Jamaica

Haiti

Bermuda

St. Kitts

Nevis

Antigua

Montserrat

Grenada

St. Lucia

Trinidad & Tobago

Barbados

St. Vincent

Guiana

Surinam

SOUTH AMERICA

Brazil

ATLANTIC OCEAN

ASIA

Hooghly

Calcutta

Bengal

Vishakhapatnam

Machilipatnam

Madras

Trincomali

Ceylon (Sri Lanka)

Surat

Karwar

Colombo

Bombay

Tellicherry

Scotland

Ireland

ENGLAND

NETHERLANDS

EUROPE

FRANCE

PORTUGAL

SPAIN

Naples

Gibraltar

Malta

INDIAN OCEAN

Gorée

AFRICA

Seychelles

Mauritius

Mozambique

Sierra Leone

Quelimane

Accra

Cape Coast Castle

Cape of Good Hope

St. Helena

REVOLT AND THE RISE OF EMPIRE

THE ACCESSION OF GEORGE I (1660–1727) IN 1714 MARKED THE BEGINNING OF THE GEORGIAN era, a century-plus-long succession of four monarchs that coincided with Britain's rise to become the greatest maritime, industrial, and colonial power on Earth. It also marked the start of the Hanoverian dynasty, a line of kings and queens with origins in what is now Germany. The dynasty survives to the present day, though the family name changed to Windsor in 1917. George acceded not by direct hereditary right but by an act of Parliament, the Protestant Stuart line having died out with Queen Anne. The line of Catholic heirs, however, remained long, with some 50 Stuart descendants reputedly boasting a better claim to the throne than George's.

George's claim originated with Elizabeth Stuart, a daughter of James I. In 1613 Elizabeth married Frederick V of the Rhine. Among their 13 children was Sophia, who in 1658 married the Ernst Augustus, Elector of Hanover. Sophia's Stuart and Protestant credentials saw her nominated as the successor to Britain's childless royal heir, Anne, in 1701. With Sophia's death in 1714, her son, George, was next in line.

For the most part, George's succession passed quietly, at least in England and Wales. In previous centuries, rival royal claimants had fought wars. By 1714, however, political expediency took precedence over hereditary right. Henceforth Britain's monarchs would reign rather than rule, with power passing more definitively to Parliament and politicians.

Rival royal claimants still created problems, however, such as uprisings in favor of James II's Catholic heirs. These struggles were known as the Jacobite Rebellions (from the Latin Jacobus, or

James; see pages 206–207). Initially, they centered on James's son, James Stuart, known as the Old Pretender. Then they shifted to James Stuart's son, Charles Edward Stuart, the Young Pretender, better known as Bonnie Prince Charlie (see pages 208–209).

While the Hanoverian succession was secured with relative ease, George I remained a personally unpopular king. Bad tempered and charmless, he spoke virtually no English and had little time for Britain or the British. Nor did the British have much time for him, as they resented his obvious preference for Hanover and his expectation that Britain would pay for its wars.

In 1720, Britons had even greater cause to dislike George, due to his possibly corrupt involvement in the collapse of the South Sea Company. Founded in 1711, the company was intended to trade in South America, in part to help reduce Britain's national debt. When George I became its governor, frantic speculation saw its stock soar. When the bubble burst

Wealth of nations *(previous pages)* The elegant sweep of Lansdown Crescent in the city of Bath, England. Built between 1789 and 1793, the street is typical of the neoclassic style found in many towns and cities transformed by the wealth of the Georgian era. The crescent, a protected historic monument, survives to this day. An oil-on-canvas portrait of King George II *(page 195)*, the second monarch of the Hanoverian dynasty and king of Great Britain between 1727 and 1760.

TIME LINE

1714
George I takes the throne

1727
George I dies; his son George II
succeeds him

1746
Battle of Culloden

1756-1763
Seven Years' War

1759
British general James Wolfe
defeats French at Quebec

1760
George III succeeds grandfather George II

1763
Treaty of Paris: Indian, Canadian,
and West Indian land granted to English

1772
Richard Arkwright creates first textile
factory in Derbyshire

1775–1783
American Revolutionary War

1781
British general Cornwallis
surrenders at Yorktown.

1783
Treaty of Paris: Britain formally recognizes
American independence

1786
British establish colony on Malay Peninsula

1793
French king Louis XVI is executed;
France declares war on Britain

1801
The Act of Union comes into effect,
creating the United Kingdom
of Great Britain and Ireland

1805
Battle of Trafalgar

1807
Parliament passes Abolition of
the Slave Trade Act

1812–1815
War of 1812

1815
Battle of Waterloo

in September 1720, the crash ruined many, including leading figures in royal and political circles.

The aftermath threatened political and economic disaster. A rambunctious landowner turned politician, Sir Robert Walpole (1676–1745), managed the fallout. George I's poor English and frequent absences in Hanover had already seen the rise in power of a cabinet of leading parliamentarians. Higher ranked politicians who chaired the cabinet's meeting became known as first and (later) prime ministers. After 1721, these first ministers included Walpole, who as a perk of his position accepted a small town house in a new development at 10 Downing Street, close to Westminster.

■ THE PATH OF PROSPERITY

George I died in 1727 after a reign of just 12 years and 10 months. Buried in Germany and little lamented, he was succeeded by his son, George II (1683–1760), who, while marginally more popular, was irritable and indolent, and he still spoke English with a pronounced German accent. His first passion was military uniforms, his second a string of mistresses, though the popularity of his long-suffering queen, Caroline of Brandenburg-Ansbach, was vital in helping endear the British to the Hanoverian dynasty.

Walpole's carefully cultivated relationship with Caroline meant that he enjoyed the new king's favor, for while Parliament's power was now paramount, monarchs still appointed cabinets and ministers (an anomaly that continued to create problems as the century progressed). Walpole's policy to avoid costly foreign wars helped produce two decades of relative peace. He also promoted trade and expansion overseas, including the creation of Georgia, named after George II, which was added to Britain's dominions in North America in 1732.

The new American possession became part of Britain's expanding colonial jigsaw. India represented another, increasingly important component (see pages 220–221), while the pioneering voyages of James Cook (1728–1779) and others laid the foundations of territorial expansion in Australasia.

Empire and commerce—including a burgeoning trade in slaves (see pages 210–213)—transformed Georgian society. Money poured into the country and financed new commercial ventures and an increasingly leisured middle class. It also paid for fine country houses and elegant new quarters in towns and cities, as well as providing an environment in which art, culture, and intellectual life flourished (see pages 228–231).

■ SCOTLAND AND IRELAND

Walpole's peace crumbled in 1739, when a halfhearted war against Spain precipitated his resignation in 1742. He had served for 20 years and 314 days (1721–1742), still the longest term of any British political administration. The Spanish war broke out partly over

"Sir Robert Walpole, the son of a middling Norfolk squire, was a mountain of a man, with a gigantic appetite: for food and drink, sex, money, power and work. He was shrewd and affable (when it suited him) and knew the price of everything and everyone."

DAVID STARKEY, *CROWN & COUNTRY*, 2010

HOUSE OF HANOVER
1714-1815

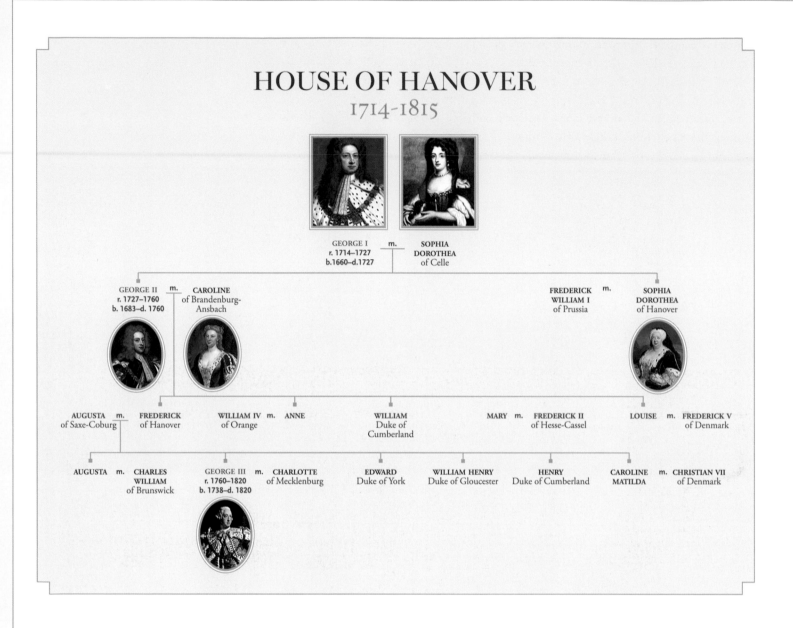

GEORGE I
r. 1714–1727
b.1660–d.1727
m.
SOPHIA DOROTHEA
of Celle

GEORGE II
r. 1727–1760
b. 1683–d. 1760
m.
CAROLINE
of Brandenburg-Ansbach

FREDERICK WILLIAM I
of Prussia
m.
SOPHIA DOROTHEA
of Hanover

AUGUSTA m. **FREDERICK**
of Saxe-Coburg of Hanover

WILLIAM IV m. **ANNE**
of Orange

WILLIAM
Duke of Cumberland

MARY m. **FREDERICK II**
of Hesse-Cassel

LOUISE m. **FREDERICK V**
of Denmark

AUGUSTA m. **CHARLES WILLIAM**
of Brunswick

GEORGE III m. **CHARLOTTE**
r. 1760–1820 of Mecklenburg
b. 1738–d. 1820

EDWARD
Duke of York

WILLIAM HENRY
Duke of Gloucester

HENRY
Duke of Cumberland

CAROLINE MATILDA m. **CHRISTIAN VII**
of Denmark

trade and piracy, and partly at the urging of a brilliant young parliamentarian, William Pitt (1708–1778), who would take Walpole's place as the country's leading politician.

The year 1745 saw the reappearance of the Jacobites, when Bonnie Prince Charlie landed in Scotland in the hope of fomenting a wider rebellion (see pages 206–207). His army marched deep into England before being defeated at the Battle of Culloden in April 1746. The rebellion produced a popular song, of vague origins, set to an old Tudor or French tune. It implored God to "save our gracious King" and "send him victorious, happy and glorious." The words were first sung in London theaters as Charles threatened the capital, and they survive to this day in the national anthem of the United Kingdom.

With Stuart hopes crushed, and despite the fact that many of its inhabitants had nurtured Jacobite sympathies, Scotland began to prosper. Edinburgh, in particular, became the focus of the Scottish Enlightenment, part of a wider European revolution in rational and secular thought (see pages 228–229). Literary, artistic, and architectural life also flourished, and Scottish expertise contributed greatly to the advances that informed the era's burgeoning agricultural and industrial revolutions (see pages 214–215).

Ireland, too, had its writers and thinkers, not the least Jonathan Swift and Edmund Burke (see pages 230–231), though both had to travel to England to find renown. In Ireland, they left a country dominated by an Anglican (Protestant) Anglo-Irish elite, and one in which the Catholic majority remained largely powerless and impoverished.

Ireland remained sullen and mostly subdued until the 1790s, when rebellion flared. Among the rebels were independence-minded Protestants who felt disenfranchised by the tight ruling clique of Anglo-Irish aristocrats. Partly to address their concerns, the Act

of Union came into effect in 1801, creating the United Kingdom of Great Britain and Ireland. The act contained other reforms, which, although partial, initially won over many Irish Catholics with the promise of Catholic emancipation. When George III revoked the promise, however, centuries-old problems returned as powerful, and as suppressed, as before.

Tea party Drinking tea was one of many genteel pursuits that became popular in the Georgian era among an increasingly leisured and affluent middle class.

■ FROM DISASTER TO MILITARY TRIUMPH

On the wider stage, Britain's imperial ambitions in 1756 brought it yet again into conflict with its oldest enemy, France. Unlike the past, where the country's differences had usually been settled on European soil, the colonial reach of both countries now meant battles were fought on a wider stage. At stake were possessions on four continents, and, by implication, the overseas trade on which national prosperity now rested.

Britain retained an army, but in the 18th century its main hope for foreign domination rested with the navy. Innovation and seamanship had defined the country's maritime endeavors since Tudor times. Enlightened leadership and technological advances now sharpened Britain's naval edge. Ships, and their guns in particular, were improved, along with vital refinements such as the chronometers of John Harrison after 1735. These painstakingly designed devices allowed mariners to calculate longitude by comparing the position of the sun against precisely known local and other times. It is no coincidence that one of Britain's most stirring patriotic songs, "Rule, Britannia!," with its assertion that Britannia ruled the waves, dates from 1740.

Not that the assertion carried much weight in 1756, when Britain suffered a humiliating naval defeat against France near Minorca, in the Mediterranean. The defeat marked the start in Europe of the Seven Years' War (see pages 222–223), a widespread Anglo-French conflict that most historians date from 1756 to 1763.

Rich and poor A London street scene from the 1770s. Like other British cities, the capital grew rapidly during the Georgian era, bringing great wealth but also increased levels of urban poverty as agricultural and industrial changes transformed patterns of settlement and employment.

The war continued to go badly as Britain suffered setbacks around the globe. Under the dynamic leadership of William Pitt, however, the tide gradually turned. A naval blockade proved decisive in the key area of North America, where the French held swathes of territory that threatened the American colonies. Here, British ships starved them of supplies and helped General James Wolfe (1727–1759) win a daring victory at Quebec in 1759. Similar triumphs were shared by Robert Clive (1725–1774) in India and by the Royal Navy in the West Indies and off the African coast.

In 1756, Britain had been one of several European powers of similar stature. However, the terms it secured after the war at the Treaty of Paris in 1763, when France was forced to the negotiating table, saw it stand alone as acknowledged master of India, Canada, much of the West Indies, and a wide swathe of North America.

■ THE LOSS OF THE 13 COLONIES

Conflict was expensive, however. Robert Walpole and his colleagues had spent the early part of the 18th century grappling with the financial fallout from the wars against France. His successors now battled to pay for a war that had been fought on four continents.

First, though, Britain greeted a new king, George III (1738–1820), who succeeded his grandfather, George II, in 1760. The new George was the first Hanoverian born in Britain, and the first to speak English without a German accent. Like his Georgian predecessors, however, he still required a German wife. Charlotte of Mecklenburg arrived in London on September 8, 1761, and married George, sight unseen, the same day. Remarkably, the blind match lasted 57 years and produced 15 children.

George saw himself as a patriot who was born to serve. "I glory in the name of Briton," he announced at his coronation. He was devout and diligent, often stubborn and superior, but also a more cultured and sympathetic character than George I and George II.

George III was also more constitutionally assertive, but not necessarily shrewder, than his predecessors. He was unfortunate in having to contend with one of his eventual prime ministers, Lord North, who held office in a critical period starting in 1770. North was agreeable as a man but ineffectual as a politician. He had been, said George, "very much my last choice."

Both George and North were involved the events that led to the Revolutionary War (see pages 224–227), known in Britain as the American War of Independence (1775–1783). The conflict was sparked by the imposition of taxes and duties designed to make the American colonies contribute to their defense, a task hitherto largely underwritten by British taxpayers. The Americans, for their part, complained they were being taxed without political representation. Britain, stung by the vehemence of the colonists' complaints and by boycotts of imported goods, repealed most of the new taxes.

The about-face proved too little too late, and exacerbated by heavy-handedness on the part of the British, events spiraled into all-out war after 1775. The conflict ebbed and flowed, the colonists inspired to victories by commanders such as George Washington, a former British army officer. The British also won battles, only to be undermined by long supply lines to the troops and the guerrilla tactics of their opponents.

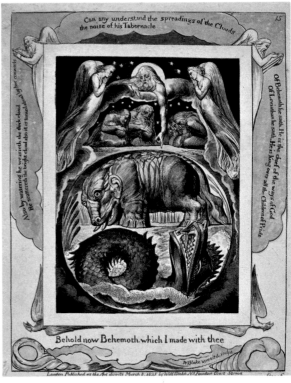

Man of vision "Behemoth and Leviathan" (1793), from the Book of Job, an engraving by poet and artist William Blake. Culture blossomed as society became wealthier and more sophisticated during the Georgian era.

Final freedom *(below)* A medal struck to commemorate the passing of the Slavery Abolition Act (1833), which outlawed slavery across the British Empire

Rebel victory *(bottom)* British general John Burgoyne surrenders at Saratoga in 1777, a turning point of the American Revolutionary War.

The breakthrough came in 1781, when the intervention of the French on the American side proved decisive. A French force at Chesapeake Bay saw off the Royal Navy, stretched by commitments elsewhere. Britain's army at Yorktown, Virginia, deprived of relief, was left no option but surrender. Britain recognized American independence with the Treaty of Paris in 1783.

■ **REVOLUTION AND VICTORY**

Although Britain would go to war with the United States again in 1812—a futile conflict over trade and borders—the loss of the American colonies was of little lasting economic consequence. The reason was the increasing wealth from Britain's remaining colonies, the vigor of mercantile endeavor, and the profound changes and rising prosperity that flowed from the beginning of Britain's Industrial Revolution (see pages 214–215).

In the political sphere, William Pitt's son, William Pitt the Younger (1759–1806), became prime minister in 1783 at just 24 years old (still a record) and proved as capable as his father. In 1787, the Society for the Abolition of the Slave Trade was founded in London as part of a long campaign that achieved partial success in 1806, when Parliament passed an act prohibiting British subjects from the trade in slaves.

George III continued as king but increasingly succumbed to bouts of mental illness (probably caused by porphyria, a hereditary complaint). His first major collapse occurred in 1788, a year before the French Revolution and the start of 25 years of conflict. Many in Britain initially supported the revolution in France, but attitudes changed after the execution of the French king, Louis XVI, in 1793. French armies quickly sought to spread the revolution abroad, and within two weeks of the king's execution France declared war on Britain.

In 1797, a young French officer, Napoleon Bonaparte (1769–1821), was dispatched to attack British interests in Egypt. He was thwarted at the Battle of the Nile (1798), a triumph for an up-and-coming British seaman, Horatio Nelson, but went on to victories in Italy, Russia, and Austria. By 1804, he was emperor of France.

A year later, Napoleon threatened to invade Britain but once again fell foul of Nelson, whose decisive naval victory at the Battle of Trafalgar is one of the most celebrated in British history (see pages 232–233). Napoleon suffered further setbacks in Russia in 1812, but regrouped for a second assault on Europe in 1814 to 1815. This time, he was decisively—if narrowly—defeated by an alliance of the British, Dutch, and Prussians at the Battle of Waterloo (see pages 234–235).

The demise of Napoleon, and the eclipse of France, set the stage for a century in which Britain would stand virtually unchallenged on the world stage. ∎

Old and new In an age when iron was superseding wood, and steam power was replacing the forces of wind and water, this painting of a new bridge on the River Wear, from 1796, when Britain's industrial revolution was well under way, represents a meeting of a new world and one that was about to disappear.

"The history of the present King of Great Britain [George III] is a history of repeated injuries and usurpations, all having in direct object the establishment of an absolute Tyranny over these States."

UNITED STATES DECLARATION OF INDEPENDENCE, 1776

BRITAIN AND EMPIRE

Old Foes, Distant Lands, New Colonies

Britain came late to colonialism. Under Elizabeth I, the nation had largely looked on as Spain and Portugal overran the New World. Under the Stuarts, Britain grew bolder as parts of North America, the Caribbean, and outposts in India and Asia fell to British rule. But in the 18th century it came of age, and by 1814 Britain boasted an empire on four continents: North and South America, Asia, and Africa.

One reason was technological change. Britain had always had remarkable seafarers. The likes of Frobisher and Drake had pushed to the ends of the earth (see pages 136–139), but they had done so armed with little more than bravery and blind faith. Now sailors had better ships and a better grasp of navigation.

Another factor was political stability. Trade was the bedrock of any nation, especially an island nation like Britain. But a nation distracted by the traumas of the Reformation, or the bloodletting of a civil war, could hardly focus on the requirements of its entrepreneurs. It was no coincidence that once Britain settled its internal affairs, its gaze began to turn to the wider world.

A third reason for Britain's new colonial reach was money. Not that Britain was producing more of it—not yet, anyway—but its elite was learning new ways to make it work. First, there was the Bank of England (founded 1694), whose banknotes were soon in widespread circulation. Then came joint-stock companies, which shared risk—but also reward—among investors. As a result, money became more fluid and capital easier to obtain.

When it came to putting capital to work, the vast profits already flowing in from the American and Caribbean colonies meant investors did not have far to look. Profits were reinvested either in new ventures or in the houses and high living that characterized wealthier Georgian society (see pages 216–219).

Colonial gifts "The East Offering Its Riches to Britannia." This allegorical painting, the work of Roma Spiridione, was commissioned by the East India Company for its London headquarters in 1778. The company, a private mercantile enterprise, was founded in 1600. After being displaced by the Dutch in the Far East, it moved its focus to India, where by the end of the 18th century it controlled much of the south and north of the country.

It might almost have been called a virtuous circle, but for the fact that much of the wealth that flowed from these colonial ventures flowed in turn from Britain's substantial trade in slaves (see pages 210–213). Much of this wealth might also have been feared lost when Britain suffered its most serious overseas setback, the loss of the American colonies in 1783 (see pages 224–227).

In fact, trade with the new United States actually increased, but the events in North America underlined the realities of colonialism: Other countries also wanted colonies, new possessions had to be defended, and conflicts that once had been confined to Europe were now played out on a world stage.

An old foe, France, became Britain's chief rival. The two powers had clashed over Canada in the previous century, and the French had become U.S. allies in the Revolutionary War. Again they jockeyed for power in Canada in the Seven Years' War (see pages 222–223) and in countless naval engagements in the Caribbean and the Mediterranean.

Away from the Americas, other earlier British colonial trends continued. By 1800, most of India and 30 million of its people were effectively ruled by Britain's East India Company (see page 164). Colonial footholds were established on the Malay Peninsula, at Penang, in 1786, and British traders became active in the intra-Asian trade of the region—the tea, opium, cotton, and other goods that moved among India, China, and the East Indies.

In the Pacific, James Cook (1728–1779) made far-reaching voyages that, among other things, included the first recorded European landing in Hawaii—or the Sandwich Islands, as Cook preferred it. More to the colonial point, he also made the discovery that led to the 1787 founding of New South Wales, Britain's first territory in Australia. ■

New worlds A watercolor depicting Grace Bay in Antigua, one of several Caribbean islands colonized by the British in the 17th century. Here and elsewhere, the indigenous Carib population was quickly subdued and slaves brought in huge numbers from West Africa to work on white-owned sugar plantations.

"For better or worse—fair and foul—the world we know today is in large measure a product of Britain's age of empire. The question is not whether British imperialism was without blemish. It was not. The question is whether there could have been a less bloody path to modernity."

NIALL FERGUSON, *EMPIRE*, 2003

Imperial game The figures in these Indian ivory chess pieces from about 1795 represent officers of Britain's East India Company and one of its Indian rivals, Tipu Sultan.

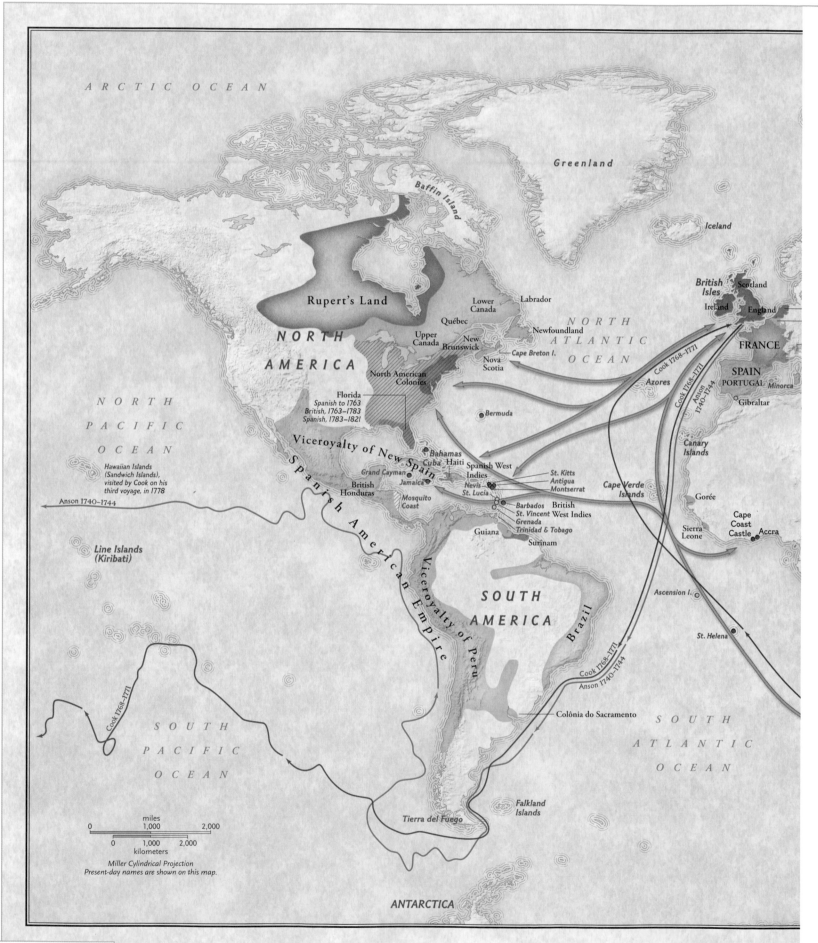

ARCTIC OCEAN

Greenland

Baffin Island

Iceland

Rupert's Land

British Isles
Scotland

Lower Canada
Labrador

NORTH ATLANTIC OCEAN

Ireland
England

Québec

NORTH AMERICA

Upper Canada
New Brunswick

Newfoundland

FRANCE

SPAIN
PORTUGAL
Minorca

Cape Breton I.

Nova Scotia

Cook 1768–1771

North American Colonies

Azores

Cook 1768–1771
Anson 1740–1744

Gibraltar

NORTH PACIFIC OCEAN

Florida
Spanish to 1763
British, 1763–1783
Spanish, 1783–1821

Bermuda

Canary Islands

Hawaiian Islands (Sandwich Islands), visited by Cook on his third voyage, in 1778

Viceroyalty of New Spain

Bahamas
Cuba
Haiti
Spanish West Indies

St. Kitts
Antigua
Montserrat

Cape Verde Islands

Anson 1740–1744

Grand Cayman

British Honduras

Jamaica

Mosquito Coast

Nevis
St. Lucia

Gorée

Line Islands (Kiribati)

Spanish American Empire

Barbados
St. Vincent
Grenada

British West Indies

Sierra Leone

Cape Coast Castle
Accra

Guiana
Trinidad & Tobago

Surinam

Viceroyalty of Peru

SOUTH AMERICA

Brazil

Ascension I.

Cook 1768–1771

St. Helena

SOUTH PACIFIC OCEAN

Colônia do Sacramento

SOUTH ATLANTIC OCEAN

Cook 1768–1771
Anson 1740–1744

miles
0   1,000   2,000

0   1,000   2,000
kilometers

Falkland Islands

Tierra del Fuego

Miller Cylindrical Projection
Present-day names are shown on this map.

ANTARCTICA

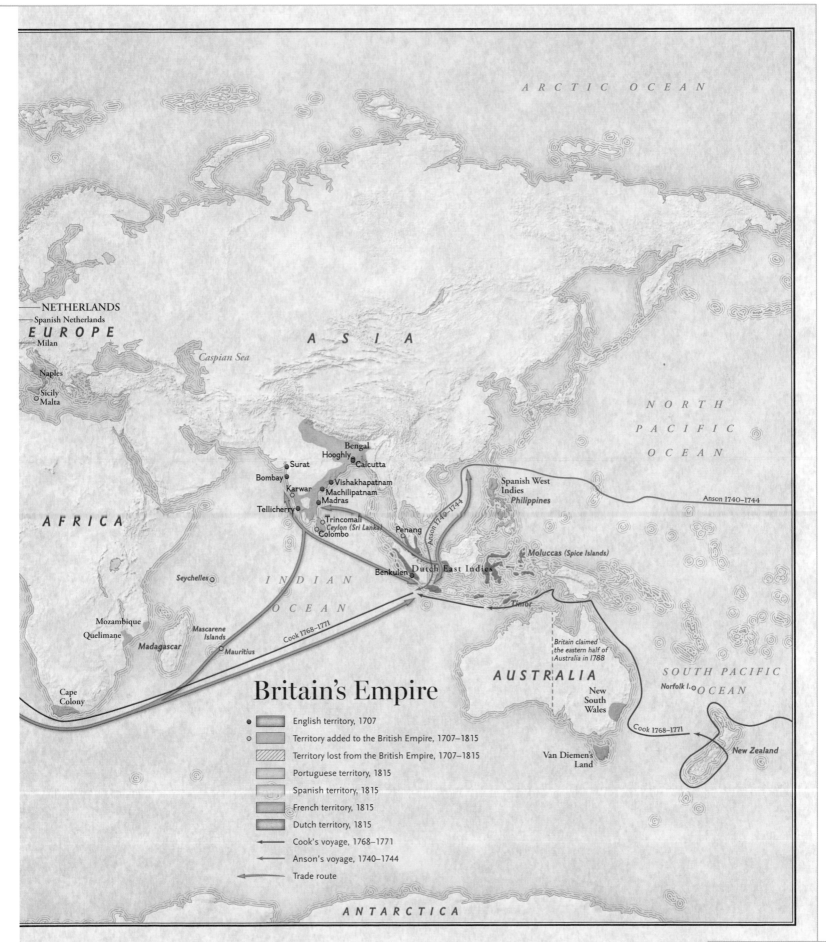

ARCTIC OCEAN

EUROPE

ASIA

Caspian Sea

NETHERLANDS
Spanish Netherlands
Milan

Naples

Sicily
Malta

NORTH

PACIFIC

OCEAN

AFRICA

Bengal
Hooghly
Surat
Bombay
Karwar
Vishakhapatnam
Machilipatnam
Tellicherry
Madras
Calcutta

Spanish West
Indies
Philippines

Anson 1740–1744

Trincomali
Ceylon (Sri Lanka)
Colombo
Penang

INDIAN

OCEAN

Seychelles

Benkulen
Dutch East Indies

Moluccas (Spice Islands)

Mozambique
Quelimane

Mascarene
Islands

Cook 1768–1771

Timor

Britain claimed
the eastern half of
Australia in 1788

SOUTH PACIFIC

OCEAN

Madagascar

Mauritius

AUSTRALIA

New
South
Wales

Norfolk I.

Cook 1768–1771

Cape
Colony

Britain's Empire

- English territory, 1707
- Territory added to the British Empire, 1707–1815
- Territory lost from the British Empire, 1707–1815
- Portuguese territory, 1815
- Spanish territory, 1815
- French territory, 1815
- Dutch territory, 1815
- Cook's voyage, 1768–1771
- Anson's voyage, 1740–1744
- Trade route

Van Diemen's
Land

New Zealand

ANTARCTICA

THE JACOBITE REBELLIONS

A Doomed Struggle for a Long-Lost Throne

The Stuart kings had a long history, first in Scotland and then in England, Wales, and Ireland. They had survived much: the execution of a matriarch, Mary, Queen of Scots; a regicide in the shape of Charles I; and an eventful return to power in the person of Charles II. So if Parliament thought it was done with James II, Charles II's Stuart heir, when he was deposed in the Glorious Revolution of 1688 (see pages 188–189), it was wrong: Rebellions to return James and his successors to the throne continued through the reigns of five monarchs until 1746.

The Stuarts had many supporters. Some—those known as Jacobites, from the Latin *Jacobus*, or James—were usually genuine; others, notably the French, were fair-weather allies anxious to inconvenience the English.

Jacobite backing came from several sources. James was Catholic, a religious allegiance that seduced many in Catholic Ireland. Scotland, too, had its Catholics, as did England, where Jacobite recruits also included those unhappy with their "foreign" kings, William of Orange and George I. Many Scots disenchanted with the Act of Union (1707), which yoked England and Scotland, also rallied to the cause.

Time and again these disparate allies fomented rebellion, and time and again they were put down. Parts of Scotland were changed in the process, not the least by networks of new British forts such as Fort William, and by the military roads of General George Wade (1673–1748), many of which survive to this day.

But while the rebellions were disruptive, they threatened little. Many ended in fiasco; others simply fizzled out. James II's son and successor, the would-be James III (1688–1766), didn't help. Gloomy and lackluster, he was a figure of whom even his supporters despaired. He was a prince "who dwelt in a maze of unrealities," said one, "who expected every moment to set sail for England or Scotland, but who did not know very well for which."

But for France, then often fighting on several fronts in Europe, the rebellions might have withered completely. In supporting the Jacobites, the French aim was to distract Britain. Sadly for the Stuarts, there was a catch when it came to France: The Jacobites could realistically rebel only with French backing, but the French invariably required evidence of powerful Jacobite support before showing their hand. Only once, in 1715, did the two events more or less coincide, when James raised an army of around 16,000 and secured the backing of Pope Clement XI, Philip V of Spain, and Louis XIV of France.

As ever, indecision and incompetence ruined the day. Worse, the further repression the 1715 rebellion brought to Scotland more or less killed Jacobite aspirations. The truth was that by now many in Britain were becoming reconciled to the Hanoverians, Protestantism, and even the Union. One glimmer of Jacobite hope remained: James's son, the charismatic Charles Stuart, better known as Bonnie Prince Charlie (see pages 208–209). ■

Royal pretender This engraving shows James Stuart (1688–1766) landing at Peterhead in northeast Scotland in 1715. James was the son of James II, whose Catholic sympathies saw him deposed as Britain's king in 1688. James's rebellion of 1715–1716 was one of several attempts to reclaim the throne, but by the time of the event depicted here, James's armies had suffered several defeats across England and Scotland. The rebellion soon petered out, but James's son, Bonnie Prince Charlie, took up the Stuart cause again in 1745.

Scottish turncoat Simon Fraser, 11th Lord Lovat, was a Highland clan chief who supported the Hanoverian kings and Stuart Jacobite cause in turn. He was arrested for treason and in 1747 became the last man to be beheaded publicly in Britain.

Bloody battle An archival map shows the site of the Battle of Culloden (April 16, 1746), the final confrontation of the Jacobite risings.

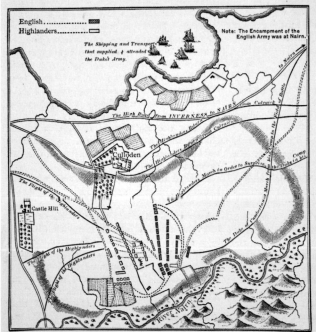

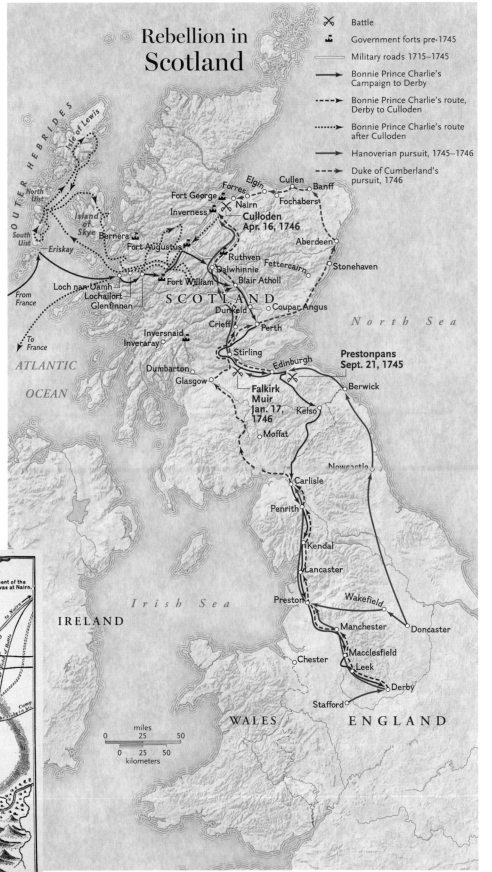

Rebellion in Scotland

✂ Battle

⛫ Government forts pre-1745

— Military roads 1715–1745

→ Bonnie Prince Charlie's Campaign to Derby

⇢ Bonnie Prince Charlie's route, Derby to Culloden

⋯⋯➤ Bonnie Prince Charlie's route after Culloden

→ Hanoverian pursuit, 1745–1746

⇢ Duke of Cumberland's pursuit, 1746

OUTER HEBRIDES

Isle of Lewis

North Uist

Island of Skye

South Uist

Bernera

Eriskay

From France

To France

ATLANTIC OCEAN

Loch nan Uamh
Lochailort
Glenfinnan

Fort William

Fort Augustus

Fort George
Inverness

Forres Elgin Cullen Banff
Fochabers
Nairn

Culloden Apr. 16, 1746

Ruthven Fettercairn
Dalwhinnie
Blair Atholl

Aberdeen

Stonehaven

SCOTLAND

Dunkeld Coupar Angus

Inversnaid
Inveraray

Crieff Perth

Stirling

Dumbarton
Glasgow

Edinburgh

Prestonpans Sept. 21, 1745

Berwick

Falkirk Muir Jan. 17, 1746

Kelso

Moffat

North Sea

Newcastle

Carlisle

Penrith

Irish Sea

Kendal

Lancaster

Preston Wakefield

IRELAND

Manchester Doncaster

Chester Macclesfield
Leek

Derby

Stafford

WALES ENGLAND

miles
0   25   50

kilometers
0   25   50

BONNIE PRINCE CHARLIE

Romance, Revolt, and the Death of a Dynasty

The Bonnie Prince, or Charles Edward Stuart (1720–1788), to give him his proper name, was the son of the Old Pretender, the would-be James III (1688–1766). Charles was brought up in exile in Rome, alongside his father, whose hopes of a return to the British throne had been dashed during the earlier Jacobite Rebellions (see pages 206–207).

By the 1740s, Britain's Hanoverian kings were well established and few paid much heed to the Stuarts or their long-lapsed claims to the throne. But royal bloodlines proved hard to extinguish, especially when France still saw Scotland and the Stuarts as a back door to England—and even more so in 1745, when a French victory over the British in Belgium rendered England more than unusually vulnerable.

For the Bonnie Prince, just 24 and fired by the enthusiasm of youth, it was a timely moment to take up the old Stuart cause. On July 25, 1745, with a handful of men, he landed in the Hebrides, off the west coast of Scotland.

Scotland was an obvious choice for rebellion. Some there still resented the Act of Union (1707), which had linked England and Scotland; many in the Highlands, the country's mountainous heart, were Catholic, as were the Stuarts; and many Scots retained an ancestral sympathy to a dynasty with deep Scottish roots.

To these advantages Charles added charm and charisma, and by the time he reached Edinburgh he had an army of several thousand men. Scotland's capital rose to meet him, its women in particular seduced by his brown eyes and fine features. It was here he was first acclaimed by his nickname, Bonnie, a Scottish word for "beautiful" or "attractive."

With Britain's main armies busy in France, Charles easily defeated an inexperienced Hanoverian force sent to meet him. He then marched into England, where he triumphed in a succession of northern cities. By December he was marching on Derby, just 125 miles from London.

The poorly defended capital panicked. December 4—Black Friday—saw a run on the banks as people rushed to withdraw funds. Even George II was ready to flee: He packed his bags and had gold transferred to the royal yacht.

And then, as in the past, it all went wrong. First, a hoped-for uprising in England failed to materialize. Then rival Irish and Scottish officers in Charles's army began to argue over strategy. Finally, and fatally, Charles's poorly equipped troops (who were paid only in food) began to hanker for home.

After reluctantly turning north, Charles was pursued by the Duke of Cumberland, newly arrived with a British army from France. The two forces eventually met at Culloden, in northeast Scotland, on April 16, 1746. In the ensuing battle—the last on British soil—Charles's ineptitude (standing his men in marshy, open ground before ordering them into Cumberland's guns) contributed to a bloody and comprehensive defeat.

Cumberland went on to earn himself the epithet "Butcher" for the ruthlessness with which he dealt with the remnants of the Stuart army and the subsequent brutality he visited on the Highland clans.

Charles fled with a bounty on his head. None betrayed him. Evading capture for almost six months, he was eventually helped to escape, disguised as a maid, by the young Flora Macdonald. The event entered Scottish folklore and has been celebrated ever since, unlike Charles's subsequent career, which saw his return to Rome and a slide into penury and alcoholism. ■

The Bonnie Prince Charles Stuart was the grandson of James II. He was young, dashing, and handsome—*bonnie* is a Scottish word meaning "attractive"—but when he attempted to claim the British throne after landing in Scotland in 1745, his charm and charisma could not make up for his military shortcomings and the lack of English support for his claims.

Fit for a king A ceremonial targe—a traditional battle shield from the Highlands of Scotland, made from wood, pigskin, and silver. Supporters presented it to Bonnie Prince Charlie in 1740.

Bonnie Prince Charlie

Culloden
Apr. 16, 1746
SCOTLAND

Falkirk
Jan. 17, 1746
Prestonpans
Sept. 21, 1745

IRELAND

North Sea

Baltic Sea

Derby
ENGLAND

English Channel

Dunkirk
Gravelines
Bouillon
Paris
Fontainebleau

Nantes

FRANCE

Lyon

Genoa
Savona
Avignon
Massa
Antibes
Lucca

Ohlau

After his failed invasion of England and exile from France, Charles spent the rest of his life moving around Europe, at times using aliases to hide his identity.

Innsbruck

Trento
Verona
Bologna
Florence

Lived in exile, 1774

ITALY

Rome
Gaeta
Naples

Observed a siege, 1734

In the early 1740s, Charles attempted to raise an army in France, to invade England and reclaim the throne.

ATLANTIC OCEAN

Born, Dec. 31, 1720
Died, Jan. 31, 1788

Mediterranean Sea

Battle

miles
0   200   400
0   200   400
kilometers

"Mourn, hapless Caledonia, mourn . . . Thy sons, for valour long renown'd, Lie slaughter'd on their native ground . . . Thy towering spirit now is broke, Thy neck is bended to the yoke."

TOBIAS SMOLLETT, "THE TEARS OF SCOTLAND," 1746

Wishful thinking (right) A garter insignia belonging to the Bonnie Prince. It is inscribed *Honi soit qui mal y pense,* the motto of the Order of the Garter, the highest chivalric honor a British monarch can bestow.

Family fortunes (below) A letter written in French, from Florence, by Bonnie Prince Charlie. It is addressed to his brother and heir, Henry, a cardinal, and asks him to recognize the rights of Charles's daughter, Charlotte. By the time it was written, in 1784, the prince had lost all hope of reclaiming the British throne.

SLAVERY AND ABOLITION

A Belated Triumph of Principle Over Profit

B ritain was not the first country to take part in the Atlantic slave trade; Portugal and then Spain had sold slaves from West Africa during the 15th century. But once Britain embarked on the trade, it did so on a vast scale, becoming the largest single carrier of slaves from Africa to the colonies of the Caribbean and the Americas.

Figures connected with slavery are difficult to assess, partly because of the many slaves who died before or during their voyages into servitude, and partly because it was in the interests of traders to falsify or neglect documentation to avoid paying duties on their "cargo." But in the 1760s, it is likely that of some 80,000 slaves being transported annually, British ships were carrying at least 40,000 of them, probably more. Research suggests that of all slaves traded across the Atlantic between 1519 and 1867—a figure put at 12 million or more—around 3.1 million (only 2.7 million of whom survived) were traded to British territories, and even more were traded by British companies on behalf of other countries.

Britain's earliest involvement in the trade began with Sir John Hawkins, an Elizabethan seafarer, who in 1562 captured a Portuguese ship off the coast of Sierra Leone and traded its

Sold into slavery *(top)* Slaves being bought from African traders prior to transportation across the Atlantic. Slaves were often bartered for cheap, British-made goods. The painting is by French artist François-Auguste Biard (1798–1882).

Scale of suffering *(above)* A model of the slave ship *Brookes*, which antislavery campaigner William Wilberforce used in Parliament to help illustrate the conditions of those transported from West Africa to Britain's colonies.

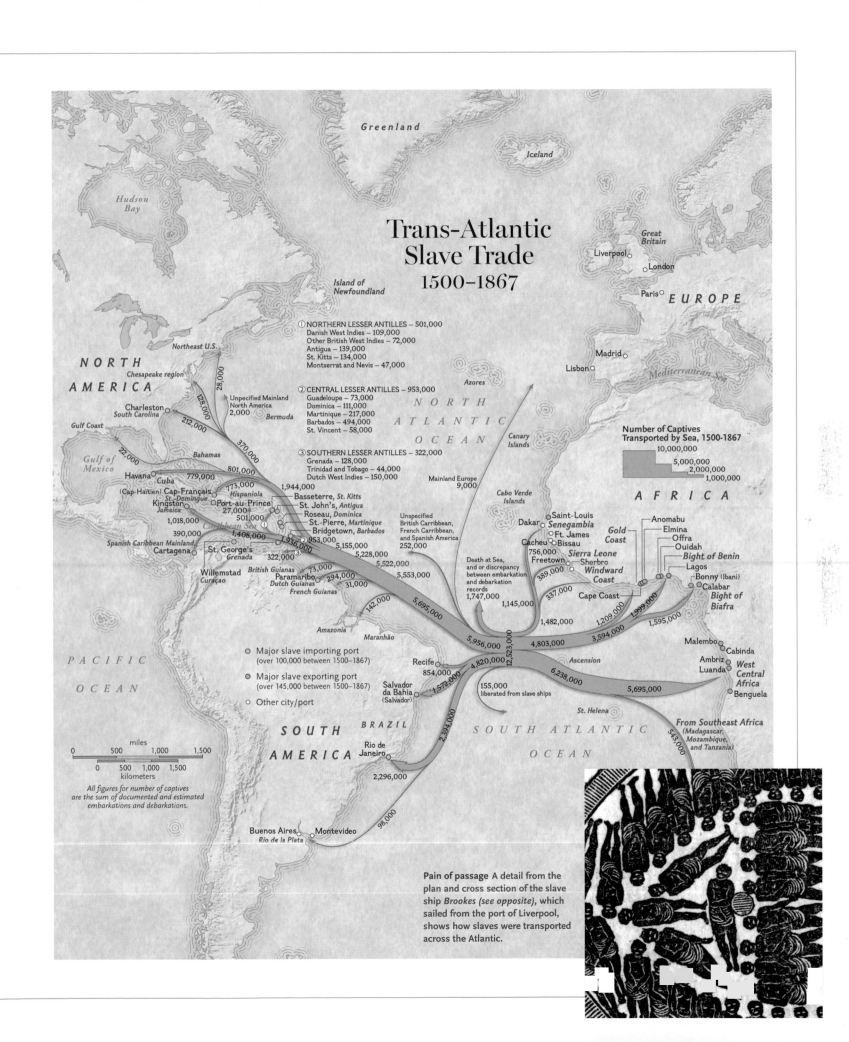

Trans-Atlantic Slave Trade
1500–1867

① NORTHERN LESSER ANTILLES – 501,000
Danish West Indies – 109,000
Other British West Indies – 72,000
Antigua – 139,000
St. Kitts – 134,000
Montserrat and Nevis – 47,000

② CENTRAL LESSER ANTILLES – 953,000
Guadeloupe – 73,000
Dominica – 111,000
Martinique – 217,000
Barbados – 494,000
St. Vincent – 58,000

③ SOUTHERN LESSER ANTILLES – 322,000
Grenada – 128,000
Trinidad and Tobago – 44,000
Dutch West Indies – 150,000

**Number of Captives
Transported by Sea, 1500-1867**
10,000,000
5,000,000
2,000,000
1,000,000

Greenland

Iceland

Hudson
Bay

*Island of
Newfoundland*

Great
Britain

Liverpool○
○London

Paris○   EUROPE

Madrid○

Lisbon○   *Mediterranean Sea*

Northeast U.S.

NORTH
AMERICA

Chesapeake region

Charleston○
South Carolina

Gulf Coast

*Gulf of
Mexico*

Bermuda

Unspecified Mainland
North America
2,000

Azores

NORTH
ATLANTIC
OCEAN

Canary
Islands

*Cabo Verde
Islands*

AFRICA

Mainland Europe
9,000

28,000
128,000
212,000
22,000
370,000

Havana○ *Cuba*
(Cap-Haïtien) Cap-Français○
St.-Domingue
Kingston○
Jamaica
Port-au-Prince○

801,000
779,000
173,000
1,944,000
27,000
501,000
1,018,000

Bahamas

Hispaniola

Basseterre, *St. Kitts*
St. John's, *Antigua*
Roseau, *Dominica*
St.-Pierre, *Martinique*
Bridgetown, *Barbados*

①

390,000
1,408,000
1,936,000
② 953,000
③ 322,000

Caribbean Sea

Spanish Caribbean Mainland
Cartagena○

St. George's○
Grenada

Willemstad○
Curaçao

British Guianas
Paramaribo○
Dutch Guianas

73,000
294,000
31,000

French Guianas

5,155,000
5,228,000
5,522,000
5,553,000

Unspecified
British Carribbean,
French Carribbean,
and Spanish America
252,000

Saint-Louis○
Dakar○ *Senegambia*
Cacheu○ ○Ft. James
○Bissau
756,000
Freetown○ *Sierra Leone*
○Sherbro
*Windward
Coast*
389,000
337,000
Cape Coast

Anomabu○
○Elmina
*Gold
Coast*
○Offra
○Ouidah
○*Bight of Benin*
Lagos○

Bonny○ (Ibani)
○Calabar
*Bight of
Biafra*

Death at Sea,
and or discrepancy
between embarkation
and debarkation
records
1,747,000

1,145,000
1,482,000
1,209,000
1,999,000
1,595,000
3,594,000
4,803,000

142,000
5,695,000
5,956,000
12,523,000

Malembo○ ○Cabinda
Ambriz○ *West
Luanda○   Central
Africa*
○Benguela

PACIFIC
OCEAN

Amazonia

Maranhão

○ **Major slave importing port**
(over 100,000 between 1500–1867)

◉ **Major slave exporting port**
(over 145,000 between 1500–1867)

○ **Other city/port**

Recife○
854,000

Salvador
da Bahia○
(Salvador)

4,820,000
1,572,000

155,000
liberated from slave ships

Ascension

6,238,000
5,695,000

SOUTH
AMERICA

BRAZIL

Rio de
Janeiro○

2,296,000

2,394,000

St. Helena

SOUTH ATLANTIC
OCEAN

From Southeast Africa
*(Madagascar,
Mozambique,
and Tanzania)*
543,000

miles
0   500   1,000   1,500
0   500 1,000 1,500
kilometers

*All figures for number of captives
are the sum of documented and estimated
embarkations and debarkations.*

Buenos Aires○ ○Montevideo
Río de la Plata

98,000

Pain of passage A detail from the
plan and cross section of the slave
ship *Brookes (see opposite)*, which
sailed from the port of Liverpool,
shows how slaves were transported
across the Atlantic.

301 slaves in Santo Domingo, in the present-day Dominican Republic. The first recorded African slave landed in Jamestown, Virginia, in 1619, though at that time Britain was still more concerned with trading ivory, gold, indigo, and other African produce than with buying and selling slaves.

All that changed in the 1640s after the Dutch introduced sugar into the Caribbean. Sugar made enormous profits, but its production was labor-intensive. Indigenous workers were few, and they quickly succumbed to European diseases. Convict labor brought to the colonies also proved inadequate. The answer was slaves, willingly traded by African tribal leaders and all but unquestionably accepted by the European powers with colonies in the Americas.

As Britain's Caribbean and American colonies proliferated, and as cotton and tobacco were added to the crops requiring labor, so Britain's participation in the business of slaves increased. Merchants quickly pioneered a triangular trade, whose seductive symmetry saw profits at every stage. Basic, cheap goods were shipped to Africa, where African traders exchanged them for slaves. The slaves were then packed into the same ships for transport across the Atlantic. Then the slaves were sold and the empty ships laden again, this time with sugar, rum, tobacco, rice, cotton, and other goods for sale on the ships' return to Britain.

The profits were considerable, but how considerable is a matter of debate. Many Britons grew rich directly, others indirectly: England's second city, Birmingham, for example, boasted 4,000 gunmakers, who by the 1780s were producing 100,000 guns annually simply for barter in African slave markets. In its earliest days, Manchester's textile industry sent around half its finished cloth to the same African markets and the other half to the West Indies. Elsewhere, banks and other financial institutions benefited, as did ports such as Bristol and Liverpool, while London boomed on the back of the vast quantities of colonial goods processed or reexported to Europe and beyond.

Some of the cultural glories and many of the new domestic comforts of the Georgian age had manifest links to the profits generated by the slave trade. But most historians have moved on from the idea that the wealth generated by the trade directly underpinned the Industrial Revolution and Britain's inexorable rise to power in the 19th century. At a best guess, economists suggest that of every £20 circulating in Britain in the late 18th century, perhaps £1 was derived directly from the slave trade. Indirect derivation was another matter. Whatever the profit, however, and whatever its effect, attitudes about slavery changed during the Georgian

William Wilberforce Member of Parliament Wilberforce (1759–1833) was a leading light in the long campaign for the abolition of slavery, which was achieved in the year of his death.

Made to pay *(opposite)* Slaves working on a British-owned Caribbean sugar plantation in a watercolor from 1823. Slaves helped realize immense profits from what otherwise would have been a prohibitively costly and labor-intensive enterprise.

Olaudah Equiano

Little is known of Olaudah Equiano's early life. He was probably kidnapped as a child in present-day Nigeria around 1745. He was transported and sold as a slave in Virginia. Years later, he bought his freedom and settled in London, where he married an Englishwoman, Susanna Cullen, with whom he had two daughters. In 1789, he wrote his autobiography, one of the first books published by an African writer *(left)*. The work became a best seller, brought Equiano fame, and served as a powerful instrument for the abolitionist cause.

era. Britain might have been shamed by its involvement with the trade, but it was also extraordinarily vocal in the campaign for its abolition. Quakers were among the first to object to the trade on moral grounds. Later they were joined by other Nonconformist and Evangelical Christians, including politician William Wilberforce (1759–1833), who spent 27 years spearheading the parliamentary campaign for abolition.

Wilberforce was also a guiding light of the Society for the Abolition of the Slave Trade, founded in 1787. Among the earliest mass-protest movements, the society was remarkable for its time. Its members were tireless in organizing petitions and boycotts of sugar and in slowly but inexorably changing public opinion.

The society did not act alone. Innumerable individual contributions and legal landmarks stood out on the road to eventual abolition (see sidebar, opposite), along with changing social and economic attitudes on a wider stage promulgated by the French Revolution, the Enlightenment, and the rise of free-market thinking.

After years of work and setbacks, Parliament finally passed the Abolition of the Slave Trade Act on February 23, 1807, by a vote of 283 to just 16. Although this act was by no means the end of slavery—which would not be outlawed across the empire until 1833—Britain actively pressured other countries to give up the trade and employed the Royal Navy to hunt down the slavers and liberate their slaves. ∎

Personal property *(below)* An iron used to brand slaves to denote ownership. Abolitionists displayed objects such as irons and shackles as they toured Britain in an attempt to mobilize public opinion against slavery.

THE INDUSTRIAL REVOLUTION

Field to Factory, Water to Steam

Britain's Industrial Revolution saw the most dramatic social and economic changes in the nation's history. Its course and causes were long and interwoven, but by 1850, its effect had been to transform a predominantly rural country into the "workshop of the world."

First came advances in agriculture, freeing rural laborers to work in factories and producing the food required to feed them. Many changes were continuations of existing trends—notably enclosure, or the consolidation of land into more efficient units. A better understanding of soil management and crop rotation increased yields. Selective breeding created better livestock. Devices such as Jethro Tull's mechanical seed drill (1701) epitomized the many improvements in technology.

One effect of such changes was the reduction of rural employment. Some former laborers went to the cities; others developed small cottage industries in their homes. The latter invariably involved spinning and weaving, and here, too, the advent of new technology was transformative. Among many innovations were James Hargreaves's spinning jenny (1764) and Richard Arkwright's spinning frame (1769), a machine that revolutionized cotton production.

Arkwright's invention was one of several that took textile manufacture out of the home and into the factory. Arkwright himself opened the first such factory, at Cromford, Derbyshire, in 1772. A five-story mill, it employed 200 unskilled men, women, and children to operate rows of spinning frames, carding machines, and mechanized looms.

Steam was Britain's next innovation. Cromford was revolutionary, but like all similar ventures of the time it was water driven. Thomas Savery had patented a steam pump in 1698, and Thomas Newcomen produced a working steam engine in 1712, but it was improvements to Newcomen's engine made by James Watt and Matthew Boulton between 1763 and 1775 that proved commercially decisive.

Steam transformed not only factories but also the mining industry, as more powerful engines could drain deeper mines. As coal production soared, improved communications were required to move it around the country, along with increasing quantities of other goods and raw materials. As a result, canals proliferated after 1741, peaking in the 1790s.

Roads also improved. Most at the time were the responsibility of local parishes and had languished untouched for centuries. Now main routes were transformed by turnpike trusts. A stagecoach journey between London and Manchester, a distance of around 200 miles that had taken 80 hours in 1750, took just 30 hours in 1820.

Perhaps Britain's greatest industrial innovation, however, had taken place even before the advent of steam, roads, and canals. In 1709, Abraham Darby had devised a way to smelt iron in a manner that used coke, made from coal, rather than the limited and centuries-old method of burning charcoal. The site of his first blast furnace, Coalbrookdale in Shropshire, is known today as the cradle of the Industrial Revolution. ∎

The die is cast The bridge spanning the River Severn near Coalbrookdale, in western England, was the world's first to be fabricated from cast iron. Erected in 1779, it was the work of Abraham Darby III, the grandson of Abraham Darby, who in 1709, in the same area, was the first to perfect the process of creating iron using coke, rather than charcoal, in a blast furnace. The process revolutionized iron production and saw Coalbrookdale dubbed the cradle of the industrial revolution. The bridge survives to this day.

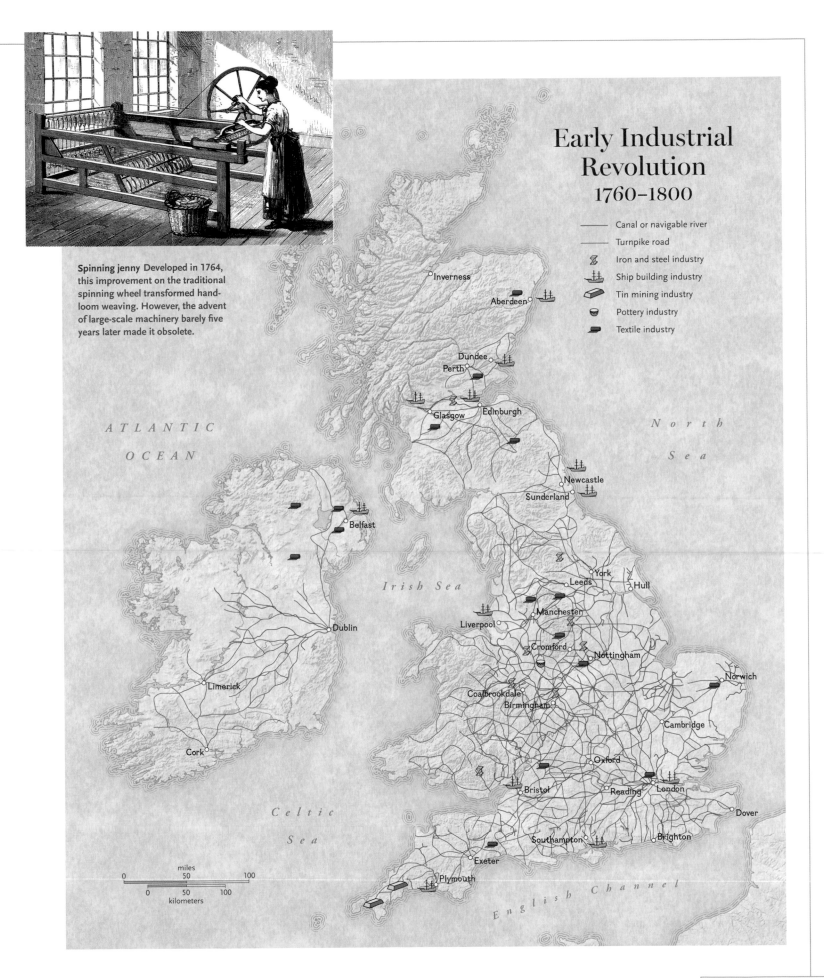

Early Industrial Revolution
1760–1800

Spinning jenny Developed in 1764, this improvement on the traditional spinning wheel transformed hand-loom weaving. However, the advent of large-scale machinery barely five years later made it obsolete.

Canal or navigable river	
Turnpike road	
Iron and steel industry	
Ship building industry	
Tin mining industry	
Pottery industry	
Textile industry	

ATLANTIC OCEAN

North Sea

Irish Sea

Celtic Sea

English Channel

Inverness

Aberdeen

Dundee
Perth
Glasgow   Edinburgh

Newcastle
Sunderland

Belfast

Dublin

Limerick

Cork

York
Leeds   Hull
Liverpool   Manchester
Cromford
Nottingham
Norwich
Coalbrookdale
Birmingham
Cambridge
Oxford
Bristol   Reading   London
Dover
Southampton   Brighton
Exeter
Plymouth

miles
0   50   100

0   50   100
kilometers

THE GEORGIAN WORLD

Life and Leisure, Town and Country

ritain in the 18th century was a perfect storm of prosperity. At its center was the maelstrom of wealth unleashed by empire—new markets, new raw materials, and new opportunities for trade. Around these whirled political change—a move to stable government, an end to internal dissent—and a flood of scientific, agricultural, and technological innovation. In their wake came a financial revolution—insurance, joint-stock companies, and more sophisticated methods of banking.

Caught up in the whirlwind was society itself, transformed as more people acquired more money than ever before. Many contrived to spend or invest their newfound wealth. Those with the most invested in art and houses, while those with less bought novel luxury goods and mass-produced items for home and hearth. A new, largely urban class evolved as wealth trickled down—"the middle sort," in the words of writer Daniel Defoe, "who live well."

Not that everyone benefited. It is estimated that in 1801, the date of Britain's first census, a third of the country's wealth was held by just 5 percent of the population. Much of Britain and Ireland also remained deeply rural, wedded to old ways of life that had barely changed since medieval times. If anything, rural hardships and the number of the rural dispossessed increased, mainly because enclosure, a blight on previous centuries, was now actively encouraged.

But where wealth was evident, it changed much of Britain, and many of these changes remain evident today. For while the country had been prosperous before, the material monuments to that wealth—Stonehenge, say, or the palaces of Tudor England—are now relatively rare. The Georgian world, by contrast, is a world that survives, and one into which we can step. Entire city quarters, for example, retain their Georgian appearance; the slave traders' beautiful country houses still sit in their verdant acres; and the artifacts of the age—the silver, furniture, paintings, and more—fill homes, museums, and antique stores the length of the land.

■ HOUSE AND GARDEN

As cities grew (see sidebar), entire new Georgian districts were laid out, with elegant squares and spacious terraces built on the ordered neoclassic lines inspired by Andrea Palladio and other Italian architects. Some survive in London, where they were diminished by World War II bombing, but the finest are found in Bath, Edinburgh, and Dublin, which for a period in the middle of the 18th century was the world's second-largest English-speaking city after London.

New homegrown architects championed the transformation. Charlotte Square, in Edinburgh, is one of the masterpieces of Robert Adam (1728–1792), also a renowned furniture and interior designer, whose services were much in demand in the period. In Bath, John Wood (1728–1782) laid out the Royal Crescent, still one of the finest pieces of urban architecture in Europe. In London, Chiswick House and Burlington House are memorials to Richard Boyle (1694–1753), third Earl of Burlington.

Adam and other architects also worked on the many great country homes of the period, some newly built, others remodeled to Georgian tastes as new money flowed into old landowning families. Stourhead, near Bristol, was among the former, built for a second-generation banker, Henry Hoare, in the 1720s; Stowe, north of Oxford, was among the latter. Both were distinguished by their gardens,

The Growth of Cities

Cities were the most obvious manifestation of the new wealth of the Georgian age. Many grew apace. London led the way—its population more than doubled to 1.4 million in the hundred years between 1714 and 1814—but Dublin and Edinburgh *(below)* were not far behind. The huge growth of Britain's industrial cities, such as Leeds, Glasgow, and Manchester, was still to come, but preempting them were port cities such as Bristol and Liverpool, which expanded as trade—particularly in slaves—increased. The rise of cities was reflected in England's rising overall population, which from around 5.05 million in 1701 rose to just 5.75 million in 1751 (with average male life expectancy around 36), but which in the next hundred years surged to 16.8 million (when men and women could live to around 40). Historians dispute the reasons, but increased material well-being was among them. In Scotland, Ireland, and Wales, which remained poorer longer and saw more emigration, the population remained depressed. But overall, more people were living better lives: The proportion of children born in London who died before the age of five decreased from two-thirds between 1730 and 1749 to one-third between 1810 and 1829.

Belton House Work on this stately home in Lincolnshire, eastern England, began in 1685. It anticipated the restrained neoclassic style that became popular in the Georgian period of the 18th century. The Brownlow family, which owned the house until 1984, made many alterations over the years, but the exterior survives largely as it is portrayed here in around 1720.

Landed gentry Thomas Gainsborough's "Mr. and Mrs. Andrews" (ca 1750), showing a couple on their estate, evokes the comfortable wealth of the upper classes during the Georgian era. Gainsborough's masterly depiction of changing weather and a naturalistic landscape was unusual at the time.

some of the glories of the age. Stowe's gardens were remodeled by the genius of Georgian garden design, Lancelot "Capability" Brown (1716–1783).

Inside, these same houses were filled with paintings by some of the greatest British artists of this or any age. Often, as in the work of Thomas Gainsborough (1727–1788) and Sir Joshua Reynolds (1723–1792), they were portraits of the owners themselves; later, they might be the landscapes of John Constable (1776–1837) or J. M. W. Turner (1775–1851). New money also attracted artists from abroad, notably the Venetian Canaletto (1697–1768), who lived and worked in London from 1746 to 1755.

■ GEORGIAN LIFE AND TIMES

As towns and cities changed, so, too, did the lives of their inhabitants. The wealthy might divide their time between a home in town and a home in the country. A social "season," marked by balls, parties, and sporting events, developed. Café society, already established in London's coffeehouses, proliferated elsewhere. Affluence increased leisure time. Women promenaded and played bridge or the piano; men went to their clubs, to the races, or on a grand tour—the cultural perambulation around Europe without which a gentleman's (or, on occasion, a lady's) education was considered incomplete.

Richard Boyle This Georgian architect was responsible for several projects in and around London, including Chiswick House *(opposite)*.

Life at the top was nothing if not genteel. In 1660, tea drinking was still an exotic pastime, and diarist Samuel Pepys could write that after talking with friends he "afterwards did send for a Cupp of Tee (a China drink) of which I never drank before." By 1800, however, it was commonplace.

So, too, was the drinking of gin, known as "Dutch courage" after its arrival in quantity from the Netherlands with William of Orange in 1688. Commentators at the time lamented its catastrophic effect on the urban poor (they called it "mother's ruin"). It was incredibly cheap—it was said you could "get drunk for a penny, and dead drunk for tuppence"—and widely available: In the 1730s, one in every 11 London dwellings was reputed to be a "gin house."

Gin's effects were overstated, though the commentators' implication of a rise in an underclass was real enough. Crime was a problem, and in an age without a coherent police force, it produced draconian measures: In 1815, more than 280 offenses were punishable by death, including shoplifting and stealing a sheep. Even if you avoided death, you might be deported: The first ships (11 in all) for Britain's new penal colony in Australia set sail in 1787.

Not all was doom and deportation, however, or fine houses and high living. The Georgian world also created writers and thinkers of the first rank. It also had civic spirit to go with its cultural élan—London's British Museum, for example, was founded in the period, in 1753. Above all, Georgians had a social conscience, manifest in religious and other radicals (see pages 228–229); the rise of philanthropy; and men and women such as William Wilberforce, who brought about the abolition of slavery (see pages 210–213). ■

Chiswick House Richard Boyle *(left)* built this villa near London in 1729 not as a residential home but to entertain and to house his art collection. The design, which was bold for its time, paid homage to Italian architect Andrea Palladio (1508–1580), whose neoclassic ideas found favor in many buildings of the Georgian era. The house survives to this day.

Made to measure *(right)* A table from Chiswick House, one of many items created specifically for the villa's sumptuous interiors.

"London is literally new to me, new in its streets, houses, even its situation . . . What I left open fields, producing hay and corn, I now find covered with streets and squares, and palaces and churches."

TOBIAS SMOLLETT, *THE EXPEDITION OF HUMPHRY CLINKER*, 1771

THE BRITISH IN INDIA

A Country Conquered in the Name of Commerce

Britain acquired empire in many ways, but until its first steps in India, colonies had largely been founded for just that: colonization. New lands were there to be settled. If they had indigenous populations, the incomers usually found them reassuringly small and easy to overcome. India, though, was different. India was not there to be settled—it already had a population of many millions. Britain therefore needed a new kind of colonialism that involved subduing and administering a large population.

The pioneer of this new colonialism was the East India Company, a trading enterprise founded by London merchants in 1600. It established its first trading posts in India after 1608 and added many more in the decades thereafter, usually in cooperation with the country's Mogul emperors.

By the middle of the 18th century, however, a decline in Mogul power left India divided into hundreds of weaker kingdoms. One of these kingdoms, Bengal, was home to Calcutta (now Kolkata), the company's headquarters and most important trading post. In 1756, the local ruler, Sirāj al-Dawlah, attacked the post, in part prompted by the French (stirred to action against British interests by the advent of the Seven Years' War). Captured Europeans were incarcerated in a subterranean prison—the "black hole of Calcutta"—where more than 120 of them may have died.

The East India Company's response was decisive. Its powerful private army, led by Robert Clive (1725–1774), recaptured Calcutta, where 3,000 troops—or, rather, their cannon—defeated 50,000 Indians. The army then deposed Bengal's ruler and replaced him with a company stooge. In 1765, a treaty forced on the Mogul emperor granted Clive the right to collect revenues across Bengal and other similarly subdued provinces.

Collecting revenues required administration and compliance, which in turn meant that the East India Company soon effectively ruled much of northeast India. It used its authority to raise taxes fivefold; to establish company monopolies on grain; to prohibit the "hoarding" (storing) of rice; and to insist that land given over to food be turned over to cash crops (not the least opium). The consequence was a famine that by 1773 killed an estimated third of Bengal's 30 million inhabitants.

The story of conquest was repeated, with minor variations, in southern and eastern India. By 1800, the East India Company controlled much of the country. Calcutta, a tiny trading post in 1690, became the second city of empire, with a population of more than 200,000, of whom just 1,000 were British. ∎

Ruling class Officials of the East India Company observe a cockfight at Lucknow, India, in a scene painted by Johann Zoffany in 1790, by which time the British trading company effectively ruled large areas of India. The Indians wait their turn to watch, and the women stand separately in a group to the left.

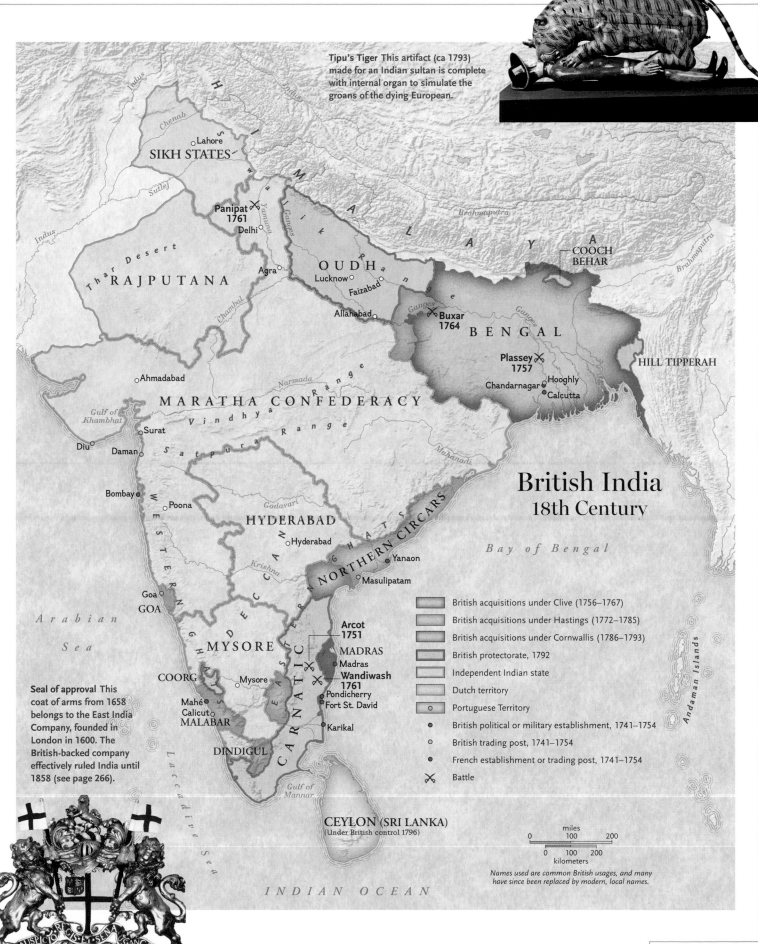

Tipu's Tiger This artifact (ca 1793) made for an Indian sultan is complete with internal organ to simulate the groans of the dying European.

SIKH STATES

Lahore

Panipat
1761

Delhi

Agra

RAJPUTANA

Thar Desert

OUDH

Lucknow

Faizabad

Allahabad

Buxar
1764

COOCH
BEHAR

BENGAL

Plassey
1757

HILL TIPPERAH

Chandarnagar

Hooghly

Calcutta

Ahmadabad

MARATHA CONFEDERACY

Narmada

Vindhya Range

Gulf of
Khambhat

Surat

Satpura Range

Mahanadi

Diu

Daman

Bombay

Poona

Godavari

Hyderabad

HYDERABAD

Hyderabad

British India
18th Century

Krishna

NORTHERN CIRCARS

Yanaon

Masulipatam

Bay of Bengal

Goa

GOA

MYSORE

Arcot
1751

MADRAS

Madras

Wandiwash
1761

Pondicherry

Fort St. David

Andaman Islands

Arabian
Sea

COORG

Mysore

Mahé

Calicut

MALABAR

Karikal

DINDIGUL

Laccadive Sea

Gulf of
Mannar

British acquisitions under Clive (1756–1767)

British acquisitions under Hastings (1772–1785)

British acquisitions under Cornwallis (1786–1793)

British protectorate, 1792

Independent Indian state

Dutch territory

Portuguese Territory

British political or military establishment, 1741–1754

British trading post, 1741–1754

French establishment or trading post, 1741–1754

Battle

CEYLON (SRI LANKA)
(Under British control 1796)

miles
0   100   200

0   100   200
kilometers

Names used are common British usages, and many
have since been replaced by modern, local names.

Seal of approval This coat of arms from 1658 belongs to the East India Company, founded in London in 1600. The British-backed company effectively ruled India until 1858 (see page 266).

INDIAN OCEAN

AUSPICIO REGIS ET SENATUS ANGLIÆ

THE SEVEN YEARS' WAR

Naval Disaster, Total War, Military Triumph

The Seven Years' War (1756–1763) had its roots in Europe, where Britain and its ally, Prussia, confronted an alliance of France, Spain, and Russia. Winston Churchill called it the first "world war," for it quickly spread to the colonies and trading posts of the belligerent powers in four major theaters: Canada, Africa, India, and the West Indies.

It got off to bad start, at least for the British, who in 1756 lost the strategic island of Minorca and thus control of the western Mediterranean. The loss led to the return to office of William Pitt the Elder (1708–1778), a new breed of politician and a man who had a clear strategy and demanded and received the means to see it through. Wars in Europe were costly and difficult. Pitt insisted that Britain would give money, but few troops, to Prussia. Wars overseas were another matter, however. Both men and money would be targeted at France's colonial possessions. The Royal Navy, fast becoming a fine fighting force, would deliver the knockout blows.

In America, the French and Indian War was already underway. In 1754, for example, a young British officer named George Washington had been involved in early skirmishes against the French. So-called New France—French North American territory—all but encircled the 13 Colonies, from Canada in an arc toward Louisiana. By 1758, Britain had made major gains, notably in the Ohio Valley, where one of the captured French forts, Duquesne, was renamed Fort Pitt (later Pittsburgh) after the British prime minister.

Elsewhere, the Royal Navy fought well in the Mediterranean, as well as at Quiberon Bay (1759), off Brittany, where it defeated France's main northern and southern fleets. It also triumphed in West Africa, where parts of French Senegal fell, and in the Caribbean, where Martinique and Guadeloupe were captured. In Asia, a string of victories by Britain's East India Company, notably at Madras (Chennai), Calcutta (Kolkata), and Pondicherry, all but eliminated French power in India.

Even greater gains were made in Canada, where a blockade by the Royal Navy, which now had the ships, men, and equipment to make long sea voyages, had starved French forces of supplies and reinforcements. By 1759, the army was ready to take advantage, which it did to most spectacular effect in the battle for the pivotal French city of Quebec.

Here, Gen. James Wolfe (1727–1759) commanded the British forces. The French, under Gen. Louis-Joseph de Montcalm, occupied the city's cliff-top plateau above the St. Lawrence River. On September 12, Wolfe's men rowed upstream under cover of night, their oars muffled. After clambering ashore, they climbed the cliffs, left undefended by the French, who had assumed them unassailable. At dawn, 4,800 British redcoats confronted the unsuspecting French. Montcalm, attacking in panic, was defeated.

Wolfe died in his moment of triumph, and Montcalm with him, but in Britain the mood was celebratory: The British called 1759 an annus mirabilis, or year of miracles. "Our bells," observed writer Horace Walpole, "are quite worn threadbare with ringing for victories." Britain ended the war with its empire increased and its power unchallenged. ■

Cover of night British forces under Gen. James Wolfe scale the cliffs beneath Quebec in 1759. The daring maneuver surprised the defending French and helped secure victory in the decisive battle of the Seven Years' War.

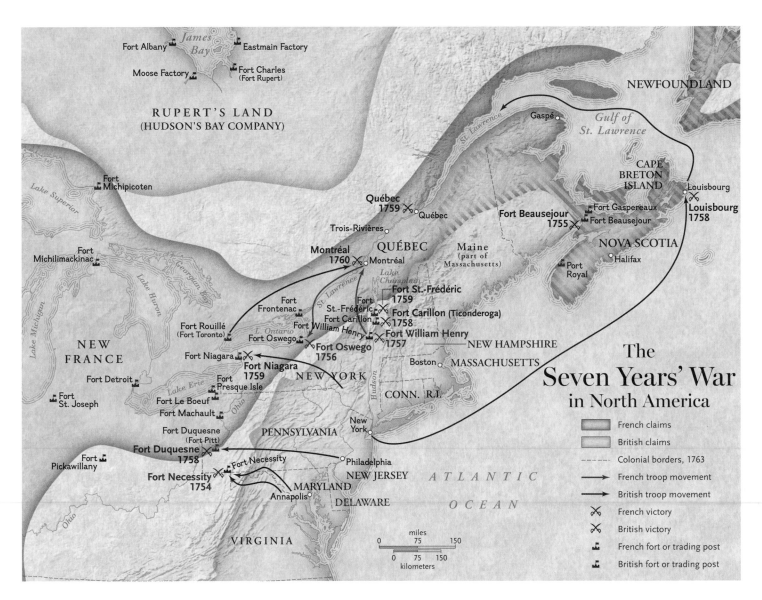

The Seven Years' War
in North America

Fort Albany
James Bay
Eastmain Factory
Moose Factory
Fort Charles
(Fort Rupert)

NEWFOUNDLAND

Gaspé
*Gulf of
St. Lawrence*

RUPERT'S LAND
(HUDSON'S BAY COMPANY)

CAPE
BRETON
ISLAND

Louisbourg
**Louisbourg
1758**

Fort
Michipicoten

Lake Superior

**Québec
1759** Québec

Fort Gaspereaux
**Fort Beausejour
1755** Fort Beausejour

Trois-Rivières

Fort
Michilimackinac

Georgian Bay

Lake Huron

**Montréal
1760** Montréal

QUÉBEC

Maine
(part of
Massachusetts)

NOVA SCOTIA

Halifax

Port
Royal

Fort
Frontenac

Fort
St.-Frédéric

**Fort St.-Frédéric
1759**

*Lake
Champlain*

Fort Rouillé
(Fort Toronto)

Fort
Carillon

**Fort Carillon (Ticonderoga)
1758**

NEW
FRANCE

L. Ontario
Fort Oswego

Fort William Henry

**Fort William Henry
1757**

**Fort Oswego
1756**

Fort Niagara

**Fort Niagara
1759**

NEW YORK

NEW HAMPSHIRE

Lake Michigan

Fort Detroit

Lake Erie

Fort
Presque Isle

Boston MASSACHUSETTS

Fort
St. Joseph

Fort Le Boeuf

Fort Machault

Ohio

CONN. R.I.

Hudson

Fort Duquesne
(Fort Pitt)

**Fort Duquesne
1758**

PENNSYLVANIA

New
York

Fort
Pickawillany

Fort Necessity

Philadelphia

ATLANTIC

**Fort Necessity
1754**

MARYLAND

NEW JERSEY

DELAWARE

OCEAN

Annapolis

Ohio

VIRGINIA

	French claims
	British claims
---	Colonial borders, 1763
→	French troop movement
→	British troop movement
✗	French victory
✗	British victory
⌂	French fort or trading post
⌂	British fort or trading post

miles
0   75   150
0   75   150
kilometers

Opening shots French naval forces defeat the British in the Mediterranean at Minorca in 1756, one of the first battles of the Seven Years' War. The defeat led to a public clamor for the return of politician William Pitt to organize the British response. It also led to the court-martial of the British admiral, John Byng, who was unjustly executed on his own quarterdeck. French writer Voltaire referred to the execution ironically in *Candide* (1759), in which he noted it was wise to execute an admiral from time to time *pour encourager les autres*—to encourage the others.

THE REVOLUTIONARY WAR

The Loss of the Colonies, the Birth of a Nation

George Washington The future first U.S. president portrayed at Dorchester Heights, above Boston, after being made commander in chief of the Continental Army in 1775

The Seven Years' War brought Britain huge gains but at huge cost. The national debt doubled to £140 million. Interest payments alone amounted to four million pounds, or half of all tax revenues. The cost of empire also increased. New borders had to be defended. Nowhere was this truer than on the long and ever increasing frontiers of the 13 Colonies in North America. Costs there since the war had increased fourfold, to £350,000 per annum. London claimed that annual net taxes from these same colonies amounted to £14,000.

Yet many in Britain argued that the Seven Years' War had benefited none so much as the Americans: The French, the principal threat to the colonies, had been defeated, along with the French allies among American Indians hostile to the colonists. In 1755, British politician William Pitt had observed that "the present war was undertaken for the long-injured, long-neglected, long-forgotten people of America."

The sense in Britain was that America should help pay its way, and that hitherto the colonies, while prospering, had enjoyed an easy ride in the matter of taxes and their collection. Britain claimed that its grave finances demanded change.

Thus, there was little fuss in February 1765 when Parliament passed the Stamp Act, which imposed a duty on American property and legal transactions. Despite protests in the colonies, Parliament introduced more taxes and increased levies on tea, sugar, and other luxury goods. In America, the response was outrage.

Startled by the reaction, Parliament backed down. Most of the new levies were repealed, though Parliament, whose Members were anxious to defend the institution's sovereignty and primacy in deciding colonial policy, refused to compromise on the principle that it could pass laws for British colonies "in all cases whatsoever." The colonists, by contrast, turned a rallying principle of the English Civil War back on the British by insisting there should be "no taxation without representation."

In Britain, the Revolutionary War is known as the American War of Independence, but many British writers maintain that it was nothing of the sort, at least at the outset. Simon Jenkins, a former editor of the *Times* newspaper, suggests that the conflict was "essentially an argument between loyalist and radical British subjects over trade and taxes, only gradually acquiring the rhetoric of civil rights and liberties."

Final Surrender

Considering all the battles of the Revolutionary War, the two sides were evenly matched. For every Saratoga, the Americans' great victory in 1777, there was a Brandywine, a triumph for the British. The arrival of the French in 1778 helped tip the balance. The Spanish (in 1779) and Dutch (1780) followed, as they were similarly keen to undermine an isolated Britain. Britain's Royal Navy was forced to fight in the Caribbean, the Mediterranean, and elsewhere. Stretched thin, it proved unable to offer adequate support to British forces on America's east coast. Matters came to a head at Yorktown, Virginia, to which Charles Cornwallis, the British general *(below)*, had retreated to await relief from the navy. Against him was a combined U.S. and French force under George Washington and the Comte de Rochambeau. On September 5, 1781, a French armada fought off the British relieving fleet in the Chesapeake Bay. It was a decisive moment, consolidated by the arrival of additional colonial forces. Under intense bombardment, Cornwallis had no option but to surrender. The Revolutionary War was effectively over. All that remained was for Britain's defeat to be recognized via the Treaty of Paris in 1783.

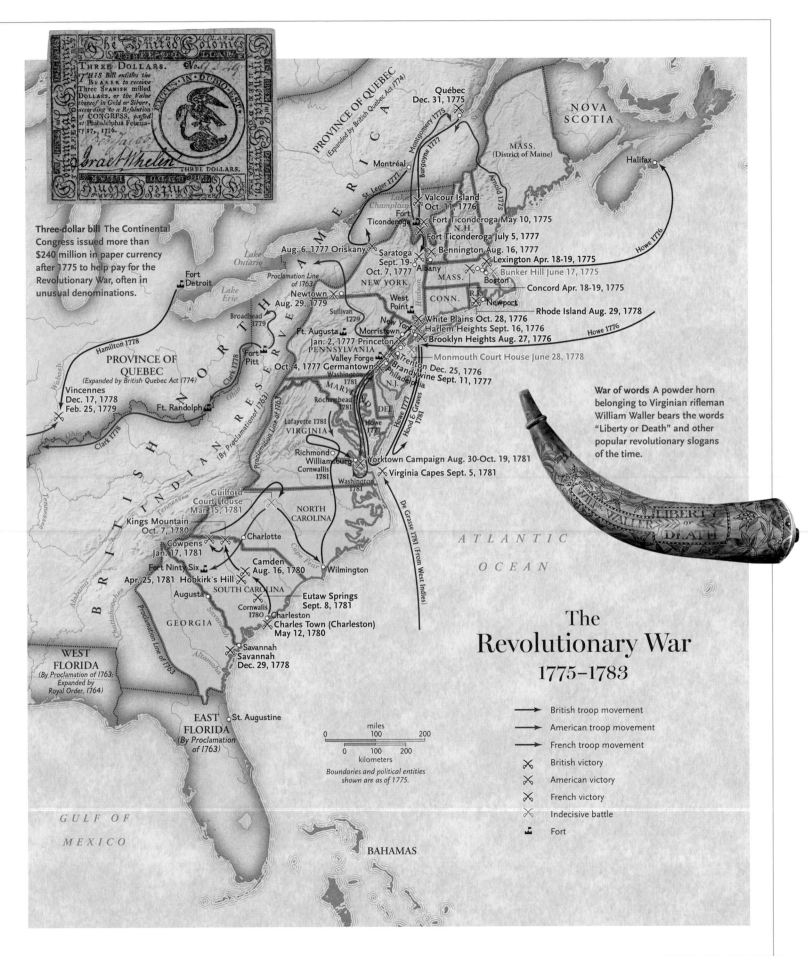

Three-dollar bill The Continental
Congress issued more than
$240 million in paper currency
after 1775 to help pay for the
Revolutionary War, often in
unusual denominations.

War of words A powder horn
belonging to Virginian rifleman
William Waller bears the words
"Liberty or Death" and other
popular revolutionary slogans
of the time.

NOVA
SCOTIA

MASS.
(District of Maine)

Halifax

Québec
Dec. 31, 1775

Montréal

PROVINCE OF QUEBEC
(Expanded by British Quebec Act 1774)

Valcour Island
Oct. 11, 1776

Fort
Ticonderoga

Fort Ticonderoga May 10, 1775

N.H.

Fort Ticonderoga July 5, 1777

Aug. 6, 1777 Oriskany

Bennington Aug. 16, 1777

Lexington Apr. 18-19, 1775

Saratoga
Sept. 19-
Oct. 7, 1777

Albany

Bunker Hill June 17, 1775

Boston

Concord Apr. 18-19, 1775

NEW YORK

MASS.

Fort Detroit

Lake
Ontario

Proclamation Line
of 1763

Newtown
Aug. 29, 1779

Sullivan
1779

CONN.

R.I.

Newport

Rhode Island Aug. 29, 1778

Lake
Erie

West
Point

Howe 1776

Broadhead
1779

Ft. Augusta

New York

White Plains Oct. 28, 1776

Harlem Heights Sept. 16, 1776

Morristown

Hamilton 1778

PROVINCE OF
QUEBEC
(Expanded by British Quebec Act 1774)

Fort
Pitt

Clark 1778

Jan. 2, 1777 Princeton

Brooklyn Heights Aug. 27, 1776

PENNSYLVANIA

Valley Forge

Monmouth Court House June 28, 1778

Oct. 4, 1777 Germantown

Trenton Dec. 25, 1776

Vincennes
Dec. 17, 1778
Feb. 25, 1779

Ft. Randolph

MARYLAND

Washington
1781

Brandywine Sept. 11, 1777

Philadelphia

N.J.

Clark 1778

Rochambeau
1781

DEL.

Howe 1777

Hood & Graves
1781

Lafayette 1781

VIRGINIA

Howe
1777

Richmond

Williamsburg

Yorktown Campaign Aug. 30-Oct. 19, 1781

Cornwallis
1781

Washington
1781

Virginia Capes Sept. 5, 1781

Guilford
Court House
Mar. 15, 1781

NORTH
CAROLINA

De Grasse 1781 (From West Indies)

ATLANTIC

OCEAN

Kings Mountain
Oct. 7, 1780

Charlotte

Cowpens
Jan. 17, 1781

Fort Ninety-Six

Camden
Aug. 16, 1780

Wilmington

Apr. 25, 1781 Hobkirk's Hill

SOUTH CAROLINA

Augusta

Eutaw Springs
Sept. 8, 1781

Cornwallis
1780

Charleston

GEORGIA

Charles Town (Charleston)
May 12, 1780

The
Revolutionary War
1775–1783

WEST
FLORIDA
(By Proclamation of 1763;
Expanded by
Royal Order,
1764)

Savannah
Savannah
Dec. 29, 1778

EAST
FLORIDA
(By Proclamation
of 1763)

St. Augustine

miles
0   100   200

0   100   200
kilometers

Boundaries and political entities
shown are as of 1775.

British troop movement

American troop movement

French troop movement

British victory

American victory

French victory

Indecisive battle

Fort

GULF OF

MEXICO

BAHAMAS

Whatever the causes, events moved quickly to confrontation. One of the sparks was the Boston Tea Party in 1773, when colonists, protesting the last of the disputed taxes (on tea), boarded three ships in Boston Harbor and threw 343 chests of tea overboard. Because news of the event was garbled in the weeks it took to cross the Atlantic, London overreacted. After the tea party, Parliament passed five so-called Coercive Acts that further restricted the colonists' freedoms.

In response, the Americans called the First Continental Congress in Philadelphia and set out a declaration of rights; they also boycotted British goods and demanded a repeal of laws that "penalized" American trade. London's response was to dispatch troops. Local American militias, composed of soldiers known as minutemen because they were supposed to be ready at a minute's notice, began to mobilize. The first shots were fired in April 1775, when the British governor of Massachusetts attempted a preemptive strike to deprive the patriot militias at Concord and Lexington of their weapons.

A month later, in May, the Second Continental Congress convened in Philadelphia to coordinate the colonies' response. On June 15, the congress appointed George Washington as commander in chief of the Continental Army. War was now joined in earnest.

The following year, the Philadelphia congress convened again. Where once the delegates had sought reconciliation, they now issued the Declaration of Independence, largely the work of a Virginian plantation owner, Thomas Jefferson. On July 4, 1776, in the words of Simon Jenkins, "England's most successful creation, the United States of America, was born."

The war, meanwhile, for all its many battles, became a stalemate. Britain's assumed early victory did not materialize. The militias performed better than expected, and as time went on, the British and American forces appeared to be evenly matched. Yet many in London realized it was a conflict that could not be won. America's resources were vast, and its soldiers knew the immense terrain. British supply lines were long, and while victories might be secured, they could rarely be exploited.

In the end, the outcome turned on an irony. Among the claims of the Declaration of Independence was the assertion that America could seek alliances where it wished. In 1778, its likeliest ally was England's oldest enemy, France. Anxious to avenge its defeat in the Seven Years' War, France was only too happy to oblige. America's new-forged nation, founded on republican ideals, therefore entered a marriage of convenience with the most uncompromising absolute monarchy in Europe. France's intervention, at Yorktown, in 1781, would prove decisive (see sidebar, p. 224). ■

"May our land be a land of liberty, the seat of virtue, the asylum of the oppressed, a name and a praise in the whole Earth, until the last shock of time shall bury the empires of the whole world."

JOSEPH WARREN, BOSTON MASSACRE ORATION, 1772

Heat of battle A camp stove in iron and copper, designed to hold hot coals and used in the field by American officers during the Revolutionary War

A nation born This John Trumbull painting of the signing of the Declaration of Independence, commissioned in 1817, portrays Thomas Jefferson presenting the declaration to John Hancock, president of the Continental Congress.

American arms A rare surviving musket from the Rappahannock Forge in Stafford, Virginia, is one of many weapons made here between 1776 and 1782.

RADICALS AND THINKERS

Ideas and Ideology, Religion and Revolution

A revolution called the Enlightenment (also called the age of reason) swept Western thought in the 18th century. It transformed life at the time and provided the foundations of secularism, liberal capitalism, and other social and political ideas that inform many aspects of the Western world. Britain had been at the forefront of the Enlightenment, with the work of men such as Sir Francis Bacon and Sir Isaac Newton in the 17th century (see pages 186–187). It remained in the vanguard as the new century progressed, part of a cosmopolitan ferment of ideas that found particularly powerful expression in France and the writings of Voltaire (1694–1778) and Jean-Jacques Rousseau (1712–1778).

Many of Britain's greatest 18th-century thinkers were Scottish (see sidebar), but England and Ireland also had their champions, not the least Thomas Paine (1737–1809) and Edmund Burke (1729–1797). Paine was a difficult character, chaotic in his private life and often spectacularly unkempt. But he was also passionate in his libertarian principles, and in 1774, attracted by the tumult of the American Revolution, he settled in Philadelphia and became a vocal advocate of the colonists' cause. In 1792, again anxious to be at the heart of revolutionary turmoil, he traveled to France during its revolution.

Dublin-born Burke also supported the American colonists but opposed the French Revolution. He presciently forecast the latter's descent into tyranny: It was an event, he wrote, that had "subverted monarchy, but not recovered freedom." His credo was conservative, and he advocated gradual change in tandem with wider social and political advances. Burke penned several well-known maxims, including "Those who don't know history are doomed to repeat it" and "The only thing necessary for the triumph of evil is for good men to do nothing."

Britain also produced female radicals, not the least Mary Wollstonecraft (1759–1797), whose espousal of women's rights was remarkable at a time when an Englishman could freely beat his wife provided the stick was no thicker than his thumb. Women such as Elizabeth Heyrick (1769–1831) and Anne Knight (1786–1862) were also part of the radical lobby that achieved the abolition of slavery; they joined the campaign because as women they were denied more direct parliamentary involvement. The antislavery movement also included religious radicals, such as William Wilberforce and Unitarian industrialist Josiah Wedgwood (1730–1795). Many had close links to John Wesley (1703–1791), the force behind Methodism, as his simplicity and practical Christianity spoke loudly to the poor in the new industrial cities no longer reached by a worldlier Anglican church. ■

The Scottish Enlightenment

Some of Britain's finest 18th-century minds were nurtured in Scotland. The country's intellectual leading lights were David Hume (1711–1776) *(left)*, an influential theorist and philosopher; pioneering sociologist Adam Ferguson (1723–1816); and Adam Smith (1723–1790), whose views on free markets shape economic thinking to this day. Among many scientists and engineers were James Watt (1736–1819), who revolutionized the technology of steam power, and John McAdam (1756–1836), whose macadam surface would transform roads worldwide.

Capital ideas Parliament Square in Edinburgh, a city that in the 18th century was at the heart of a ferment of progressive literary, intellectual, and scientific endeavor known as the Scottish Enlightenment. While parts of the square portrayed in this painting have since been rebuilt, the figure of King Charles II at its heart—Britain's oldest equestrian statue (1685)—survives to this day.

"Common Sense" Thomas Paine's 1776 pamphlet was a rallying cry for the American Revolution. Paine was born in England but was largely reviled in his own country.

"*But what is liberty without wisdom and without virtue? It is the greatest of all possible evils; for it is folly, vice, and madness, without tuition or restraint.*"

EDMUND BURKE, *REFLECTIONS ON THE REVOLUTION IN FRANCE, 1790*

Edmund Burke This Irish-born thinker espoused gradual political change in step with wider social changes. He supported the American colonists in 1776 but warned that the French Revolution would end in tyranny.

THE LITERARY WORLD

Novels, Satire, and the Rise of the Printed Word

Literary endeavor in the 18th century continued the rich traditions of the previous century—the poetry of Donne, Milton, and Marvell; the delightful musings of men such as Samuel Pepys; and the great drama of the Jacobean and Restoration eras. It also saw the beginning in Britain of the novel—the form that in the following century would yield some of the greatest glories of the English language.

No novelist of the era is more celebrated than Jane Austen (1775–1817), best known for works, such as *Pride and Prejudice* (1813), that combine timeless dissections of character with a nuanced portrait of the Georgian gentry. Earlier novelists include Daniel Defoe, celebrated for *Robinson Crusoe* (1719); Samuel Richardson, best known for *Pamela* (1740), considered one of the first modern novels; and Henry Fielding, remembered for *The History of Tom Jones, a Foundling* (1749).

Also popular was satire, exemplified by Alexander Pope's "The Rape of the Lock" (1712–1717), a delicious mock-heroic poem that elevates a vain woman's loss of a lock of hair to the epic world of the gods: "Charms strike the sight," cautions Pope, "but merit wins the soul."

Pope's close friend, Dublin-born Jonathan Swift, is best known for *Gulliver's Travels* (1726), but almost as celebrated is "A Modest Proposal" (1729), a scurrilous satire that suggested poor Irish children might be less of a burden if their parents sold them as food to the wealthy: "A young healthy child well nursed, is, at a year old, a most delicious nourishing and wholesome food, whether stewed, roasted, baked, or boiled."

Ireland also produced dramatist Oliver Goldsmith, best known for the humorous *She Stoops to Conquer* (1773), while one of Scotland's most loved literary sons is Robert Burns (1759–1796). Burns wrote with flair in conventional English but is most remembered for his songs and poems in a Scots dialect, "Auld Lang Syne" (1788) being the most famous. Other mavericks included William Blake (1757–1827), whose visionary poems, prints, and paintings are some of the most singular of any British artist or writer.

Literary endeavor flourished in many other fields and was avidly consumed by a public that had become voracious for the printed word. Essays, periodicals, and pamphlets proliferated. Thomas Paine and Edmund Burke (see pages 228–229) were the most prominent of the political pamphleteers—Paine's rallying cry for the American Revolution, "Common Sense," sold more than 100,000 copies in 1776 alone. Magazines also came to the fore, notably *The Spectator*, devoted to news and comment. First published in 1711, it sold 4,000 copies a day, and it is still in print today. Newspapers, too, became popular. *The Daily Universal Register*, first published in 1785, is now better known as *The Times,* the title it adopted in 1788. ■

Required reading A 1720 edition of Daniel Defoe's *Robinson Crusoe*. This famous tale of a shipwrecked sailor helped popularize the novel as a literary genre in Britain.

The Wit and Wisdom of Samuel Johnson

Britain had some 20 dictionaries at the turn of the 17th century. The oldest, called *Wordbook*, from 1538, merely translated Latin to English. Another, Cawdrey's *Table Alphabeticall* (1604), featured vocabulary entering English from the "far journied gentlemen who pouder their talke with oversea language," but it had just 2,449 words, and none beginning with *W, X,* or *Y*. It was left to Samuel Johnson (1709–1784) to produce Britain's first comprehensive dictionary (1746–1755), a 46,000-word best seller celebrated for its wit and scholarship: A *boat*, in Johnson's definition, was a "prison with a chance of drowning"; *fishing* a "stick and a string, with a worm on one end and a fool on the other"; *oats* a "grain which in England is generally given to horses but in Scotland supports the people." Johnson was also the subject of James Boswell's (1740–1795) celebrated *The Life of Samuel Johnson* (1791), which collects many of Johnson's aphorisms, such as "Patriotism is the last refuge of the scoundrel" and the warning that entering into a second marriage represents "the triumph of hope over experience."

> *"This sensation of listlessness, weariness, stupidity, this disinclination to sit down and employ myself, this feeling of everything's being dull and insipid about the house! I must be in love . . ."*

JANE AUSTEN, *EMMA*, 1815

Sir Walter Scott Born in Edinburgh in 1771, Scott combined a legal career with writing and achieved international success with a series of historical novels—such as *Waverley* (1814) and *Rob Roy* (1817)—many of which were rooted in his native Scotland.

Hand in hand Mr. Darcy and Elizabeth Bennet, the protagonists of Jane Austen's novel *Pride and Prejudice* (1813). Austen's sublime novels contain timeless elements of humor, irony, plot, and character, but also offer a fine portrait of contemporary life among the landed gentry of the Georgian period.

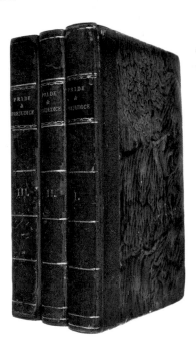

Mass appeal Early editions of novels by Jane Austen. Britain acquired a voracious appetite for the printed word during the Georgian era, which saw the proliferation of books, magazines, and newspapers.

NELSON AND TRAFALGAR

A Life Lost, a Battle Won, a Hero Born

In 1805, Napoleon was close to the height of his power. Much of Western Europe had bowed its knee, and now it was Britain's turn. The French emperor was planning an invasion, but it could not succeed without naval superiority. This Napoleon could achieve either by engaging and destroying the British fleet or by tempting it to the Caribbean to leave the way clear for invasion. Were the Royal Navy vanquished, few Britons would put much faith in their army.

Despite complex thrust and counterthrust, France failed in its first objective—to lure the British fleet away from the English Channel. This left the option of direct confrontation and, with it, a moment of destiny for one of the most famous names in British history.

Horatio Nelson (1758–1805) was born in Norfolk, close to the sea. He joined the navy at age 12, saw action at 16, and gained his first command at 20. At 35, he lost an eye (fighting off Corsica), and four years later he lost an arm in a battle off Tenerife. At Cape St. Vincent (1797), he ignored orders but still helped defeat the Spanish; in 1798, at the Battle of the Nile, he annihilated the French, partly by fighting at night; at Copenhagen (1801), against the Danish and the Norwegians, he won the day by turning a blind eye to orders to withdraw.

Nelson's triumphs became the talk of England, as did his affair with Lady Emma Hamilton, wife of Britain's ambassador to Naples. The pair remained married to their respective spouses, but in 1801 they had a child and christened her Horatia—hardly a name designed to keep her paternity secret. Rather than causing public outrage, Nelson's racy love life only increased his celebrity status.

Four years after Horatia's birth, on September 15, Britain's fleet arrived at Cape Trafalgar, off the Spanish coast. A 33-ship Franco-Spanish force destined for the invasion of Britain lay nearby in the port of Cádiz. When Nelson arrived to take command of the fleet on September 29, his presence had an immediate effect on his men: "a sort of general joy has been the consquence," wrote one of his

Frontal assault Nelson's flagship H.M.S. *Victory* at the Battle of Trafalgar. Nelson demanded his ship be at the heart of the action and died as a result, but not before learning that the battle was won.

captains; "Everything seemed, as if by enchantment, to prosper under his direction," observed another.

Nelson's plan for the coming battle was simple but fraught with danger. It was also typically unorthodox but, if successful, would deliver not only victory, but also Britain's long-term strategic goal: the elimination of France as a naval power.

Conventional engagements of the time were fought by two lines of ships abreast, firing broadsides at one another from side-mounted guns. As such, they usually became battles of attrition that ended in stalemate. At Trafalgar, by contrast, Nelson divided his 27 ships into smaller squadrons. Two columns would approach the enemy line head-on, at right angles. Their unarmed bows would be exposed to devastating broadsides, and their gunners would be unable to return fire. But the ships would present a narrow target, and once they broke the French line, would be able to fire up and down the enemy formation at will. Just as important, many of the French guns would now be directed at empty sea.

Nelson would use his own flagship, *Victory,* to defeat the *Bucentaure,* flagship of the French commander, Admiral Villeneuve. Deprived of its commander, the enemy fleet would scatter. Nelson trusted his captains to do the rest. He would also hold back 15 ships to reinforce his first wave and either pick off the enemy as it scattered or prevent the segmented French line from rejoining battle.

It all worked. At 11:48 a.m., on October 19, 1805, Nelson raised the most famous signal in British naval history: "England expects that every man will do his duty." At the day's end, his fleet was victorious—better led, better gunned, better crewed, better trained. The man himself, though, was dead. At 1:15 p.m., as Nelson walked *Victory*'s decks in the thick of battle, he was struck by a musket ball from a French sniper. The shot ruptured an artery and lodged in his spine. At 2:30 p.m. his flag captain, Thomas Hardy, informed him of the battle's triumphal outcome. Two hours later, in his hour of glory, Nelson died, his nation saved from invasion, her supremacy of the sea secured for a century. ∎

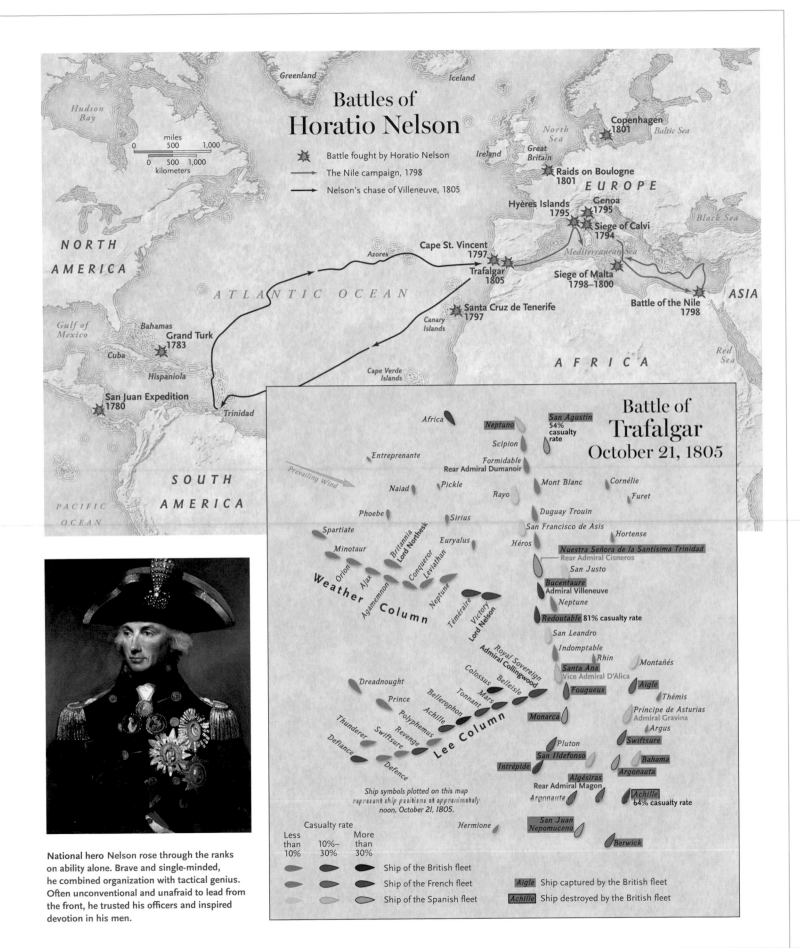

Battles of Horatio Nelson

✸ Battle fought by Horatio Nelson
→ The Nile campaign, 1798
→ Nelson's chase of Villeneuve, 1805

Greenland

Iceland

Hudson Bay

miles
0 500 1,000

kilometers
0 500 1,000

North Sea
Baltic Sea

Copenhagen 1801

Great Britain

Ireland

Raids on Boulogne 1801

EUROPE

Hyères Islands 1795
Genoa 1795
Siege of Calvi 1794

Black Sea

NORTH AMERICA

Azores

Cape St. Vincent 1797
Trafalgar 1805

Mediterranean Sea

ATLANTIC OCEAN

ASIA

Siege of Malta 1798–1800

Battle of the Nile 1798

Gulf of Mexico
Bahamas
Grand Turk 1783
Cuba
Hispaniola

Santa Cruz de Tenerife 1797

Canary Islands

Red Sea

AFRICA

Cape Verde Islands

San Juan Expedition 1780

Trinidad

SOUTH AMERICA

PACIFIC OCEAN

National hero Nelson rose through the ranks on ability alone. Brave and single-minded, he combined organization with tactical genius. Often unconventional and unafraid to lead from the front, he trusted his officers and inspired devotion in his men.

Battle of Trafalgar
October 21, 1805

Prevailing Wind →

Africa
Neptuno
San Agustín 54% casualty rate
Scipion
Entreprenante
Formidable
Rear Admiral Dumanoir
Mont Blanc
Cornélie
Naiad
Pickle
Rayo
Furet
Phoebe
Sirius
Duguay Trouin
San Francisco de Asís
Hortense
Spartiate
Euryalus
Héros
Nuestra Señora de la Santísima Trinidad
Rear Admiral Cisneros
Minotaur
Britannia Lord Northesk
Conqueror
Leviathan
San Justo
Orion
Ajax
Agamemnon
Neptune
Bucentaure Admiral Villeneuve
Neptune
Weather Column
Téméraire
Redoutable 81% casualty rate
Victory Lord Nelson
San Leandro
Indomptable
Rhin
Montañés
Royal Sovereign Admiral Collingwood
Santa Ana Vice Admiral D'Alica
Aigle
Dreadnought
Belleisle
Fougueux
Thémis
Colossus
Mars
Prince
Tonnant
Monarca
Príncipe de Asturias Admiral Gravina
Bellerophon
Argus
Achille
Polyphemus
Swiftsure
Revenge
Lee Column
Pluton
Intrépide
San Ildefonso
Bahama
Thunder
Swiftsure
Defiance
San Juan Nepomuceno
Argonaute
Algésiras Rear Admiral Magon
Argonauta
Achille 64% casualty rate
Defence
Hermione
Berwick

Ship symbols plotted on this map represent ship positions at approximately noon, October 21, 1805.

Casualty rate

Less than 10%	10%–30%	More than 30%	
			Ship of the British fleet
			Ship of the French fleet
			Ship of the Spanish fleet

Aigle Ship captured by the British fleet
Achille Ship destroyed by the British fleet

THE BATTLE OF WATERLOO

A Narrow Victory and the End of an Emperor

Duke of Wellington *(above)* The Iron Duke, the victor of Waterloo, went on to a career in politics. *(below, right)* Wellington's pencil-written orders for the battle

Horatio Nelson defeated Napoleon at sea in 1805. The Russian winter helped defeat Napoleon on land in 1812. In 1815, after a French resurgence, it fell to Britain and allies to defeat him again.

Two armies were marshaled for the task. One, led by Gebhard von Blücher, was made up of Prussians. The other, an Anglo-Dutch force, was led by Arthur Wellesley, Duke of Wellington (1769–1852).

The Prussians were first into the fray. Sensing defeat if his two still-separate enemies joined forces, Napoleon made a failed attempt to destroy Blücher's army in Belgium between June 12 and 16, 1815. Two days later, knowing that Blücher was on the march, he turned his attention to Wellington. With 72,000 men to his opponent's 68,000, and twice as many guns, Napoleon expected an easy victory. Wellington had seen action in India and in the Peninsular War (1807–1814), the campaign to dislodge Napoleon from Spain and Portugal, but had never faced the emperor in person.

On the morning of battle, Wellington kept his main force back. Instead, he placed men and guns in farms and strongpoints along a ridge near the town of Waterloo. Having learned the art of defense in the Peninsular War, he knew how to lure an enemy to exhaust itself by attacking heavily fortified redoubts. As planned, Napoleon's guns pounded the positions, but to little avail.

Only when the French infantry attacked did Wellington introduce his troops. His men, also battle hardened and disciplined by the Peninsular War, formed tight squares and held firm, their musket volleys flaying wave after wave of French infantry. Napoleon's cavalry then entered the fray. A vital farm, La Haye Sainte, at the fulcrum of the battle, fell. The tide seemed to turn. Defeat for Wellington appeared imminent.

At this moment, Blücher's 48,000 troops arrived and immediately engaged the main French force. Napoleon's personal guard made an assault on the British center. It was a final fling, and when it faltered, the entire French army broke and fled.

Napoleon was defeated, but it was, as Wellington later observed, "the nearest-run thing you ever saw in your life." Some 17,000 British, 7,000 Prussian, and 26,000 French soldiers died, and 8,000 Frenchmen were captured. Wellington refused to gloat. "It is quite impossible to think of glory at the moment of victory," he said. "Next to a battle lost, the greatest misery is a battle gained." Napoleon, for his part, was finished. He abdicated on June 22 and surrendered on July 15. Six years later, at age 51, he was dead. ■

The Napoleonic Wars

Napoleon Bonaparte (1769–1821) rose to prominence during the upheavals that followed the French Revolution. As the revolution took hold after 1789, other powers feared the spread of revolutionary fervor to their own countries. As a result, between 1792 and 1802, several states and coalitions fought the French Revolutionary Wars against the new republic. Austria was drawn into the fray in 1792, Britain in 1793, and Russia in 1798.

France more than held its own, not the least because of Napoleon, whose military genius saw him go from a young artillery officer in 1793 to emperor of France and ruler of much of Europe by 1804. "I never see a throne," he said, "without feeling the urge to sit on it." In 1805, Nelson's victory at Trafalgar (see pages 232–233) forestalled Napoleon's attempts to invade Britain, but in the same year Napoleon had his greatest triumph when he crushed Russia and Austria at the Battle of Austerlitz. In 1807 and 1808, his attempt to take the Spanish crown provoked the Peninsular War, in which Britain joined Spanish and Portuguese rebels to resist him, and what Napoleon called the "Spanish ulcer" constantly diverted troops from more pressing campaigns.

In 1812, winter undid his attempt to invade Russia, a failure that, combined with defeat in the Peninsular War in 1814, precipitated his fall and exile. In 1815, however, he returned and raised another army. This marked the so-called Hundred Days of the Napoleonic Wars—the period between Napoleon's return and his defeat at Waterloo.

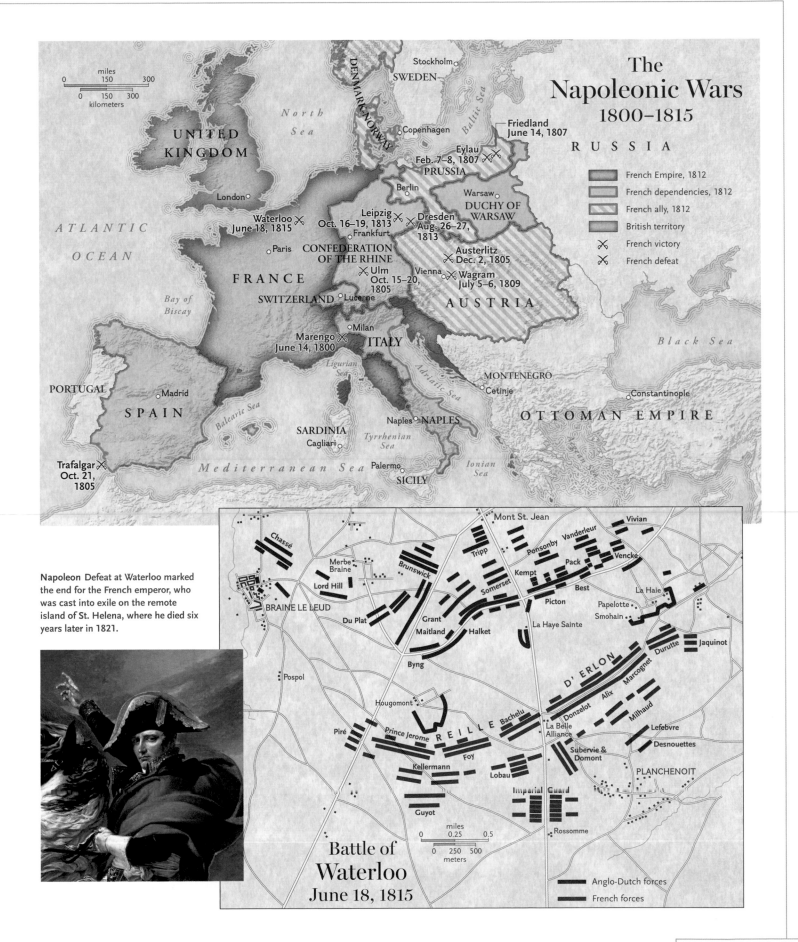

The Napoleonic Wars
1800–1815

French Empire, 1812
French dependencies, 1812
French ally, 1812
British territory
✕ French victory
✕ French defeat

UNITED KINGDOM

ATLANTIC OCEAN

North Sea

DENMARK-NORWAY

SWEDEN

Stockholm

Copenhagen

Baltic Sea

RUSSIA

Eylau
Feb. 7–8, 1807

Friedland
June 14, 1807

PRUSSIA

Berlin

Warsaw

DUCHY OF WARSAW

London

Waterloo
June 18, 1815

Leipzig
Oct. 16–19, 1813

Dresden
Aug. 26–27, 1813

Frankfurt

Paris

CONFEDERATION OF THE RHINE

Austerlitz
Dec. 2, 1805

Ulm
Oct. 15–20, 1805

FRANCE

Vienna

SWITZERLAND

Lucerne

Wagram
July 5–6, 1809

AUSTRIA

Bay of Biscay

Milan

Marengo
June 14, 1800

ITALY

Ligurian Sea

Adriatic Sea

Black Sea

MONTENEGRO

Cetinje

Constantinople

PORTUGAL

Madrid

SPAIN

Balearic Sea

SARDINIA

Cagliari

Tyrrhenian Sea

Naples NAPLES

OTTOMAN EMPIRE

Trafalgar
Oct. 21, 1805

Mediterranean Sea

Palermo

SICILY

Ionian Sea

Napoleon Defeat at Waterloo marked the end for the French emperor, who was cast into exile on the remote island of St. Helena, where he died six years later in 1821.

Battle of Waterloo
June 18, 1815

Mont St. Jean

Chassé
Merbe Braine
Brunswick
Tripp
Vivian
Vanderleur
Ponsonby
Pack
Vencke
Lord Hill
Somerset
Kempt
Best
La Haie
BRAINE LE LEUD
Picton
Papelotte
Smohain
Du Plat
Grant
Maitland
Halket
La Haye Sainte
Byng
D' ERLON
Durutte
Jaquinot
Pospol
Marcognet
Alix
Hougomont
Milhaud
Piré
Prince Jerome
REILLE
Bachelu
Donzelot
La Belle Alliance
Lefebvre
Desnouettes
Foy
Lobau
Subervie & Domont
PLANCHENOIT
Kellermann
Imperial Guard
Guyot
Rossomme

Anglo-Dutch forces
French forces

THE AGE OF EMPIRE
1815–1914

"*We seem, as it were, to have conquered and peopled half the world in a fit of absence of mind.*"

SIR JOHN ROBERT SEELEY, 1883

Britain's Empire

1815–1901

- British territory, 1815
- British territory, 1901
- British territory lost between 1815 and 1901
- Belgian territory, 1901
- Dutch territory, 1901
- French territory, 1901
- German territory, 1901
- Italian territory, 1901
- Portuguese territory, 1901
- Spanish territory, 1901

Tonga

Ellice Islands (Tuvalu)

Fiji

New Zealand

Norfolk Island

Cook Islands

Gilbert Islands

Tasmania

PACIFIC OCEAN

Solomon Islands

Australia

AUSTRALIA

Line Islands

Papua

Pitcairn Islands

North Borneo

Cocos Islands

Brunei

Fort York

Hong Kong

Singapore

Malaya   Malacca

Weihaiwei

Penang

NORTH AMERICA

Canada

ASIA

Nicobar Islands

Andaman Islands

British Honduras

India

Cayman Islands

Jamaica

Bahamas

Ceylon (Sri Lanka)

Newfoundland

Turks and Caicos Is.

Bermuda

UNITED KINGDOM

Laccadive Islands

Virgin Islands

Heligoland

Qatar

Maldive Islands

Leeward Islands

Cyprus

Kuwait

Oman

Windward Islands

Dominica

Ionian Islands

Trucial States

INDIAN

Trinidad   Barbados

Malta

Hadramaut

OCEAN

Tobago

Gibraltar

Egypt

Aden

Chagos Islands

British Guiana

ATLANTIC

British Somaliland

SOUTH AMERICA

OCEAN

Anglo-Egyptian Sudan

Seychelles

British East Africa

Mauritius

Bathurst   Gambia

AFRICA

Zanzibar

Uganda

Sierra Leone

Nyasaland

Nigeria

Rhodesia

Transvaal

Gold Coast

Natal

Falkland Islands

Accra

Bechuanaland

Basutoland

Ascension Island

Cape Colony

South Georgia

Walvis Bay

Tristan da Cunha

St. Helena

Gough Island

BRITAIN AT THE PEAK OF ITS POWER

BRITAIN EMERGED VICTORIOUS FROM THE NAPOLEONIC WARS IN 1815. BUT THE NATION HAD paid a high price, and it suffered a painful transition to a peacetime economy. Munitions factories closed, some 200,000 demobilized soldiers and sailors flooded the labor market, and a series of poor harvests led to increased food prices. Protectionist measures made matters worse, notably the Importation Act, or Corn Laws, of 1815, which imposed tariffs on imports of foreign wheat to help bolster prices for British producers. The cost of bread increased, compounding economic and social unrest elsewhere—notably the Luddite riots in northern England, in which skilled workers smashed new factory machinery that they blamed for lower wages and unemployment.

Worse followed. In 1819, some 60,000 men, women, and children gathered for a demonstration in St. Peter's Fields in Manchester. The city's magistrates panicked and ordered troops to charge the throng. In the chaos that ensued, 11 or more demonstrators were killed and more than 400 injured. The event caused outrage and was dubbed the Peterloo Massacre, an ironic reference to the recent victory at Waterloo.

As with the Luddite disturbances, the government's reaction was repressive. Memories of the French Revolution (1789) were fresh, and fear of similar events in Britain ran high. The prime minister, Robert Banks Jenkinson, Earl of Liverpool—a man so conservative it is said he would have opposed creation to preserve chaos—passed six acts restricting freedom of speech, expression, and assembly.

In 1820, the unpopular George IV (1762–1830) died after ten years on the throne. *The Times* wrote that there had never been "an individual less regretted by his fellow creatures than this deceased king." His chief defects, in the words of the Duke of Wellington, were those caused by "Strong liquors taken too frequently and in too large quantities."

As well as being a drunk, George was a conservative. Although kings in his time exercised less power than did monarchs in previous centuries, they were still a constitutional consideration. George's death, and the accession of his brother, the more amenable William IV (1765–1837), removed one of the obstacles to change. With fear of revolution ran an understanding that it might be averted via reform. Nowhere was reform more needed than in Parliament, where seats in the lower house no longer reflected the enormous demographic changes wrought by the industrial revolution. Qualifications for those eligible to vote were haphazard, and they varied across the nation; voting procedures in many areas were also corrupt.

New power *(previous pages)* A view of Stockport in northwest England, in a scene painted around 1845. Early textile mills, such as those illustrated, relied on water, but during the 19th century, steam power revolutionized Britain's mines and factories. After 1830, steam also led to the rapid growth of railroads. Britain's position as the world's first industrialized nation accounted for much of the country's wealth during the Victorian age.

TIME LINE

1819
The Peterloo Massacre

1830
George IV dies; his brother,
William IV, succeeds him

1830
Britain's first time-tabled railroad runs
between Liverpool and Manchester

1832
The Great Reform Act

1837
William IV dies; Victoria is named queen

1839–1842
First Opium War; Britain secures
the island of Hong Kong

1845–1851
Famine in Ireland

1853–1856
The Crimean War

1854
The Charge of the Light Brigade

1857–1858
Indian troops of the British East India
Company revolt

1858
The Raj: British rule replaces
East India Company's control of India

1859
Darwin publishes theory of evolution in
On the Origin of Species

1880–1881
First Boer War

1899–1902
Second Boer War

1901
Queen Victoria dies; her son Edward VII
assumes throne

1904
Entente Cordiale: Britain allies
with France in treaty

1907
Britain enters into treaty with Russia,
forming Triple Entente among Russia,
Britain, and France

1912
The R.M.S. *Titanic* sinks

Landowners largely benefited from the status quo and thwarted several attempts at change before the passing of the Great Reform Act in 1832. A radical departure for the time, the act addressed certain parliamentary shortcomings and modestly increased the number of voters. More social and economic reforms followed in prisons, mines, factories, and elsewhere, some introduced by the modernizing Conservative prime minister, Sir Robert Peel (1788–1850). Further acts that extended the vote were passed in 1867 and 1884–1885, but Parliament resisted full, universal suffrage until 1928.

Elsewhere, in 1830, Britain's first railroad service opened between Liverpool and Manchester. Railroads transformed much of Britain and Ireland in the next 50 years (see pages 254–255), as did the continued and intense industrialization of areas such as South Wales, Glasgow, Belfast, and central and northern England.

In the following year, 1831, a young naturalist named Charles Darwin set sail for the southern oceans aboard the H.M.S. *Beagle* (see pages 272–273). In 1834, a group of Dorset agricultural workers, the Tolpuddle Martyrs, was threatened with a voyage of a different kind: deportation to Australia, for attempting to form a "friendly" society, or trade union. In the face of public opposition the sentence was repealed, and the event marked a stage in the slow evolution of Britain's labor movement (see pages 278–279).

■ FROM THE GEORGIAN TO THE VICTORIAN AGE

In 1837, William IV died without a direct heir. His niece, Victoria (1819–1901), the daughter of the king's younger brother, Edward, became queen. Among many other things, Victoria's 63-year reign, the longest of any British monarch to that point, saw the further expansion of Britain's empire (see pages 248–249). While she was on the throne, not a year passed in which Britain was not at war.

Colonial wars had already started in India and Burma (in 1817 and 1824), and they continued soon after Victoria's accession with rebellions in Upper and Lower Canada (after 1837); the First Opium War in China (1839); the First Anglo-Afghan War (1839); the Anglo-Sindh War of 1843 (in present-day Pakistan); the First Sikh War (1845); and the Maori Wars, or New Zealand Wars, of 1845. Many more followed.

Events closer to home turned to Ireland, where a potato blight in 1845 resulted in a famine that killed more than a million people over seven years and resulted in the emigration of perhaps two million more (see pages 262–263).

Ireland occupied a pivotal role in British politics for the next 80 years, in part because the extension of the Catholic franchise in 1829 returned a block of Irish politicians to Parliament in London. These MPs often held the balance of power between Britain's rival political parties. With their ability to influence the ruling parties came demands for Irish land reforms—land tenure having been a root cause of events in 1845—and for Irish Home Rule, or the return of Ireland's domestic governance to a parliament in Dublin.

"Remember that you are an Englishman, and have drawn first prize in the lottery of life . . . I contend that we are the first race of the world and the more of the world we inhabit the better it is for the human race."

CECIL RHODES, BRITISH BUSINESSMAN AND POLITICIAN, 1877

Even as much of Ireland suffered, Britain was approaching the height of its industrial and imperial power. Largely at the prompting of Queen Victoria's husband, Albert, the country's achievements were celebrated in the Great Exhibition of 1851. Held in London in the vast Crystal Palace, constructed of glass and iron, the event displayed 100,000 artifacts from 14,000 European and imperial exhibitors, and was attended by six million people, or almost a third of Britain's adult population.

A new life Scottish settlers in North America portrayed in a painting by Thomas Faed (1826–1900). Emigration was a feature of life in Britain and Ireland throughout the 19th century, especially among the countries' rural and urban poor.

■ THE CRIMEA AND INDIA, IRELAND AND CULTURE

Britain would have things less its own way in the remainder of the century. Many colonial wars of the period were fought against poorly equipped indigenous peoples that were no match for British economic power and superior weaponry. In the Sudan, for example, in 1898, Britain's artillery and new Maxim machine guns killed some 10,000 Sudanese fighters, while British deaths amounted to just 47.

In 1853, however, the Crimean War (1853–1856) pitched Britain and France against a more than usually powerful foe, Russia. Britain feared Russia's moves into the territories of the declining Ottoman (Turkish) Empire, in particular into areas of the Mediterranean and central Asia that threatened Britain's interests in India. The war

HOUSES OF HANOVER AND SAXE-COBURG-GOTHA
1815-1914

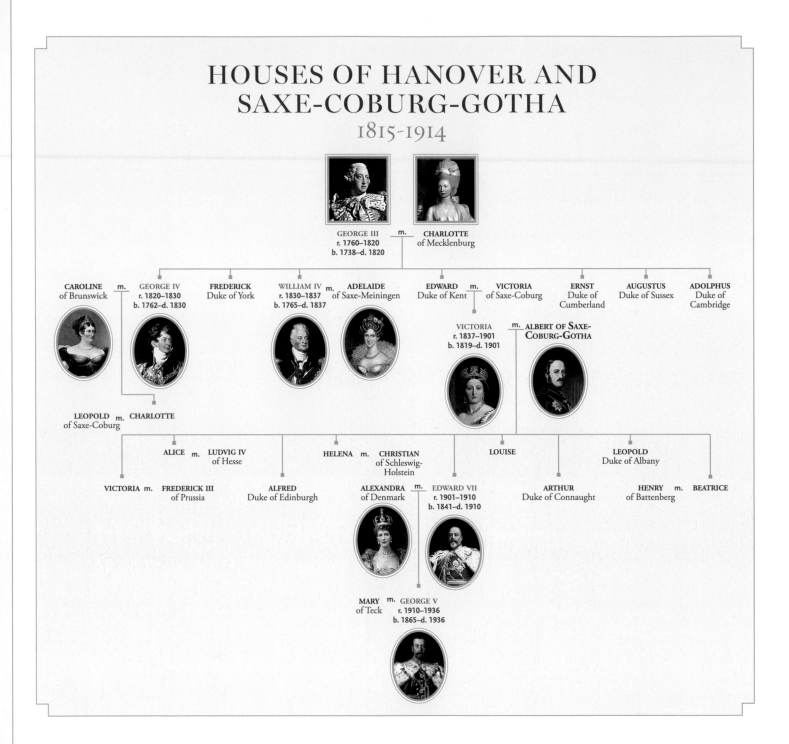

GEORGE III
r. 1760–1820
b. 1738–d. 1820
m. **CHARLOTTE**
of Mecklenburg

CAROLINE
of Brunswick
m.
GEORGE IV
r. 1820–1830
b. 1762–d. 1830

FREDERICK
Duke of York

WILLIAM IV
r. 1830–1837
b. 1765–d. 1837
m.
ADELAIDE
of Saxe-Meiningen

EDWARD
Duke of Kent
m.
VICTORIA
of Saxe-Coburg

ERNST
Duke of
Cumberland

AUGUSTUS
Duke of Sussex

ADOLPHUS
Duke of
Cambridge

VICTORIA
r. 1837–1901
b. 1819–d. 1901
m.
ALBERT OF SAXE-COBURG-GOTHA

LEOPOLD
of Saxe-Coburg
m.
CHARLOTTE

ALICE
m.
LUDVIG IV
of Hesse

HELENA
m.
CHRISTIAN
of Schleswig-
Holstein

LOUISE

LEOPOLD
Duke of Albany

VICTORIA
m.
FREDERICK III
of Prussia

ALFRED
Duke of Edinburgh

ALEXANDRA
of Denmark
m.
EDWARD VII
r. 1901–1910
b. 1841–d. 1910

ARTHUR
Duke of Connaught

HENRY
of Battenberg
m.
BEATRICE

MARY
of Teck
m.
GEORGE V
r. 1910–1936
b. 1865–d. 1936

played out largely around the Black Sea, and though Britain eventually triumphed, the battles of attrition and stalemate between larger and more modern armies foreshadowed greater wars to come.

The Crimean War is also known for the Charge of the Light Brigade (1854), when incompetence led to the needless slaughter of 300 British cavalrymen as they rode headlong into a battery of Russian guns. It is also remembered for the nursing pioneer Florence Nightingale (1820–1910), known as the "Lady with the Lamp" due to her nocturnal habit of walking the Turkish field hospital wards she helped reorganize.

"Those were . . . the days when it was glorious to be an English boy . . . You had God always behind you. You owned half the globe; you were foremost in every manly pursuit; you were clean, sober, honest; you hated injustice . . . you righted wrongs, succoured the oppressed . . . you could stand against . . . a whole foreign army."

FORD MADOX FORD, *RETURN TO YESTERDAY*, 1932

Just a year after the war's end, in 1857, Indian forces from one of the East India Company's armies in India mutinied, precipitating Britain's worst colonial crisis since the loss of the 13 American Colonies. This uprising had numerous social, economic, and religious causes (see pages 266–267), and though it was suppressed, the atrocities committed by both sides compromised Anglo-Indian relations for generations. In 1858, direct administration of India from London, known as the Raj, replaced the East India Company's rule.

At home, two prime ministers, William Gladstone (1809–1898) and Benjamin Disraeli (1804–1881), dominated domestic politics in the last third of the 19th century. They came from different parties—Whig (later Liberal) and Conservative respectively—and were men of different and complex character: Gladstone, august, high-minded, and moral; Disraeli, populist, charming, and cynical.

Bustling station An archival image shows Broad Street Railway Station (ca 1890) in London, then the world's largest city. The station opened in 1865 and was a major terminal in the city. It closed in 1986 after years of dwindling use.

Gladstone served as prime minister four times between 1868 and 1894, and he became especially associated with attempts to secure Home Rule for Ireland. Disraeli, too, was a reformer; both men understood that the times and an expanding electorate demanded progressive change. The period saw numerous improvements and reforms in education, public housing, health, factories, the civil service, the army, and the franchise. Poverty remained rife, however, especially in the cities, and was a factor in the mass emigration that characterized much of the 19th century (see pages 264–265).

There were also small political advances for Britain's labor movement, with the emergence of stronger unions after 1850 and the formation of the Scottish Labour Party in 1888 and the Independent Labour Party in Britain in 1893. Culture blossomed, too, especially among Britain's poets and novelists; the 19th century yielded some of the greatest names in the English literary canon (see pages 276–277).

In the arts, historic revivals marked a reaction against industrialization and what many saw as the materialism of Victorian culture. Neo-Gothic architecture,

for example, enjoyed considerable popularity; it was seen to most famous effect in London's Houses of Parliament, rebuilt after a fire in 1834. The Pre-Raphaelite group of painters, founded in 1848, sought refuge from the academic art of the day in a return to medievalism, while the Arts and Crafts movement under William Morris (1834–1896) championed the handmade over the mass-produced.

Second place *(above)* A British expedition led by Robert Falcon Scott in 1912 finds a tent belonging to a Norwegian expedition at the South Pole. Scott's entire team died during the return trek from the pole.

Royal portrait *(opposite)* Queen Victoria in 1859 at age 40. She would reign for 63 years.

■ GERMANY AND THE EDWARDIAN AGE

On the wider stage, Britain's domination of world affairs was increasingly challenged. By about 1870, the United States was close to domestic economic parity, and in Europe the rising industrial and imperial strength of Germany, a country forged from disparate states and kingdoms in the 1860s, threatened the continental and wider balance of power.

For all its many wars, Britain's late 19th-century foreign policy centered on a notion of "splendid isolation." In Europe, the approach had largely worked, and Britain's

"Men make the moral code and they expect women to accept it. They have decided that it is entirely right and proper for men to fight for their liberties and their rights, but that it is not right and proper for women to fight for theirs."

SUFFRAGETTE LEADER EMMELINE PANKHURST, *MY OWN STORY*, 1914

armies remained aloof from the French and other campaigns that had embroiled them in previous centuries. However, the rise of Germany, and especially its navy, made this approach increasingly untenable.   .

Anglo-German rivalry in Europe would come later: In the 1880s and beyond, it was played out largely in Africa, one of the last areas of the world in which European empires could be established. The continent had already attracted adventurers and missionaries, notably David Livingstone (1813–1873), one of many British explorers of the period (see pages 268–271). In the late 19th century, armies followed the explorers, as Germany, together with France, Italy, and Belgium, assimilated territories across the region. New German colonies in East Africa—present-day Tanzania, Rwanda, and beyond—were particular threats to British interests, but in 1899 Britain was distracted by events farther south, in a war that had more traditional colonial roots.

The Boers were descendants of Dutch settlers in the Cape Colony of southern Africa, which had passed to Britain formally in 1814. Having left the Cape and created their own colonies to the north, the Boers were forced to defend their new lands when the discovery of gold and diamonds in their homelands provided added imperial incentive to ambitious British politicians and businessmen.

The war, when it came, did not go well (see pages 280–281). The guerrilla tactics of the Boers highlighted British military shortcomings, and newspapers brought these and other controversial aspects of the conflict directly to an increasingly disenchanted British public. Most controversial of all was Britain's use of "concentration camps"—a term employed at the time—to imprison Boer women and children. Many thousands died, leading to widespread condemnation of the camps.

Britain prevailed in the war but was chastened by the international isolation it caused and by covert German support for the Boers. This isolation and other factors accounted for the Entente Cordiale, a treaty with France in 1904. A treaty with Russia followed in 1907, cementing the Triple Entente (Russia had concluded its own treaty with France in 1894). Germany, for its part, already had a treaty with

Charles Dickens The novels of Dickens (1812–1870) were among the most popular of the 19th century, a golden age for literature and the arts.

Rising tide Unemployed men marching in London. Nineteenth-century British governments remained largely fearful of the working class, which formed increasingly powerful unions but lacked a real political voice until after World War I.

Austria-Hungary (signed in 1879), and, fearful of Russian expansion, was also wooing the Ottoman (Turkish) Empire.

With Queen Victoria's death in 1901, Britain had entered the Edwardian age, named after Victoria's son and heir, Edward VII (1841–1910). It was a time of greater military expenditure, especially on the Royal Navy, a reaction to Germany's own increased spending. It was also a period in which the dissent and reform programs of the previous half century intensified. The labor movement grew in power, if not yet substantial political representation, and governments grappled with welfare and other social reforms.

The sinking of the R.M.S. *Titanic* in 1912 gripped the nation (see pages 282–283), a temporary distraction from the campaign for woman suffrage; from labor unrest on an increased scale; and from a sense that the long-running Irish Question was approaching a bloody denouement. Ireland, votes for women, and all other domestic affairs were put on hold after June 1914, however, with the assassination in Sarajevo of Archduke Franz Ferdinand, heir to the Austro-Hungarian Empire. ■

THE BRITISH EMPIRE
Colonial Power and a Century of War

In 1814 Britain was already the world's leading colonial power. Two centuries earlier, it had secured a succession of small but valuable colonies in the Caribbean. In the 18th century, it had lost its American possessions but gained territories in Canada, Australia, India, and elsewhere. After 1814, its empire grew even larger, so that by 1922 Britain ruled more than 450 million people—about a fifth of the world's population—and almost a quarter of Earth's total land area.

The reasons for this imperial success were the same as in previous centuries. Britain had a powerful navy, which with the advent and increased reach of steamships became even more powerful. Britain was wealthy and, with the advantages bestowed by the Industrial Revolution, became wealthier still. Britain was also at the forefront of technological change and, with the invention of the telegraph, among other things, acquired a system that could be used to administer its far-flung territories.

How empire happened is easier to explain than why, for Britain rarely pursued territory for its own sake. Rather, its empire often developed almost by accident, as part of an ad hoc process usually designed to protect existing trade interests. Frontiers were consolidated, buffer zones created, and rivals—such as they were—fought off.

One of the earliest conflicts inspired by trade came in Asia (see opposite), precipitated in China by Britain's trading machine par excellence, the East India Company (see page 164). Elsewhere in Asia, Britain also secured Singapore (1819), Malacca (1824), and Burma (1824–1826), often to forestall the Dutch, and, in the case of Burma, as part of a wider campaign to safeguard India from Russia and China.

Britain's conflicts with Russia became known as the Great Game, part of the attempts by both powers to fill the vacuum left by the declining Ottoman (Turkish) and Qajar (Persian) Empires. Among Britain's fears was that Russia had designs on India. Partly to create a buffer against invasion from the north, Britain attempted to subdue Afghanistan in the First

Born to serve British soldiers were involved in countless colonial wars during the 19th century. Sir John Carstairs McNeill, pictured here, fought in the Waikato War in New Zealand between 1863 and 1864.

Anglo-Afghan War (1839–1842), with disastrous results. Further disaster threatened in India itself in 1857, when a mutiny among Indian troops under British control led to some of the bloodiest events in Britain's colonial history (see pages 266–267).

Russia appeared elsewhere in 1853, when its incursions into the Balkans threatened British interests in the Mediterranean and the Middle East. In response Britain fought and checked Russia in the Crimean War (1853–1856), though discord between the countries simmered until treaties of 1878 and 1907.

By this period, however, British attention had turned elsewhere. Colonial progress in many of Britain's so-called white dominions—European-dominated Canada, Australia, and New Zealand—had been relatively smooth. The discovery of gold gave a new impetus to settlement in Australia, and wars and treaties had quelled New Zealand's indigenous Maori population.

In Africa, though, it was a different story. By the 1890s, countries such as France, Belgium, and above all Germany were beginning to match Britain's industrial might. They soon sought empires of their own, and Africa was the last continent that offered substantial opportunities for imperial gain.

Britain already had a toehold in West Africa, where Nigeria, the Gold Coast (Ghana), and Sierra Leone were in part a legacy of the slave-trading era. It also had a presence in the Cape Colony in the south, where confrontation with the Boer descendants of the original Dutch colonists would lead to the Boer Wars of 1881 and 1899–1902 (see pages 280–281). In the north, Britain had effective control of Egypt and had secured Sudan and Somaliland to the south, largely to secure routes to India. After 1880, Britain felt forced to act in the east and took Uganda (1894) and British East Africa (1895)—present-day Kenya—to forestall Germany, which had established colonies in what are now Tanzania, Rwanda, and Burundi.

Europe's so-called Scramble for Africa, and the rise of competing industrial powers, presaged a far more direct and bloody confrontation barely a generation later, in the events of 1914–1918. ∎

Drug war *(above)* Opium ships in China. Although China banned trade in opium in China, Britain still used the drug to pay for Chinese tea, silks, and spices. China's confiscation of 20,000 chests of the drug in 1839 compounded other trading and diplomatic disputes that led to the First Opium War (1839–1842). The British won swiftly and, in the treaty that followed *(right)*, secured rights to the then little known island of Hong Kong.

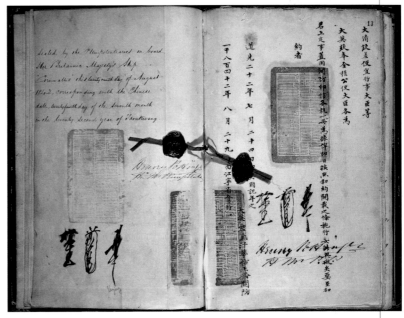

"Take up the White Man's burden, Send forth the best ye breed / Go bind your sons to exile, to serve your captives' need . . . And reap his old reward: The blame of those ye better, The hate of those ye guard."

RUDYARD KIPLING, "THE WHITE MAN'S BURDEN," 1899

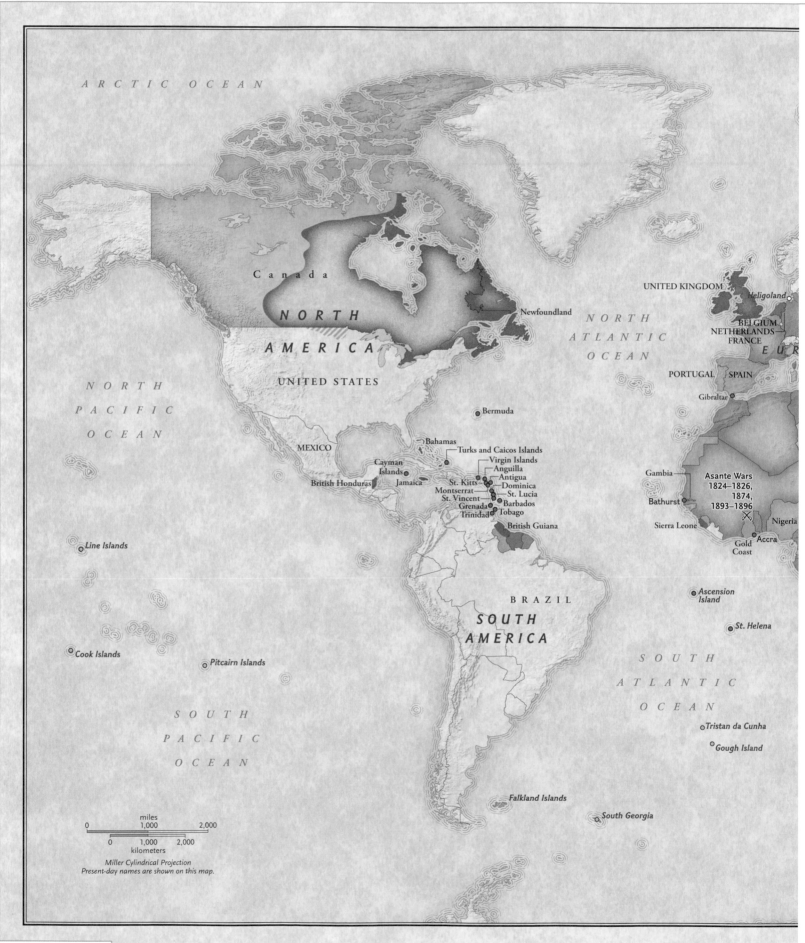

ARCTIC OCEAN

Canada

NORTH

AMERICA

UNITED STATES

Newfoundland

NORTH
ATLANTIC
OCEAN

UNITED KINGDOM

Heligoland

BELGIUM
NETHERLANDS
FRANCE

EUR

PORTUGAL   SPAIN

Gibraltar

NORTH

PACIFIC

OCEAN

Bermuda

MEXICO

Bahamas

Turks and Caicos Islands

Virgin Islands

Cayman
Islands

Anguilla

Antigua

St. Kitts

Dominica

British Honduras

Jamaica

Montserrat

St. Lucia

St. Vincent

Barbados

Grenada   Tobago

Trinidad

British Guiana

Gambia

Bathurst

Sierra Leone

Asante Wars
1824–1826,
1874,
1893–1896

Nigeria

Gold
Coast

Accra

Line Islands

BRAZIL

SOUTH
AMERICA

Ascension
Island

St. Helena

Cook Islands

Pitcairn Islands

SOUTH
ATLANTIC
OCEAN

SOUTH

PACIFIC

OCEAN

Tristan da Cunha

Gough Island

Falkland Islands

South Georgia

miles
0   1,000   2,000

0   1,000   2,000
kilometers

Miller Cylindrical Projection
Present-day names are shown on this map.

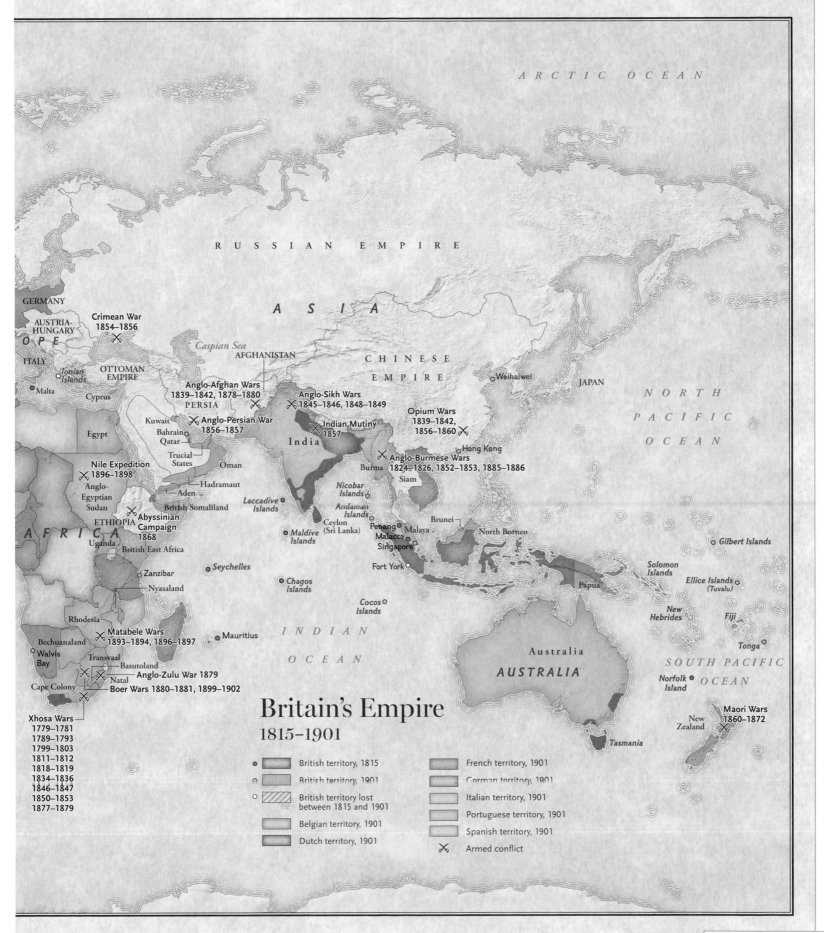

ARCTIC OCEAN

RUSSIAN EMPIRE

A S I A

GERMANY

**Crimean War
1854–1856**

AUSTRIA-
HUNGARY

Caspian Sea

AFGHANISTAN

CHINESE
EMPIRE

ITALY

*Ionian
Islands*

OTTOMAN
EMPIRE

○ *Malta*

Cyprus

PERSIA

**Anglo-Afghan Wars
1839–1842, 1878–1880**

**Anglo-Sikh Wars
1845–1846, 1848–1849**

○ Weihaiwei

JAPAN

NORTH

PACIFIC

OCEAN

Kuwait

Egypt

Bahrain
Qatar

**Anglo-Persian War
1856–1857**

India

**Indian Mutiny
1857**

**Opium Wars
1839–1842,
1856–1860**

○ Hong Kong

**Nile Expedition
1896–1898**

Anglo-
Egyptian
Sudan

Trucial
States

Oman

Burma

**Anglo-Burmese Wars
1824–1826, 1852–1853, 1885–1886**

Siam

Hadramaut

Aden

British Somaliland

*Laccadive
Islands*

*Nicobar
Islands*

ETHIOPIA

**Abyssinian
Campaign
1868**

*Maldive
Islands*

Ceylon
(Sri Lanka)

*Andaman
Islands*

Brunei

A F R I C A

Uganda

British East Africa

○ Zanzibar

Seychelles

Penang
Malacca
Singapore

Malaya

North Borneo

Gilbert Islands

Nyasaland

*Chagos
Islands*

Fort York

*Solomon
Islands*

Rhodesia

**Matabele Wars
1893–1894, 1896–1897**

○ *Mauritius*

*Cocos
Islands*

Papua

*Ellice Islands
(Tuvalu)*

Bechuanaland

○ Walvis
Bay

Transvaal

Basutoland

I N D I A N

*New
Hebrides*

Fiji

Anglo-Zulu War 1879

Natal

OCEAN

Australia

AUSTRALIA

SOUTH PACIFIC

Tonga

Cape Colony

Boer Wars 1880–1881, 1899–1902

**Xhosa Wars
1779–1781
1789–1793
1799–1803
1811–1812
1818–1819
1834–1836
1846–1847
1850–1853
1877–1879**

*Norfolk
Island*

OCEAN

**Maori Wars
1860–1872**

New
Zealand

Tasmania

Britain's Empire
1815–1901

●	British territory, 1815	French territory, 1901
◖	British territory, 1901	German territory, 1901
○	British territory lost between 1815 and 1901	Italian territory, 1901
	Belgian territory, 1901	Portuguese territory, 1901
	Dutch territory, 1901	Spanish territory, 1901
		✕ Armed conflict

INDUSTRIAL REVOLUTION

Britain Becomes the Workshop of the World

Britain's wealth in the 19th century was based on the country's empire, which provided raw materials and markets for its goods, and on its status as the world's first—and, for decades, only—mature industrialized nation. Until around 1870, when the United States caught up, the result was a remarkable near monopoly in countless areas of commerce and manufacture.

The country's industrial transformation began in the 18th century with improvements in technology and transport, and with the advent of mechanization and steam power. It continued along similar lines in the Victorian age, but on a larger scale and with a more furious rate of expansion. The growth of railroads, in particular, was vital (see pages 254–255), but stable government and the emergence of financial institutions able to marshal capital and investment were also vital.

Textile production led the way, as it had in the 18th century, especially in the booming cities of northern England (by 1830 cotton goods accounted for more than half of all British exports by value). But other industries soon caught up—pottery in Staffordshire, for example; shipbuilding in Glasgow, Belfast, and Newcastle; and toys, buttons, munitions, and more in Birmingham. As a result, Britain at its peak produced around 40 percent of the world's manufactured goods and accounted for two-thirds of its coal, half its iron, and three-quarters of its steel and ships.

Towns, ports, and cities expanded as industrialization took hold. For example, the population of Bradford, a textile center in England's northern industrial heartland, grew from 16,000 in 1800 to 182,000 by 1850. London became the world's first modern city with more than a million inhabitants, and the population of England and Wales almost doubled to 32,526,000 in the years 1850 to 1900. Scotland's population rose 70 percent in the same period. Only in Ireland, where poverty was more acute and industrialization more sporadic, did the population falter.

Such rapid growth brought intense poverty and squalor for many, and though some of the period's worst iniquities were not addressed until later in the 19th century—notably child labor, horrible housing, and unjust working hours and conditions—the rise of social radicalism, religious revivalism, and the birth of the labor movement (see pages 278–279) had their roots in the era's teeming slums and factories. At the same time, the period also saw the widespread introduction of gas, water, lighting, and sewers and transit, telegraph, and telephone networks, along with the creation of schools, museums, universities, public libraries, and other modern civic institutions. ∎

Power of progress A steam hammer, invented in 1832 by James Nasmyth (1808–1890) and pictured in his foundry near Manchester in 1842. Steam power and numerous other technological advances helped fuel the rapid pace of Britain's industrial revolution in the 19th century.

"Earth and air seem impregnated with fog and soot . . . factories . . . one after another . . . like economical and colossal prisons, thousands of workmen . . . masses of livid children, dirty and flabby of flesh."

HIPPOLYTE TAINE ON MANCHESTER, 1859

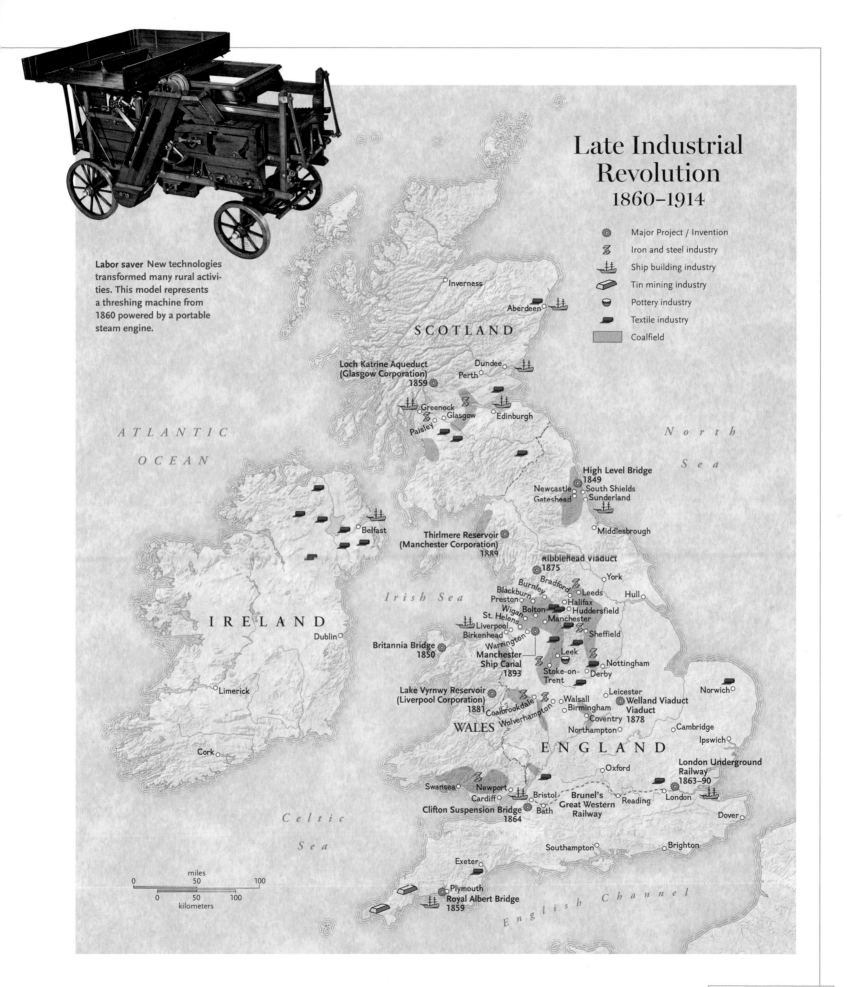

Late Industrial Revolution
1860–1914

Labor saver New technologies transformed many rural activities. This model represents a threshing machine from 1860 powered by a portable steam engine.

Legend:
- Major Project / Invention
- Iron and steel industry
- Ship building industry
- Tin mining industry
- Pottery industry
- Textile industry
- Coalfield

SCOTLAND

ATLANTIC OCEAN

North Sea

Inverness

Aberdeen

Loch Katrine Aqueduct (Glasgow Corporation) 1859

Dundee
Perth

Greenock
Glasgow
Paisley
Edinburgh

High Level Bridge 1849

Newcastle
South Shields
Gateshead
Sunderland

Middlesbrough

Thirlmere Reservoir (Manchester Corporation) 1889

Ribblehead Viaduct 1875

Bradford
Burnley
Blackburn
Preston
Wigan
Bolton
St. Helens
Liverpool
Birkenhead
Warrington

Leeds
York
Hull
Halifax
Huddersfield
Manchester
Sheffield

Belfast

IRELAND

Dublin

Irish Sea

Britannia Bridge 1850

Manchester Ship Canal 1893

Leek
Nottingham
Stoke-on-Trent
Derby

Limerick

Lake Vyrnwy Reservoir (Liverpool Corporation) 1881

Coalbrookdale

Walsall
Birmingham
Coventry

Leicester
Welland Viaduct 1878

Norwich

WALES
Wolverhampton
Northampton
Cambridge
Ipswich

ENGLAND

Cork

Swansea
Newport
Cardiff
Bristol
Bath

Oxford
Reading

London Underground Railway 1863–90

London

Brunel's Great Western Railway

Clifton Suspension Bridge 1864

Dover

Celtic Sea

Southampton
Brighton

Exeter

miles
0 50 100

kilometers
0 50 100

Plymouth
Royal Albert Bridge 1859

English Channel

THE RAILROAD AGE

Britain Transformed by Steam and Speed

Tracked transport in Britain was nothing new: Wooden and later iron rails had been used with horse-drawn wagons in mining areas since the Tudor period. But after the experiments with steam engines by Watt, Boulton, and Newcomen in the 18th century, it was a short step to powered locomotion and the creation of a railroad network that would transform Britain and Ireland.

The first journey by steam took place in 1804, courtesy of a Cornish mining engineer, Richard Trevithick *(below).* The first steam service to carry passengers appeared in 1825, on a line in northeast England between Stockton and Darlington. Its first engine was *Locomotion No. 1,* built by George Stephenson (1781–1848), who in 1830 created the world's first time-tabled passenger line from Manchester to Liverpool. Stephenson also designed the line's most famous locomotive, *Rocket,* whose top speed of around 30 miles an hour was remarkable at a time when the greatest distance that might be covered in a day (on a galloping horse) was around 80 miles.

The revolutionary nature of the first railroads, not to mention the vast profits they generated, fired the public imagination. Within a decade, Britain was gripped by what became known as Railway Mania. Two intense speculative bursts, in 1836 to 1837 and 1844 to 1847, coupled with a less frenzied expansion of the network to the end of the century, transformed the British landscape (and ruined and enriched investors large and small in the process).

By 1845, 2,441 miles of railroads, whose trains carried 30 million passengers a year, were in operation. By 1900, the figures were 18,680 miles of track and 1.1 billion passengers. More important, and (after about 1852) more profitable than the passengers, was the carriage of freight, and of bulk raw materials in particular, a vital factor in the nation's booming economy. British engineering expertise, along with the men and materials to build railroads, was exported worldwide.

Once companies had obtained a government charter to build (272 were granted in 1846 alone), the early development and running of the railroads was virtually unregulated. The result was that rival companies duplicated many routes (one reason London has a dozen major termini) and built innumerable tiny and ultimately uneconomic rural branch lines. Many of these closed in time—some not until the 1960s—and consolidation eventually reduced the number of companies. The effects on Britain's economy, however, and the changes railroads wrought in the working and recreational lives of people, remained some of the most profound in the country's history. ■

Over and under Railroad construction in London in 1837. After 1860, the difficulty of obtaining land in the center of the capital forced companies to build underground.

Railroads and Time

One of the railroads' most remarkable impacts was their effect on timekeeping. Hitherto, Britain had no standard point of reference for its clocks, and time varied across the country by as much as 20 minutes. After 1840, the adoption of "Railway" or "London" time meant that Britain marched in step for the first time in its history. The invention of the telegraph in 1837 and its diffusion across the rail network—vital in many other respects—allowed the correct time to be relayed from station to station. *(Left)* Richard Trevithick (1771–1833) was first to use high-pressure steam to drive an engine.

Railroads
built by 1840

—— Railroad built by 1840

SCOTLAND

ATLANTIC
OCEAN

North
Sea

Glasgow   Edinburgh

Newcastle

Belfast

Irish Sea

IRELAND
Dublin

Manchester

Birmingham

WALES   ENGLAND

Celtic
Sea

Cardiff   London

English Channel

miles
0   50   100

0   50   100
kilometers

FRANCE

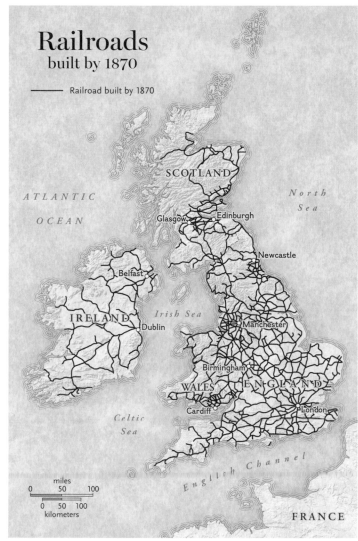

Railroads
built by 1870

—— Railroad built by 1870

SCOTLAND

ATLANTIC
OCEAN

North
Sea

Glasgow   Edinburgh

Newcastle

Belfast

Irish Sea

IRELAND
Dublin

Manchester

Birmingham

WALES   ENGLAND

Celtic
Sea

Cardiff   London

English Channel

miles
0   50   100

0   50   100
kilometers

FRANCE

Coast to coast *(above)* Railroads spread quickly across much of the British Isles after the creation of the first lines in 1825 and 1830. The locomotive *Rob Roy (left)*, photographed in 1873, belonged to the Midland Great Western Railway, Ireland's third-largest railroad company.

ISAMBARD KINGDOM BRUNEL

Man of Vision and Engineering Genius

In 2002, Britain's state broadcasting organization, the BBC, conducted an online poll in an attempt to determine the 100 Greatest Britons of all time. Some of the results were controversial, but there were few complaints about the eventual winner, the nation's wartime leader, Sir Winston Churchill, or about the man who came second, engineer Isambard Kingdom Brunel (1806–1859).

Brunel was the son of an Englishwoman, Sophia Kingdom, and a Frenchman, Sir Marc Isambard Brunel, an engineer who fled the French Revolution in 1799 to live in England. After a higher education in France, young Brunel returned to England in 1822. Three years later, he assisted his father on the Thames Tunnel (1825–1843), the world's first foot and rail tunnel under a navigable river. A feature of London's docklands, it remains part of the capital's rail network to this day.

Several men died on the project, and Brunel himself was badly injured in 1828 when part of the roof collapsed. During his six-month recuperation, he drew up several plans for a bridge across the Avon Gorge near Bristol, in southwest England. The plan that succeeded resulted in the Clifton Suspension Bridge (1831–1864), the longest spanned bridge in the world on its completion. Like the Thames Tunnel, it is still in use.

Soon afterward, Brunel became involved in his most ambitious venture, the construction of a railroad from London to Bristol. As ever, he was meticulous in his planning. Riding on horseback along the 110 miles of the route, he plotted a line with the gentlest curves and the shallowest gradients. At one point, at Box, near Swindon, he planned a railroad tunnel that at 1.83 miles was the world's longest when it opened in 1841. When the two teams digging the shaft from each end met in the middle, they were a mere inch and a quarter out of alignment.

Brunel's Great Western Railway opened to Bristol in 1841, the engineer having also designed many of its stations, including its London terminus at Paddington. A year later the line welcomed Queen Victoria, whose short journey from Slough (near Windsor Castle) to London on June 13 represented the first rail journey by a reigning monarch.

Brunel envisioned that passengers on his railroad would be able to buy a single ticket between London and New York. To this end, he built the first of three great vessels, the S.S. *Great Western,* launched in 1837. A wooden paddle-powered steamer, it was the first passenger steamship to run a regular transatlantic service (and the world's longest vessel, at 236 feet). The journey took about 15 days—half the time of the fastest sailing ship.

In 1843, Brunel launched an even larger ship, the 322-foot S.S. *Great Britain,* the world's first large iron-hulled, steam-powered, and screw propeller–driven vessel. Not everything Brunel touched turned to gold, however, and his third ship, the immense S.S. *Great Eastern,* launched in 1858, proved a commercial failure. But as Brunel's friend and colleague, Daniel Gooch, remarked on Brunel's death a year later, "great things are not done by those who count the cost of every thought and act." ■

Miracles of the age *(left)* When it opened in 1864, the Clifton Suspension Bridge over the Avon Gorge, Bristol, in southwest England, had the longest span of any bridge in the world. It was one of the earliest engineering masterpieces of Isambard Kingdom Brunel, pictured opposite in front of chains used during the 1858 launch of his ship the S.S. *Great Eastern.*

QUEEN VICTORIA

Embodiment of Empire, the Symbol of an Age

Queen Victoria (1819–1901) ruled Britain for 63 years. By the end of her reign, the country had been transformed in countless ways, not the least in the manner in which it was governed, the limited role of an aristocratic elite at her accession 1837 having given way to a recognizable democracy in which the monarchy played the mostly ceremonial role it performs today.

Victoria the person is often confused with the age she embodied—one supposedly hidebound by prudishness, for example, or constrained by social convention—but the queen's character was more complicated than her public image suggested. Like an earlier queen, Elizabeth I, she endured a difficult upbringing following the early death of a parent—in this case her father, Edward, the fourth son of George III. She spent much of her childhood in thrall to her German mother, with little more than a dour Teutonic governess and a collection of 132 dolls for company.

Groomed for the throne from a young age ("I will be good," she was reported to have said on hearing the news), she responded to her coronation in 1837, at age 19, with a dignity and self-composure that immediately endeared her to her subjects. Despite, or because of, her small stature—she was around five feet tall—she was forthright and assertive. She was also clever without being intellectual; warm but quick-tempered; and perfectly capable of passion, something that became evident when she met her first cousin, Albert of Saxe-Coburg-Gotha, a minor German prince and her future husband (see sidebar).

Alfred's unexpected death in 1861 was a turning point in Victoria's life, and she chose to wear widow's black for the rest of her life (she also hung a portrait of Albert on his deathbed over every bed she slept in thereafter). It also caused her to withdraw from public life, a lapse that led to a dramatic fall in her popularity. Her absence was not helped by rumors of an inappropriate closeness to one of her Scottish servants, John Brown, a lock of whose hair was placed in her coffin.

She returned to the public eye in the mid-1870s, largely through the careful offices of prime minister Benjamin Disraeli, one of ten premiers who came and went during her reign. Some of these were favored, such as the avuncular Lord Melbourne, who took her in hand at her accession; others, notably William Gladstone, were roundly disliked. Personal preference aside, Victoria tried to remain above party politics, much in the manner of modern British monarchs, for whom she and Albert largely established the current constitutional model of duty and discretion. To an ultimately adoring public, she remained unimpeachable, the embodiment of national greatness, feted at her Golden and Diamond Jubilees in 1887 and 1897, and mourned at her death in 1901 in a funeral of unparalleled pomp and ceremony. ■

◆ KEY DATES ◆

MAY 24, 1819 Alexandrina Victoria, the future Queen Victoria, is born in London, the daughter of Edward, fourth son of George III.

JUNE 20, 1837 Victoria succeeds her uncle, William IV, at the age of 18. She reigned for 63 years.

FEBRUARY 10, 1840 Victoria marries her first cousin, Albert, a German prince, with whom she has nine children.

DECEMBER 14, 1861 Albert dies, devastating Victoria, whose extended retreat from public life undermines support for the monarchy.

JUNE 20, 1897 Victoria's Diamond Jubilee, marking 60 years on the throne, is the occasion of national celebration. The queen dies three years later, on January 22, 1901, at age 81.

Prince Albert and Married Life

" He is perfection in every way—in beauty, in everything," wrote Victoria of her future husband, Albert *(left)*: "broad in the shoulders and a fine waist." Of her wedding night, she noted in her diary, "We did not sleep much." The two would have nine children—"nasty objects," in Victoria's view, that she only "occasionally" found "agreeable or easy." Albert, admired rather than loved by the British people, proved a cultured, serious, and conscientious consort and public servant. Victoria was devastated by his unexpected death in 1861.

Long to reign Victoria was the first British monarch to be photographed. Here, she is portrayed in the official picture taken for her Golden Jubilee in 1887 after 50 years as queen.

"I shall do my utmost to fulfil my duty towards my country; I am very young and . . . inexperienced, but I am sure that very few have more real good will and more real desire to do what is fit and right than I have."

QUEEN VICTORIA, DIARY, JUNE 20, 1837

Perfect match *(above)* A ring bearing portraits of Victoria and Albert, created in 1840, the year of their marriage. Victoria wore black for 40 years after Albert's death in 1861.

Family affair *(left)* Victoria and Albert with five of their eventual nine children in an 1846 painting. Victoria was known as the "grandmother of Europe," as her descendants married into the royal families of Russia, Germany, Denmark, Greece, Norway, Romania, Spain, and Sweden.

DISSENT AND REFORM

Calls for Change Addressed and Ignored

The British Parliament in 1832 was in a sorry state. It had steered the country through the momentous events of the 18th century but in many respects had remained unchanged for hundreds of years. Somewhere between 200,000 and 450,000 men— no women—were eligible to vote (in a population of 24,132,294 in 1831), but among a maze of voting qualifications was legislation from 1430 that excluded "people of small substance and no value" and factors as arbitrary as residence, property ownership, and membership in civic institutions. In Ireland, votes were excluded from most Catholics but granted to "potwallopers," or those who controlled their own front doors and cooking facilities.

Votes were also dubiously sought and randomly distributed. In Britain's many "rotten" boroughs, for example, a handful of voters elected one or more Members of Parliament (MPs). The most notorious was Old Sarum in Wiltshire, where in 1802 and 1803 just seven electors returned two MPs. Many such seats were the domain of powerful Tory landowners, who, because voting was public, were often able to influence their client voters. By contrast, the new industrial cities of Leeds, Bradford, and Manchester, among others, had no MPs at all.

Events came to a head in 1830. One reason was the election—for all the bias of the system— of a more progressive Whig government under Lord Grey. Others included the continued rise of an industrial entrepreneurial class, which gravitated toward the economically liberal Whigs; the appearance of a more vocal middle class; and the work of grassroots radicals such Henry Hunt and William Cobbett, who mobilized large popular movements for reform. The last reason was important. Demographic changes aside, the recent memory of the French Revolution produced a fear of similar events in Britain. Like many among the ruling class, Grey realized the pragmatic need for change. "The principle of my reform," he told Parliament, "is to prevent the necessity for revolution . . . reforming to preserve, not to overthrow."

The Tory landowners in Parliament saw things differently and battled to prevent Whig reforms. In the end, a threat from William IV to create enough Whigs in the House of Lords to force through the changes won the day. The result was the Great Reform Act of 1832, often seen as a turning point in Britain's democratic development.

In truth, the passing of the act, while a dramatic event for the time, did enough to ward off discontent without addressing many of Parliament's problems. "Rotten" boroughs were abolished, however, and new seats created or redistributed more fairly, though voting remained public, franchise anomalies persisted, and voters still numbered only 814,000, or about one in five adult males, and came from a now narrow property and landowning base.

Clamor for further reform began almost immediately. It found its most powerful grass-roots voice among the Chartists, a working-class movement that took its name from the People's Charter of 1838. Among other things, this charter called for secret ballots, paid MPs, and universal male suffrage. Huge open-air meetings took place in many industrial cities, and in 1839, a petition of 1.3 million signatures was presented to Parliament.

Chartism faded as a force, and further reform was slow to arrive. An act in 1867 made only piecemeal changes; secret ballots were introduced as late as 1872; and despite several reforms between 1883 and 1885, the 19th century ended with only 60 percent of men eligible to vote. Votes for women (those over 30) would not arrive until 1918 (see page 288). ∎

Mass appeal *(above)* The Great Chartist Meeting on Kennington Common, London, in 1848. Chartism was a working-class mass movement that called for political and other reforms. Despite their numbers, the Chartists were ignored and then suppressed by Parliament, and they faded as a force after the 1850s.

Voices for change *(opposite)* John Arthur Roebuck (1802–1879) was one of many radical writers, orators, and politicians who called for social and parliamentary reforms during the 19th century.

THE IRISH FAMINE

Hunger and Disease, Death and Emigration

The famine—also known as the Great Hunger—in Ireland between 1845 and 1851 was a watershed in the country's social, cultural, and demographic history. It remains a contentious subject to this day. The catastrophe began around 1844, when a blight, *Phytophthora infestans,* arrived in Europe, probably from Mexico by way of ships from North America. In 1845, it devastated potato harvests across the continent, but in Ireland, where at least a third of the rural poor relied on the potato for subsistence, its effects were devastating.

The reliance on the potato stemmed from a historic system of land tenure based on large estates, most of which were owned by absentee landlords, many of them British or Anglo-Irish. Almost all such estates were given over to livestock and cash crops, tenants having long lost the best land or holdings of sufficient size to feed their families on anything but a crop—the potato—that could be grown in quantity in poor soils.

Meat, grain, and other foodstuffs therefore continued to be exported in large amounts during the famine. And it is for this reason, and events during the even worse harvests of 1846 and 1847, that some historians talk of an "artificial" famine that might have been prevented. "The Almighty, indeed, sent the potato blight," wrote Irish nationalist John Mitchel in 1861, "but the English created the Famine."

In fact, the British government (responsible for Ireland since 1801) did react. Maize and cornmeal were ordered from the United States, but the provisions were slow to arrive and proved difficult to process. An effective soup-kitchen scheme fed three million people daily at its peak in July 1847 but was discontinued after six months. A vast government works plan was instigated in the winter of 1846 to 1847, but it was badly administered and wound down too soon (and the wages it paid were too low to cover the inflated price of food).

Behind these and other shortcomings lay both the scale of the disaster and powerful contemporary orthodoxies. One was the doctrine of laissez-faire—of not interfering with the economy. It was for this reason that prices were unregulated; grain and other exports from Ireland were allowed to continue; little was done to prevent the forced eviction of tenants unable to pay their rents; and assisted passage was withheld from those wishing to emigrate.

A second orthodoxy was a notion that relief and charity would undermine self-reliance. This was reinforced by a long-standing prejudice among some Britons that the Irish were inherently feckless, and that the famine was a timely, providential, and morally corrective act. Both ideas accounted for the fact that programs of public assistance were short-lived and that deliberate tests and obstacles were placed in the way of those seeking relief. ∎

Death and destitution An Irish family evicted from their home during the famine of 1846 to 1851, in a painting by Frederick Goodall (1822–1904). Disease and starvation during and after the famine resulted in at least a million deaths and perhaps double that number lost to emigration. Even today, the population of the island of Ireland, at around six million, remains below its prefamine peak of just over eight million.

The Irish Famine
1845–1852

Excess Death Rate 1846-51

- Over 20%
- 10-19%
- 5-9%
- 1-4%
- Population gain
- Soup ration area, 1847

Emigration by county, 1851-1911

- 545,000
- 300,000
- 200,000
- 100,000
- 31,000

SCOTLAND

North Channel

Lough Foyle

Londonderry (Derry)

DERRY

ANTRIM

Carrickfergus

Belfast Lough

DONEGAL

TYRONE

Lough Neagh

Belfast

Bann

Donegal Bay

Lower Lough Erne

Enniskillen

FERMANAGH

Upper Lough Erne

ARMAGH

Strangford Lough

DOWN

Sligo

MONAGHAN

Dundalk

Dundulk Bay

SLIGO

Lough Allen

LEITRIM

CAVAN

LOUTH

Lough Conn

MAYO

ROSCOMMON

Shannon

LONGFORD

MEATH

Drogheda

Irish Sea

Lough Mask

Lough Ree

Boyne

Trim

Lough Corrib

GALWAY

WESTMEATH

I R E L A N D

Dublin

DUBLIN

Galway

Galway Bay

Lough Lee

KING'S COUNTY (OFFALY)

KILDARE

ATLANTIC OCEAN

Lough Derg

QUEEN'S COUNTY (LAOIS)

WICKLOW

Shannon

CLARE

CARLOW

Mouth of the Shannon

Limerick

TIPPERARY

Kilkenny

Barrow

KERRY

LIMERICK

Clonmel

Suir

KILKENNY

WEXFORD

New Ross

Wexford

Wexford Harbour

Dingle Bay

Blackwater

WATERFORD

Dungarvan

Waterford

Waterford Harbour

St. George's Channel

CORK

Youghal

Glengarriff

Cork

Kenmare River

Bandon

Cork Harbour

Bantry Bay

C e l t i c   S e a

miles
0   25   50

0   25   50
kilometers

EMIGRATION

A Search for a New Life in New Lands

People had always left the British Isles, from the Celtic migrations that followed the collapse of Rome to the settlers who stepped onto the shores of Britain's fledgling North American colonies. But during the 19th century, emigration took place on an unprecedented scale, with perhaps 17 million people seeking a new life overseas.

Statistics can be misleading, however, for while the number of emigrants grew, so did the overall population: Between 1821 and 1911, the population of England and Wales increased from 20.9 million to 45.2 million; that of Scotland rose from 2.1 to 4.8 million. Only Ireland's fell, from 8.2 million in 1841 to 4.4 million in 1911.

Migration within the British Isles was also a factor in population change. Many Irish immigrated to North America, but many also moved to Britain's booming ports and industrial cities. In 1891 the population of the United States included 1,872,000 emigrants of Irish birth (in a total European-born U.S. population of over 63 million); in England, in the same year, the figure was 458,000.

When emigrants did move abroad, it was usually to North America. Definitive figures are elusive until the late 19th century, but a total of 9.6 million people probably left the United Kingdom for the United States in the 90 years leading up to 1911 (57 percent of all overseas emigrants), while 3.4 million, or 20 percent of the total, traveled to Canada.

These trends prevailed for much of the 19th century, but as the reach of steamships increased—and their levels of comfort and safety improved—proportionately larger numbers of Britons immigrated to other, mostly English-speaking and culturally familiar countries such as Australia, South Africa, and New Zealand. Australia was especially popular: Of its 668,650 inhabitants of European descent in 1891, 218,830 were born in Britain and Ireland. This was on top of an earlier generation of forced emigrants—the 161,700 transported as criminals (of whom 25,000 were women) between 1788 and 1868.

Rural poverty was the main motive for emigration, especially in Ireland and Scotland, and especially after the Irish famine of 1845 to 1851 (see pages 262–263) and the Highland Clearances (see sidebar). But many urban dwellers also emigrated—men and women, many of whom were skilled, who left Britain and Ireland not out of abject need but to seek better economic and social opportunities. Many of these people reacted to economic booms in their chosen destinations—one reason for spikes in immigration to North America in the 1880s and after 1901. ■

Fond farewell Emigrants board a ship in the aftermath of the Irish famine of 1845 to 1851, when as many as two million Irish citizens sought a new life overseas.

The Clearances

The Highland Clearances—the removal of small tenant farmers from large estates to make way for more profitable sheep rearing—undermined a distinct clan culture and were a major impetus for emigration from Scotland in the 19th century. They began around 1780 and continued for at least 70 years, with the most traumatic removals taking place in the Highlands, Scotland's mountainous heart. Planned towns and new industrial cities claimed some of the displaced population, but many Scots immigrated to Canada, Australia, New Zealand, and the United States.

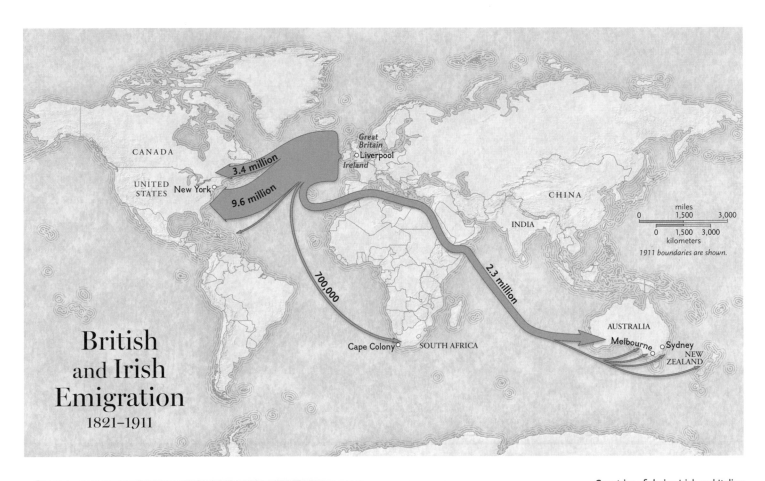

British and Irish Emigration
1821–1911

CANADA

UNITED STATES

New York

3.4 million

9.6 million

Great Britain

Liverpool

Ireland

CHINA

INDIA

miles
0   1,500   3,000

0   1,500   3,000
kilometers

1911 boundaries are shown.

700,000

2.3 million

Cape Colony   SOUTH AFRICA

AUSTRALIA

Melbourne   Sydney

NEW ZEALAND

Countries of choice Irish and Italian
emigrants at Ellis Island, New York.
An estimated 9.6 million, or 57
percent, of all those who left Britain
and Ireland between 1821 and 1911
immigrated to the United States.
A further 3.4 million, or 20 percent,
moved to Canada.

THE INDIAN MUTINY

Culture Clash, Massacre, and Reform

By the 1850s, most of India was ruled by the East India Company, a British mercantile enterprise founded in 1600 (see page 164). The company employed armies of local soldiers (sepoys) under British control, and it was a mutiny, uprising, rebellion, or war of independence—commentators give it different names—by elements of one of these armies that sparked Britain's biggest colonial crisis since the Revolutionary War.

The mutiny of 1857 to 1858 had many cultural, religious, and economic causes, but its trigger was the introduction of new ammunition that required soldiers to bite off pregreased cartridges to release their firing powder. When rumors took hold that the grease contained beef or pork fat—clearly offensive to the armies' Hindu and Muslim troops—they sparked a series of incidents that came to a head in the city of Meerut on May 10, 1857.

The East India Company maintained three main Indian armies: the Bengal, the Madras, and the Bombay. Meerut was garrisoned by the first, which was made up largely of upper-caste Indians, the group that had lost most in terms of wealth and social prestige under British rule.

Meerut's garrison mutinied when around 80 soldiers who had refused to use the new ammunition were sentenced to ten years' hard labor. After releasing the imprisoned men, Indian soldiers killed British officers and their families, along with Indians who tried to protect Europeans in the city beyond. The revolt spread immediately to nearby Delhi, and then through other areas of northern and central India. The complex causes of this wider uprising were reflected in the fact that the Madras and Bombay armies remained loyal, and that many areas of India remained untouched by violence.

Events at Meerut, though, set a bloody tone for what was to follow. Both sides committed atrocities, especially in the wake of events in June 1857 at Cawnpore (now Kanpur), where British women, children, and wounded soldiers, having apparently been offered safe passage, were taken hostage and massacred. When the British retook the city, the sepoys were murdered in turn, some by being strapped to cannon and blown up, others after being made to lick the dried blood of the hostages from their prison walls.

The British response to these and other events, notably the sieges of Delhi and Lucknow in 1857, was initially confused. But the Indian forces also lacked coherence, and it was only a matter of time before superior British arms and organization brought the revolt under control. Although direct rule from Britain (the Raj) replaced the East India Company, and some attempts were made to address Indian grievances, the mutiny compromised Anglo-Indian relations until Indian independence in 1947 (see pages 324–325). ∎

Heroes and villains This painting by Louis Desanges (1822–1887) depicts British army captain Charles Gough saving his brother during the Indian Mutiny, an action for which he won the Victoria Cross, Britain's highest military award for gallantry. Despite the heroic actions of some, the mutiny was marked by numerous civilian deaths, and by massacres and other atrocities on both sides.

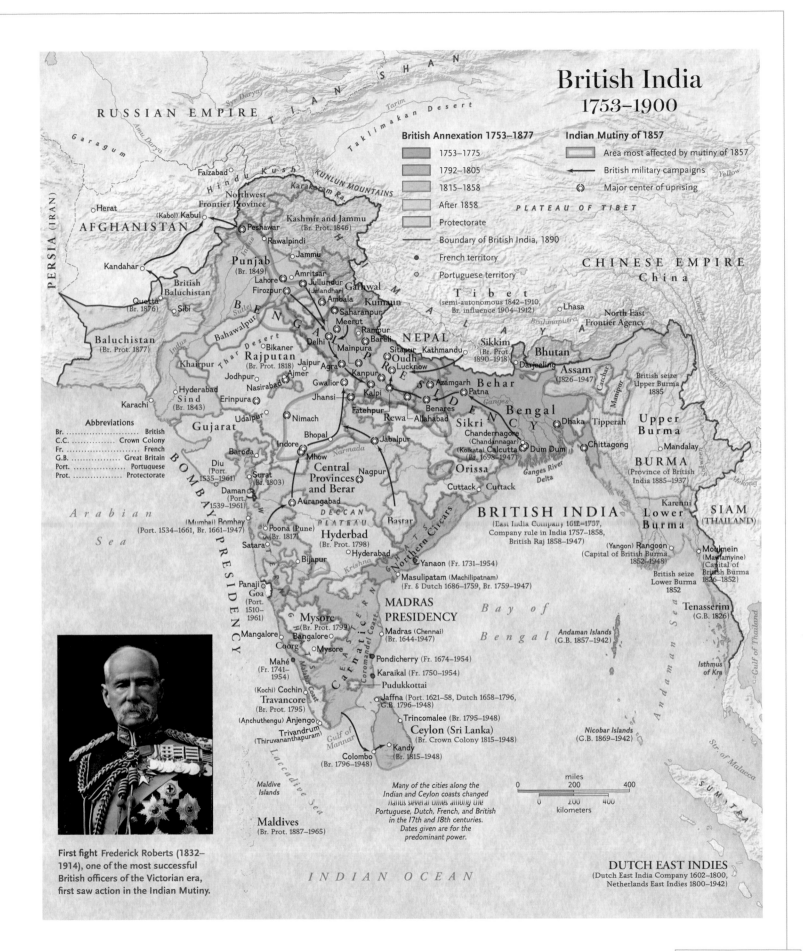

British India
1753–1900

British Annexation 1753–1877
- 1753–1775
- 1792–1805
- 1815–1858
- After 1858
- Protectorate
- Boundary of British India, 1890
- French territory
- Portuguese territory

Indian Mutiny of 1857
- Area most affected by mutiny of 1857
- British military campaigns
- Major center of uprising

Abbreviations

Br.	British
C.C.	Crown Colony
Fr.	French
G.B.	Great Britain
Port.	Portuguese
Prot.	Protectorate

Many of the cities along the Indian and Ceylon coasts changed hands several times among the Portuguese, Dutch, French, and British in the 17th and 18th centuries. Dates given are for the predominant power.

First fight Frederick Roberts (1832–1914), one of the most successful British officers of the Victorian era, first saw action in the Indian Mutiny.

THE AGE OF EXPLORATION

Africa to Australia, the Arctic to the Americas

Britain and Ireland's explorers ranged the globe in the years to 1914, much as they had done for centuries, pursuing journeys to some of the most extreme places on Earth. Some were inspired by the old imperatives—science, knowledge, and adventure—others by a new evangelical zeal.

The most famous among the latter was David Livingstone (1813–1873). "The opening of [a] new . . . country . . ." he wrote in 1857, "is a matter of congratulations only in so far as it opens up a prospect for the elevation of the inhabitants . . . I view the end of the geographical feat as the beginning of missionary enterprise."

In the course of a remarkable 30-year career, Livingstone covered an estimated 29,000 miles in Africa, much of it on foot, and became the first European to cross the continent from west to east. When he disappeared in the African interior in 1865, he was famously "discovered" by another writer and explorer, Henry Morton Stanley, who greeted him in 1871 with the (possibly apocryphal) words

Polar picture An ice grotto photographed during Robert Falcon Scott's expedition to the Antarctic (1910–1912). Scott's ship, an old whaler, the S.S. *Terra Nova*, can be seen in the background. Its wreck was discovered on the seabed off Greenland in 2012.

"Dr. Livingstone, I presume . . ."

Other African explorers included Richard Burton and John Speke, renowned for their exploration of Africa's great lakes (1856–1860), as well as one of Britain's first female explorers, Mary Kingsley (1862–1900), who on several expeditions to West Africa between 1893 and 1895 explored uncharted territories in present-day Gabon and pioneered a new route up Mount Cameroon, West Africa's highest mountain.

In Australia, Gregory Blaxland (1778–1853) made some of the first forays into the interior of New South Wales and became the first European to cross the Blue Mountains in 1813. Matthew Flinders (1774–1818) and Charles Sturt (1795–1869) also made incursions into the country's interior, and an 1860–1861 expedition led by William John Wills and Robert O'Hara Burke became the first to cross the continent from south to north.

Scottish explorers proved their mettle in North America, where in 1793 Alexander Mackenzie (ca 1764–1820) completed the first east-to-west crossing of North America north of Mexico. Simon Fraser (1776–1862) explored the majestic Western Canadian river that bears his name, and David Thompson (1770–1857) explored immense areas of northern Canada, as well as becoming the first European to navigate the length of the Columbia River in 1811.

Elsewhere, a renewed search for the long-sought Northwest Passage from the Atlantic to the Pacific drew several explorers, most famously Sir John Franklin (1786–1847), remembered for his last voyage, when Franklin, his ships, and his crew disappeared in the icy wastes of northern Canada.

Similarly ill-fated was Robert Falcon Scott (1868–1912), who, after pioneering Antarctic expeditions from 1901 to 1904 with another polar explorer, the Anglo-Irishman Ernest Shackleton (1874–1922), failed in an attempt to be the first to reach the South Pole. Roald Amundsen and his Norwegian expedition, which arrived in late 1911, beat Scott by 34 days. Scott and his party died on the 800-mile return trek, but it was the final act of self-sacrifice by Captain Lawrence Oates, along with his immortal valedictory words (recorded in Scott's diary), that has entered British lore:

"This was the end," Scott wrote in his journal. "He slept through the night before last, hoping not to wake; but he woke in the morning—yesterday. He said, 'I am just going outside and may be some time.' He went out into the blizzard and we have not seen him since . . . we knew that poor Oates was walking to his death, but though we tried to dissuade him, we knew it was the act of a brave man and an English gentleman." ∎

Perils of the bush Explorer and missionary David Livingstone is mauled while helping defend an African village from a lion in 1844. The wounds to Livingstone's shattered arm disabled him for the rest of his life.

Explorer's aid The boat's compass used by David Livingstone during his first expedition on the Zambezi River in 1853 to 1856, when he became probably the first European to see Mosi-oa-Tunya, or Victoria Falls.

Sir John Franklin The British naval officer and Arctic explorer disappeared with his ships and crew in 1847 during an expedition to discover the Northwest Passage. Franklin's precise fate and that of his men remain unknown to this day.

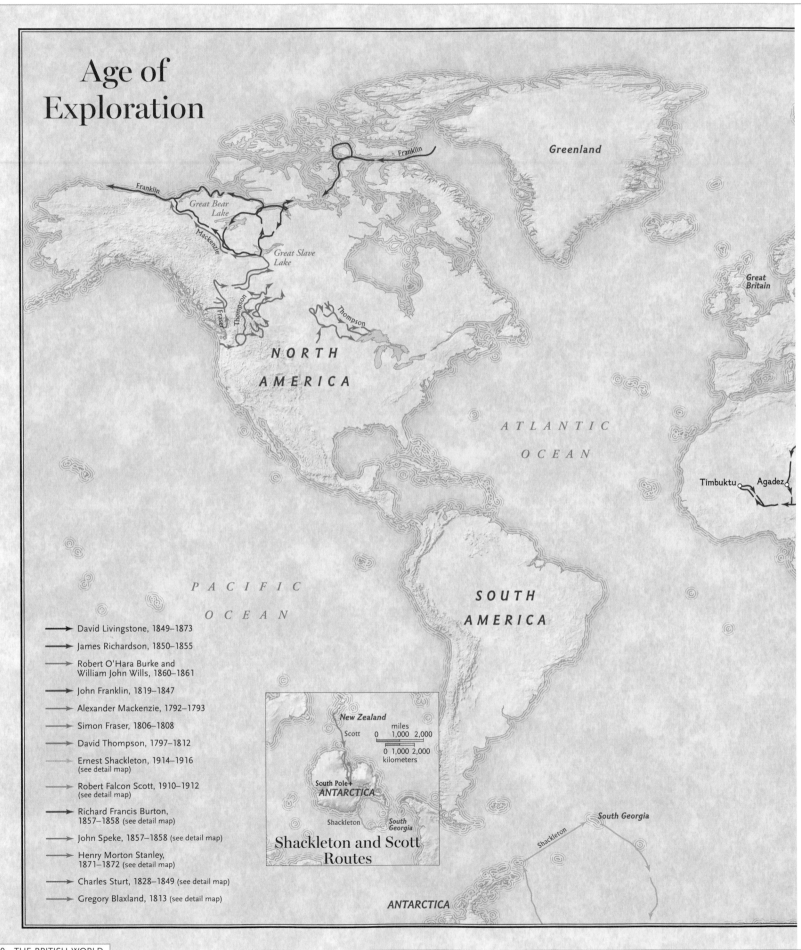

Age of Exploration

Greenland

Great Britain

Franklin

Great Bear Lake

Mackenzie

Great Slave Lake

Franklin

Thompson

Fraser

Thompson

NORTH AMERICA

ATLANTIC OCEAN

Timbuktu○ Agadez

PACIFIC OCEAN

SOUTH AMERICA

→ David Livingstone, 1849–1873

→ James Richardson, 1850–1855

→ Robert O'Hara Burke and William John Wills, 1860–1861

→ John Franklin, 1819–1847

→ Alexander Mackenzie, 1792–1793

→ Simon Fraser, 1806–1808

→ David Thompson, 1797–1812

→ Ernest Shackleton, 1914–1916 (see detail map)

→ Robert Falcon Scott, 1910–1912 (see detail map)

→ Richard Francis Burton, 1857–1858 (see detail map)

→ John Speke, 1857–1858 (see detail map)

→ Henry Morton Stanley, 1871–1872 (see detail map)

→ Charles Sturt, 1828–1849 (see detail map)

→ Gregory Blaxland, 1813 (see detail map)

New Zealand

Scott

miles
0   1,000 2,000

0 1,000 2,000
kilometers

South Pole +
ANTARCTICA

Shackleton   *South Georgia*

Shackleton and Scott Routes

South Georgia

Shackleton

ANTARCTICA

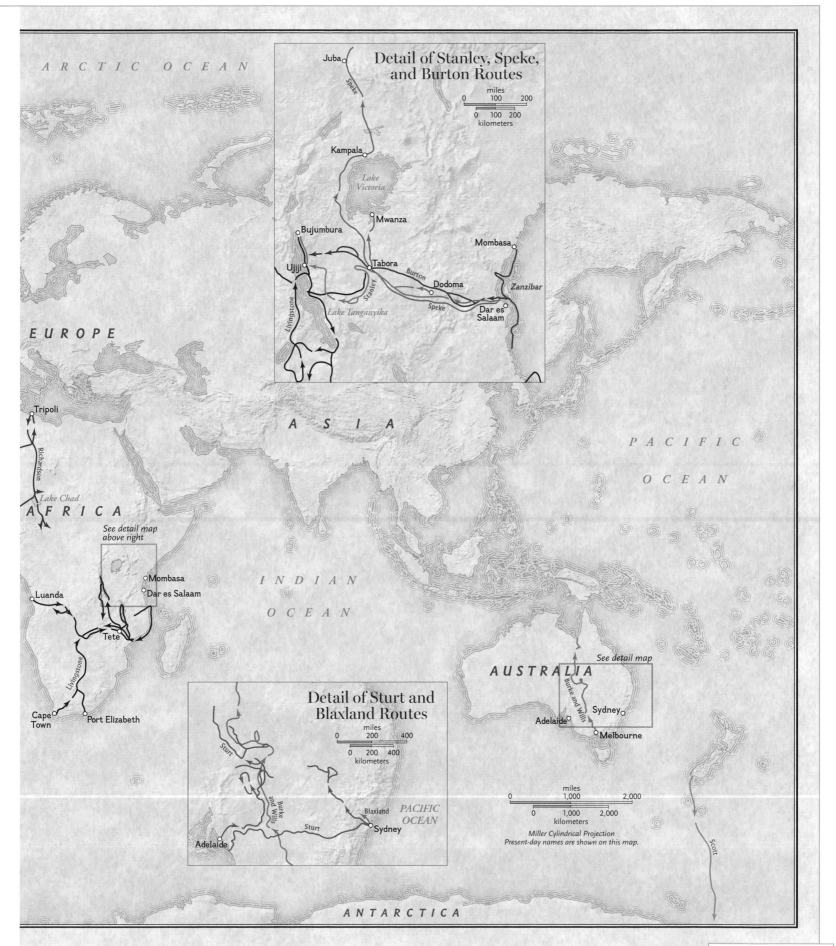

ARCTIC OCEAN

Detail of Stanley, Speke, and Burton Routes

Juba

Speke

Kampala

Lake Victoria

Mwanza

miles
0   100   200

0   100   200
kilometers

Bujumbura

Mombasa

Tabora

Ujiji

Burton

Dodoma

Zanzibar

Stanley

Livingstone

Speke

Dar es Salaam

Lake Tanganyika

EUROPE

Tripoli

Richardson

A S I A

PACIFIC

OCEAN

Lake Chad

AFRICA

See detail map
above right

Mombasa

Dar es Salaam

INDIAN

Luanda

OCEAN

Tete

Livingstone

See detail map

AUSTRALIA

Burke and Wills

Sydney

Adelaide

Melbourne

Cape Town

Port Elizabeth

Detail of Sturt and Blaxland Routes

Sturt

miles
0   200   400

0   200   400
kilometers

Burke and Wills

Blaxland

PACIFIC
OCEAN

Sturt

Sydney

Adelaide

miles
0   1,000   2,000

0   1,000   2,000
kilometers

Miller Cylindrical Projection
Present-day names are shown on this map.

Scott

ANTARCTICA

CHARLES DARWIN

Evolution and Revolution in the World of Science

Charles Darwin (1809–1882) was born in Shrewsbury, in central England, to Robert Darwin, a prosperous doctor, and Susannah, the daughter of industrialist Josiah Wedgwood. He attended the universities of Edinburgh (from 1825 to 1827) and Cambridge (1828 to 1831), where he rebelled first against his father's wish that he study medicine and then, troubled by religious doubts, against a career as a clergyman. On leaving Cambridge, he secured a place as an informal "gentleman" naturalist aboard H.M.S. *Beagle,* a Royal Navy research ship bound for the southern oceans.

Remaining with the *Beagle* for five years (1831–1836) as it sailed to South America and beyond (see map opposite), Darwin collected data and nurtured the evolutionary theories that later would make his name. In 1842, having married, he moved to Knole, a village in Kent about 15 miles from London, which would remain his home and a base for his research and writing for 40 years.

In the same year, Darwin made one of the first manuscript sketches of his ideas. He drew on others' research into areas as diverse as dinosaurs and population, and in particular the work of Charles Lyell (1797–1875), a geologist who had studied incremental changes to the physical landscape over time. Yet Darwin, aware of the furor that the revolutionary content of his ideas would create, hesitated to publish them. Instead, he refined and experimented, tirelessly seeking evidence to substantiate his theories.

In the end, the similar conclusions of another scientist, Alfred Russel Wallace (1823–1913), were brought to his notice in June 1858, thus forcing his hand. Honorable to a fault, Darwin insisted on a joint presentation of his and Wallace's ideas at the Linnean Society of London on July 1, 1858, one of the landmark dates in the history of science. A year later, he finally published his thesis in *On the Origin of Species,* a work that suggested a natural rather than divine theory of evolution. He made his even more famous assertion that humans descended from apes later, in *The Descent of Man,* published in 1871.

Because they challenged religious orthodoxies, both works generated controversy, yet many of the increasingly secular elements in Victorian society gradually accepted them. Darwin's ideas were also embraced by the majority of his peers, whose efforts ensured that he received the honor of a state funeral in London's Westminster Abbey, the pantheon of many of Britain's greatest men and women. ■

Charles Darwin The great Victorian scientist is remembered for his theories on the natural, rather than divine, origins and evolution of humans and the physical world.

Science and Scientists

Charles Darwin was one among many scientific pioneers during the Victorian age. Others included Joseph Lister (1827–1912) *(left)*, a pioneer of antiseptic surgery; Michael Faraday (1791–1867), remembered for his work with electricity; John Dunlop (1840–1921), the inventor of the pneumatic rubber tire; Joseph Swan (1828–1914), who helped create incandescent lightbulbs; Charles Babbage (1791–1871), known for his calculating machines; and William Ramsay (1852–1916), awarded the Noble Prize in 1904 for his discovery of the inert noble gases.

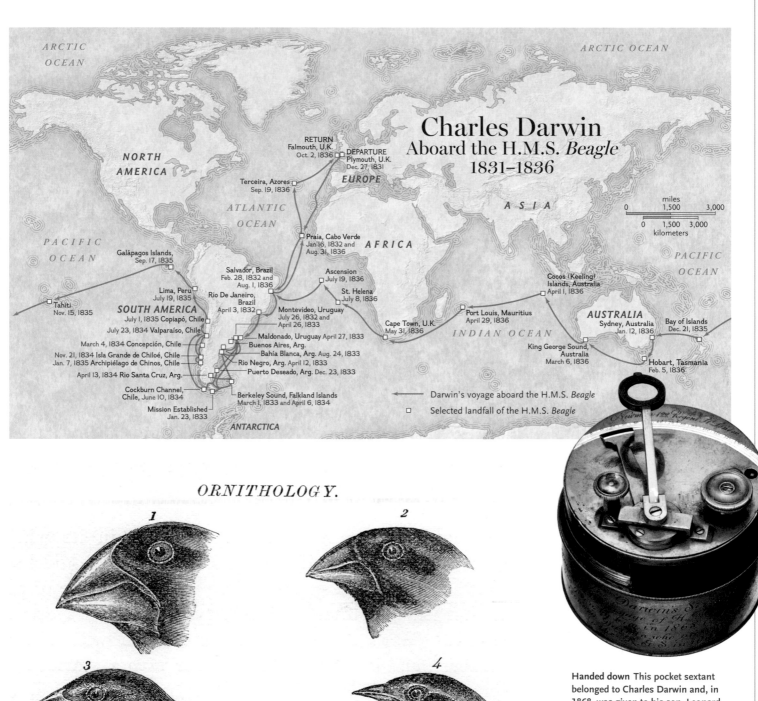

Charles Darwin
Aboard the H.M.S. *Beagle*
1831–1836

ARCTIC OCEAN

ARCTIC OCEAN

NORTH AMERICA

RETURN
Falmouth, U.K.
Oct. 2, 1836

DEPARTURE
Plymouth, U.K.
Dec. 27, 1831

Terceira, Azores
Sep. 19, 1836

EUROPE

ATLANTIC OCEAN

ASIA

PACIFIC OCEAN

Galápagos Islands,
Sep. 17, 1835

Praia, Cabo Verde
Jan. 16, 1832 and
Aug. 31, 1836

AFRICA

PACIFIC OCEAN

Tahiti
Nov. 15, 1835

Lima, Peru
July 19, 1835

Salvador, Brazil
Feb. 28, 1832 and
Aug. 1, 1836

Rio De Janeiro,
Brazil
April 3, 1832

Ascension
July 19, 1836

St. Helena
July 8, 1836

Cocos (Keeling)
Islands, Australia
April 1, 1836

SOUTH AMERICA

July 1, 1835 Copiapó, Chile

July 23, 1834 Valparaíso, Chile

March 4, 1834 Concepción, Chile

Nov. 21, 1834 Isla Grande de Chiloé, Chile
Jan. 7, 1835 Archipiélago de Chinos, Chile

April 13, 1834 Rio Santa Cruz, Arg.

Cockburn Channel,
Chile, June 10, 1834

Mission Established
Jan. 23, 1833

Montevideo, Uruguay
July 26, 1832 and
April 26, 1833

Maldonado, Uruguay April 27, 1833
Buenos Aires, Arg.
Bahía Blanca, Arg. Aug. 24, 1833
Rio Negro, Arg. April 12, 1833
Puerto Deseado, Arg. Dec. 23, 1833

Berkeley Sound, Falkland Islands
March 1, 1833 and April 6, 1834

Cape Town, U.K.
May 31, 1836

Port Louis, Mauritius
April 29, 1836

INDIAN OCEAN

AUSTRALIA
Sydney, Australia
Jan. 12, 1836

King George Sound,
Australia
March 6, 1836

Bay of Islands
Dec. 21, 1835

Hobart, Tasmania
Feb. 5, 1836

ANTARCTICA

miles
0   1,500   3,000

0   1,500   3,000
kilometers

→ Darwin's voyage aboard the H.M.S. *Beagle*

□ Selected landfall of the H.M.S. *Beagle*

ORNITHOLOGY.

1

2

3

4

1. Geospiza magnirostris.
2. Geospiza fortis.
3. Geospiza parvula.
4. Certhidea olivacea.

Handed down This pocket sextant belonged to Charles Darwin and, in 1868, was given to his son, Leonard, who bequeathed it to the Royal Geographical Society in 1912.

Evolutionary clue Darwin collected several finches—now usually classified as part of the subfamily Geospizinae—in the Galápagos Islands during his voyage aboard H.M.S. *Beagle* between 1831 and 1836. He came to understand that the different beaks of otherwise similar birds that had evolved from a single species had been "taken and modified," in his words, as a result of their adaptation to different food sources. The observations were a cornerstone of his theories on evolution and natural selection.

IRISH HOME RULE

Land and Liberty, Catholic and Protestant

Home Rule was the demand that the government of Ireland be returned from Westminster to an Irish parliament in Dublin. This issue, along with the closely connected question of Irish land reform, dominated British and Irish politics for much of the second half of the 19th century. Although unresolved by 1914, it formed part of the centuries-long historical process that culminated in the creation of Northern Ireland and the independent Irish Free State in 1921 (see page 306).

Ireland had possessed a parliament until 1801, when the Act of Union dissolved it and made Ireland one of the four constituent countries of the United Kingdom. Irish voters, such as they were, returned Members of Parliament to sit with English, Welsh, and Scottish MPs in London. This parliament legislated for the countries of the United Kingdom, along with the colonies of the British Empire.

The complex politics of Home Rule provoked powerful divisions in Parliament and beyond. Broadly, the Conservatives, who made up one of the U.K.'s two main parties, were against it: Although other so-called white colonies such as Canada, Australia, and New Zealand were being given self-governing dominion status, the Conservatives deemed similar consideration for Ireland a dangerous subversion of empire. Instead, they hoped land reform would buy off Irish discontent.

Their Whig (later Liberal) opponents, by contrast, were more sympathetic, but divisions within their ranks over what became known as the Irish Question eventually split the party. Ireland's Unionist Protestants—those in favor of the union of the United Kingdom—especially those of Ulster in the northeast, were vehemently against Home Rule, as they feared Catholic domination and economic decline under a Dublin parliament.

Key to the parliamentary maneuvers provoked by the issue, and the reason the mainstream parties could not ignore Ireland, was the fact that Irish and other MPs in favor of Home Rule often commanded enough seats to hold the balance of power between Whig and Conservative MPs. As such, they were able to negotiate concessions as a price for supporting one or the other party in government.

William Gladstone (1809–1898), prime minister on four occasions in a career spanning more than 60 years, was the key British player. A Liberal, he disestablished the Anglican (Protestant) Church of Ireland in 1869 (to which Catholics had been forced to pay tithes) and then passed the Irish Land Act of 1870 in an only modestly successful attempt to improve tenants' rights. He then moved to establish Home Rule in two failed parliamentary bills in 1886 and 1893.

His key Irish counterpart was Charles Stewart Parnell (1846–1891), a Protestant landowner and therefore an unlikely champion of Ireland's rural Catholic majority. A consummate politician, and widely admired, even by opponents, Parnell drew strength from his combined leadership of political and other organizations devoted to both Home Rule and land reform. Parnell powerfully advanced both causes before being undermined by a scandalous divorce case in which he was implicated.

A third Home Rule bill was finally passed in 1914, but it was not implemented due to the outbreak of World War I. By the time the war was over, the issue of Home Rule had been overtaken by events. ■

Charles Stewart Parnell *(left)* Although he was a Protestant landowner, Parnell emerged as a champion of Ireland's Catholic rural poor and enjoyed popularity and some success as a politician before his early death in 1891.

Front-page news *(opposite)* A report on the Phoenix Park Murders, in which members of the Irish National Invincibles, a radical group that sought Irish independence, fatally stabbed two leading Anglo-Irish politicians on the outskirts of Dublin in 1882

POLICE THE ILLUSTRATED NEWS

LAW COURTS AND WEEKLY RECORD

No. 1,274.   SATURDAY, JULY 14, 1888.   Price One Penny.

FATAL BOATING ACCIDENT ON THE THAMES

SHOOTING CASE IN BLOOMSBURY

PARNELLISM AND CRIME O'DONNELL VERSUS 'TIMES'.

WATCHING THE HOUSE

DEATH TO A TRAITOR SECRET COUNCIL

MURDER OF MR JOYCE AND FAMILY

MURDER OF LORD CAVENDISH AND MR BURKE
PHOENIX PARK

A LANDLORD

SECRET VENGEANCE

MAIMING CATTLE

WHAT TIM BRYAN WILL GET IF HIS RINT IS PAID CAPTAIN MOONLIGHT

DEATH OF CAREY

THE INFORMER

FATAL ACCIDENT IN THE HAYFIELD

EVICTING A MAN IN HIS COFFIN'

VICTORIAN LITERATURE
Wordsworth to Wilde, Keats to Kipling

The literary history of Britain and Ireland is a treasury of great names, but few periods produced as fine a flowering of poets, novelists, and playwrights as the years before, during, and just after the Victorian age. Above all, it was an era of great novelists, as well as a period in which women writers came to the fore. George Eliot, best known for *Middlemarch* (1871–1872), and Emily Brontë, remembered for *Wuthering Heights* (1847), stand out among the latter, but Mary Wollstonecraft Shelley, the author of *Frankenstein; or, The Modern Prometheus* (1818); Emily's sister, Charlotte Brontë; and Elizabeth Gaskell all left a mark on their times.

Elizabeth Gaskell was one of many writers of the period who, in novels such as *North and South* (1854–1855), addressed the social and other issues of a rapidly changing Britain. Others included Benjamin Disraeli, Thomas Carlyle, John Stuart Mill, John Ruskin, and William Cobbett, though none achieved the fame of Charles Dickens, who in serialized novels such as *David Copperfield* (1849–1850) and *Bleak House* (1852–1853) painted a vivid and often damning picture of the times.

Another feature of the age were sprawling, epic narratives such as those of Dickens and the novels of Anthony Trollope, John Galsworthy, Wilkie Collins, and William Thackeray. So, too, were works that arguably lay outside the mainstream, such as Lewis Carroll's *Alice's Adventures in Wonderland* (1865); Arthur Conan Doyle's tales of his fictional detective, Sherlock Holmes (after 1887); the science fiction of H. G. Wells; and Robert Louis Stevenson's *Treasure Island* (1883).

A similarly wide range of sensibilities marked the many poets of the 19th century, beginning with the Romantic poets (see sidebar), through the names that dominated the high Victorian period—Robert Browning (1812–1889) and Alfred, Lord Tennyson (1809–1892)—to the more modern outlook of writers such as W. B. Yeats (1865–1939).

Other late Victorian writers whose work often seems to strike a more contemporary note include Rudyard Kipling (1865–1936), known above all for *The Jungle Book* (1894) and his ambivalent tales of empire; playwright and poet Oscar Wilde; and poet and novelist Thomas Hardy (1840–1928), in many of whose works the vagaries of fate and a changing world often undercut a timeless English pastoralism. ∎

Joseph Conrad English was Conrad's third language—he was born in Russian-dominated Ukraine to Polish parents—but after settling in Britain in 1894, after 20 years at sea, he became widely celebrated for novels such as *Nostromo* and *Heart of Darkness.*

The Romantic Poets

Britain's quintet of great Romantic poets—William Wordsworth, Percy Bysshe Shelley, Lord Byron, Samuel Taylor Coleridge, and John Keats *(left)*—dominated the early part of the 19th century. Part of a wider European movement, they rejected many of the rational principles of the Enlightenment in favor of the intensity and passion of individual experience. They were fired by ideals of liberty and relished the primal power of love and landscape. Many traveled and lived abroad, remembered as much for their tumultuous lives and often -early deaths as for their art.

> *"Everything in moderation, including moderation . . . Hard work is simply the refuge of people who have nothing whatever to do . . . We are all in the gutter, but some of us are looking at the stars . . . I can resist anything except temptation . . ."*

SELECTED QUOTATIONS, OSCAR WILDE

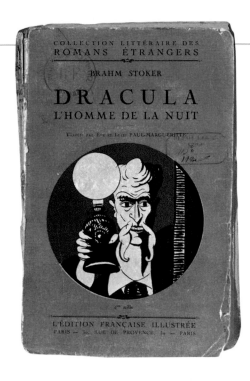

Man of the night Dublin-born writer Bram Stoker (1847–1912), a civil servant and actor's manager, would have remained little known but for *Dracula,* his celebrated tale of vampirism published in 1897.

Charles Dickens Among the most famous and prolific novelists of the Victorian era, Dickens combined acute social criticism with vivid characterization and compelling storytelling in a career that spanned almost half a century.

Oscar Wilde Born in Dublin in 1854, Wilde enjoyed a glittering career as a wit and playwright before a homosexual scandal saw him jailed in 1895. He was released in 1897 and died in Paris in 1900.

THE LABOR MOVEMENT

A Slow March to Power and Parliament

The 19th century produced one of the largest mass movements in British history—the vast numbers of workers created by the climax of the Industrial Revolution—and yet for the best part of a hundred years that group remained almost entirely without power or political representation. Organized labor made its presence felt early, however. In 1811, groups of artisans known as Luddites (after Ned Ludd, a possibly mythical figure) broke into textile mills and destroyed some of the new machines of mass production. Most were hand weavers or others wedded to outmoded skills, and many had lost their jobs to unskilled workers or had been forced to accept lower factory wages.

From 1824 to 1825, an impediment to organized labor was removed when the Combination Acts of 1799 and 1800 were repealed. The acts, which had prohibited the formation of unions, had been passed during the Napoleonic Wars to prevent strikes that might damage the war economy. The repeal did nothing to help the Tolpuddle Martyrs, a celebrated group of rural workers condemned to deportation (but later reprieved) for forming a society to campaign for higher wages in 1834. Unions remained weak in the 1840s, when labor concerns were often voiced through broader political movements such as Chartism. This changed after the 1850s, when improved economic conditions and higher wages facilitated the formation of more powerful unions. An umbrella organization, the Trades Union Congress, was founded in Manchester in 1868, and union membership rose from around 100,000 in 1850 to around a million by 1874. Equally as important as unions was the cooperative movement, made up of self-help organizations that pooled resources and shared profits. The first appeared in 1844; by 1899, there were 1,531 organizations with 1.6 million members. Just as crucial were friendly societies—organizations that provided help in everything from insurance against sickness to the provision of a respectable funeral.

Cooperative and friendly societies, like unions, were concentrated in Britain's industrial heartlands. Their evolution was largely a reaction to two realities of Victorian life: one, a disdain for the state provision of assistance for the poor, which was seen by some as morally corrupting and liable to encourage dependency and idleness; and two, the almost complete lack of parliamentary representation for the country's vast constituency of workers (estimated at 5.7 million in 1881).

After 1874, unions helped finance sympathetic Liberal parliamentary candidates, but even at its peak, in 1885, the support resulted in the election of just 12 MPs. Even when J. Keir Hardie (1856–1915) helped found the Independent Labour Party, a party of labor, in 1893, its 28 candidates—with suffrage still limited—mustered only 44,325 votes and finished last in every poll they contested. Even by 1906, MPs with links to labor numbered 29 out of a total of 670.

In the meantime, many people worked for the advancement of labor in other ways. Intellectuals such as Beatrice and Sidney Webb founded the Fabian Society (1884), which advocated a gradual, nonrevolutionary path to the emerging doctrine of socialism. On the ground, the increasing power and public profile of labor were reflected in events such as the matchgirls' strike of 1888, when some of London's poorest workers secured victory over their employers, and an influential countrywide strike of dockworkers in 1889. A new century would be well under way, however, before the strands of the labor movement were backed by sufficient political representation to obtain real power in the aftermath of World War I. ■

Mass movement A 1908 march in London by hop pickers and producers demanding levies on cheap foreign hops. Lack of political representation often forced workers of the period onto the streets to make their voices heard.

"*The present day is a Mammon worshipping age. Socialism proposes to dethrone the brute god Mammon and to lift humanity into its place.*"

J. KIER HARDIE, PARLIAMENTARY SPEECH, 1901

Sidney Webb A co-founder of the Fabian Society, Webb was one of many middle- and upper-class writers and intellectuals who supported the labor and other radical movements during the Victorian age and beyond.

THE BOER WARS

The British Meet Their Match in Africa

The Boer Wars (also known as the Anglo-Boer Wars or the South African War) were fought between the British and the Boers (or Afrikaners) between 1899 and 1902. The Boers were mostly descendants of the original Dutch settlers of the Cape Colony, on Africa's southern tip, which was ceded to Britain in 1814 after the Napoleonic Wars. After the arrival of British rule, many Boers left the Cape to establish their own republics in the Transvaal and the Orange Free State to the north.

The status of these colonies was doubtful, at least in British eyes, and became more so after the 1860s, when gold and diamonds were discovered in the Boer homelands. Britain attempted to annex the Transvaal in 1877, only to be driven back by the Boers between 1880 and 1881 in what is often known as the First Boer, or First South African, War.

The spark for the second war came from Cecil Rhodes (1853–1902), an ambitious mining magnate and Cape politician who envisaged a British sphere of influence stretching the length of Africa. In December 1895, possibly with the support of the British government, Rhodes instigated the Jameson Raid, a clumsy mercenary attempt to overthrow the Transvaal government and to foment rebellion among the many foreign (and often badly treated) prospectors attracted to the goldfields.

Full-scale war broke out in 1899. The first phase saw numerous Boer successes, especially in the Sieges of Ladysmith, Mafeking, and Kimberley. Tough and self-reliant, the Boers were formidable fighters who employed guerrilla tactics that often confounded Britain's orthodox military thinking.

A second phase of the war began when a new British chief of staff, Lord Kitchener, dispatched 200,000 regular soldiers to the region. At that time it was the largest British force ever seen in a foreign conflict. Although the tide turned and the most pressing sieges were lifted, the Boers returned to the hills to stage a renewed guerrilla war, with the help of the wider Boer population.

Kitchener's response was a scorched-earth policy that saw farms razed, crops burned, livestock killed, food supplies cut, and wells poisoned. He also instigated 40 tented internment camps for families suspected of collaboration or forced from their homes. Inadequate food and sanitation in the camps saw the death from hunger and disease of almost 28,000 Boer women and children and, at the least, 14,000 African internees caught up in the British campaign.

The camps caused widespread domestic and international condemnation. In Britain, a country unused to military setbacks and the visceral reality of conflict, the already somber mood darkened further. Many began to oppose the war. In 1902, the Boers were forced to the negotiating table, but their defiance continued: By 1910, the Union of South Africa, comprising four former British and Boer colonies, was a self-governing dominion, and, after 1934, it was an all but independent state. ■

Temporary relief British troops greet the relieving force at the Siege of Ladysmith in 1900 during the Boer Wars. The lifting of the siege brought rejoicing in Britain, but attitudes changed in the wake of a guerrilla campaign by the Boers and Britain's use of internment camps in which thousands of civilians died.

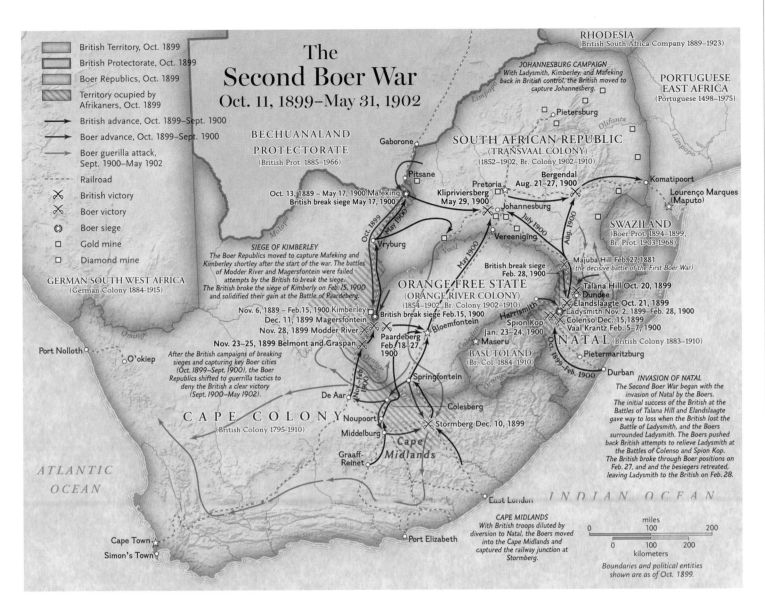

The
Second Boer War
Oct. 11, 1899–May 31, 1902

Legend:
- British Territory, Oct. 1899
- British Protectorate, Oct. 1899
- Boer Republics, Oct. 1899
- Territory occupied by Afrikaners, Oct. 1899
- British advance, Oct. 1899–Sept. 1900
- Boer advance, Oct. 1899–Sept. 1900
- Boer guerilla attack, Sept. 1900–May 1902
- Railroad
- British victory
- Boer victory
- Boer siege
- Gold mine
- Diamond mine

RHODESIA
(British South Africa Company 1889–1923)

JOHANNESBURG CAMPAIGN
With Ladysmith, Kimberley, and Mafeking back in British control, the British moved to capture Johannesberg.

PORTUGUESE EAST AFRICA
(Portuguese 1498–1975)

BECHUANALAND PROTECTORATE
(British Prot. 1885–1966)

Gaborone

Pietersburg

SOUTH AFRICAN REPUBLIC
(TRANSVAAL COLONY)
(1852–1902, Br. Colony 1902–1910)

Pitsane

Oct. 13, 1889 – May 17, 1900 Mafeking
British break siege May 17, 1900

Pretoria
Klipriviersberg May 29, 1900

Bergendal Aug. 21–27, 1900

Komatipoort
Lourenço Marques (Maputo)

Johannesburg
Vereeniging

Vryburg

SWAZILAND
(Boer Prot. 1894–1899, Br. Prot. 1903–1968)

GERMAN SOUTH WEST AFRICA
(German Colony 1884-1915)

SIEGE OF KIMBERLEY
The Boer Republics moved to capture Mafeking and Kimberley shortley after the start of the war. The battles of Modder River and Magersfontein were failed attempts by the British to break the siege. The British broke the siege of Kimberly on Feb. 15, 1900 and solidified their gain at the Battle of Paardeberg.

British break siege Feb. 28, 1900

Majuba Hill Feb. 27,1881
(the decisive battle of the First Boer War)

Talana Hill Oct. 20, 1899
Dundee
Elandslaagte Oct. 21, 1899
Ladysmith Nov. 2, 1899–Feb. 28, 1900
Colenso Dec. 15,1899
Vaal Krantz Feb. 5–7, 1900

ORANGE FREE STATE
(ORANGE RIVER COLONY)
(1854–1902, Br. Colony 1902–1910)

British break siege Feb.15, 1900

Harrismith

Spion Kop
Jan. 23–24, 1900

Nov. 6, 1889 – Feb.15, 1900 Kimberley
Dec. 11, 1899 Magersfontein
Nov. 28, 1899 Modder River
Nov. 23–25, 1899 Belmont and Graspan

Bloemfontein

Paardeberg Feb. 18–27, 1900

Maseru

N A T A L (British Colony 1883–1910)

After the British campaigns of breaking sieges and capturing key Boer cities (Oct. 1899–Sept. 1900), the Boer Republics shifted to guerrilla tactics to deny the British a clear victory (Sept. 1900–May 1902).

BASUTOLAND
(Br. Col. 1884–1910)

Pietermaritzburg

Durban

Port Nolloth

O'okiep

Springfontein

De Aar

Colesberg

Noupoort
Middelburg
Graaff-Reinet

Stormberg Dec. 10, 1899

Cape Midlands

C A P E   C O L O N Y
(British Colony 1795-1910)

INVASION OF NATAL
The Second Boer War began with the invasion of Natal by the Boers. The initial success of the British at the Battles of Talana Hill and Elandslaagte gave way to loss when the British lost the Battle of Ladysmith, and the Boers surrounded Ladysmith. The Boers pushed back British attempts to relieve Ladysmith at the Battles of Colenso and Spion Kop. The British broke through Boer positions on Feb. 27, and and the besiegers retreated, leaving Ladysmith to the British on Feb. 28.

ATLANTIC OCEAN

East London

I N D I A N   O C E A N

CAPE MIDLANDS
With British troops diluted by diversion to Natal, the Boers moved into the Cape Midlands and captured the railway junction at Stormberg.

Port Elizabeth

Cape Town
Simon's Town

miles / kilometers
0 100 200

Boundaries and political entities shown are as of Oct. 1899.

"ALL RED NOW JOEY"

"A sordid and criminal war, and in everyway shameful and excuseless . . . My head is with the British, but my heart and such rags of morals as I have are with the Boer."

MARK TWAIN, FROM A LETTER, 1900

Patriotic pride This cartoon probably dates to 1900, when the fall of the Boer capital, Pretoria, seemed to promise Britain's defeat of the Boer republics. Red was the color on maps given to areas of the British Empire. "Joey" was pro-war British politician Joseph Chamberlain.

THE *TITANIC*

The First—and Final—Voyage of a Doomed Ship

The R.M.S. (Royal Mail Steamer) *Titanic* was the most famous ship in the world upon her launch in Belfast, Northern Ireland, on May 31, 1911. For her brief life, she was the largest (but not technically most advanced) passenger liner ever built—882 feet 9 inches long and 175 feet high, with a displacement of 52,310 tons. She was also the most luxurious ship afloat, at least in first class, which was equipped with libraries, onboard telephones, barbershops, a gym, a squash court, a Turkish bath, a swimming pool, and even a newfangled Electric Bath, or sunbed.

A total of 2,223 people were on board during *Titanic*'s maiden voyage from Southampton, England, to New York City on April 10, 1912. Four days into the journey, at 11:40 p.m. ship's time, she struck an iceberg some 375 miles from the coast of Newfoundland. Two hours and 40 minutes later she sank, and 1,517 lives were lost. Just 706 people, along with three small dogs, were rescued at dawn by the liner *Carpathia*.

One reason for the tragedy was the fact that *Titanic* was traveling at close to her top speed of 21 to 23 knots. This meant that although the iceberg was spotted five minutes before impact, and despite a change of course, the ship's momentum took her into the ice. Then there was the vessel's design. In theory, *Titanic* could remain afloat with breaches to four of her 16 major "watertight" compartments,

but on the night of April 14, five or six were ruptured. Worse, the compartments' low transverse bulkheads—horizontal metal walls dividing the hull—allowed water to rush into the unbreached compartments as the ship tilted. The compartments also retained water in the bow, thus exaggerating the tilt, leading many to suggest *Titanic* might actually have survived longer—perhaps long enough to rescue its passengers—without the bulkheads intended to make her "practically unsinkable."

According to research on the wreck in 1985, better materials might also have extended *Titanic*'s life. Scientists showed that the boat's cheap iron (rather than steel) rivets had sheared badly. They also showed that under certain conditions, including severe cold, the type of steel used in the hull rendered it liable to sudden, brittle fracture rather than slower deformation (which might have prevented the catastrophic hull breaches).

In addition, fewer might have died had the *Titanic* carried more than 20 lifeboats, which had room for just 1,178 passengers. Reflecting the conviction that the ship was "practically unsinkable," her lifeboats were intended only to pick up survivors from other stricken ships. Worse, on the night of the disaster, many lifeboats left the ship partially empty: 31.6 percent of *Titanic*'s passengers survived; had the boats been filled, the figure would have been 53.4 percent. ■

Life and loss Newsboy Ned Parfett announcing the sinking of the *Titanic* outside the London offices of its owners, the White Star Line, on April 16, 1912, two days after the disaster. The loss of the ship and more than 1,500 lives represented an immense human tragedy, but also constituted a heavy blow to Britain's prestige at a time when the country was close to the height of its imperial and industrial powers. Parfett was killed in France during World War I, at age 22, in 1918.

Stop the clocks *(below)* A watch belonging to one of the victims of the *Titanic* disaster. Survivors or victims' families donated similar artifacts to museums around the world. Canadian coastguardsmen also gathered many objects in the aftermath of the disaster.

A final line Some of *Titanic*'s 1,324 passengers wait to board the ship for its doomed maiden voyage: 492 would survive, including 61 percent of first class but only 24 percent of third-class passengers; 20 percent of men and 75 percent of women were saved; 685 of the 899 crew members perished.

WHITE STAR LINE.

"OLYMPIC." 45000 TONS.
"TITANIC." 45000 TONS.
THE LARGEST STEAMERS IN THE WORLD.

To NEW YORK.
From SOUTHAMPTON-CHERBOURG-QUEENSTOWN.
From LIVERPOOL-QUEENSTOWN.
To BOSTON.
From LIVERPOOL-QUEENSTOWN.

For Freight and Passage apply to

THOS. COOK & SON.
31, Fargate, SHEFFIELD;
18, Clumber Street and
27, Derby Road, NOTTINGHAM;
and Gallowtree Gate, LEICESTER.

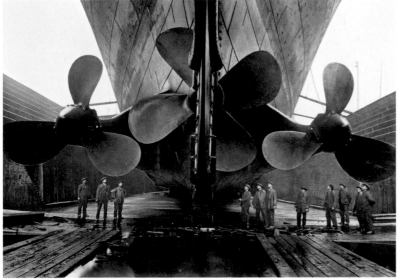

Height of ambition The *Titanic* in the Harland & Wolff shipyard's Thompson Graving Dock, then the world's largest dry dock, in a photograph taken in 1910 or 1911

Two lost A poster for the *Titanic* and a sister ship, the *Olympic,* which remained in service until 1935. A third ship in the class, *Britannic,* struck a mine and sank in 1916.

"*It seemed as if once everybody had gone, drowned, finished, the whole world was standing still. There was nothing, just this deathly, terrible silence in the dark night with the stars overhead.*"

EVA HART, *TITANIC* SURVIVOR, 1993

THE MODERN AGE
 1914–present

"*In Flanders fields, the poppies blow, between the crosses row on row. That mark our place; and in the sky the larks, still bravely singing, fly. Scarce heard amid the guns below.*"

LT. COL. JOHN MCCRAE, CANADIAN DOCTOR, "IN FLANDERS FIELDS," 1915

Europe in 1914

Reykjavík — ICELAND (Denmark)

ATLANTIC OCEAN

Faroe Is. (Denmark)

Shetland Is.

Outer Hebrides

Orkney Is.

NORTH SEA

GREAT BRITAIN

NORWAY

SWEDEN

FINLAND

White Sea

Archangel

Dvina

Torne

Kristiania (Oslo)

Stockholm

Gulf of Bothnia

Lake Onega

Lake Ladoga

Helsinki

Petrograd (St. Petersburg)

Reval (Tallinn)

Lake Peipus

Volga

Moscow

RUSSIAN EMPIRE

Skagerrak

Gothenburg

Baltic Sea

Riga

Daugava

Vilna (Vilnius)

Minsk

Oka

UNITED KINGDOM

IRELAND

Glasgow

Dublin

Leeds

Liverpool

Birmingham

Cardiff

Bristol

London

Portsmouth

English Channel

DENMARK

Copenhagen

Hamburg

NETH.

Amsterdam

Hanover

Elbe

Berlin

GERMAN EMPIRE

Oder

Danzig (Gdańsk)

Königsberg (Kaliningrad)

Vistula

Posen

Warsaw

Poland

Pinsk

Kiev

Dnieper

Kharkov

Ukraine

Brussels

Lille

BELGIUM

LUX.

Düsseldorf

Cologne

Frankfurt

Magdeburg

Leipzig

Dresden

Breslau

Prague

Cracow

Lemberg

Dniester

Rostov

Rouen

Reims

Paris

Nancy

Rhine

Nuremberg

Brünn

Czernowitz

Prut

Kishinev

Odessa

Sea of Azov

Kuban

Nantes

Seine

Loire

FRANCE

Stuttgart

Munich

Bern

SWITZ.

Danube

Vienna

Budapest

Theiss

AUSTRO-HUNGARIAN EMPIRE

Graz

Debrezin

Jassy (Iaşi)

Crimea

Bordeaux

Lyons

Garonne

Rhône

Turin

Milan

Venice

Po

Trieste

Drava

Sava

Beograd (Belgrade)

KINGDOM OF ROMANIA

Bucharest

BLACK SEA

Oporto

PORTUGAL

Duero

Ebro

ANDORRA

Marseille

Nice

Genoa

Bologna

Florence

Livorno

Adriatic Sea

SAN MARINO

Sarajevo

KINGDOM OF MONTENEGRO

KINGDOM OF SERBIA

Danube

KINGDOM OF BULGARIA

Sofia (Sofiya)

Madrid

Tagus

SPAIN

Barcelona

Valencia

Corsica (France)

Rome

KINGDOM OF ITALY

Cetinje

Tirana

ALBANIA

Constantinople (Istanbul)

Angora (Ankara)

Lisbon

Guadiana

Guadalquivir

Málaga

Balearic Islands

Sardinia (Italy)

Tyrrhenian Sea

Naples

Salonika (Thessaloniki)

KINGDOM OF GREECE

Aegean Sea

OTTOMAN EMPIRE

Tangier (France)

GIBRALTAR (United Kingdom)

SPANISH MOROCCO (Spanish Protectorate)

Alger (Algiers)

Palermo

Messina

Sicily (Italy)

Catania

Ionian Sea

Athens

Smyrna (Izmir)

Aleppo (Haleb)

Fez

Tunis

Tripoli

MALTA (British Crown Colony)

Crete

ITALIAN DODECANESE (Italy)

CYPRUS (annexed by United Kingdom 1914)

Beirut
Damascus

MOROCCO (French Protectorate)

FRENCH ALGERIA (France)

TUNISIA (French Protectorate)

MEDITERRANEAN SEA

Jerusalem

Banghazi

Alexandria

Cairo

Nile

miles

0   100   200   300   400

0   100   200   300   400

kilometers

1914 Political boundaries and entities are shown.
Present-day coastlines and rivers are shown.
Present-day names in parentheses.

ITALIAN LIBYA (Italian Protectorate)

EGYPT (occupied by United Kingdom)

TWO WORLD WARS DEFINED TODAY

BRITAIN BEGAN THE 20TH CENTURY AS THE LARGEST IMPERIAL POWER ON EARTH, WITH A SUPErior military, financial, and industrial presence. In the century that followed, the story of the land and its people changed dramatically as the country grappled with the loss of its empire and the development of a new modern identity. The British fought valiantly in two world wars. They emerged from World War I with their global status still strong. After the Second World War, however, as Britain's position as world leader began to diminish, the nation entered a new phase of massive social and cultural change—defined by an innovative welfare state and large-scale immigration—forever altering the fabric of this historic land.

■ WORLD WAR I

World War I looms large in the minds of the British to this day. The war burdened Britain's economy with huge war debts and weakened industries. More than eight million soldiers across Europe, nearly a million of whom were British, were killed in the fighting. Estimates of total British casualties, including those killed, wounded, and missing, exceed three million. Almost one in three British men born between 1890 and 1895 was killed, and tens of thousands were in mental hospitals for shell shock, a disorder that came from seeing comrades killed and mutilated in artillery barrages and attacks.

The Germans hoped that Britain would not enter the Great War. They had convinced themselves that the British would not stand by their commitments to France and Russia. Germany also believed Britain would be occupied by a civil war, since

Ireland was venting its frustration at being part of the British Empire. Since the late 19th century, Britain had come to view the emergence of a strong Germany with alarm, as German efficiency and educational prowess threatened British dominance. Also, the strong nationalism that ran through Europe included the United Kingdom. Still, in 1914, Britain had little interest in unleashing a major conflict. But its efforts at peacemaking and mediation came too late to halt the slide into war. Germany declared war on Russia on August 1 and on France two days later. But it was the German invasion of Belgium on August 4 that propelled Britain into the conflict, as the British had pledged to defend Belgian independence in the 1839 Treaty of London.

By the end of 1914, a trench line had been dug from the English Channel to the Swiss border (see page 296). For the next four years, most inventions of modern history—airplanes,

Soldiers to the front *(previous pages)* British troops in silhouette advance toward trenches in the First Battle of Ypres in World War I. Fighting back, the British and French blocked the German advance to English Channel ports, but the Allied counterattack failed. In the second battle, a year later, the Germans first used poisonous chlorine gas. The Allies soon followed suit. Despite its dreadful effects, gas killed far fewer soldiers than did shells and machine guns.

TIME LINE

1914–1918
World War I

1916
Easter Rising in Ireland

1916
Battle of the Somme

1917
The Balfour Declaration

1921
The Anglo-Irish Treaty

1922–1923
Irish Civil War

1936
King George V dies; Edward becomes king

1936
Edward VIII abdicates; King George VI
ascends to the throne

1939–1945
World War II

1940
The Battle of Britain

May 1940
Winston Churchill becomes prime minister

1940–1941
The Blitz

June 6, 1944
D-Day

1947
Pakistan and India gain independence
from Britain

1952
King George VI dies; Elizabeth II
becomes queen

1969–1998
The Troubles in Northern Ireland

1979
Margaret Thatcher becomes
the first female prime minister

1997
Britain returns Hong Kong to China

April 29, 2011
Prince William and
Catherine Middleton marry

2014
Scotland votes to remain in
the United Kingdom

poison gas, machine guns, tanks, flamethrowers, and submarines—were turned to the task of mass destruction. Britain and its empire fought in an alliance with France, Russia, and Italy. In 1917, Russia collapsed due to dwindling food supplies, poor transportation, lack of replacement parts, and a heavy death toll. The United States entered the conflict that year and, more than offsetting the collapse of Russia, turned the tide with an injection of men and matériel. By November 1918, World War I was over. The conflict had proved to be so destructive and widespread that it was called "the war to end all wars."

■ AFTERMATH OF WORLD WAR I

In the aftermath of the war, for all of its trauma, Britain recovered and the population at large had more of a chance to enjoy the comforts and fun of modern living. Many were able to afford homes and cars and to enjoy theaters, dance halls, and foreign travel. All men older than 21 and women over the age of 30 (who met a property qualification) were granted the right to vote in 1918, thus increasing the electorate from 8 million to 21 million. Women older than 21 acquired the vote in 1928, thus achieving the same voting rights as men.

There was still poverty, and in the recessions of 1920 to 1921 and 1929 to 1932, millions of people were thrown into unemployment. But many in the 1920s and 1930s also shared in the advances. For example, housing improved with slum-clearance plans and government homebuilding.

"To the north of Ypres the Germans, by employing
a large quantity of asphyxiating bombs, the effect of which
was felt for a distance of a mile and a quarter
behind our lines, succeeded in forcing us to retire."

OFFICIAL COMMUNIQUÉ, APRIL 23, 1915

American celebrities, movies, popular music, and dance crazes influenced British pop culture. Factory girls dressed up like actresses, and electricity zoomed from 1 house in 17 in 1920 to two-thirds of the houses in Britain in 1939.

And yet, trouble loomed. The dream of returning London to the center of the financial world resulted in the return of the gold standard in 1925. The move raised the cost of British exports and drove wages down, worsening the fate of struggling industries. Coal-mining owners, in an attempt to match foreign competition, asked for lower wages and longer working hours, and the coal miners objected. They struck nationwide, and the trade unionists in support of them stopped work as well. This resulted in the General Strike of 1926, although the government used emergency measures to assure essential services would continue. The union called off the strike after nine days without a single concession, but some of the coal miners struck for another six months.

In 1929, the Great Depression slowed business and caused worldwide unemployment. The fall began in October with the market crash on Wall Street in New York City. The crash had less impact on Britain than on the United States, but it nevertheless brought misery for millions who experienced the era as the "hungry thirties." The situation improved significantly when the British government initiated rearmament in response to the threat of Nazi Germany, imperial Japan, and fascist Italy, thus spurring economic growth.

In January 1936, King George V died, and his eldest son, Edward, became king of the United Kingdom (see page 310). Months into his reign, the new king proposed to American socialite Wallis Simpson, who was divorced, and the country faced a moral crisis. Edward VIII finally abdicated to marry Simpson, and his younger brother Albert became King George VI on December 11.

■ WORLD WAR II

The Treaty of Versailles in 1919 had put extreme restrictions on Germany—15 years of Allied occupation and heavy reparation payments. Then Adolf Hitler stepped into the picture in 1921 as leader of the Nazi Party. Twelve years later, in 1933, he became chancellor on a program aimed at restoring Germany as a major power. Prime Minister Neville Chamberlain tried to appease Hitler, but when the latter's forces first occupied Czechoslovakia in March 1939 and then invaded Poland in September, Britain's agreements forced it into the war to defend several countries against Germany's aggression.

The war began badly for Britain. Unlike in 1914, when French and British armies had managed to halt the German advance, they were humiliatingly defeated in May 1940 and forced to retreat to the port of Dunkirk, where every boat that could be mustered rescued them. The result of this defeat was to bring the Conservative warhorse Winston Churchill to office as prime minister, replacing Chamberlain.

German bombing of the cities of England by airplanes and rockets caused 43,000 deaths—about half of them in London—but British Spitfires and Hurricanes cleared the skies of bombers in the Battle of Britain (see pages 312–313). German submarines interrupted British supply lines by sinking ships until U.S. and British warships began accompanying the convoys.

The United States entered the war in 1941, after the bombing of Pearl Harbor, Hawaii, but the conflict still favored the Axis (Germany, Japan, and Italy) over the Allies (Britain,

"You are the man I want" *(above)* In a 1914 recruitment poster for World War I, Lord Kitchener, war minister, seemingly points at a camera and makes a statement. The photo was actually taken from a magazine cover, and the arm was painted on. New research indicates the poster was never used for recruitment purposes.

World War I aircraft *(opposite)* A British-built Sopwith fighter plane has just returned from bombing Essen, Germany, on the Western Front. World War I was the first war to see the large-scale employment of airplanes, which were used mostly for scouting before pilots realized they could use them in battle, too.

HOUSE OF WINDSOR
1914-Present

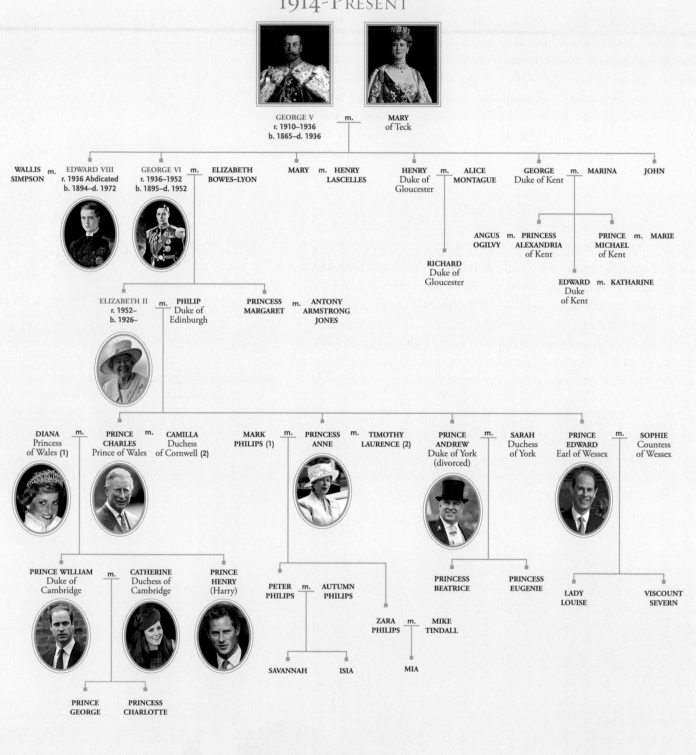

GEORGE V
r. 1910–1936
b. 1865–d. 1936

m.

MARY
of Teck

WALLIS
SIMPSON

m.

EDWARD VIII
r. 1936 Abdicated
b. 1894–d. 1972

GEORGE VI
r. 1936–1952
b. 1895–d. 1952

m.

ELIZABETH
BOWES-LYON

MARY

m.

HENRY
LASCELLES

HENRY
Duke of
Gloucester

m.

ALICE
MONTAGUE

GEORGE
Duke of Kent

m.

MARINA

JOHN

RICHARD
Duke of
Gloucester

ANGUS
OGILVY

m.

PRINCESS
ALEXANDRIA
of Kent

PRINCE
MICHAEL
of Kent

m.

MARIE

EDWARD
Duke
of Kent

m.

KATHARINE

ELIZABETH II
r. 1952–
b. 1926–

m.

PHILIP
Duke of
Edinburgh

PRINCESS
MARGARET

m.

ANTONY
ARMSTRONG
JONES

DIANA
Princess
of Wales (1)

m.

PRINCE
CHARLES
Prince of Wales

m.

CAMILLA
Duchess
of Cornwell (2)

MARK
PHILIPS (1)

m.

PRINCESS
ANNE

m.

TIMOTHY
LAURENCE (2)

PRINCE
ANDREW
Duke of York
(divorced)

m.

SARAH
Duchess
of York

PRINCE
EDWARD
Earl of Wessex

m.

SOPHIE
Countess
of Wessex

PRINCE WILLIAM
Duke of
Cambridge

m.

CATHERINE
Duchess of
Cambridge

PRINCE
HENRY
(Harry)

PETER
PHILIPS

m.

AUTUMN
PHILIPS

ZARA
PHILIPS

m.

MIKE
TINDALL

PRINCESS
BEATRICE

PRINCESS
EUGENIE

LADY
LOUISE

VISCOUNT
SEVERN

PRINCE
GEORGE

PRINCESS
CHARLOTTE

SAVANNAH

ISIA

MIA

> *"You must not lose faith in humanity. Humanity is an ocean;*
> *if a few drops of the ocean are dirty, the ocean does not become dirty."*

MAHATMA GANDHI (1869–1948)

France, the United States, and Russia). By autumn 1942, the latter stages of the war turned in favor of the Allies, as Britain recovered, American industries geared up, the Free French (the government-in-exile led by Charles de Gaulle) fought with the Allies, and Russia (and its winter) proved to be too much for the Axis powers.

After the Allies landed at Normandy in June 1944 (see pages 320–321), battles mostly turned against the Axis powers, and the Germans retreated across the continent. On May 4, 1945, Germany surrendered, and the war in Europe was officially over at midnight on May 8.

■ POSTWAR BRITAIN

Britain was impoverished after World War II, its economy ruptured and its population diminished. Nearly 400,000 British people had lost their lives in the conflict—about 330,000 members of the military and 60,000 civilians. In 1945, the Labour Party, enthusiastically supported by a people who believed they deserved better lives as a result of bearing up under the war, came to office in an electoral landslide. Labour leader Clement Attlee replaced Churchill as prime minister, but the latter remained leader of the Conservative Party.

Industries were run-down, and the investment required to rebuild them only would have added to the austerity of the people who had voted in the new government. The coal industry was nationalized, as were electricity and gas, the Bank of England, rails

Leader of Indian independence Mahatma Gandhi, political and spiritual leader of India, believed in nonviolence in achieving independence from Britain. British authorities repeatedly arrested him. Whereas he had supported the British war effort in World War I, by 1939 he opposed Indian mobilization for war against Germany and Japan. In January 1940, following India's independence, a radical Hindu assassinated him.

SUNNY RHYL
FOR GOLDEN SANDS & SUNSHINE
SERVED BY THE LMS MAIN LINE.

Sunny destination A poster advertises Rhyl on the coast of Wales after World War II. Once an elegant Victorian resort, the popular vacation spot became awash with people from Liverpool and Manchester as growing affluence gave the broader public access to travel, vacations, and swimming.

War bride *(left)* In 1940, Ena Squire-Brown, an international dancer known for the Dove Dance, leaves her recently bombed home for church to marry a Royal Air Force flying officer. The German effort to break British resolve backfired.

London Underground *(opposite)* Passengers in the 1920s descend to and ascend from trains of the London Underground—the first underground subway in the world. When it became operational in 1863, the railway was just under the ground. Circular tunnels were cut much deeper later, and the system became known as the Tube. Today, it encompasses more than 250 miles.

and canals, road transport, and iron and steel. A universal health system guaranteed that no one would go untreated in case of sickness or accident (see pages 322–323).

But an empire was waning (see pages 324–325). Ireland, whose fortunes have been linked to Britain since people began crossing the Irish Sea, had gained its independence between the wars. In 1916, a rebellion took place in Dublin during Easter week, and British leaders, wanting to squash it, sent a strong message by executing 16 nationalist leaders and imprisoning or interning more than a thousand (see page 306). In 1921, after two years of violent struggle against the British and civil war, Ireland became an independent state, and Northern Ireland—largely Protestant—remained as a dominion within the British Commonwealth.

This loss was small compared with the wave of independence that followed World War II, beginning with India. British merchants and soldiers had subordinated India to British rule in the 18th century. In the course of the 19th century, the Raj replaced rule by the East India Company, and Queen Victoria was declared the empress of India. But the more Britain became involved in the government of India, the more independence-minded Indians became. By the beginning of the 20th century, Indians—Muslims and Hindus alike—increasingly resented and resisted British rule. After decades of struggle, led most notably by Mahatma Gandhi, partition occurred. India gained independence on August 15, 1947. Pakistan had become independent a day earlier (see pages 324–325).

"These are not dark days; these are great days   the greatest days our country has ever lived; and we must all thank God that we have been allowed, each of us according to our stations, to play a part in making these days memorable in the history of our race."

WINSTON CHURCHILL, OCTOBER 29, 1941

Flower Power *(above)* A Mini with a painted pattern bespeaks London in the 1960s, when the mood changed from staid to irreverent. The land of the bowler hat and tea turned to stylish art and protests as young people rebelled against their parents and the establishment.

Hot spot of fashion *(below)* Shoppers on London's Carnaby Street wear short skirts on their way to buy the latest mod fashions in the late 1960s. Young people drove pop culture: Girls dressed differently from their parents, and boys wore their hair long.

"Ancient elegance and new opulence are all tangled up in a dazzling blur of op and pop. [London] is alive with birds (girls) and beatles, buzzing with minicars and telly stars, pulsing with half a dozen separate veins of excitement."

PIRI HALASZ, *TIME* MAGAZINE, APRIL 1966

After India's independence, Burma (Myanmar) followed suit, becoming an independent state in January 1948, and Ceylon (Sri Lanka) became independent a month later in February. Nigeria, Kenya, Tanganyika (Tanzania), the Gold Coast (Ghana), Sudan, and other African countries rapidly took first steps toward self-government. "The sun never sets on the British Empire" was true no more.

Nevertheless, the United Kingdom became more egalitarian than ever before. By the 1960s people had more money to spend, the young were more rebellious, and social mores relaxed. The Beatles invaded the scene, the fashion shops of Carnaby Street became a tourist attraction, and Mary Quant's miniskirt became the icon of the decade (see page 326).

Meanwhile, in Northern Ireland, the "swinging 60s" ended on a far more bitter note. Britain had not paid much attention to Northern Ireland from the 1920s to the 1960s. And when the Protestant majority was allowed to discriminate against the Catholic minority, violence broke out and British troops were sent to quell it. By 1969, a bitter struggle began between the nationalist terrorists of the Irish Republican Army (IRA), Protestant paramilitaries, and the British Army (see pages 328–329).

Past and present The old and the new are juxtaposed as the Tower Bridge and the glass city hall appear at dusk. Symbol of the new London, the hall is home to the mayor, the London Assembly, and the 600 or so permanent staff who work there.

■ THE LAST DECADES

In 1979, Britain turned away from the welfare state as an answer to economic problems when the Conservative Party came to power and Margaret Thatcher, its leader, was named first female prime minister (see pages 330–331). Thatcher, who headed the British government for 11 years, became the most controversial British leader of the 20th century for her outspokenness, directness, and uncompromising policies. She believed in unfettered free-market capitalism and the end of government interference in the economy. Her controversial program of market reforms was made easier to swallow by the victory over Argentina in the Falklands War in 1982, and patriotic fervor raised her standing among the electorate.

At the same time, the House of Windsor, led by Queen Elizabeth II (1926–), encountered its share of ups and downs. Prince Charles, the heir apparent, married Lady Diana Spencer in 1981. Fifteen years later, amid disclosures of adultery on both sides, the marriage ended. The unions of Prince Andrew and Princess Anne also ended in divorce, and the private lives of the royals once again became tabloid fodder. Called the "people's princess," Diana was beloved by the people. Her sudden death in a car crash on August 31, 1997, resulted in an extraordinary outpouring of grief.

The Diamond Jubilee, commemorating Elizabeth's 60th anniversary as queen, was marked with lavish celebrations in June 2012. Today, the monarchy is as popular as ever, largely due to respect for the queen and her venerable tenure, and the glamour and appeal of the younger generation of royals (see pages 332–333). ■

THE WESTERN FRONT

Key Conflict to Central and Allied Forces

The Western Front was the name given to an enormous network of trenches and fortifications that ran from the Swiss border to the North Sea. Germany opened the front by invading Belgium in August 1914. For four bitter years, both sides launched offensives across these lines. After Germany defeated Russia in 1917, it was on the Western Front that Germany was broken in 1918.

Britain, France, and Russia formed the Triple Entente, which was eventually joined by the United States. Germany, Italy, and Austria-Hungary formed the Central Powers. Later, the Ottoman Empire joined the Central Powers, as did Bulgaria. In 1916, Romania joined the Triple Entente.

Neither side thought the war would last very long. The Germans figured they would knock out the French on the Western Front quickly, before the Russians on the Eastern Front could get organized. The French army proved strong and Britain came into the war immediately in August, after Germany invaded Belgium.

The British, thinking the conflict would be over by Christmas, volunteered for duty in droves. Clerks and factory workers were willing to join in the fight, as the average Briton was extremely patriotic and believed the cause was just. The call to arms was issued for 100,000 volunteers, and about 175,000 Britons came forward in the first week. Also contributing to the overwhelming response was British propagandists' message that this was a battle between civilization and barbarism—that the "Huns" had massacred civilians and brought wanton destruction on Belgium.

The daunting job of training the thousands of civilian volunteers required many months. In the meantime, the country had to rely on its regular army, the small British Expeditionary Force, which arrived in France in August and positioned itself along the northern line.

In August and September 1914, the Germans advanced after their thrust through Belgium, and it looked as if a quick victory were in sight. The British and their allies, the French, retreated from Mons and Le Cateau in late August, and, figuring the war was lost, Sir John French, head of the British Expeditionary Force, planned to withdraw his forces. Horatio Kitchener, the war minister in London, overruled French, and together the British and French forces drove back the Germans in the First Battle of the Marne, in which both sides settled in to slow trench warfare.

Preparing for the front lines Newly arrived British soldiers rest in France after arriving across the English Channel. When the Ottoman Turks opposed Russia, the conflict spread to the Middle East, but the Western Front was considered the deciding battlefield.

Murder in Bosnia *(opposite)* The assassination of Archduke Franz Ferdinand of Austria and his wife, Sophie, in Sarajevo by a Bosnian Serbian nationalist sparked the outbreak of World War I.

*"The plunge of civilization into this abyss of blood and darkness
by the wanton feat of two infamous autocrats . . .
is too tragic for any words."*

ANGLO-AMERICAN WRITER HENRY JAMES, IN A LETTER ABOUT THE OUTBREAK OF WORLD WAR I

Within the opposing trench lines lived thousands of men who planned offensives and died during them, fought off diseases, and coped with death all around. Parts of the trenches filled with water during rains, and though modern medicine took care of some illnesses, new ones reared their ugly heads. Trench foot—caused by standing for days in cold water—and all kinds of dysentery appeared, but none of them served to disable opposing forces. Plus, an enormous logistical system enabled by modern railways helped the armies to keep fighting.

The British trenches were in three lines: the front, for command and firing; the middle, for support; and the reserve, behind which was positioned the artillery. Trench lines ran at right angles, connecting the three main trenches for communication. Wired telephone lines, pigeons, dogs, and semaphores were all used to pass messages. Barbed-wire entanglements were in No Man's Land, the ground between the opposing trenches. Germany's fortifications, organized by depth and provided with deep concrete emplacements, were superior to those of the British and French.

Fighting in the heavily fortified line created a new kind of warfare. With the armies held immobile for months on end by fierce machine-gun and artillery fire, small-scale raids were done with knives, clubs, and grenades. Periscopes were useful in spying on the enemy without exposing oneself, and wire cutters were used to cut barbed-wire entanglements before and during an attack. Lice were a constant problem; they caused trench fever, a disease with high fever and severe pain. Huge rats, fat from feeding on corpses, gnawed holes in men's packs to reach morsels of food. After several months of this life on the Western Front, a man was beyond his prime as an efficient soldier.

Troops at the front included volunteers from Britain's empire; men from Australia, New Zealand, and Canada responded to the call. Protestants and Catholics from Ulster in the north of Ireland offered their services to the British Army. Men from India rallied to the cause as well.

The losses were staggering. Soldiers and their leaders were accustomed to marching toward their opponents and overwhelming them with their numbers and tactics. Instead, machine guns mowed them down. Explosive artillery shells killed men as they cowered in the trenches. Tens of thousands of British lives were lost for minimal gains. In the opening three months of the war, 89,864 British casualties occurred on the Western Front—more than the entire 84,000 British Expeditionary Force at the beginning of the conflict. The Germans, too, suffered enormous losses, and French casualties were as great or greater.

The Americans, embittered against the Germans when U.S. citizens were lost in the sinking of the passenger liner *Lusitania,* joined the war effort in 1917 after remaining neutral

Reviled and respected General Douglas Haig was appointed head of the British forces in World War I. He was blamed for the casualties at the Battle of the Somme in 1916—almost 60,000 in the first day—and repeated the heavy losses at Passchendaele. Even so, he was named commander of home forces when he returned to England.

for three years. The Central Powers had begun to use German submarines in unfettered attacks on ships, and this unrestricted warfare was pivotal in President Woodrow Wilson's decision to declare war on Germany.

Like Britain before it, the United States, a young and untouched country, took more than a year to train its army. In the meantime, in March 1918, the Germans, believing the Western Front held the key to the war, launched a last offensive. At first they were successful, pushing the British and the French back within 62 miles of Paris. Then resistance stiffened as the Allies came under Marshal Ferdinand Foch as supreme commander. In summer 1918, American soldiers arrived at the front and bolstered the British and French forces lost in previous fighting. In July 1918, the Battle of Château-Thierry, a victory for the Allies, proved the quality of the new U.S. Army.

The British Army pierced German lines in August. Germany was exhausted. Defeat and retreat along the entire Western Front was the story of October 1918, as the fighting spirit passed out of the German army. Early in November, British and Canadian troops were in Valenciennes, and the Americans were in Sedan. The Western Front had indeed held the key to victory for the Allies. ■

Explosives you could throw Grenades were useful in trench warfare. These British-made ones were handy in dealing with machine guns. Soldiers hurled the grenades forward to destroy an entire gun crew and its implement of death.

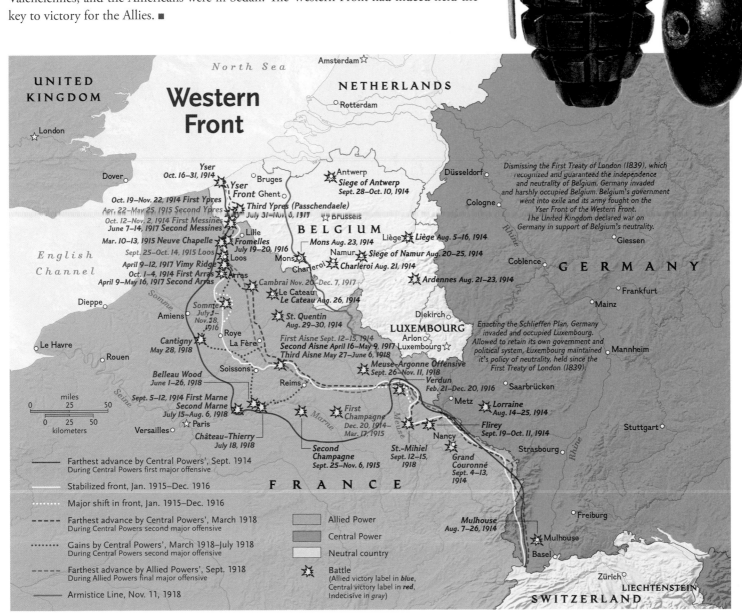

Western Front

Dismissing the First Treaty of London (1839), which recognized and guaranteed the independence and neutrality of Belgium, Germany invaded and harshly occupied Belgium. Belgium's government went into exile and its army fought on the Yser Front of the Western Front. The United Kingdom declared war on Germany in support of Belgium's neutrality.

Enacting the Schlieffen Plan, Germany invaded and occupied Luxembourg. Allowed to retain its own government and political system, Luxembourg maintained it's policy of neutrality, held since the First Treaty of London (1839).

Yser Oct. 16–31, 1914
Oct. 19–Nov. 22, 1914 First Ypres
Apr. 22–May 25, 1915 Second Ypres
Oct. 12–Nov. 2, 1914 First Messines
June 7–14, 1917 Second Messines
Third Ypres (Passchendaele) July 31–Nov. 6, 1917
Mar. 10–13, 1915 Neuve Chapelle
Sept. 25–Oct. 14, 1915 Loos
April 9–12, 1917 Vimy Ridge
Oct. 1–4, 1914 First Arras
April 9–May 16, 1917 Second Arras
Fromelles July 19–20, 1916
Mons Aug. 23, 1914
Siege of Antwerp Sept. 28–Oct. 10, 1914
Liège Aug. 5–16, 1914
Siege of Namur Aug. 20–25, 1914
Charleroi Aug. 21, 1914
Ardennes Aug. 21–23, 1914
Cambrai Nov. 20–Dec. 7, 1917
Le Cateau Aug. 26, 1914
St. Quentin Aug. 29–30, 1914
Somme July 1–Nov. 18, 1916
First Aisne Sept. 12–15, 1914
Second Aisne April 16–May 9, 1917
Third Aisne May 27–June 6, 1918
Cantigny May 28, 1918
Meuse-Argonne Offensive Sept. 26–Nov. 11, 1918
Belleau Wood June 1–26, 1918
Verdun Feb. 21–Dec. 20, 1916
Sept. 5–12, 1914 First Marne
Second Marne July 15–Aug. 6, 1918
First Champagne Dec. 20, 1914–Mar. 17, 1915
Lorraine Aug. 14–25, 1914
Château-Thierry July 18, 1918
Flirey Sept. 19–Oct. 11, 1914
Second Champagne Sept. 25–Nov. 6, 1915
St.-Mihiel Sept. 12–15, 1918
Grand Couronné Sept. 4–13, 1914
Mulhouse Aug. 7–26, 1914
Mulhouse

Legend:
— Farthest advance by Central Powers', Sept. 1914 During Central Powers first major offensive
— Stabilized front, Jan. 1915–Dec. 1916
⋯ Major shift in front, Jan. 1915–Dec. 1916
- - - Farthest advance by Central Powers', March 1918 During Central Powers second major offensive
⋯⋯ Gains by Central Powers', March 1918–July 1918 During Central Powers second major offensive
- - - Farthest advance by Allied Powers', Sept. 1918 During Allied Powers final major offensive
— Armistice Line, Nov. 11, 1918

Allied Power
Central Power
Neutral country

✸ Battle (Allied victory label in *blue*, Central victory label in *red*, Indecisive in *gray*)

miles 0 25 50
kilometers 0 25 50

UNITED KINGDOM
NETHERLANDS
North Sea
Amsterdam
London
Dover
Rotterdam
Bruges
Ghent
Antwerp
Brussels
BELGIUM
Lille
Mons
Namur
Charleroi
Liège
Düsseldorf
Cologne
GERMANY
Giessen
Coblence
Arras
Le Cateau
Amiens
Roye
La Fère
Soissons
Reims
Diekirch
LUXEMBOURG
Arlon
Luxembourg
Frankfurt
Mainz
Mannheim
Saarbrücken
Metz
Nancy
Le Havre
Rouen
Dieppe
English Channel
Paris
Versailles
FRANCE
Verdun
Strasbourg
Stuttgart
Freiburg
Basel
Zürich
LIECHTENSTEIN
SWITZERLAND
Somme
Seine
Marne
Meuse
Rhine

THE BATTLE OF THE SOMME

Britain Endures Biggest Casualties in a Single Day

The opening day of the Battle of the Somme, July 1, 1916, was the worst military disaster in British history. Nearly 60,000 casualties were suffered within a matter of hours, a third of them dead. The battle is cited for Britain's reluctance to become involved in World War II 20 years later. Nothing was worth another Somme, some said.

The carnage was blamed on the mistakes of Sir Douglas Haig, named field marshal for all of the British Expeditionary Force when Sir John French was dismissed. Haig is not without his supporters, who said that after all, he was on the winning side. But his detractors abhor the biggest casualty figures of any British battle.

Haig ordered the attack at the Somme River in northern France as a means of decreasing the pressure on the French at Verdun, who were reeling. Reasons for the high casualty figure were many and varied. Haig had been a member of the cavalry for nine years, chiefly in India, and believed that horses were necessary in battle. He was convinced that with a sustained blast from the big guns, his forces would strike holes in the barbed wire and the enemy would be devastated. His infantry would advance slowly and take over the abandoned German trenches, and the cavalry would pursue the fleeing enemy.

The British artillery preceded the attack with a weeklong barrage, which warned the Germans that an attack was coming. German soldiers simply retreated into their substantial concrete bunkers and waited out the pounding of the artillery. When the barrage lifted and the British blew their whistles to begin the offensive, the Germans emerged and set up their machine guns. The British advanced at a slow walk—the better to maintain control—and the Germans mowed them down.

The conflict lasted from July 1 until November 13, 1916. Britain suffered more than 400,000 casualties in that time, France about 200,000. And more than 600,000 casualties were inflicted on Germany. According to noted military historian John Keegan, the Somme resulted in "the end of an age of vital optimism in British life."

After months of frontal attacks, Haig called an end to the Somme campaign, and in 1917 he undertook a similar offensive in Ypres. In this campaign, he aimed at perfecting the tactic he had tried at the Somme. When rains came and the battleground turned to mud and shell holes filled with water, more men died of drowning than at any land battle in British history. The final assault carried the village of Passchendaele, but the casualty figure was another 325,000 British men. ■

Keeping watch A British lookout creeps to the edge of a captured trench in the Battle of the Somme. Known for high losses in the battle, the British suffered 420,000 casualties, the French about 200,000, and the Germans more than 600,000. The British hurled 1.6 million shells at the Germans over a week's time, and were so confident of success that General Haig ordered his troops to walk to the German trenches. Haig's soldiers fell in swathes before machine guns, which the Germans, now deep in trenches, had set up when the attack began.

Poison Gas Used

British machine gunners, hooded by gas masks, fire a Vickers machine gun at the Germans during the Battle of the Somme in 1916. Gas was first used by the Germans at Ypres in 1915, but it was soon adopted by the Allies. It appeared first as a yellow-green cloud that, when inhaled, destroyed the victim's respiratory organs, which brought on choking attacks and death. The gas, though horrible, was responsible for only 12,000 deaths in the British ranks. Soldiers wore gas masks to help protect themselves against the airborne toxin.

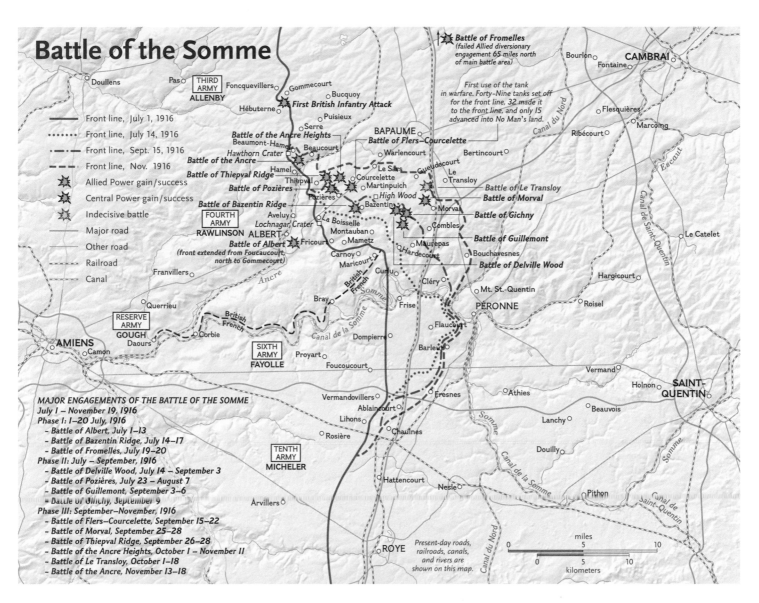

Battle of the Somme

Battle of Fromelles (failed Allied diversionary engagement 65 miles north of main battle area)

First use of the tank in warfare. Forty-Nine tanks set off for the front line, 32 made it to the front line, and only 15 advanced into No Man's land.

THIRD ARMY ALLENBY

First British Infantry Attack

Battle of the Ancre Heights
Battle of the Ancre
Battle of Thiepval Ridge
Battle of Poziéres
Battle of Bazentin Ridge

FOURTH ARMY RAWLINSON ALBERT

Battle of Albert (front extended from Foucaucourt, north to Gommecourt)

Battle of Flers–Courcelette
Battle of Le Transloy
Battle of Morval
Battle of Gichny
Battle of Guillemont
Battle of Delville Wood

- Front line, July 1, 1916
- Front line, July 14, 1916
- Front line, Sept. 15, 1916
- Front line, Nov. 1916
- Allied Power gain/success
- Central Power gain/success
- Indecisive battle
- Major road
- Other road
- Railroad
- Canal

RESERVE ARMY GOUGH

SIXTH ARMY FAYOLLE

TENTH ARMY MICHELER

MAJOR ENGAGEMENTS OF THE BATTLE OF THE SOMME
July 1 – November 19, 1916
Phase I: 1–20 July, 1916
– Battle of Albert, July 1–13
– Battle of Bazentin Ridge, July 14–17
– Battle of Fromelles, July 19–20
Phase II: July – September, 1916
– Battle of Delville Wood, July 14 – September 3
– Battle of Poziéres, July 23 – August 7
– Battle of Guillemont, September 3–6
– Battle of Gichny, September 9
Phase III: September–November, 1916
– Battle of Flers–Courcelette, September 15–22
– Battle of Morval, September 25–28
– Battle of Thiepval Ridge, September 26–28
– Battle of the Ancre Heights, October 1 – November 11
– Battle of Le Transloy, October 1–18
– Battle of the Ancre, November 13–18

Present-day roads, railroads, canals, and rivers are shown on this map.

miles 0 5 10
kilometers 0 5 10

Captured soldiers A column of German prisoners marches to the place of internment, guarded by British soldiers during the Battle of the Somme. Few POWs were taken in World War I on the Western Front until the final offensives in the summer and autumn of 1918. By the end of the war, 115,000 German POWs were held in camps in the United Kingdom.

"It was a magnificent display of trained and disciplined valor . . . only failed of success because dead men can advance no further."

MAJOR GENERAL SIR HENRY DE BEAUVOIR DE LISLE, ON THE FIRST
DAY OF THE BATTLE OF THE SOMME, JULY 1, 1916

WORLD WAR

Conflict and Casualties Spread Around the Globe

e know it today as World War I, but participants in the conflict knew it as the Great War and "the war to end all wars." Centered in Europe, the conflict quickly widened to become global. Britain brought its empire, by far the largest the world has ever seen, into the fray, as did France and Russia, and the war involved a wide range of ethnicities and nationalities from countries such as India, Algeria, Tunisia, Vietnam, and Japan. The battleground on land and sea ultimately extended from the waters around the British Isles to northern France and Italy, the eastern Mediterranean, Eastern Europe from the Baltic to the Black Sea, East and West Africa, Mesopotamia, the South Pacific, and northeast China.

On the Western Front, the Germans battled the British, the French, and later the United States; on the Eastern Front, Austria-Hungary's troops—augmented by the Germans—fought the Russians. Also in the European theater were the Italian and Balkan Fronts, where combat took place in more confined areas.

Japan joined the Allies in 1914 and attacked German colonial concessions in China. Brazil and China, which initially had stayed neutral, entered on the side of the Allies in 1917.

In October 1914, the Ottoman Empire joined the Central Powers of Germany, Austria-Hungary, and Bulgaria, and brought into the conflict its colonial dependencies. Much of 1915 was dominated by Allied actions against the Ottomans. First, in March, the British launched a failed assault on the Dardanelles, a strait in northwestern Turkey. Next, in late April, British and ANZAC (Australia and New Zealand) troops landed in Gallipoli, Turkey, to the west of the Dardanelles, and again Turkish resistance was strong. After eight months of fighting with high casualties on both sides, Allied troops pulled out in January 1916.

In the first years of the 19th century, Britain and Germany had engaged in a fierce naval arms race. And the big battleships known as dreadnoughts clashed inconclusively at Jutland, Denmark, in 1916. The actual decisive naval battle in World War I was between the U-boats and the blockading navies of Britain, France, and eventually the United States. The German U-boats did terrible damage to unprotected shipping, and the losses mounted after January 1917 and the declaration of unrestricted U-boat warfare. Their sinking of American ships eventually brought the United States into the war in April 1917. Russia had bowed out in 1917, but the entry of the United States tipped the scales toward the Allies. With the British, American, and French navies combined, Germany never had enough resources to cut off the transatlantic supply lines.

The war ended in fall 1918 when members of the Central Powers signed armistice agreements one by one. In October 1918, Germany, the last to do so, asked for an armistice, which it signed on November 11 in a railway car near the front lines. The war didn't officially end until the Treaty of Versailles in June 1919. Altogether, the ruinous conflict cost the lives of more than 16 million soldiers and civilians.

The global impact of World War I lasted well into the 20th century. The conflict contributed to the downfall of monarchies in Russia, Austria-Hungary, Germany, and the Ottoman Empire. And it severely fractured the British economy—allowing for the beginning of a power shift from the United Kingdom to the United States. ∎

Lawrence of Arabia

Thomas Edward (T. E.) Lawrence, born in 1888 in Wales, was a British military officer who traveled to Cairo with the British Army to contribute his knowledge of Arabic gained through his work as an archaeologist in the Middle East. In 1916, he was sent as a liaison officer to accompany Prince Feisal in his revolt against the Turks. With guerrilla tactics and guns that Lawrence supplied to the Arabs, they struck at Turkish lines of communication. In 1917, Lawrence joined Feisal in crossing hundreds of miles of Arabian Desert to hit the Turks at Aqaba, a valuable port town and Turkish fort. The Arabs won a stunning victory by hitting the enemy from the rear, where they least expected it. American war correspondent Lowell Thomas traveled with Lawrence in the desert, and Thomas's coverage made Lawrence a household name. After writing his war memoirs, called *Seven Pillars of Wisdom,* Lawrence tried to disappear, joining the Royal Air Force as a mechanic and later the British Army as a private. He retired in Britain and died in 1935 after losing control of his motorcycle. A popular movie, *Lawrence of Arabia,* was made about his life in 1962.

Moroccan horsemen A regiment of Spahis is awarded for bravery during World War I. Established in 1914, the First Moroccan Spahi Regiment was a mounted cavalry unit recruited primarily from indigenous horsemen. The regiment saw service on both the Eastern and the Western Fronts.

"At eleven o'clock this morning came to an end the cruellest and most terrible war that has ever scourged mankind. I hope we may all say that thus, this fateful morning, came to an end all wars."

PRIME MINISTER DAVID LLOYD GEORGE,
SPEECH IN THE HOUSE OF COMMONS, NOVEMBER 11, 1918

Recruiting troops Proclaiming "Our Ancestors Fought for Our Freedom," a 1914 recruitment poster for WWI encourages British youth to join the effort against Germany and her allies. During the war, some 200 recruiting posters were designed by the Parliamentary Recruiting Committee.

World War I
1914–1918

ATLANTIC

OCEAN

A detailed map of the Western Front appears on page 299.

Allied Powers (including commonwealths, colonies, protectorates, and territories)

Neutral state that joined Allied Powers

Central Powers

Neutral state that joined Central Powers

Remained neutral

1914 Farthest advance by Allied Powers (with date of advance)

1914 Farthest advance by Central Powers (with date of advance)

Armistice lines

Battles (Allied victory label in *blue*, Central victory label in *red*, Indecisive in *gray*)

Faroe Is. (Denmark)

Shetland Is.

Orkney Is.

Outer Hebrides

Scotland

Glasgow

UNITED
IRELAND
KINGDOM GREAT
BRITAIN

Dublin

Liverpool
Manchester

Wales England
Birmingham
Cardiff
Bristol

London

Portsmouth

English Channel

FRANCE

Bay of
Biscay

Nantes

Bordeaux

Lyons

Oporto

Lisbon

PORTUGAL

SPAIN

Madrid

Valencia

Barcelona

Málaga

Str. of Gibraltar
(Fr.) Tangier
GIBRALTAR
(U.K.)
SPANISH MOROCCO
(Sp. Prot.)

Alboran Sea

Fez

MOROCCO
(Fr. Prot.)

FRENCH ALGERIA
(France)

Alger
(Algiers)

NORWAY

SWEDEN

Finland

Kristiania
(Oslo)

Helsinki

Stockholm

Skagerrak

NORTH SEA

DENMARK
Copenhagen

Kattegat

Gulf of Bothnia

Gulf of Finland
Reval
(Tallinn)

Riga

Mar. 1918

BALTIC SEA

Jutland
May 31–June 1, 1916

Dogger Bank
Jan. 24, 1915

Heligoland Bight
Aug. 28, 1914

Hamburg

NETH.
Amsterdam

Berlin

Brussels

Lille

BELGIUM
LUX.

Rouen

Paris

Nancy

Stuttgart

Munich

Bern

SWITZ.

Milan

Turin

Genoa

Nice

Marseille

Corsica
(France)

ANDORRA

Toulouse

Ligurian Sea

Florence
Livorno

Rome

SAN
MARINO

Naples

Tyrrhenian Sea

Sardinia
(Italy)

Palermo
Messina
Catania

Sicily
(Italy)

Ionian Sea

Tunis

TUNISIA
(Fr. Prot.)

Gulf of Hamamet

MALTA
(Br. Crown Colony)

MEDITERRANEAN SEA

GERMAN EMPIRE

Königsberg
(Kaliningrad)
Danzig
(Gdańsk)

Posen

Warsaw

Łódź
Nov. 11–Dec. 6, 1914

Poland

Breslau

Cracow

Prague

Dresden

Leipzig

Hanover

Magdeburg

Düsseldorf

Nuremberg

Brünn

Vienna

Graz

AUSTRIA-HUNGARY

Budapest

Debrezin

Sarajevo

KINGDOM OF SERBIA

Beograd
(Belgrade)

KINGDOM OF
MONTENEGRO

Cetinje
(capital 1910–1916)

ALBANIA

KINGDOM
OF
GREECE

Athens

Smyrna
(Izmir)

Riga Offensive
Sept. 1–3, 1917

First Masurian Lakes
Sept. 7–14, 1914

Lake Naroch Offensive
Mar. 18–
Apr. 14, 1916

Vilna
(Vilnius)

Minsk

Second Masurian Lakes
Feb. 7–22, 1915

Baranovichi Offensive
July 3–25, 1916

Tannenberg
Aug. 26–30, 1914

Vistula River
Sept. 29–Oct. 31, 1914

Pinsk

Krásnik
Aug. 23–25, 1914

Komarów
Aug. 30–Sept. 2, 1914

Lutsk
June 4–6, 1916

Galicia
Aug. 23–Sept. 11, 1914

Gorlice-Tarnów Offensive
May 2–June 22, 1915

Lemberg

Brusilov Offensive
June 4–
Sept. 20, 1916

Siege of Przemyśl
Sept. 24, 1914–Mar. 22, 1915

Kerensky Offensive
July 1–19, 1917

Czernowitz

Iasi Jassy
(capital 1916–18)

Asiago May 15–June 10, 1916

Caporetto Oct. 24–Nov. 12, 1917

Third Isonzo Oct. 18–Nov. 3, 1915
Sixth Isonzo Aug. 6–17, 1916
Tenth Isonzo May 10–June 8, 1917
Eleventh Isonzo Aug. 18–Sept. 12, 1917

Vittorio Veneto
Oct. 24–Nov. 3, 1918

Venice
Trieste

Piave River
June 15–23, 1918

Bologna

Adriatic Sea

KINGDOM OF ROMANIA

Bucharest
(capital 1881–1916)

Jan. 1917

Danube

KINGDOM OF
BULGARIA

Sofia
(Sofiya)

Vardar Offensive
Sept. 14–29, 1918

Monastir Offensive
Sept. 12–Dec. 11, 1916

Salonika Front
Oct. 21, 1915–Sept. 30, 1918

Salonika
(Thessaloniki)

Gallipoli Campaign
Apr. 25, 1915–Jan. 9, 1916

Dec. 1915

Aegean Sea

Crete

ITALIAN
DODECANESE
(Italy)

MEDITERRANEAN

Banghazi

Gulf of Sidra

ITALIAN LIBYA
(It. Prot.)

KINGDOM OF ITALY

Belligerents of World War I

July 28, 1914 .... Austria-Hungary declares war on Kingdom of Serbia
Aug. 1 .... German Empire declares war on Russian Empire
Aug. 3 .... German Empire declares war on France
Aug. 4 .... German Empire declares war on Belgium
Aug. 4 .... United Kingdom declares war on German Empire
Aug. 5 .... Kingdom of Montenegro declares war on Austria-Hungary
Aug. 6 .... Austria-Hungary declares war on Russian Empire
Aug. 6 .... Kingdom of Serbia declares war on German Empire
Aug. 9 .... Kingdom of Montenegro declares war on German Empire
Aug. 11 .... France declares war on Austria-Hungary
Aug. 12 .... United Kingdom declares war on Austria-Hungary
Aug. 22 .... Austria-Hungary declares war on Belgium
Aug. 23 .... Empire of Japan declares war on German Empire
Aug. 25 .... Empire of Japan declares war on Austria-Hungary
Nov. 1 .... Russian Empire declares war on Ottoman Empire
Nov. 2 .... Kingdom of Serbia declares war on Ottoman Empire
Nov. 3 .... Kingdom of Montenegro declares war on Ottoman Empire

Nov. 5 .... United Kingdom declares war on Ottoman Empire
Nov. 5 .... France declares war on Ottoman Empire
May 23, 1915 ... Kingdom of Italy declares war on Austria-Hungary
June 3 .... San Marino declares war on Austria-Hungary
Aug. 21 .... Kingdom of Italy declares war on Ottoman Empire
Oct. 14 .... Kingdom of Bulgaria declares war on Kingdom of Serbia
Oct. 15 .... United Kingdom declares war on Kingdom of Bulgaria
Oct. 15 .... Kingdom of Montenegro declares war on Kingdom of Bulgaria
Oct. 16 .... France declares war on Kingdom of Bulgaria
Oct. 19 .... Kingdom of Italy declares war on Kingdom of Bulgaria
Oct. 19 .... Russian Empire declares war on Kingdom of Bulgaria
Mar. 9, 1916 ... German Empire declares war on Portugal
Mar. 15 .... Austria-Hungary declares war on Portugal
Aug. 27 .... Kingdom of Romania declares war on Austria-Hungary
Aug. 27 .... Kingdom of Italy declares war on German Empire
Aug. 28 .... German Empire declares war on Kingdom of Romania
(continued on next page)

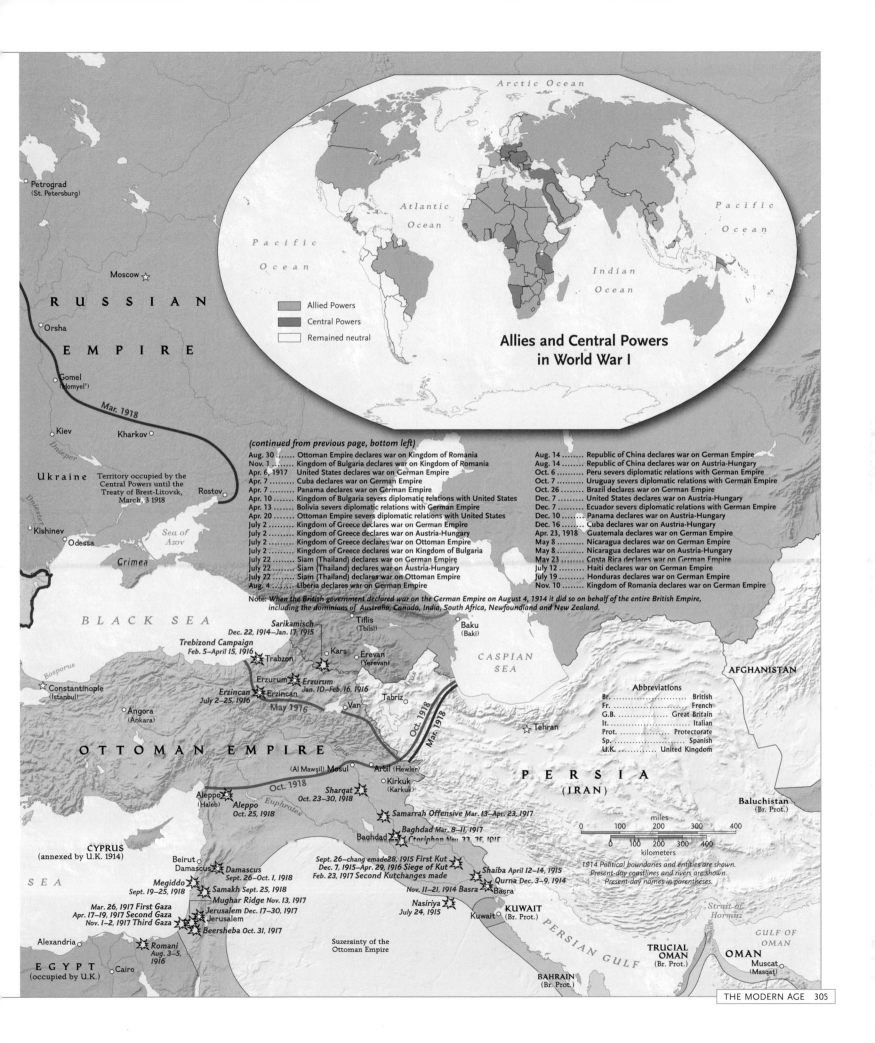

Petrograd
(St. Petersburg)

R U S S I A N

Orsha

E M P I R E

Moscow ✦

Gomel
(Homyel')

Mar. 1918

Kiev   Kharkov

U k r a i n e   Territory occupied by the
Central Powers until the
Treaty of Brest-Litovsk,
March, 3 1918

Rostov

Kishinev

Odessa   Sea of
Azov

Crimea

Dnieper

Dniester

Arctic Ocean

Atlantic
Ocean   Pacific

Ocean

Pacific

Ocean   Indian
Ocean

**Allies and Central Powers
in World War I**

Allied Powers

Central Powers

Remained neutral

(continued from previous page, bottom left)

Aug. 30 .... Ottoman Empire declares war on Kingdom of Romania
Nov. 1 .... Kingdom of Bulgaria declares war on Kingdom of Romania
Apr. 6, 1917   United States declares war on German Empire
Apr. 7 .... Cuba declares war on German Empire
Apr. 7 .... Panama declares war on German Empire
Apr. 10 .... Kingdom of Bulgaria severs diplomatic relations with United States
Apr. 13 .... Bolivia severs diplomatic relations with German Empire
Apr. 20 .... Ottoman Empire severs diplomatic relations with United States
July 2 .... Kingdom of Greece declares war on German Empire
July 2 .... Kingdom of Greece declares war on Austria-Hungary
July 2 .... Kingdom of Greece declares war on Ottoman Empire
July 2 .... Kingdom of Greece declares war on Kingdom of Bulgaria
July 22 .... Siam (Thailand) declares war on German Empire
July 22 .... Siam (Thailand) declares war on Austria-Hungary
July 22 .... Siam (Thailand) declares war on Ottoman Empire
Aug. 4 .... Liberia declares war on German Empire

Aug. 14 .... Republic of China declares war on German Empire
Aug. 14 .... Republic of China declares war on Austria-Hungary
Oct. 6 .... Peru severs diplomatic relations with German Empire
Oct. 7 .... Uruguay severs diplomatic relations with German Empire
Oct. 26 .... Brazil declares war on German Empire
Dec. 7 .... United States declares war on Austria-Hungary
Dec. 7 .... Ecuador severs diplomatic relations with German Empire
Dec. 10 .... Panama declares war on Austria-Hungary
Dec. 16 .... Cuba declares war on Austria-Hungary
Apr. 23, 1918   Guatemala declares war on German Empire
May 8 .... Nicaragua declares war on German Empire
May 8 .... Nicaragua declares war on Austria-Hungary
May 23 .... Costa Rica declares war on German Empire
July 12 .... Haiti declares war on German Empire
July 19 .... Honduras declares war on German Empire
Nov. 10 .... Kingdom of Romania declares war on German Empire

*Note: When the British government declared war on the German Empire on August 4, 1914 it did so on behalf of the entire British Empire,
including the dominions of Australia, Canada, India, South Africa, Newfoundland and New Zealand.*

B L A C K   S E A

Sarikamisch
Dec. 22, 1914–Jan. 17, 1915

Trebizond Campaign
Feb. 5–April 15, 1916   Trabzon   Kars

Tiflis
(Tbilisi)

Baku
(Baki)

Erevan
(Yerevan)

CASPIAN
SEA

AFGHANISTAN

Bosporus

Constantinople
(Istanbul)

Erzurum
Erzurum   Erzurum
Jan. 10–Feb. 16, 1916

Erzincan
July 2–25, 1916   Erzincan

May 1916   Van

Tabriz

Oct. 1918

Mar. 1918

Tehran

Angora
(Ankara)

Abbreviations

Br. .... British
Fr. .... French
G.B. .... Great Britain
It. .... Italian
Prot. .... Protectorate
Sp. .... Spanish
U.K. .... United Kingdom

O T T O M A N   E M P I R E

(Al Mawṣil) Mosul   Arbil (Hewler)

Kirkuk
(Karkuk)

P E R S I A
(IRAN)

Euphrates

Tigris

Baluchistan
(Br. Prot.)

Aleppo
(Haleb)   Aleppo
Oct. 25, 1918

Oct. 1918

Sharqat
Oct. 23–30, 1918

Samarrah Offensive Mar. 13–Apr. 23, 1917

Baghdad Mar. 8–11, 1917

Baghdad   Ctesiphon Nov. 22–25, 1915

miles
0   100   200   300   400

0   100   200   300   400
kilometers

Beirut
Damascus   Damascus
Sept. 26–Oct. 1, 1918

Sept. 26–changemade28, 1915 First Kut
Dec. 7, 1915–Apr. 29, 1916 Siege of Kut
Feb. 23, 1917 Second Kutchanges made

Shaiba April 12–14, 1915
Qurna Dec. 3–9, 1914

CYPRUS
(annexed by U.K. 1914)

*1914 Political boundaries and entities are shown.
Present-day coastlines and rivers are shown.
Present-day names in parentheses.*

S E A

Megiddo
Sept. 19–25, 1918

Samakh Sept. 25, 1918

Mughar Ridge Nov. 13, 1917

Mar. 26, 1917 First Gaza
Apr. 17–19, 1917 Second Gaza
Nov. 1–2, 1917 Third Gaza   Jerusalem Dec. 17–30, 1917
Jerusalem

Beersheba Oct. 31, 1917

Nov. 11–21, 1914 Basra   Basra

Nasiriya
July 24, 1915

KUWAIT
(Br. Prot.)

Kuwait

Strait of
Hormuz

Alexandria

EGYPT
(occupied by U.K.)   Cairo

Romani
Aug. 3–5,
1916

Suzerainty of the
Ottoman Empire

P E R S I A N   G U L F

GULF OF
OMAN

TRUCIAL
OMAN
(Br. Prot.)

OMAN

Muscat
(Masqat)

BAHRAIN
(Br. Prot.)

THE PARTITION OF IRELAND

Free State Declared; North Stays With Britain

In 1914, the decision of whether or not to support Britain in the Great War split the Irish Nationalist movement. The majority of the nationalist Irish Volunteers supported Britain's war, as did the Ulster Volunteers, made up of Protestants. About 30,000 Irishmen would lay down their lives. But a minority formed the Irish Republican Brotherhood (IRB), which saw the war as an opportunity to overthrow British rule. The IRB appealed to the Germans, who agreed to supply arms, and a revolution was planned for Easter week 1916.

In April, the British captured a ship carrying German rifles and ammunition off the coast of Ireland. Orders were circulated to cancel the uprising, but a hard core of about 1,600 armed IRB men went ahead anyway. On April 24, they marched down Sackville Street in Dublin, took over the post office, and declared Ireland an independent republic. The army in Ireland, angry at this stab in the back during wartime, rushed troops to the scene and brutally put down the uprising. More than 400 people died in the fighting. On April 30, the uprising collapsed, the IRB surrendered, and Britain executed 16 leaders of the organization, thus making martyrs of the men and drawing many to their cause.

Ireland relapsed into a bitter calm. In 1918, when the last German offensive crashed into Britain's lines, the government in London ordered implementation of both Home Rule for Ireland and conscription. The result was hostility: Catholic priests denounced conscription, the Irish nationalists quit Parliament at Westminster, and in December 1918, when elections were held, 73 radical Irish known as Sinn Féin were elected. Instead of taking their seats in the House of Commons, they set up the Dáil Éireann, an Irish parliament in Dublin, to rule the republic that had been declared in the 1916 Easter Rising.

In 1919, the Irish Republican Army (IRA) orchestrated a campaign of ambush and assassination, to which the British responded

Easter Rising The Easter Rising of 1916 on Dublin's Sackville Street by Irish nationalists caused devastation. After independence, the street was renamed O'Connell after Daniel O'Connell, a 19th-century Irish political leader.

with recently demobilized soldiers. These undisciplined troops terrorized the Catholic population, and the IRA in turn assassinated village policemen. In December 1921, desperate to solve the Irish problem after months of killings, the British government agreed to the Anglo-Irish Treaty, which established the Irish Free State with its capital in Dublin. The treaty let Northern Ireland decide if it wanted to stay or not, and in 1922, six of Ulster's nine counties opted to remain in the United Kingdom.

The agreement, which required members of the Irish parliament to swear fealty to the British monarch, split the Sinn Féin party. As Michael Collins, mastermind of the IRA, backed the compromise, Éamon de Valera, first president of the republic, rallied the anti-treaty forces. In 1922, Ireland slipped into a civil war that claimed as many lives as the war against the British. Among the casualties was Collins, ambushed by his former IRA comrades. A cease-fire was finally concluded in 1923. Though the anti-treaty forces had been defeated, in 1932 Éamon de Valera was elected prime minister, and he declared Eire (Ireland) a fully independent country.

The Catholic minority in mostly Protestant Northern Ireland suffered decades of discrimination before a protest movement erupted in the 1960s and, after 1968, escalated into the violence of the Troubles (see pages 328–329). For 30 years, nationalists, loyalist paramilitaries, and the British Army clashed.

Relations between Northern Ireland and the United Kingdom began to normalize in the 1970s, when both joined the European Economic Community. By the time peace was finally achieved with the Good Friday Agreement of 1998, some 3,500 people had been killed and more than 47,000 injured—the vast majority of them civilians. ■

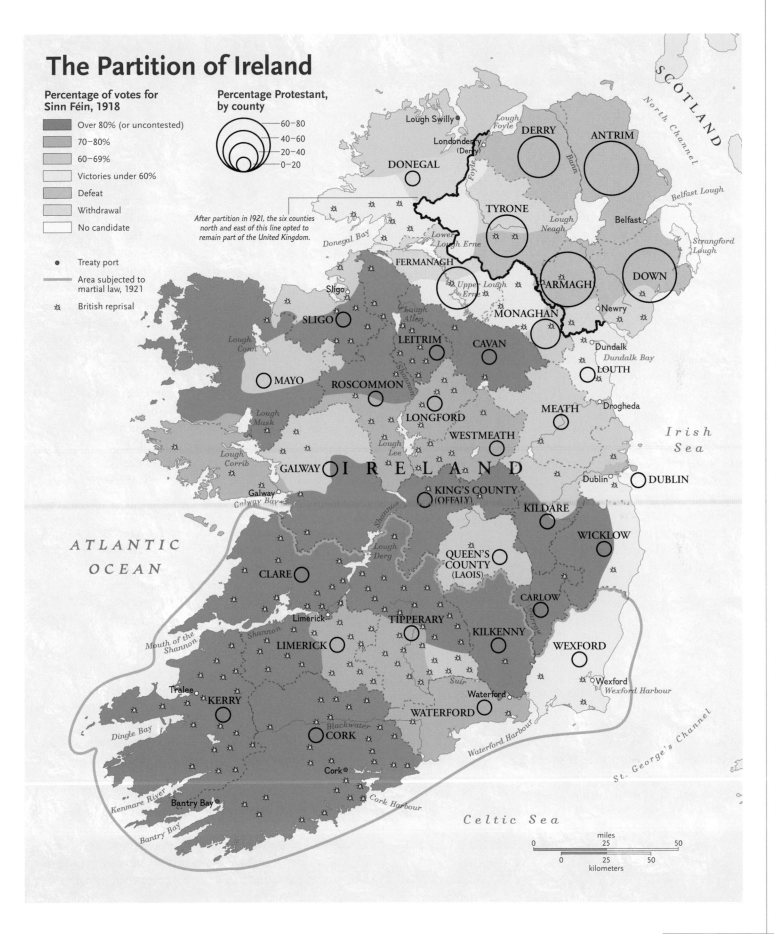

The Partition of Ireland

Percentage of votes for Sinn Féin, 1918

- Over 80% (or uncontested)
- 70–80%
- 60–69%
- Victories under 60%
- Defeat
- Withdrawal
- No candidate

Percentage Protestant, by county

- 60–80
- 40–60
- 20–40
- 0–20

After partition in 1921, the six counties north and east of this line opted to remain part of the United Kingdom.

- ● Treaty port
- ── Area subjected to martial law, 1921
- ✳ British reprisal

SCOTLAND

North Channel

Lough Swilly

Lough Foyle

Londonderry (Derry)

DERRY

ANTRIM

DONEGAL

Belfast Lough

Belfast

Strangford Lough

TYRONE

Lough Neagh

Bann

Donegal Bay

Lower Lough Erne

FERMANAGH

Upper Lough Erne

ARMAGH

DOWN

Sligo

Lough Allen

MONAGHAN

Newry

Dundalk

Dundalk Bay

SLIGO

LEITRIM

CAVAN

LOUTH

MAYO

ROSCOMMON

Shannon

LONGFORD

WESTMEATH

MEATH

Drogheda

Lough Conn

Lough Mask

Lough Lee

Lough Corrib

GALWAY

I R E L A N D

Dublin

DUBLIN

Irish Sea

Galway

Galway Bay

KING'S COUNTY (OFFALY)

KILDARE

WICKLOW

ATLANTIC OCEAN

Lough Derg

CLARE

QUEEN'S COUNTY (LAOIS)

CARLOW

Shannon

Limerick

TIPPERARY

KILKENNY

WEXFORD

Mouth of the Shannon

LIMERICK

Suir

Waterford

Wexford

Wexford Harbour

Tralee

KERRY

WATERFORD

Waterford Harbour

Dingle Bay

Blackwater

CORK

St. George's Channel

Cork Harbour

Cork

Kenmare River

Bantry Bay

Bantry Bay

Celtic Sea

miles
0 25 50
kilometers
0 25 50

BRITAIN AND THE MIDDLE EAST

Carving Up the Ottoman Empire

Since the 19th century, Britain had considered the passage to India by way of the Middle East as part of its sphere of strategic interest. In the Crimean War of the 1850s, Britain and France had fought to defend Turkey against Russian aggression. In 1914, the Ottoman Empire joined Germany and Austria-Hungary in the war against Britain, France, and Russia. It was out of World War I that the fraught politics of the modern Middle East would emerge.

In 1915, to raise a rebellion against the Ottomans, the British promised Sharif Hussein bin Ali, Emir of Mecca, control of the Arabian Peninsula, Iraq, and Syria. At Russia's instigation, in the secret Sykes-Picot Agreement of 1916, the French and the British carved up the Ottoman Empire between them, and

Balfour Declaration In 1917 Lord Balfour made a statement in a letter to Baron Walter Rothschild of the Zionist League that the British government thought the Jewish people should have a homeland in Palestine.

Syria and modern Lebanon were allocated to the French sphere of influence. In 1917, to compound the confusion, the Balfour Declaration promised Zionist activists the establishment of a home in Palestine. This promise came in the form of a letter from A. J. Balfour, British foreign secretary, to Baron Walter Rothschild, the famous banker and putative leader of the British Jewish community.

In the aftermath of the war, the result was not peace, but a chain reaction of violence with which the world is still dealing today. By 1922, the League of Nations had distributed a mandate over Palestine, Syria, and Iraq between the French and the British. Iraq was cobbled together from disparate religious and tribal elements. The French army suppressed an Arab nationalist uprising in Syria. In Palestine, the British presided over simmering tension between the Palestinians and the Jews.

In 1850, under the Ottomans, the Jewish minority had numbered 4 percent of the population. By 1920, the Jewish share in the Palestinian mandate's population of 700,000 had risen to nearly 11 percent. In the 1920s and 1930s, both the Arab and the Jewish populations expanded rapidly, and the British struggled to hold the balance. Britain's efforts to contain the crisis included tight controls on Jewish immigration even at the height of the Nazi persecution in the 1930s and 1940s. As a result, the British faced not only resentment of the Arab population but also armed resistance by Jewish underground groups.

After World War II, with the population of Palestine having swollen to 1.9 million—of which 32 percent were Jews, mostly refugees from Europe and survivors of the Holocaust—Britain decided to withdraw from the British Mandate of Palestine. London turned to the United Nations, which approved the 1947 UN Partition Plan to divide the mandated area into two states roughly the same size. At midnight on May 14, 1948, the British Mandate of Palestine officially expired and Jewish leadership declared the independent State of Israel. This resulted in the 1948 Arab-Israeli War, which lasted until March 1949. Better prepared than its Arab neighbors, Israel prevailed.

Despite its exit from Palestine, Britain withdrew only reluctantly from the Middle East. In 1956, 40 years after Sykes-Picot, the French and the British again collaborated in landing troops in Egypt to seize back control of the Suez Canal from President Nasser (see page 325). It was local Arab resistance and the disapproval of the United States that finally brought Britain's ill-fated imperial influence in the Middle East to an end. ■

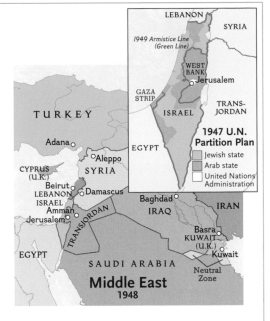

1947 U.N. Partition Plan

Jewish state
Arab state
United Nations Administration

Ottoman Empire, 1299–1922

The Islamic state was founded in Anatolia in 1299. It spanned more than 600 years, and at its height in 1683, controlled most of southeastern Europe, western Asia, North Africa, and parts of the Arabian Peninsula. The secret Sykes-Picot Agreement of 1916 carved up the empire between France and Britain after World War I. The sultanate was abolished in 1922, and the new state of Turkey emerged in 1923.

British Mandate, 1922–1948

As part of the settlement ending World War I, Britain governed Palestine with a League of Nations Mandate. Under the British, Jewish immigration steadily increased, alarming local Arabs. Riots and terrorism erupted as both sides lashed out at each other—and the British. As pressure mounted after World War II, Britain turned to the United Nations. This led to the 1947 UN Partition Plan (see inset map).

After Israel's Independence, 1948

When Britain withdrew in 1948, Israel declared its independence and five neighboring Arab governments mobilized for war. Well armed and better organized, Israel repulsed the Arab armies and seized more of Palestine than the UN plan had prescribed, uprooting 750,000 Palestinians. Jordan annexed Jerusalem's Old City and the West Bank, while Egypt occupied the Gaza Strip.

Camel caravan British soldiers trek along a desert ridge in Palestine during World War I. Arabs had been told their reward for playing a part in defeating the Ottoman Empire would be independence. However, agreements made by the British and the French contradicted this outcome and resulted in long-standing tensions that exist to this day.

THE TWENTIES AND THIRTIES

Britain in Debt, but Some Live It Up

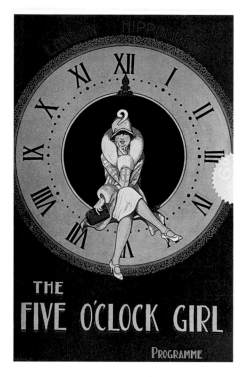

London Hippodrome A 1929 theater program encourages Londoners to attend a popular musical titled *The Five O'Clock Girl.*

The 20 years between the World Wars were marked by great economic and social change. While the country faced severe debt, a worldwide depression, and unemployment, it also experienced rapid social change.

During World War I, Britain had borrowed heavily from others in its empire and from the United States. Factories had focused on war production during the conflict, and afterward the country found it impossible to recover lost markets. The shipbuilding industry, robust during the war, lost its competitive edge. Unemployment rose sharply in 1921 and remained high until World War II.

Then, in 1929, the Great Depression struck. International trade decreased, currencies were devalued, banks collapsed, and unemployment soared. Working people in Britain felt they had fought a war and deserved to be better off than they had been before, but the shaky economy made it difficult.

While working-class communities of the industrial north struggled, many in the south of Britain were starting to live it up. People began enjoying greater freedoms, going to movies, playing sports, and visiting cocktail bars and the theater—in general, having more fun. American celebrities like Clark Gable and Greta Garbo influenced the young, and the national grid spread electricity across the country.

The position of women improved. Those over 21 got the vote in 1928, and although they were replaced in the factories when the men came home from war, by the early 1930s, three quarters of a million more women were employed than had been 20 years earlier. Young women found jobs in cafés, dance halls, and musicals, as well as in offices and industry.

In the domestic realm, housework became easier thanks to electrical appliances such as refrigerators, stoves, heaters, radios, and the first televisions. Telephones with rotary dials made their appearance in the 1930s, almost always in black. A £25 deposit and easy credit from a building society could buy you a house.

Britain remained deeply divided by class and money. People on modest pensions that had been extended to the workforce after the war were a far cry from those who held middle-class jobs. And poorhouses of the 19th-century type still existed.

Even so, the working class began to see a better life. People took more vacations to seaside resorts, and a growing number of people could afford to travel abroad. Suburban streets, gas stations, houses with garages, cars, and affordable goods promised a better future. ■

Playboy King

Prince Edward was a dashing figure and popular as the Prince of Wales. The American press described him as the "idol of bachelors, and dream of spinsters." He met Wallis Simpson at a party in London, where she had moved with her second husband, and they became constant companions. His parents—King George V and Queen Mary—were displeased with his choice. When George died in January 1939, Edward succeeded him and ruled until December. When the press broke its self-imposed silence about the king's relationship with Simpson, the topic became top news, with sympathy from extremists and rebuke from the British establishment, which gave Edward a choice: marriage or the throne. Simpson fled, urging Edward to keep the throne, but the king chose marriage. He abdicated on December 10, 1936, saying in a speech that he found it impossible to "discharge my duties as king as I would wish to do without the help and support of the woman I love." His brother became King George VI, and Edward was given the title Duke of Windsor. In 1937, he married Simpson in France. They lived the life of the jet set. Edward died in 1972, his wife in 1986.

> *"Fish and chips, art-silk stockings . . .
> the movies, the radio, strong tea,
> and the Football pools have
> between them averted revolution."*
>
> BRITISH NOVELIST GEORGE ORWELL,
> *THE ROAD TO WIGAN PIER*, 1937

Dining out A 1930 oil painting, called "The Mannequins," shows fashionably dressed men and women eating out in an elegant restaurant—an increasingly popular activity in the 1930s.

Stage review *(above)* Theater was big after the war, and posters and magazines exploited the interest in fun and dramatic activities. The cover of the *Theatre World and Illustrated Stage Review* of 1926 shows two dancers in a stage review.

Cabaret music hall *(left)* A program for "Ca C'est Paris," shown at London's Prince of Wales Theatre shows near nudity. Morals relaxed after the war; Britons had more money and went to theaters and dance halls more often.

THE BATTLE OF BRITAIN

Spitfire and Hurricane Pilots Fend Off the Luftwaffe

The Battle of Britain was a World War II air campaign waged by the Luftwaffe, or German Air Force, from July to October 1940, to gain control over Britain's Royal Air Force (RAF). A month before the battle began, Winston Churchill coined the conflict's name in a rousing speech to the House of Commons: "What General Weygand called the Battle of France is over. I expect that the Battle of Britain is about to begin. Upon this battle depends the survival of Christian civilization."

The British had declared war on Germany after the invasion of Poland on September 3, 1939. At first, Britain—supported by the Commonwealth—and France were outclassed by Germany and its blitzkrieg tactics, which quickly took over the Netherlands and Norway and then subdued Denmark, Belgium, and France. France's surrender left Britain on its own, and the British soldiers were driven back to a perimeter at Dunkirk in June 1940. It was a devastating defeat.

That summer, England prepared for an amphibious and airborne German invasion. Hitler, intending to attack and prevail over Britain, hoped for a humiliating peace settlement by mid-July. But first, he had to command the skies over England or British planes would destroy his navy as it transported German soldiers across the English Channel.

Hitler's plans for air dominance were foiled when Spitfire and Hurricane pilots held off the Luftwaffe from successfully bombing the airfields of eastern England. This was a fight for which the RAF had long prepared. With the help of newly developed radar, which could track German bombers and their fighter escorts from the time they left airfields in Europe, British airmen intercepted the Luftwaffe bombers and fighters before they reached the RAF's infrastructure. Britons could see the contrails of the vicious aerial combat and witness the planes crashing into the channel and the fields. In this campaign, England's fliers were helped by the injection of skilled pilots from the British colonies and occupied Europe, for though planes were never in short supply, pilots were. These pilots hailed from Poland, Czechoslovakia, and Belgium, as well as New Zealand, Australia, the United States, and Canada.

On September 15, 1940, now known as the Battle of Britain Day, about a thousand German aircraft attacked southern England. A raging battle ensued, and British air defenses held. Soon afterward, Hitler called off his invasion plans indefinitely but, thinking that the British people would pressure their government to end the conflict, continued mass bombing raids on Britain's cities.

Hitler's failure to achieve his goal of destroying Britain's air defenses is considered Germany's first major defeat and a critical turning point in the war. ∎

Inflated defense Barrage balloons moored to the ground during the Battle of Britain were supposed to keep low-flying enemy planes away from London and other British cities. In 1940 there were 1,400 balloons in all, of which one-third were around London. The balloons proved most effective against low-flying cruise missiles at the end of the war.

Radar in War

In World War II, a member of the Women's Auxiliary Air Force uses radio waves to track aircraft in flight. Both the Allies and the Axis powers used radar during the war to locate planes, ships, and submarines, even at night. First demonstrated in the United States in 1934, the basic technology of radio-based detection was developed in the late 1930s. During the war radar relied on a semiconductor crystal, or rectifier, which translated the radio signal into a current that could be seen on a screen. Use of this revolutionary new system was vital to the success of the Battle of Britain.

Battle of Britain
July 10–Oct. 31, 1940

ATLANTIC

OCEAN

Scotland

Firth of Forth

Edinburgh

Glasgow

**RAF Fighter
Command
13 Group**

Range of high-level radar
(aircraft detection at 15,000 feet)

NORTH SEA

*Range of low-level radar
(aircraft detection at 500 feet)*

Newcastle
Newcastle

miles

0   100   200   300   400

0   100   200   300   400

kilometers

Present-day coastlines and rivers are shown.

Northern
Ireland

Belfast

IRISH SEA

Liverpool

Manchester

IRELAND

Dublin

U N I T E D

**RAF Fighter Command
12 Group**

Watnall

K I N G D O M

Birmingham

Wales

England

Coventry

Amsterdam

NETHERLANDS
(occupied by Germay May 1940–May 1945)

Rhine

*CELTIC
SEA*

Cardiff

Rudloe

Bristol Channel

Stanmore

Uxbridge

London

Thames

BELGIUM
(occupied by Germay
May 1940–Feb. 1945)

Brussels

**RAF Fighter Command
11 Group**

Strait of Dover

Dunkirk

**RAF Fighter
Command
10 Group**

Portsmouth

Brighton

Lille

Luftwaffe Luftlotte 2

Exeter

*Range of low-level radar
(aircraft detection at 500 feet)*

Amiens

Plymouth

ENGLISH CHANNEL

*Range of high-level radar
(aircraft detection at 15,000 feet)*

Allied

Area occupied by Axis

Neutral

Le Havre

Channel Islands
(occupied by Germay
June 1940–May 1945)

Caen

Seine

Paris

Marne

RAF Fighter Command

■ Command headquarters

— Group boundary

● Group headquarters

⊥ Fighter base

High-level radar station

Low-level radar station

Luftwaffe Command

— Air fleet boundary

■ Air fleet headquarters

Bomber base

⊥ Fighter base

Luftwaffe Luftlotte 3

F R A N C E
(occupied by Germay May 1940–Sept. 1944)

Rennes

Orleans

THE BLITZ

London and Other Cities Endure Bombing Raids

After the Royal Air Force prevailed in the Battle of Britain, Germany continued relentless bombing of more than 15 British cities, especially London, primarily to destroy British infrastructure and to break the spirit of the British people.

The months-long operation known as the Blitz had the opposite effect. The British endured the destruction of their cities; rather than breaking their morale, as Hitler had intended, a sense of defiance in the face of the enemy settled over most people. They had entered the war without enthusiasm, but they had gained a better understanding of the demands of the conflict during World War I. Thus, they were better prepared to deal with conscription, rationing, blackouts, bombing raids, and the removal of children to rural areas where they would be safer.

Witness to demolition Prime Minister Winston Churchill views the ruins after a German bombing of the British House of Commons. His visits to bombing sites were designed to raise morale, and despite some skepticism, the tours were welcomed.

Beginning on September 7, 1940, waves of German bombers wreaked havoc on cities in the British Isles for eight months. The damage was terrific; communities were devastated; and by the end of the war's second year, there had been more civilian deaths than soldiers killed as a result of enemy actions. About half of the 43,000 casualties in 1940 and 1941 were in London. During the Blitz, some 177,000 people slept in London Underground stations on makeshift beds, with no privacy and poor sanitary facilities. In their backyards people built and put to use more than three million corrugated steel shelters that could be covered with soil.

The bombed cities included Birmingham, Liverpool, Portsmouth, Southampton, Plymouth, Bristol, and Glasgow. Coventry, an important engineering and manufacturing center before the war, was particularly hard hit. The city had few prepared defenses against an aerial attack, though it had two types of natural defense: The city was situated in a slight dip, and fog often covered it, especially in the colder months. The night of November 14, 1940, was cold, but there was no fog and the moon was full. That night and in the early hours of the next day, 400 bombers dropped their high explosives and incendiaries on the city. More than 33 percent of Coventry's factories were destroyed, 41,500 homes were damaged, and trams and tramlines were so badly compromised they never ran again. In 1940, these conditions were landmarks of aerial destruction. By the end of the war, however, the damage done to Germany by Allied bombers would eclipse that of Coventry many times over.

Throughout the Blitz, Britons' resolve held up better than British authorities had expected. In fact, the nation's leaders had been extremely anxious beforehand. Members of the government and royal family were able to visit recently bombed areas with the expectation of a warm greeting. Support of the war allowed the government to exercise control without seeming oppressive.

The Royal Air Force's destruction of many German bombers during the Battle of Britain also contributed to the Blitz's failure. British Hurricanes had downed some 80 percent of the German aircraft, although the sleek and faster Spitfires had won most of the publicity. Strategic bombing "makes headlines, kills people, and smashes property," intoned radio correspondent Edward R. Murrow. "But it does not win wars," he concluded, "and will not cause this country to collapse."

The Blitz ended on May 16, 1941, when Hitler stopped the bombing raids and moved his military east to fight in the invasion of Russia. ∎

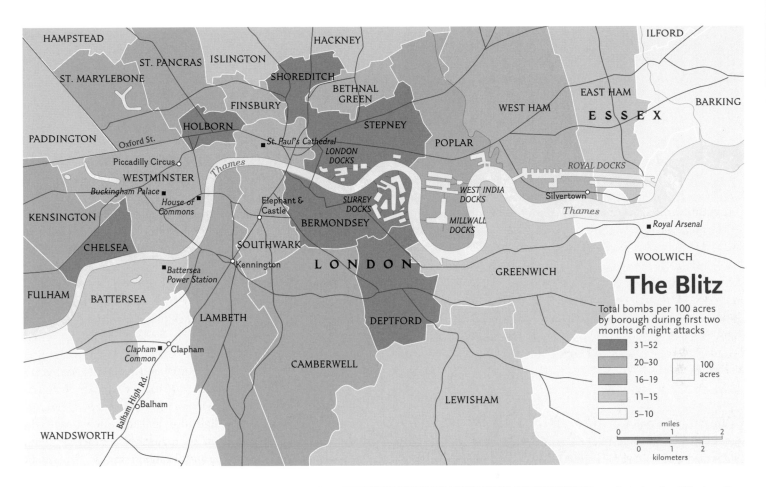

The Blitz

Total bombs per 100 acres
by borough during first two
months of night attacks

31–52
20–30
16–19
11–15
5–10

100 acres

miles
0　　　1　　　2

0　　　1　　　2
kilometers

A city burning This view of smoke rising from London was taken from St. Paul's Cathedral during the Blitz. After Hitler failed in the Battle of Britain by mid-September 1940, he undertook eight months of mass-bombing raids on several cities.

SIR WINSTON CHURCHILL

Prime Minister Leads the Country Through War

S on of a conservative politician and a beautiful American heiress, Winston Churchill was born in 1874 in Oxfordshire. He loved the action of war, a characteristic that was evident early on when he joined the Queen's Royal Hussars in 1895 as a cavalry officer in British India and in Sudan. Churchill served as a correspondent for the *Morning Post* in South Africa and reported on the Boer Wars. He wrote two books about his experiences, including being captured by the Boers, escaping, and trekking almost 300 miles to Portuguese territory. In 1900, he began his first term as an MP.

In 1911, Churchill was appointed First Lord of the Admiralty and continued in the position until the First World War. He resigned after the disastrous Battle of Gallipoli, which he had not led but had backed. The Conservative politician was humiliated, but he worked his way back into the government, first under Lloyd George and then under Stanley Baldwin in the 1920s. In 1929, when Labour won, his career seemed over. His hostility to Gandhi and Indian nationalism made him seem like a political dinosaur. But as Hitler became more powerful, he gave Churchill another chance. Churchill issued ominous warnings about the German threat, backed rearmament, and opposed the appeasement of Hitler.

In September 1939, Neville Chamberlain appointed Churchill First Lord of the Admiralty again. When Germany's invasion of Norway succeeded in April 1940, Chamberlain resigned after losing a confidence vote and Churchill was named prime minister in May.

During World War II, the inveterate politician raised the morale of the British people with rousing speeches and catchphrases, such as "we shall never surrender." In the Battle of Britain, when Allied pilots held off the Luftwaffe, he coined the slogan, "Never in the field of human conflict was so much owed by so many to so few."

Churchill was dedicated to defeating Hitler, and, despite his contempt of communism, he allied with Soviet leader Joseph Stalin. In February 1945, Churchill traveled to the Yalta Conference, where he met with U.S. president Franklin D. Roosevelt and Stalin to plan the final stages of the war and the postwar world. While there, Churchill was replaced by Clement Attlee, whose Labour Party won an unexpected landslide victory in the 1945 general election. Churchill returned as prime minister in 1951 but relinquished the office in 1955. He died in 1965. ∎

Portrait of a student Churchill as a young man was an independent and rebellious student in Dublin, Ireland, where he studied while his parents were in London. His father died when he was 20, and Winston wrote to his mother to urge her to come visit him, which she rarely did.

Churchill the Hero

The British mourned for more than a week when Winston Churchill died, and they gave him a hero's funeral parade on Whitehall with Big Ben in the background. The man who had guided them through World War II was voted out as prime minister in 1945. The public saw him as a wartime prime minister—too old and conservative to lead the country into peacetime reconstruction. Churchill returned as prime minister in 1951 but retired in 1955 after a series of strokes. He suffered a severe stroke in 1965 and died nine days later at the age of 90.

Cheering the boys Prime Minister Churchill shares a laugh with Field Marshal Bernard Law Montgomery and Monty's troops at Caen, France, in 1944. Churchill's speeches were a great inspiration to Britons. He once said, "What is our aim? I can only answer in one word: victory. Victory at all costs."

"We shall fight on the seas and oceans . . .
We shall fight on the beaches . . .
we shall fight in the hills;
we shall never surrender."

PRIME MINISTER WINSTON CHURCHILL,
SPEECH TO THE HOUSE OF COMMONS, 1940

War correspondent To earn extra money during the Second Boer War in South Africa, Churchill wrote for several London newspapers and wrote books about the fighting. A lover of combat, he never followed promotion through army ranks but planned to use family influence to join military campaigns.

LIFE ON THE HOME FRONT

Civilians Do Their Part for the War Effort

I n 1940, Winston Churchill understood that total mobilization of the home front was key to victory over Germany. The effort to maintain public support required identifying potential workers, assigning the right skills to the right task, increasing output to replenish supplies, rationing, and boosting civilian morale.

Britons responded wholeheartedly. More than a million men, usually too old for the draft, signed up for the Home Guard militia to fight the Germans should they invade England. In summer 1940, people prepared for the expected invasion by collecting scrap metal for armaments and building concrete dug-in guard posts in suburban parks.

Women played a crucial role in the effort. They worked on munitions and as air-raid wardens, engineers, and fire-engine drivers. More than 80,000 women joined the Women's Land Army, working on farms to provide food. The Women's Voluntary Service worked in cities to support victims of the Blitz and those in London Underground shelters. Some two million women were employed in arms factories and 500,000 in noncombat roles in the armed forces.

Keeping up morale proved to be particularly challenging, especially in the midst of the brutal Blitz and the fear it engendered. Still, a strong sense of community developed and, as a result, a collective stoicism settled in among the people. At first, the government assumed that 87 percent of those needing protection would use home shelters or find cover under stairs in their homes. However, the people took matters into their own hands; they removed the government-installed chains on the Underground shelters and slept there every night by the thousands. Most people found safety, with one or two exceptions. In one case, a bomb hit the road, fell into the Tube station, and killed more than 200 people. Corrugated steel shelters were given out to millions of civilians to give them a safe place in case of attack from the air. Half-buried with dirt, they were usually cold and damp and offered minimal protection from enemy raids.

The propaganda machine was busy, staging campaigns to try to boost the population's oftentimes struggling morale and sometimes refusing to let newspapers publish pictures of bombed-out areas in case spirits might be dampened. In one instance, in an effort to show that life was unchanged, the government indicated that people were partying and visiting clubs as usual in London's West End. The plan backfired when East Enders, angry and looking for shelter, burst into the Savoy Hotel. The people soon retreated, having made the point that they, too, needed safe shelter.

Food became less available, and the British made good through rationing and a huge increase in domestic farm production. Before the war, Britain had imported 55 million tons of food over a year; during the war, the country imported only 12 tons. Britain also endured rationing of other products, such as furniture, clothing, and gasoline for cars. The controls created a booming black market of people called spivs, who dealt in nylon stockings, car and truck parts, cigarettes, alcohol, eggs, and canned meat. A popular item on the black market was SPAM—a combination of ham and other meats brought to Britain by American soldiers. Not until 1954 did rationing finally end, when limits on the purchase of meat were lifted.

The influx of some two million American GIs in 1943 and 1944 had a considerable impact on British society. English comedian Tommy Trinder referred to them as "over-paid, over-sexed, and over here." GI brides sailing to the United States numbered as many as 100,000. ■

Working alongside men Women add components to bombs in a munitions factory in 1941. The British knew that to win the war all members of society would have to pitch in, and so women filled jobs that men had occupied.

"Britain could not have emerged victorious in 1945 without the help of the many who selflessly worked all the hours they could to provide the materials the British Army and Allied troops used to defeat the Germans."

SIMON FOWLER, WAR HISTORIAN

Women of Britain A poster urges British women to contribute to the war effort. Every woman aged 18 to 60 was registered, and by mid-1943, almost 90 percent of single women and 80 percent of married women were involved in essential work on the home front.

WOMEN OF BRITAIN

COME INTO THE FACTORIES

ASK AT ANY EMPLOYMENT EXCHANGE FOR ADVICE AND FULL DETAILS

D-DAY

War Turns Bloody as Allies Invade Normandy

The Normandy landings, also known as D-Day, began the 1944 invasion of German-occupied Western Europe. German forces expected an attack on northern France from the Allies but thought it would be at Calais, at the other end of the shortest trip from England across the English Channel. Instead, British, Canadian, and American troops took the long way to France; they set sail from Portsmouth and Southampton in the south of England and landed on the open beaches of Normandy on June 6, 1944.

The Allies rehearsed their landings by role-playing months before the initial attack on the beaches. German torpedo boats crashed one of those rehearsals, on April 28, and 638 American soldiers and sailors were killed in the waters off the southeastern English coast.

Supreme Commander Dwight Eisenhower had selected June 5 as the day for the invasion, but inclement weather settled over the area. At a vital meeting shortly before the invasion was to occur, the chief meteorologist to Eisenhower said that a one-day lull in the bad weather would take place on June 6. And so Eisenhower gave the go-ahead to proceed with the landings on that day.

The Germans thought the weather would keep the Allies from landing. Several German officers were away for the weekend, and Field Marshal Erwin Rommel, commander of the defense forces, had taken a few days' leave to celebrate his wife's birthday.

The invasion began with overnight parachute drops, glider landings, air attacks, and naval bombardments by British, Canadian, and American troops. Early in the morning, troops from Britain, Canada, the United States, and the Free French (Charles de Gaulle's government-in-exile) landed on the five beaches along 50 miles of Normandy's coast.

The largest single invasion of all time, it consisted of nearly 160,000 Allied troops, who set out for beaches code-named Gold, Omaha, Juno, Utah, and Sword. The fleet consisted of nearly 7,000 ships from eight different navies.

The British and the Canadians, facing light opposition, secured the eastern beaches of Gold, Juno, and Sword, and the Americans captured Utah. The worst fighting of the day was at Omaha, where the United States suffered more than 2,000 casualties. Allied plans had called for the capture of Saint-Lo, Caen, Carentan, and Bayeux the first day, but they remained in German hands. The day ended with the beaches secured, yet only two—Juno and Gold—were linked. All five were finally connected on June 12.

While the Allies did not achieve all of their goals on the first day, the operation opened the door to the liberation of Western Europe from Nazi control the following year and the partitioning of Germany between Western powers and Stalin's Red Army. ∎

Normandy Invasion Ships crowd Normandy Beach on D-Day, and barrage balloons are moored to prevent low-flying planes from gunning down troops. For two years, the Allies planned to invade France, but the Germans didn't know where they would land. Several deceptions took place to fool Germany about the precise locations of the landings, and when the invasion took place at Normandy, Hitler thought it was a feint.

Europe, June 6, 1944

- Allied-controlled area
- Axis-controlled area
- Neutral country

D-Day
Invasion forces

→ American
→ British
→ Canadian

UNITED KINGDOM

LONDON

Southampton
Weymouth
Portland
Dartmouth
Portsmouth
Shoreham by Sea
Calais
Lille
Amiens
Rouen
Le Havre
Cherbourg
Bayeux
Saint-Lô
Caen
NORMANDY
FRANCE
PARIS

North Sea
English Channel

miles
0 100 200
kilometers
0 100 200

"You are about to embark upon a great crusade, toward which we have striven these many months. The eyes of the world are upon you."

SUPREME ALLIED COMMANDER DWIGHT D. EISENHOWER, IN A LETTER TO TROOPS BEFORE THE ASSAULT, JUNE 1944

Supreme Allied Commander Speaking to paratroopers just before their departure for France, American general Eisenhower tells them, "Full victory—nothing else." Eisenhower was appointed commander of Operation Overlord and had selected June 5, 1944, as the day of the invasion, but it took place a day later because of bad weather. By day's end, 156,000 Allied troops were on Normandy beaches, and more than 4,000 lost their lives.

THE WELFARE STATE

A Social Contract to Benefit the People

World War II was planned by politicians and professional soldiers but fought, as World War I had been, by a largely working-class population. One of the most popular perspectives on World War II in Britain is to see it as the "people's war," which ushered in a "people's peace." The government to which the British electorate entrusted reconstruction in July 1945 was not that of wartime prime minister Winston Churchill. Despite his legendary postwar reputation, Churchill was seen as too conservative and divisive a figure. It was the Labour Party that would rebuild Britain. Having formed two short-lived governments in the 1920s and 1930s, Labour gained a huge majority in Parliament in 1945.

The postwar Labour government in Britain was undoubtedly one of the most influential in modern British history. Above all, it introduced the National Health Service, providing health care for Britons that was free at the point of delivery and paid for through general taxation. The postwar period also saw less stigmatizing of relief for the poor and the nationalization of key industries.

Britain's reconstruction was a story of sacrifice and hard work. The Labour Party urged a continuation of the spirit of sacrifice, austerity, and collective effort that was evident in the war years. There was little choice. Though Britain's situation was better than that of mainland Europe, which had just escaped Nazi tyranny, its economic situation was dire.

Since 1941, Britain had relied on the generosity of American aid in the form of Lend-Lease to finance the joint war effort. As the war ended, Lend-Lease was canceled. This left the British economy desperate for dollars to pay for food and raw materials and to cover huge debts to the United States and its empire. Under humiliating circumstances, Britain had to negotiate with Washington, D.C., for new loans and to accept its incorporation in 1947, alongside France, Italy, and even Germany, into the Marshall Plan, named after U.S. general George Marshall, President Truman's secretary of state.

With domestic reconstruction under way and the costs of colonial wars to contend with, society actually tightened in Britain after 1945. Wartime rationing continued, and was even extended. When London hosted the Olympic Games in 1948, foreign athletes were encouraged to bring their own food. It was not until the early 1950s that the mood began to lighten.

In 1951, to celebrate the centennial of Prince Albert's Great Exhibition of 1851, the Labour government hosted the Festival of Britain, a modernist fair whose main hall can still be visited on London's South Bank. The festival was a huge success, but by 1951, Labour's popularity was in decline. Winston Churchill returned as prime minister and in 1953 put on his version of an English festival, with the coronation of the young queen, Elizabeth II, on June 2, 1953. A new Elizabethan age had begun. ∎

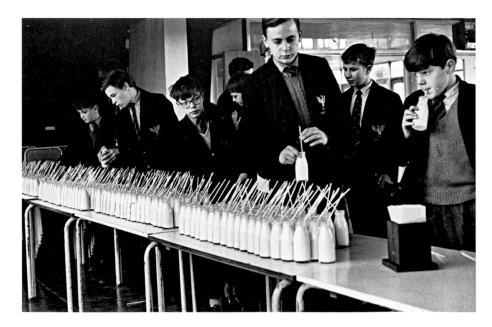

Free milk Bottles of milk line tables for students at Holloway Comprehensive School in London. The Free Milk Act passed as a measure of health and welfare in 1946, and lasted until 1971, when Margaret Thatcher as education secretary repealed it. Criticized for taking the milk away, Thatcher acquired the irreverent nickname of "Maggie Thatcher, Milk Snatcher."

National Health Service Women line up for medical examinations for foreign workers at Havant, Hampshire, in 1947. After the deprivations of war, the welfare state swept into power a Labour government that promoted decent wages, retirement, and time off for vacations. Many foreign workers, with jobs hard to get in their home country, took advantage of the prospects. But continuing 19th-century habits, Britain continued to be a society of emigrants. Emigration—above all to the destinations of the United States, Canada, and Australia—exceeded immigration until 1983.

"And no more running out at dinnertime
for a penny bag of chips to eat with your bread.
Now, . . . you got fair wages."

ALAN SILLITOE, *SATURDAY NIGHT AND SUNDAY MORNING*, 1958

THE END OF THE EMPIRE

After WWII, Colonies Clamor for Independence

Despite the wartime alliance against Hitler and Japan, both Franklin D. Roosevelt and Joseph Stalin wanted to end the empire that Churchill so loved. The opportunity came after World War II. Britain was exhausted, its economic situation was dire, and across the empire there were calls for independence. In the 19th century, Canada and Australia had evolved into autonomous dominions still joined to Britain through constitutional ties, language, economic interdependence, and emigration. South Africa had rebelled, but by 1910, the British and the Boers (or Afrikaners) ruled together under the Union of South Africa. Ireland had been granted dominion status in 1921 but had broken away to assert its full independence and neutrality during World War II. What path would the rest of the empire follow?

The call for Indian independence, which had been raised loudly since the early years of the 20th century, was deafening by 1945. The Labour Party had been in favor of Indian self-rule since the 1920s. The problem was, who would rule, and how would the transfer of power take place? Muslims and Hindus alike wanted power, and the British had encouraged the split with their divide-and-rule policy of favoring the Muslim minority. The result, as in Ireland, was partition, but on a vaster scale and with greater bloodshed. On August 15, 1947, India celebrated independence (Pakistan's was a day earlier). Although both remained in the Commonwealth and British honor was saved, for some 12 million people, this meant forced migration from one state to the other. Amid the ensuing violence and chaos, hundreds of thousands perished.

Next, Britain withdrew from Burma and Sri Lanka in 1948. In Malaya, a key rubber-growing colony, Britain fought a bitter counterinsurgency war against the Malay resistance that had first fought the Japanese. By 1957, Britain had reestablished control sufficiently to grant independence and to withdraw. A year earlier, in 1956, along with its withdrawal from Egypt, Britain had granted independence to Sudan. Ghana followed suit in 1957.

Between 1960 and 1968, Britain handed over independence to all its African holdings except Southern Rhodesia, where whites, fearing black majority rule, took over. In Kenya, this followed a brutal eight-year battle against the Mau Mau resistance. The British Army also fought a rearguard action in the Arab world in Aden and South Yemen before finally withdrawing "East of Suez," as the Labour government of the 1960s promised. A few outposts of empire remained until the end of the 20th century, most important Hong Kong, which was returned to China after expiration of the lease in 1997. The number of people under British rule overseas had fallen from 700 million in 1945 to five million in the 1970s.

As decolonization proceeded in Africa and Asia, and Ireland disowned Britain altogether, it was the Commonwealth that ostracized South Africa for its brutal policy of racial apartheid. Meanwhile, the relationship with the so-called white Commonwealth was also evolving. Canada, Australia, and New Zealand were Britain's most loyal allies in both World War I and World War II. Between 1914 and 1918, more than 60,000 Aussies were killed and 156,000 were wounded. However, the humiliation of the British Empire in Asia by Japan in 1942 irrevocably changed relations between Australia and Britain. Henceforth, Australia and New Zealand knew they must turn to the United States for protection. In 1951 the nations signed the ANZUS Treaty, creating a military alliance with the United States. But constitutional subordination to the British Parliament continued until 1986, and to this day, Elizabeth II, the descendant of the 18th-century House of Hanover, remains Queen of Australia. ■

Escaping Job Loss

Jamaican immigrants arrive aboard the former German troopship *Empire Windrush* at Tilbury Docks in Essex on June 22, 1948. More than 450 Jamaicans, mostly Royal Air Force ex-servicemen, left their homes to travel to Britain to avoid unemployment in their own country. They were part of a first wave in Britain to recruit men from the Commonwealth to fill the postwar labor shortage. The arrival of these West Indian workers marked the beginning of today's multicultural Britain.

To unify the Caribbean post-independence after 1957, Britain experimented with the West Indies Federation, a short-lived political union made up several Caribbean islands. The intent was to establish a unit that would become independent as a single state (similar to Canada or Australia). But in 1962, Jamaica, the largest member, opted for full independence, followed by Trinidad and Tobago (1962), Barbados (1966), the Bahamas (1973), and St. Lucia (1979), among others.

Suez crisis Men in a dwindling power—Sir Hugh Stockwell, commander of allied land forces (left), and Sir Charles Keightley, commander of the Middle East land forces, stand in Egypt during the Suez Crisis of 1956. Gamal Abdel Nasser, the Egyptian leader, had nationalized the Suez Canal, and Britain allied with Israel and France to seize back control of the canal. U.S. resistance to the move demonstrated British loss of prestige.

"Great Britain has lost an empire and has not yet found a role. The attempt to play a separate power role . . . based on being head of a 'commonwealth' which has no political structure, or unity, or strength . . . is about played out."

DEAN ACHESON, U.S. SECRETARY OF STATE, 1962–1963

Independence Day Indian crowds watch a motorcade pass by at an Independence Day celebration in 1947. Mahatma Gandhi, the popular leader of Indian nationalism, was killed on January 30, 1948, by a Hindu extremist shortly after independence. Lord Mountbatten was sent to India as the last viceroy with instructions to work out the political differences and to make the transfer of power.

LONDON SWINGS!

Britain's Image Is Transformed

In April 1966, *Time* magazine registered London's new status as a capital of popular culture with its cover story titled "London: The Swinging City." A change had arrived in Britain. The country of bowler hats, tea, and dignified manners was a thing of the past. Britain's image was transformed forever.

Men flocked to Carnaby Street for the latest in mod fashions; women went to King Street to pick up Mary Quant's short skirts. Twiggy, with her thin, straight figure, became a top fashion model that same year.

Beatlemania had existed in Britain for some time; the group of young men from Liverpool had formed in 1960. And the Fab Four came to international prominence when they arrived in the United States for an appearance on *The Ed Sullivan Show* in 1964. Nearly 40 percent of the U.S. population tuned in for the Beatles' debut. The appearance of the band and the wild approval by the youth of the TV world paved the way for other British groups, most notably the Rolling Stones, who offered a more rebellious alternative.

By the 1960s, affluence had come to Britain. Unemployment was virtually nonexistent. Young people had money in their pockets. Leisure time centered on the home, with television, gardening, and improvements to the house and grounds gaining popularity. Young people were prepared to spend what money they had. And there were a lot of them; the baby boom had created a public younger than it had been since Roman times. By the mid-1960s, 40 percent of the British population was under 25.

In British households, a generation gap developed between parents and their children. Schools resisted the youthful penchant for long hair and short skirts. The birth control pill became widely available. Anti-Vietnam protests took place in London. In March 1968, demonstrators clashed with police outside the U.S. Embassy in Grosvenor Square. But Britain saw nothing on the scale of the marches in Washington, D.C. There was unrest on campuses, from Essex to Cambridge, but no revolutionary atmosphere to rival that in the States. Nevertheless, the revolution of mores and manners in 1960s and 1970s Britain was dramatic and influential beyond Britain's borders. Sex, drugs, and rock and roll marked a generation.

A decline in the respect for authority was the most obvious change in British mentality. TV shows like *That Was the Week That Was* mocked the prime minister. Previously, the government had banned jokes about religion or the monarchy, and government ministers never faced hostile interviews. And as in previous moments of convulsive political and cultural change, the British political system proved responsive and resilient. Capital punishment was banned in 1965, homosexual acts between consenting adults were decriminalized in 1967, abortion was legalized, and divorce was liberalized. The first Race Relations Acts, which banned all discrimination against Britain's immigration population, were passed.

The preoccupation of many Britons is soccer, and on rare occasions, the national teams of England, Ireland, Scotland, and Wales have provided moments of delight and national unity. Most spectacularly, in 1966, England won the World Cup in a tight and controversial match against Germany in Wembley Stadium. Watched in the stadium by 98,000 people, it remains a moment of rare collective joy. ∎

Face of the Sixties English fashion model Twiggy poses beside a poster that bears her name in 1967. The fashion icon of the mid-1960s was born Lesley Hornby in London in 1949. Her mother taught her to sew at an early age. Today, she models for Marks and Spencer of London.

Fab Four Musicians George Harrison, Paul McCartney, and John Lennon rehearse for a recording at Granada TV's *Late Scene Extra* in Manchester in 1963. Together with drummer Ringo Starr, the Beatles became a world household name and took the United States by storm when they appeared on *The Ed Sullivan Show* the following year. The group changed men's hairstyles and led the way for more British groups, including the Rolling Stones, contemporaries of the Beatles. McCartney was awarded knighthood in 1997.

World Cup champs England won soccer's World Cup in 1966, the only time the country has taken first place. Here, team captain Bobby Moore holds the trophy aloft while jubilant teammates lift him. With a defeat of West Germany 4-2 in the final game, England's first World Cup victory had plenty of drama, including a goal disputed by the losing team and a theft of the cup, which was found under a hedge in southeast London.

THE TROUBLES

Deaths Occur as Protestants and Catholics Clash in Northern Ireland

◆ KEY FACTS ◆

1175 Henry II confirms England as the Irish overlord in the Treaty of Windsor.

OCTOBER 23, 1641 Irish gentry try to overthrow the English administration in Ireland to force concessions for the Catholics.

FALL 1649 Oliver Cromwell's campaigns at Drogheda and Wexford result in the death of thousands of Royalist soldiers, civilians, and priests.

JULY 1690 A Protestant army led by William III crushes rebellion by James II in the Battle of the Boyne.

JULY 23, 1803 Rebellion takes place in Dublin against Great Britain by Robert Emmet, who fled into hiding, was captured, and was executed on September 20.

JANUARY 22, 1919 Sinn Féin declares independence from the United Kingdom, and war ensues, ending with partition on July 11, 1921.

AUGUST 14, 1969 British troops are sent to Northern Ireland to quell violence, and it touches off a 30-year war.

APRIL 10, 1998 Peace is achieved with the Good Friday Agreement, which guaranteed power sharing for Catholics and Protestants in Northern Ireland.

From the 1920s on, the Irish Free State was peaceful. But in Northern Ireland, discontent simmered. The Catholic minority population suffered discrimination and exclusion. At first, this institutionalized disadvantage triggered a civil rights movement and then a violent struggle between the IRA and nationalist terrorist groups, Protestant paramilitaries, the Royal Ulster Constabulary (RUC), and the British Army.

The Troubles claimed the lives of more than 3,500 people, including 700 British soldiers, 300 members of the RUC, 370 Nationalist paramilitaries, 162 Protestant paramilitaries, and 1,840 civilians. More than 47,000 suffered wounds in shootings, violent demonstrations, and bombings. The Catholic community first welcomed British soldiers as protection against the local police force and the Protestant majority. But a house-to-house search of Catholic dwellings and curfews turned the residents against the troops and stirred up old hostilities. Eventually, the Provisional Irish Republican Army—which split off from the official IRA—launched a war of attrition to drive the British out of Ireland. Bombings and sniping were their main tactics. Fifty years after the end of the Anglo-Irish War in 1921, the first British soldier was killed in Northern Ireland in February 1971. The British responded with internment without trial of hundreds of Catholics. The following year saw a horrible escalation. On January 30, 1972, British paratroopers broke up a civil rights demonstration and shot dead 13 unarmed protesters. Over the next 12 months, 480 people were killed, the worst year in a struggle that would drag on for 30 years.

Protestant paramilitaries concentrated their violence in Northern Ireland itself. The IRA countered by attacking its Protestant opponents, as well as the RUC and the British Army. In pursuit of its goals of civil rights for Northern Irish Catholics, British withdrawal from Northern Ireland, and unification of Ireland, the IRA spread its campaign to the British mainland. Years of harassing bomb attacks on London were punctuated by dramatic attacks, such as one on Prime Minister Margaret Thatcher at the Brighton Party Conference in October 1984. After years of negotiations, the Good Friday Agreement was signed by the British and Irish and eight Northern Irish political parties on April 10, 1998. By the early 2000s, the Irish Question was settled enough that in 2011, Queen Elizabeth paid the first visit of a British monarch to Ireland since independence. ■

Grim arbiters *(above)* British troops man the barricades in Belfast in 1972, as nationalists in Northern Ireland push for Irish-wide independence.

The Troubles

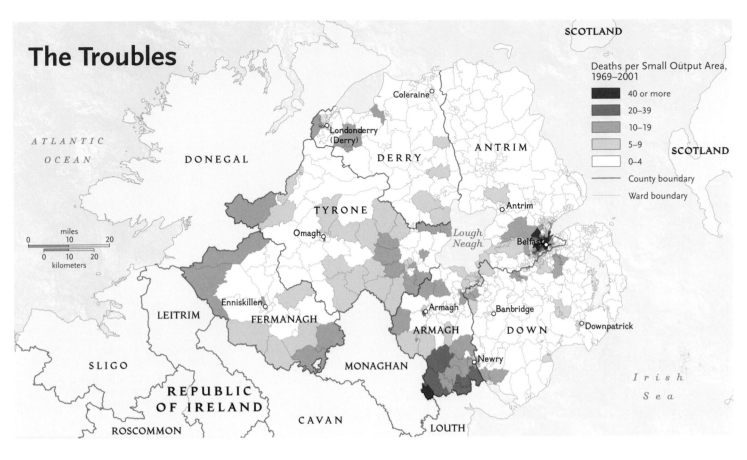

Deaths per Small Output Area, 1969–2001

- 40 or more
- 20–39
- 10–19
- 5–9
- 0–4

— County boundary
— Ward boundary

SCOTLAND

SCOTLAND

ATLANTIC OCEAN

DONEGAL

Coleraine

Londonderry (Derry)

DERRY

ANTRIM

Antrim

TYRONE

Omagh

Lough Neagh

Belfast

miles
0 10 20
0 10 20
kilometers

LEITRIM

Enniskillen

FERMANAGH

Armagh

Banbridge

Downpatrick

ARMAGH

DOWN

Irish Sea

SLIGO

MONAGHAN

Newry

REPUBLIC OF IRELAND

CAVAN

LOUTH

ROSCOMMON

The Troubles

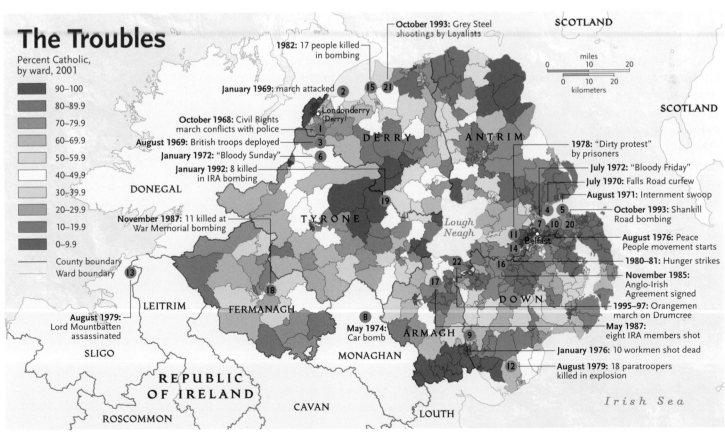

Percent Catholic, by ward, 2001

- 90–100
- 80–89.9
- 70–79.9
- 60–69.9
- 50–59.9
- 40–49.9
- 30–39.9
- 20–29.9
- 10–19.9
- 0–9.9

— County boundary
— Ward boundary

SCOTLAND

SCOTLAND

October 1993: Grey Steel shootings by Loyalists

1982: 17 people killed in bombing

January 1969: march attacked ② ⑮ ㉑

October 1968: Civil Rights march conflicts with police ①

August 1969: British troops deployed ③

January 1972: "Bloody Sunday" ⑥

January 1992: 8 killed in IRA bombing

Londonderry (Derry)

DERRY

ANTRIM

1978: "Dirty protest" by prisoners

July 1972: "Bloody Friday"

July 1970: Falls Road curfew

August 1971: Internment swoop

October 1993: Shankill Road bombing

④ ⑤

⑦ ⑩ ⑳

August 1976: Peace People movement starts

1980–81: Hunger strikes

November 1985: Anglo-Irish Agreement signed

1995–97: Orangemen march on Drumcree

May 1987: eight IRA members shot

January 1976: 10 workmen shot dead

August 1979: 18 paratroopers killed in explosion

DONEGAL

November 1987: 11 killed at War Memorial bombing

TYRONE

⑲

Lough Neagh

⑪

Belfast

⑭

⑯

㉒

⑰

DOWN

⑬

August 1979: Lord Mountbatten assassinated

LEITRIM

FERMANAGH

⑱

SLIGO

May 1974: Car bomb ⑧

ARMAGH

⑨

⑫

REPUBLIC OF IRELAND

MONAGHAN

CAVAN

LOUTH

ROSCOMMON

Irish Sea

miles
0 10 20
0 10 20
kilometers

THE THATCHER YEARS

Prime Minister Stirs Controversy and Division

The most controversial 20th-century prime minister of Britain was Margaret Thatcher, leader of the Conservative Party. Born in 1925, daughter of a Grantham grocer, Thatcher grew up in opposition to much of the drift of British politics and society in the period between 1945 and the 1970s. She opposed the Labour Party, trade unions, nationalized industries, and the welfare state. She also stood in opposition to the new culture of permissiveness that changed British culture in the 1960s and 1970s. Like her American counterpart, President Ronald Reagan, she was a neoconservative.

A graduate of Oxford University with an affluent businessman husband, she won a seat in the House of Commons in 1959. In 1970, she was appointed secretary of education by Conservative prime minister Edward Heath and infuriated opponents by taking away free school milk. In the 1970s, her strong position against the Soviet Union earned her the nickname "Iron Lady." She also adopted a strongly skeptical point of view toward the European Economic Community, which the United Kingdom had joined under Heath.

In 1975, after Heath's government was humiliated by the National Union of Mineworkers and ousted from office by Labour, Thatcher challenged him for party leadership and won. In 1979, she was swept to power as prime minister amid surging inflation and a huge wave of trade union strikes.

At first, as the U.K. economy plummeted and millions lost their jobs in the early 1980s recession, Thatcher's popularity plunged. But the Falklands War raised it again after Britain defeated Argentina in 1982 (see sidebar). A wave of patriotic feeling helped restore the Thatcher government to office.

By the time she fell from power in 1990, her government had transformed Britain. All major industries nationalized since 1945 were privatized. Millions of public-housing units were sold off to private owners. The power of the trade unions was broken by labor legislation and a brutal yearlong confrontation with the miners trade union. Tax rates were reduced for those on higher incomes. Capital markets were freed. Britain became a far more market-orientated, globalized society, but also more unequal. Thatcher's downfall came in 1990 after she backed a poll tax to pay for local government. Frustrated by her anti-European stance, the leadership of her own party unseated her and replaced her with John Major, who joined the European monetary system but otherwise continued many of Thatcher's domestic policies. After her retirement, Thatcher continued in public life until she succumbed to memory problems. She died at 87 on April 8, 2013, from a stroke. ∎

Political soul mates One of Margaret Thatcher's allies was President Ronald Reagan, a fellow conservative. The two shared similar right-wing, free-enterprise philosophies and stood closely together as allies in the final years of the Cold War.

The Falklands War

Signaling victory over Argentina in 1982, the British flag flies over Port Howard in West Falkland, thus elevating Margaret Thatcher in British minds because of her decisive and patriotic leadership and resolute nationalism. Ownership of the Falkland Islands, in the South Atlantic, was long disputed between Argentina and Britain, and the Argentines invaded the island on April 2, 1982. In response, Britain dispatched a naval and amphibious task force to the area and engaged the Argentine Air Force. On May 21, British troops landed and compelled Argentina's forces to surrender.

Bitter dispute Miners, defeated in March 1985, demonstrate in Gwent, South Wales, at the end of a nationwide miner's strike led by the National Union of Mineworkers. Thatcher ended the yearlong strike and privatized the industry, which had been nationalized since January 1947. The cost cutting and shutdowns destroyed mining communities that had been formed by the industrial revolution. British coal was replaced by imported coal and gas. Britain's new energy industry was the offshore North Sea oil industry.

"I love argument, I love debate. I don't expect anyone just to sit there and agree with me—that's not their job."

MARGARET THATCHER, 1980

The Iron Lady Margaret Thatcher sits for a formal portrait in 1985. The first woman prime minister, Thatcher is credited by some with bringing Britain back from the doldrums. Her highly personal style of leadership overshadowed her Tory successor, John Major. Tony Blair, her Labour successor, successfully modeled his prime-ministerial style on that of Thatcher.

THE BRITISH WORLD TODAY

Booming Economies, Good Times Solve Tensions

The 20th century ended, and the 21st century began with Britain on a high. Having recovered from the collapse of its 19th-century industries, the British economy grew rapidly, carried upward by financial services and a gigantic real-estate boom. After the successful peace settlement in Ireland, Scotland and Wales were granted devolved parliamentary assemblies.

The economy boomed from 1997 to 2007, with most British people benefiting from rising living standards. Wealth was unequally shared, however, as British manufacturing continued its decline and many people, working-class men in particular, found themselves without the skills necessary for the new world of work. A gain in services has compensated for the loss in industry. By the 1990s unemployment was 5.5 percent, the lowest in Europe, and migrants flooded in from all over the world. The unusually strong development of the British economy, out of step with that of the rest of Europe, led the Labour government to stay out of the eurozone. Prime Minister Tony Blair and Chancellor of the Exchequer Gordon Brown took much of the credit for the excellent economic session—the biggest factor in the Labour victories of the 2001 and 2005 elections.

With its economy fueled by its booming financial-services sector, the United Kingdom led the world into financial crisis, when, in September 2007, news broke that the Northern Rock bank was on the verge of collapse. Britain witnessed its first genuine bank run in 150 years, with depositors lining up around the block to withdraw their cash. Blair's government fell to Gordon Brown, who took effective measures to stave off the worst of the crisis but gave way in 2010 to a coalition between Conservative David Cameron and Nick Clegg, head of the Liberal Party. Cameron put into play a series of rigorous spending cuts.

Meanwhile, the politics of Scotland and England moved further apart. In the 1950s, the Tories were at an even keel with Labour in Scotland; by comparison, the electoral support of the governing party in England had fallen to below 20 percent in Scotland by the election of early 2010. Around the same time, the Labour Party was challenged by the Scottish National Party, which has governed Scotland since 2007. On September 18, 2014, with approval of the British government, the Scots hosted a hotly contested independence referendum, which voted against independence by a majority of 55.3 to 44.7 percent. David Cameron's government responded by proposing far-reaching devolution for Scotland and raising the issue of England's representation in a restructured United Kingdom.

Whatever its constitutional form, the late 20th century left the United Kingdom a transformed country in terms of its ethnic composition and relations between the sexes. In 1997, women won 120 seats as MPs, compared with 23 in early 1974. Seventy percent of women had paid employment, one of the highest rates in the world.

Today, the United Kingdom remains united beneath its official banner—the Union Jack. Adopted in 1801, the standard—reflecting a pattern of conquest and dynasties stretching back for centuries—continues to fly throughout the sovereign state. ■

More relaxed times A pedestrian strolls along a cobblestone street in the center of Belfast in Northern Ireland. Violence in the six counties that make up Northern Ireland died down after the Good Friday Agreement in 1998. The most antagonistic murals depicting military groups have been replaced by depictions of cultural heroes such as George Best and C. S. Lewis.

The new princess The Duke and Duchess of Cambridge—William and Catherine—leave London's St. Mary's Hospital on May 2, 2015, with their newly born daughter, Charlotte. The little girl is fourth in line to the British throne, after her paternal grandfather, Charles; father, William; and brother, George. A number of London landmarks including Tower Bridge were lit in pink to commemorate her birth.

APPENDIX

MONARCHS OF BRITAIN

Name	Reign	House
Egbert	802–839	Wessex
Ethelwulf	839–856	Wessex
Ethelbald	856–860	Wessex
Ethelbert	860–865	Wessex
Ethelred	865–871	Wessex
Alfred the Great	871–899	Wessex
Edward the Elder	899–924	Wessex
Ethelstan	924–939	Wessex
Edmund I	939–946	Wessex
Eadred	946–955	Wessex
Eadwig	955–959	Wessex
Edgar I	959–975	Wessex
Edward the Martyr	975–978	Wessex
Ethelred II	978–1013, 1014–1016	Wessex
Swein Forkbeard	1013–1014	Denmark
Edmund II	1016	Wessex
Cnut	1016–1035	Denmark
Harold I	1035–1040	Denmark
Harthacnut	1040–1042	Denmark
Edward the Confessor	1042–1066	Wessex
Harold II	1066	Wessex
Edgar II	1066 (never crowned)	Wessex
William the Conqueror	1066–1087	Normandy
William II	1087–1100	Normandy
Henry I	1100–1135	Normandy
Stephen	1135–1154	Normandy
Henry II	1154–1189	Plantagenet/Angevin
Richard I	1189–1199	Plantagenet/Angevin
John	1199–1216	Plantagenet/Angevin
Henry III	1216–1272	Plantagenet
Edward I	1272–1307	Plantagenet
Edward II	1307–1327	Plantagenet
Edward III	1327–1377	Plantagenet

Richard II	1377–1399	Plantagenet
Henry IV	1399–1413	Plantagenet/Lancaster
Henry V	1413–1422	Plantagenet/Lancaster
Henry VI	1422–1461, 1470–1471	Plantagenet/Lancaster
Edward IV	1461–1470, 1471–1483	Plantagenet/York
Richard III	1483–1485	Plantagenet/York
Henry VII	1485–1509	Tudor
Henry VIII	1509–1547	Tudor
Edward VI	1547–1553	Tudor
Jane Grey	1553	Tudor
Mary	1553–1558	Tudor
Elizabeth I	1558–1603	Tudor
James I	1603–1625	Stuart
Charles I	1625–1649	Stuart
Commonwealth	1649–1653	Commonwealth
Oliver Cromwell (Lord Protector)	1653–1658	Commonwealth
Richard Cromwell (Lord Protector)	1658–1659	Commonwealth
Charles II	1660–1685	Stuart
James II	1685–1688	Stuart
Mary II	1689–1694	Orange/Stuart
William III	1689–1702	Orange/Stuart
Anne	1702–1714	Stuart
George I	1714–1727	Hanover
George II	1727–1760	Hanover
George III	1760–1820	Hanover
George IV	1820–1830	Hanover
William IV	1830–1837	Hanover
Victoria	1837–1901	Hanover
Edward VII	1901–1910	Saxe-Coburg-Gotha
George V	1910–1936	Windsor
Edward VIII	1936 (abdicated)	Windsor
George VI	1936–1952	Windsor
Elizabeth II	1952–present	Windsor

For individual family trees, see pages 40–41 (Houses of Wessex and Denmark), pages 68–69 (Houses of Normandy and Plantagenet), pages 106–107 (House of Tudor), page 153 (House of Stuart), page 196 (House of Hanover), page 242 (Houses of Hanover and Saxe-Coburg-Gotha), and page 290 (House of Windsor). For a list of monarchs of Scotland, see pages 41, 69, and 106.

FURTHER RESOURCES

Innumerable books have been written on every aspect of British and Irish history. Among the many consulted for *The British World,* the titles and websites below have been particularly helpful. For readers seeking more detailed one-volume introductions to the subject, the works of Simon Jenkins, Andrew Marr, and David Starkey are especially recommended.

Ackroyd, Peter. *London: The Biography.* Chatto & Windus, 2000.

Alexander, Caroline. *Lost Gold of the Dark Ages.* National Geographic, 2011.

The Anglo-Saxon Chronicle. Michael Swanton, ed. Weidenfeld & Nicolson, 1997.

Brooke, Christopher. *London 800–1216: The Shaping of a City.* Secker & Warburg, 1975.

Cannon, Jon. *The Great English Cathedrals and the World That Made Them.* Constable & Robinson, 2007.

Carter, E. H., and R.A.F. Mears. *A History of Britain.* Vols. 2–4. Stacey International, 2010.

Crofton, Ian. *The Kings & Queens of England.* Quercus, 2011.

Ferguson, Niall. *Empire: How Britain Made the Modern World.* Penguin, 2004.

Jenkins, Simon. *A Short History of England.* Profile, 2012.

Jones, Dan. *The Plantagenets: The Kings Who Made England.* HarperPress, 2013.

Lacey, Robert. *Great Tales From English History.* Abacus, 2007.

The London Encyclopaedia. Ben Weinreb and Christopher Hibbert, eds. Macmillan, 1983.

Marr, Andrew. *A History of Modern Britain.* Pan Books, 2009.

McNay, Michael. *Hidden Treasures of England.* Random House, 2009.

The Oxford Guide to Literary Britain & Ireland, 3rd ed. Daniel Hahn and Nicholas Robins, eds. Oxford University Press, 2008.

The Penguin Illustrated History of Britain and Ireland. Penguin, 2004.

Phillips, Charles. *The Illustrated History of the Kings & Queens of Britain.* Southwater, 2012.

Saunders, Ann. *The Art and Architecture of London: An Illustrated Guide.* Phaidon, 1984.

Schama, Simon. *A History of Britain,* 3 vols. Bodley Head, 2009.

Schofield, John. *The Building of London: From the Conquest to the Great Fire.* Colonnade, 1984.

Starkey, David. *Crown & Country.* HarperPress, 2011.

Thompson, John M. *The Medieval World.* National Geographic, 2009.

Tombs, Robert. *The English and Their History.* Allen Lane, 2014.

The Travellers' Dictionary of Quotations. Peter Yapp, ed. Routledge Kegan & Paul, 1983.

Wilson, Ben. *Empire of the Deep: The Rise and Fall of the British Navy.* Weidenfeld & Nicolson, 2013.

Websites

Archives Wales. archiveswales.org.uk
BBC. bbc.co.uk/history
British Library. bl.uk
British Monarchy (official site). royal.gov.uk
British Museum. britishmuseum.org
Education Scotland (history). educationscotland.gov.uk/scotlandshistory
English Heritage (heritage body). english-heritage.org.uk, englishheritagearchives.org.uk
History Learning Site. historylearningsite.co.uk
Irish History Live. qub.ac.uk/sites/irishhistorylive
Irish History Online (excellent links). irishhistoryonline.ie
Luminarium (history, literature). luminarium.org
National Archives of Ireland. nationalarchives.ie
National Archives of Scotland. nas.gov.uk
National Library of Ireland. nli.ie
National Library of Scotland. nls.uk
National Library of Wales. cat.llgc.org.uk
National Trust (heritage body). nationaltrust.org.uk
Oxford Dictionary of National Biography. oxforddnb.com (subscription required)
Scotland (official government site). scotland.org
U.K. Government National Archives. nationalarchives.gov.uk
U.K. Parliament. parliament.uk
Visit Britain (official visitor site). visitbritain.com
Visit England (official visitor site). visitengland.com
Visit Ireland (official visitor site). visitireland.com

Visit Scotland (official visitor site).
visitscotland.com
Visit Wales (official visitor site).
visitwales.com

Map Sources

Aldcroft, Derek, and Michael Freeman. *Transport in the Industrial Revolution.* Manchester University Press, 1983.

Barnes, Ian. *The Historical Atlas of the British Isles.* Pen and Sword Books, 2011.

Barrington Atlas of the Greek and Roman World. Richard J. A. Talbert, ed. Princeton University Press, 2000.

Black, Jeremy. *Historical Atlas of Britain: The End of the Middle Ages to the Georgian Era.* Sutton Publishing, 2000.

Bradley, Richard. *The Prehistory of Britain and Ireland.* Cambridge World Archaeology, 2007.

Cowan, Helen I. *British Emigration to British North America.* University of Toronto Press, 1961.

Dalziel, Nigel. *Penguin Historical Atlas of the British Empire.* Penguin Books, 2006.

Darvill, Timothy. *Prehistoric Britain.* Yale University Press, 1987.

Divine, David. *The Northwest Frontier of Rome: A Military Study of Hadrian's Wall.* Macdonald and Co., 1969.

Eltis, David, and David Richardson. *Atlas of the Transatlantic Slave Trade.* Yale University Press, 2010.

Esposito, Vincent J. *West Point Atlas of American Wars.* Frederick A. Praeger, 1959.

Fernandez-Armesto, Felipe. *The Times Atlas of World Exploration.* Harper Collins, 1991.

Foster, R. F. *Modern Ireland, 1600–1972.* Allen Lane, the Penguin Press, 1988.

Gardiner, Samuel R. *The History of the Great Civil War, 1642–1649, Vols. 1 and 2.* Longmans, Green and Co., 1888.

Gillingham, John. *Cromwell: Portrait of a Soldier.* Weidenfeld and Nicolson, 1976.

Grove, Noel. *National Geographic Atlas of World History.* National Geographic Society, 1998.

Harris, R. Cole. *Historical Atlas of Canada: From the Beginning to 1800.* University of Toronto Press, 1987.

Hibbert, Christopher. *Agincourt.* B. T. Batsford Ltd, 1964.

Historical Atlas of the United States. National Geographic Society, 2004.

Illustrated History of South Africa: The Real Story. 3rd ed. Reader's Digest, 1994.

Isbouts, Jean-Pierre. *The Story of Christianity: A Chronicle of Christian Civilization From Ancient Rome to Today.* National Geographic Society, 2014.

Lambert, Andrew. *Nelson, Britannia's God of War.* Faber and Faber, 2004.

Loyn, Henry. *The Vikings in Britain.* Blackwell, 1994.

MacLean, Alistair. *Captain Cook.* Collins, 1972.

The MacMillan Atlas of Irish History. Duffy, Sean, ed. MacMillan, 1997.

Magocsi, Paul Robert. *Historical Atlas of Central Europe.* University of Washington Press, 1993.

Marshall, Rosalind K. *Bonnie Prince Charlie.* National Museums of Scotland, Her Majesty's Stationery Office, 1988.

McNamee, Colm. *The Wars of the Bruces.* Tuckwell Press, 1997.

Morillo, Stephen. *The Battle of Hastings.* Boydell Press, 1996.

Murdoch, Alexander. *British Emigration, 1603–1914.* Palgrave McMillan, 2004.

National Geographic Atlas of the Middle East, 2nd Edition. National Geographic Society, 2008.

PELAGIOS: A digital map of the Roman Empire. Available online at pelagios-project.blogspot.com/2012/09/a-digital-map-of-roman-empire.html.

The Penguin Illustrated History of Britain and Ireland: From Earliest Times to the Present Day. Barry Cunliffe, et al., eds. Penguin Books, 2004.

Pollard, Joshua. *Prehistoric Britain.* Blackwell Publishing, 2008.

Pollard, Justin. *Alfred the Great.* John Murray Publishers, 2005.

Quammen, David. *The Voyage of the* Beagle. National Geographic Society, 2004.

Raftery, Joseph. *Prehistoric Ireland.* B. T. Batsford Ltd, 1951.

Richards, Julian D. *Viking Age England.* B. T. Batsford Ltd, 1991.

Royal Geographical Society. *Oxford Atlas of Exploration.* Reed International Books, 1997.

Saul, Nigel. *The National Trust Historical Atlas of Britain: Prehistoric to Medieval.* Sutton Publishing, 1994.

Shepperson, W. S. *British Emigration to North America.* Blackwell, 1957.

Turnock, David. *An Historical Geography of Railways in Great Britain and Ireland.* Ashgate, 1998

Wacher, John. *Roman Britain.* Sutton Publishing, 1998.

ABOUT THE AUTHOR

Tim Jepson is a London-based British writer, traveler, and broadcaster, as well as a cultural expert for National Geographic Expeditions. After graduating from Oxford University, Jepson lived in Italy, where he worked as a mountain guide and wrote for a variety of British newspapers. He has since written more than 20 books on a wide range of subjects, including several titles for National Geographic, as well as numerous articles for magazines and other publications worldwide. He worked for several years as a travel editor for London's *Daily Telegraph*. Jepson continues to travel extensively, and in his spare time is a keen hiker and semiprofessional musician.

OTHER CONTRIBUTORS

Noel Grove was a staff writer at the National Geographic Society for 25 years. His love of history is reflected in many of his two dozen articles for *National Geographic* magazine, as well as his books for the Society, including National Geographic's *Atlas of World History* and *Inside the White House*. Grove contributed chapter 8: The Modern Age.

Adam Tooze is the Barton M. Biggs Professor of History at Yale University in New Haven, Connecticut. Born in England and raised in Germany, he taught modern history for many years at the University of Cambridge. Tooze specializes in the economic, political, and military history of the 20th century.

ACKNOWLEDGMENTS

Tim Jepson would like to thank Barbara Payne, Sanaa Akkach, Matt Propert, Carl Mehler, and their colleagues at National Geographic. Special thanks go to Professor Adam Tooze of Yale University for his insights and overview of the manuscript, and to Michelle Harris for her painstaking research.

ILLUSTRATIONS CREDITS

BI = Bridgeman Images, NGC = National Geographic Creative

Cover (UP), Antony McCallum; Cover (LO A), Roberto A. Sanchez/Getty Images; Cover (LO B), National Portrait Gallery, London, UK/BI; Cover (LO C), Pete Ryan/NGC; Cover (LO D), Kenneth Geiger/NGC; Cover (LO E), © Royal Geographical Society, London, UK/BI; Cover (LO F), Hulton-Deutsch Collection/Corbis;
Back Cover (LE), R Schultz Collection/The Image Works; Back Cover (CTR), De Agostini Picture Library/R. Merlo/BI; Back Cover (RT), Chris Jackson/Getty Images.

1, C Squared Studios/Getty Images; 2-3, Jim Richardson/NGC; 4, National Portrait Gallery, London, UK/BI; 6, © Galerie Bilderwelt/BI; 12-13, Roff Smith/NGC; 16, HIP/Art Resource, NY; 17, De Agostini Picture Library/BI; 18, Jim Richardson/NGC; 19, Joe Daniel Price/Getty Images; 20, Natural History Museum, London, UK/BI; 21 (LE), Erich Lessing/Art Resource, NY; 21 (RT), © The Trustees of the British Museum/Art Resource, NY; 22 (UP), Kazuhiko Sano/NGC; 22 (LO), Royal Albert Memorial Museum, Exeter, Devon, UK/BI; 23 (LE), Ashmolean Museum, University of Oxford, UK/BI; 23 (RT), David Newham/Alamy; 24, Oliver Uberti/NGC; 25, Richard Nowitz/NGC; 26, Ira Block/NGC; 27 (UP), © English Heritage Photo Library/BI; 27 (LO), Werner Forman/Art Resource, NY; 28, © Christie's Images/BI; 28-29, The Stapleton Collection/BI; 29 (UP), CM Dixon/HIP/The Image Works; 29 (LO), Museo Archeologico Nazionale, Naples, Italy/BI; 30 (UP), Ferens Art Gallery, Hull Museums, UK/BI; 30 (LO), Vindolanda Charitable Trust, Bardon Mill, UK; 31, Ashmolean Museum, University of Oxford, UK/BI; 32, Photo © Neil Holmes/BI; 33 (UP), Robert Clark/NGC; 33 (LO), The Israel Museum, Jerusalem, Israel/Israel Antiquities Authority/BI; 34-35, Daniel Dociu/NGC; 38, Tom Lovell/NGC/BI; 39, Robert Clark/NGC; 40 (Egbert), © Look and Learn/BI; 40 (Ethelbald), © Look and Learn/BI; 40 (Edward the Elder), © Look and Learn/BI; 40 (Alfred the Great), The Stapleton Collection/BI; 40 (Eadwig), © Mary Evans Picture Library/The Image Works; 40 (Edgar I), © Look and Learn/BI; 40 (Edward the Martyr), © Look and Learn/BI; 40 (Ethelred II), © Look and Learn/BI; 40 (Cnut), © Mary Evans Picture Library/The Image Works; 40 (Edward the Confessor), © Look and Learn/BI; 41 (Swein Forkbeard), Wikimedia Commons; 41 (Swein II), The Pierpont Morgan Library/Photo: Joseph Zehavi, 2008/Art Resource, NY; 41 (Harold II), © Mary Evans Picture Library/The Image Works; 42, © Walker Galleries, Harrogate, North Yorkshire, UK/BI; 43, The Stapleton Collection/BI; 44 (UP), © The Trustees of the British Museum/Art Resource, NY; 44 (LO), Design Pics Inc./NGC; 45, De Agostini Picture Library/BI; 46 (UP), © Lady Lever Art Gallery, National Museums Liverpool/BI; 46 (LO), Photo © Liszt Collection/BI; 47, Victoria & Albert Museum, London, UK/BI; 48, © English Heritage Photo Library/BI; 49 (UP), © Paul Williams—Funkystock/imageBROKER/Corbis; 49 (LO), © The Board of Trinity College, Dublin, Ireland/BI; 50 (LE), © British Library Board/Robana/Art Resource, NY; 50 (RT), Jim Richardson/NGC; 51, © The Trustees of the British Museum/Art Resource, NY; 52 (LE), Lindisfarne Priory Museum, UK/Ancient Art and Architecture Collection Ltd/BI; 52 (RT), Louis S. Glanzman/NGC; 53, Historiska Museet, Stockholm, Sweden/

Giraudon/BI; 54, Photo © Christie's Images/BI; 55 (LE), © Museum of London, UK/BI; 55 (RT), Ashmolean Museum, University of Oxford, UK/BI; 56, © British Library Board/Robana/Art Resource, NY; 57, Maltings Partnership, Derby, England; 58, Birney Lettick/NGC; 59, Krys Bailey/Alamy; 60-61, Wakefield Museums and Galleries, West Yorkshire, UK/BI; 64, Ian Murray/age fotostock; 65, Photo © Philip Mould Ltd, London/BI; 66, The Stapleton Collection/BI; 67, Werner Forman Archive/BI; 68 (UP A), © English Heritage Photo Library/BI; 68 (UP B), Private Collection/BI; 68 (LO A), © Look and Learn/BI; 68 (LO B), © The British Library Board. All Rights Reserved; 68 (LO C), HIP/Art Resource, NY; 68 (LO D), HIP/Art Resource, NY; 68 (LO E), Westminster Abbey, London, UK/BI; 69 (UP A), North Wind Picture Archives/The Image Works; 69 (UP B), Ken Welsh/BI; 69 (UP C), Ken Welsh/BI; 69 (UP D), The Stapleton Collection/BI; 69 (UP E), De Agostini Picture Library/BI; 69 (LO A), Photo © Philip Mould Ltd, London/BI; 69 (LO B), National Portrait Gallery, London; 69 (LO C), Society of Antiquaries of London, UK/BI; 69 (LO D), © Her Majesty Queen Elizabeth II, 2014/BI; 69 (LO E), Private Collection/BI; 69 (LO F), © Stefano Baldini/BI; 70, © Her Majesty Queen Elizabeth II, 2014/BI; 71, Society of Antiquaries of London, UK/BI; 72 (UP), © Walker Art Gallery, National Museums Liverpool/BI; 72 (LO), © Look and Learn/BI; 74, Jonathan Blair/NGC; 75 (UP), Jonathan Blair/NGC; 75 (LO), Maltings Partnership, Derby, England; 76, The Art Archive at Art Resource, NY; 77, © Look and Learn/BI; 78 (UP), © Look and Learn/BI; 78 (LO), © RMN-Grand Palais/Art Resource, NY; 79, Hamburger Kunsthalle, Germany/BI; 80, Ken Welsh/BI; 81 (UP), IIC/Axiom/Getty Images; 81 (LO), The *Irish Times;* 82 (UP), British Museum, London/BI; 82 (LO), Werner Forman Archive/Treasury of the Basilica of Our Lady, Maastrich/HIP/Art Resource, NY; 82-83, Photo © Leicester Arts & Museums/BI; 83, Erich Lessing/Art Resource, NY; 86, Jarrold Publishing/The Art Archive at Art Resource, NY; 87 (LE), National Archives, UK/BI; 87 (RT), The Stapleton Collection/BI; 88 (UP), Peter Newark Pictures/BI; 88 (LO), Smith Art Gallery and Museum, Stirling, Scotland/BI; 89, The Granger Collection, NYC—All rights reserved; 90, HIP/Art Resource, NY; 90-91, The Stapleton Collection/BI; 91, Centre Historique des Archives Nationales, Paris, France/Giraudon/BI; 92, ©The British Library/The Image Works; 93, Prado, Madrid, Spain/BI; 94 (UP), Photo © Philip Mould Ltd, London/BI; 94 (LO), © Corpus Christi College, Oxford, UK/BI; 95 (UP), © Look and Learn/BI; 95 (LO), © British Library Board. All Rights Reserved/BI; 96 (UP), Atkinson Art Gallery, Southport, Lancashire, UK/BI; 96 (LO), © Lebrecht/The Image Works; 97 (UP), Photo © Philip Mould Ltd, London/BI; 97 (LO), The Florida Center for Instructional Technology, fcit.usf.edu; 98, Public Records Office, London, UK/BI; 99, © Guildhall Art Gallery, City of London/BI; 100-101, Society of Apothecaries, London, UK/BI; 105, HIP/Art Resource, NY; 106 (Henry VII and Elizabeth of York), The Stapleton Collection/BI; 106 (Henry VIII), Palazzo Barberini, Rome, Italy/BI; 106 (Edward VI), © Richard Philp, London/BI; 106 (James IV of Scotland), Scottish National Portrait Gallery, Edinburgh, Scotland/BI; 106 (Mary), National Portrait Gallery, London, UK/BI; 106 (Elizabeth I), Private Collection/BI; 106 (James V), Photo © Philip Mould Ltd, London/BI; 106 (Mary, Queen of Scots), Victoria & Albert Museum, London, UK/BI; 106 (James I of England), Photo © Philip Mould Ltd, London/BI; 107

INDEX

Boldface indicates illustrations.

A

Aberdeen Jewel **132**
Act for the Settlement of Ireland (1652) 178
Act of Settlement (1701) 157, 206
Act of Supremacy (1534) 107
Act of Supremacy (1559) 110
Act of the Six Articles (1539) 126
Act of Uniformity (1549) 108
Act of Uniformity (1559) 110
Act of Union (1707) 157, 208
    map 148
Act of Union (1801) 197, 274
Adam, Robert 216
Adrian IV, Pope 80
Africa
    Anglo-German rivalry 246
    colonies 246, 248
    exploration 246, 268, **269**
    independence movement 294, 324
    see also Boer Wars
Age of Rationalism 186, **186, 187**
Agincourt, Battle of (1415) 96, **96,** 124
    map 97
Agriculture 134, **134, 253**
Aidan, St. **46,** 49
Alban, St. 46
Albert, Prince, consort of Victoria 241, 258, **258, 259**
Albret, Charles d' 96
Alexander II, Pope 59
Alexander III, King (Scotland) 90
Alexander III, Pope 78
Alfred Aetheling (brother of Edward the Confessor) 56
Alfred the Great, King 39, **42,** 54, **54,** 55, **55**
American War of Independence see Revolutionary
    War (1775–1783)
Amundsen, Roald 268
Andrew, Prince 295
Andrewes, Lancelot 162
Angevins 64
Angles 37, 44
    migration map 45
Anglo-Irish Treaty (1921) 306
Anglo-Saxons see Saxons
Anne, Princess 295
Anne, Queen 157, 193
Anne, Queen, consort of James I 158, **159**
Anne Boleyn, Queen 104, 107, 120, **121,** 122
Anne of Cleves, Queen 107, 120, **121**
Antonine Wall 32
    map 32

Antoninus Pius, Emperor (Rome) 32
Archaeology
    Bronze Age 16–17
    early humans 15, 20, 20
    hunters-and-gatherers 15, 20, 20, 21
    Iron Age 16–17
    Neolithic period 15–16, 18
    Stonehenge 24, 24–25, 25
Arkwright, Richard 214
Arthur, Prince 104, 114
Arts and Crafts movement 245
Attlee, Clement 291, 316
Augustine (missionary) 49
Augustus, Emperor (Rome) 28
Austen, Jane 230, 231
Australia
    as colony 164, 194, 202
    deportation to 240
    immigrants 264

B

Babbage, Charles 272
Babington, Anthony 111
Bacon, Sir Francis 114, 186, **186**
Bale, John 124
Balfour, A. J. 308, **308**
Balliol, John see John, King (Scotland)
Baltimore, Lord 164
Bamburgh Castle **44**
Bannockburn, Battle of (1314) 90, **90–91**
Barbon, Praise-God 152
Barebones Parliament 152
Barrow Hills, near Radley, Oxfordshire **23**
Bath, England **19, 190–191,** 216
Battersea Shield **17**
Battle Abbey **59**
Beatles 326, **327**
Beaufort, Margaret 112
Becket, Thomas 64, 78, **78, 79,** 94, 95
Bede, the Venerable (monk) 37, 49
Belfast, Northern Ireland **328, 332**
Bertha, Queen 48–49
Bess of Hardwick **132**
Bibles 162, **162**
Birmingham, England 212
Black Death 92, **92, 93**
    map 93
Blair, Tony 331, 332
Blake, William 199, 230
Blaxland, Gregory 268, 271
Blitz **6,** 314, **314, 315**
    map 315

Bloodworth, Sir Thomas 182
Blücher, Gebhard von 234
Boer Wars (1881 and 1899–1902) 246, 248, 280, **280, 281, 317**
    map 281
Boleyn, Anne, Queen 104, 107, 120, **121,** 122
Book of Common Prayer **127,** 128
Book of Kells **49**
Boston Tea Party (1773) 226
Boswell, James 230
Bosworth, Battle of (1485) 71, 103, 112, **113**
    map 113
Boudicca, Queen (Iceni) 28, **28**
Boyle, Richard 216, **218**
Boyne, Battle of the (1690) 188, **189**
Bradford, England 252
Bradford, William 163
Brendan, St. 46
Britain, Battle of (1940) 289, 312, **312**
    map 313
British Expeditionary Force 296, 298
British Isles
    11th–15th centuries map 62
    physical map 10–11
British Mandate (1922–1948) 308
    map 309
British Museum, London 218
Brontë, Charlotte 276
Brontë, Emily 276
Bronze Age 16–17, **17**
Brown, Gordon 332
Brown, John 258
Brown, Lancelot "Capability" 218
Bruce, Robert the, King (Scotland) 65, 90, **90–91, 91**
Brunel, Isambard Kingdom 256, **257**
Brunel, Sir Marc Isambard 256
Buckingham, George Villiers, Duke of 158, 168
Burgoyne, John **200**
Burke, Edmund 197, 228, **229,** 230
Burke, Robert O'Hara 268
Burns, Robert 230
Burton, Richard (explorer) 268, 271
Byng, John 223

C

Cabot, John 136
Caesar, Julius 17, 28, **28–29**
Calcutta (Kolkata), India 220
Caledonii tribe 32
Cameron, David 332
Camerton, near Bath **29**
Canterbury, England 49

The Canterbury Tales (Chaucer) 94, **95**
Canute (Cnut), King 42–43, **43,** 56
Caribbean colonies 164, **203,** 212, **213,** 324
Carman, Thomas **129**
Carroll, Lewis 276
Catherine, Duchess of Cambridge **333**
Catherine Howard, Queen 120, **121**
Catherine of Aragon, Queen **121**
    annulment 104, 107, **122**
    Battle of Flodden Field 116, 117
    lack of male heir 104, 120, 121, 122
    marriage to Arthur 104, 114
    marriage to Henry VIII 104, 120
Catherine Parr, Queen 120, **121,** 130
Catuvellauni tribe 28
Caxton, William 95
Cecil, William 130
Celts
    Christianity 38, 46
    Iron Age 17
    maps 51
    Roman Britain 30
    Saxons and 37–38, **50,** 50–51
Chamberlain, Joseph 281
Chamberlain, Neville 289, 316
Chancellor, Richard 136
Charge of the Light Brigade (1854) 242
Charles, Prince of Wales 295, 333
Charles I, King 168, **169**
    children **168**
    English Civil war and 150–152, 170, 172–173, 178
    money, power, and religion 149–150, 162
    trial and execution 152, 154, **173,** 174, **174–175**
Charles II, King
    armor **181**
    childhood **168**
    coronation **180–181**
    dancing at court **146–147**
    exile 152
    Great Fire of London 182
    introduction 154, 156
    rebuilding after Great Fire 184
    Restoration 180
    Scotland and 178
    statue **228–229**
    successor 188
    support for science and learning 186
Charles IV, King (France) 67
Charles V, King (Spain) 104, 107, 122
Charles VI, King (France) 96
Charles Edward Stuart (Bonnie Prince Charlie),
    Prince 193, 196, 208, **208**
    artifacts **209**
    map 209
Charlotte, Princess of Cambridge **333**
Charlotte of Mecklenburg, Queen 199
Chartists 260, **260–261**
Chaucer, Geoffrey 94, **94,** 95
China, Opium Wars **247**

Chiswick House, near London 216, **218–219**
Christianity
    Celts 38, 46
    crucifix **47**
    early Christianity **46,** 46–49, **48, 49**
    map of early Christianity 47
    Saxons 38, 46, 48–49
Church of Scotland 150
Churchill, John 157
Churchill, Sir Winston 316, **316**
    birthplace 157
    funeral 316, **316**
    as Greatest Briton of all time 256
    post-World War II 322
    Second Boer War **317**
    on Seven Years' War 222
    World War II 289, 312, **314,** 316, **317,** 318
Cities, Georgian era 216
Civil war *see* English Civil War
Claudius, Emperor (Rome) 28, **29**
Clegg, Nick 332
Clement VII, Pope 107, 122
Clement XI, Pope 206
Clifton Suspension Bridge 256, **256**
Clive, Robert 199, 220
Clothing
    1960s 294, 326
    Iron Age 26
Clovis, King (Franks) 48
Cnut, King 42–43, **43,** 56
Cobbett, William 260
Colchester, England 28, 30
Collins, Michael 306
Colonial possessions
    Africa 246, 248
    Georgian era 194, 202, **202, 203**
    India **220,** 220–221, **221**
    loss of American colonies 199–200
    maps 154, 166–167, 204–205, 221
    post-World War II wave of independence 293–
        294, 324
    settlement and exploration 164, **165**
    Seven Years' War 222–223
    wars in 243, 246, 248, **248**
    see also Boer Wars; Pilgrims; Revolutionary War;
        Slave trade
Columba, St. 46
Combination Acts (1799 and 1800) 278
Common law 54
Confessio Amantis (Gower) 95
Conrad, Joseph **276**
Constantine II, King (Scotland) 88
Constitutional monarchy, birth of 188
Cook, James 194, 202
Corn Laws (Importation Act, 1815) 239
Cornwallis, Charles 224, **224**
Coventry, England 314
Coverdale, Miles 126, 162
Cranmer, Thomas 108, 122, **122,** 126, **126,** 128, **128**

Crécy, Battle of (1346) 70, **70**
Crimean War (1853–1856) 241–242, 248, 308
Cromwell, Oliver 176
    English Civil War and 152, 170, 172, 173, 176,
        178
    execution 154
    execution of Charles I 174, 176
    as Lord Protector 152, **176**
    map of conquest of Ireland 179
    portrait **177**
    Scotland and Ireland and 178, 328
    statue **156**
    successor 180
Cromwell, Richard 152, 180
Cromwell, Thomas 107, 124
Crown Jewels **1,** 74
Crusades
    looted artifacts **67, 82**
    Richard I and 81, **82–83**
    route map 84–85
Crystal Palace, London 241
Cullen, Susanna 212
Culloden, Battle of (1746) 208
Cumberland, Duke of 208
Cuthbert, St. 116

D

Danelaw 39, 54
Darby, Abraham 214
Darnley, Henry Stuart, Lord 132
Darwin, Charles 240, 272, **272**
    artifacts **273**
    map 273
David I, King (Scotland) 90
David II, King (Scotland) 116
De Valera, Éamon 306
Declaration of Independence (United States) 186,
    226, **226–227**
Defoe, Daniel 216, 230
Denmark, House of 40–41, **40–41**
Despenser, Hugh 65, 67
Devereux, Robert, Earl of Essex 142, **142,** 172,
    173
Diana, Princess of Wales 295
Diarmait Mac Murchada, King (Leinster) 80
Dickens, Charles **246,** 276, **277**
Dictionaries 230
Disraeli, Benjamin 243–244, 258
Domesday Book 63, 76, **76, 77**
Doyle, Arthur Conan 276
Drake, Sir Francis 111, 136, 138, **130,** 164
Dublin, Ireland 216, 306, **306**
Dudley, John, Duke of Northumberland 108–109,
    126, 130
Dudley, Lord Robert 111, 130, **130,** 142
Dunlop, John 272
Durham Cathedral 116
Durrington Walls **21**

E

East Anglia (Saxon kingdom) 39
East India Company
    artifacts **203**
    artwork at headquarters **202**
    coat of arms **221**
    founding 164, 202, 220
    mutiny 243, 266, **266**
    officials **220**
    rule of India 202, 220
Easter Rising (1916) 306, **306**
Edgar I, King 39, 42
Edinburgh, Scotland 216, **228–229**
Edmund II (Ironside), King 42–43
Edmund Tudor 103, 112, 114
Edward, Prince of Wales 98, **99,** 103
Edward I "Longshanks," King 65, 74, 88, **89,** 90
Edward II, King 65, 67, 90, 91
Edward III, King 65, 67, 70, **70,** 92, 103
Edward IV, King 98, **99**
    royal seal **98**
Edward V, King 98
Edward V, Prince 98
Edward VI, King 107, 108–109, 120, 126, **126,** 132
Edward VII, King 247
Edward VIII, King 289, 310
Edward the Black Prince 70, **70**
Edward the Confessor, King 42, 43, 56, **56,** 57, 58
Edward the Elder, King 39, 88
Edward the Martyr, King 42
Edwardian age 247
Egbert, King 39
Eisenhower, Dwight D. 320, **321,** 324
Eleanor of Aquitaine, Queen 65
Elfthryth, Queen 42
Eliot, George 276
Elizabeth, Queen, consort of Edward IV 98, 103
Elizabeth, Queen, consort of Henry VII 103–104, **105,** 112, 114
Elizabeth I, Queen 110–111, 130, **130–131**
    birth 107, 120
    colonies 164
    execution of Mary, Queen of Scots 111, 116, 132, 133
    exploration 136
    Ireland and 142
    portraits **4, 110**
    religious stance 110, 126
    Spanish Armada **110,** 140
    successor 149
Elizabeth II, Queen 295, 322, 328
Ellis Island, New York **265**
Ely Cathedral **43**
Emigration
    Age of Empire **241, 264,** 264–265, **265**
    map (1821–1911) 265
    post–World War II 323
Emma of Normandy 42, 43

Emmet, Robert 328
Empire, Age of (1815–1914) 236–283
    arts 245
    dissent and reform 260, **260–261**
    emigration **241**
    Houses of Hanover and Saxe-Coburg-Gotha 242, **242**
    maps 238, 250–251
    size of empire 248
    time line 240
Enclosure (land-use practice) 134, **134**
England
    map of Tudor counties 102
    name 38
    population 252, 264
    Saxon reign 39, 42
English Bill of Rights (1689) 188
English Civil War (1642–1646) **170,** 170–173, **172, 173**
    Ireland and 178
    map 171
    precursors 150–152
    Scotland and 178
English Reformation 126, **126, 127**
Enlightenment 228, **228–229**
Entente Cordiale (1904) 246
Equiano, Olaudah 212, **212**
Essex, Robert Devereux, Earl of 142, **142,** 172, 173
Ethelbert, King (Saxons) 37–38, 46, 48–49
Ethelred, King (Saxons) 39
Ethelred II (the Unready), King 42
Ethelstan, King 39
Europe
    map (1914) 286
    map at beginning of Reformation 127
    physical map 10–11
European Economic Community 306, 330
Evelyn, John (diarist) 176, 180, 182
Evelyn, John (scientist) 184
Exploration and discovery
    Africa 246
    Age of Empire **268,** 268–271, **269**
    maps 138–139, 270–271
    North America **155**
    South Pole **245**
    Tudor seamen 136, **136–137**

F

Fabian Society 278
Fairfax, Thomas 172, **172**
Falklands War (1982) 295, 330, **330**
Faraday, Michael 272
Farynor, Thomas 182
Fawkes, Guy 74, 160, **160–161**
Feisal, Prince (Arabia) 302
Ferdinand II, King (Spain) 104
Ferguson, Adam 228
Field of the Cloth of Gold (1520) **108**

Fielding, Henry 230
Financial crisis (2007) 332
Fionnán of Clonard, St. 46
First Act of Succession (1534) 107
First Bishops' War (1639) 150
First Opium War (1839–1842) **247**
FitzAlan family 116
FitzGilbert, Richard "Strongbow" 80, **81**
Flight of the Earls (1607) 142, **142**
Flinders, Matthew 268
Flodden Field, Battle of (1514) 116, **117**
    map 117
Foch, Ferdinand 299
France
    American Revolutionary War and 200, 224, 226
    colonies 164, 222
    Crimean War 241–242
    Entente Cordiale 246
    Seven Years' War 198–199, 222, **223**
    see also World War I; World War II
Francis, St. 126
Francis I, King (France) 104, **108**
Francis II, King (France) 132
Franklin, Sir John 268, **269**
Franks 48, 49
Franz Ferdinand, Archduke (Austro-Hungarian Empire) 247, **296**
Fraser, Simon 268
French, Sir John 296, 300
French and Indian War 222
French Revolution (1789) 201, 228
Frobisher, Sir Martin 136, 138, **138**

G

Gandhi, Mahatma **291,** 293, 325
Gaskell, Elizabeth 276
Gaveston, Piers 65
George, Prince of Cambridge 333
George I, King 157, 193–194
George II, King 194, **195,** 208
George III, King 197, 199, 201
George IV, King 239
George V, King 289, 310, **310**
George VI, King 289, 310
Georgia (colony) 194
Georgian era (1714–1815) 190–235
    architecture 216, **217,** 218, **218–219**
    Britain and empire 192, **202,** 202–205, **203**
    House of Hanover 194
    ideas and ideology 228, **228–229**
    Jacobite Rebellions 206, **206, 207**
    literary world **199,** 230, **230, 231**
    maps of empire 192, 204–205
    prosperity **197,** 216, **216, 217,** 218, **218, 218–219**
    time line 194

Germany
    rising strength (late 19th-century) 245–247
    see also World War I; World War II
Gilbert, Sir Humphrey 136, 138, **138**
Gildas (monk) 37
Gin 218
Gladstone, William 243–244, 258, 274
Globe Theatre 144, **144, 145**
Glorious Revolution (1688) 188, **188, 189,** 207
Godwin, Earl of Wessex 43, 56
Goldsmith, Oliver 230
Gooch, Daniel 256
Good Friday Agreement (1998) 306, 328
Gough, Charles **266**
Gower, John 95
Grand Remonstrance (1641) 151
Grave monuments 16
Great Depression 289, 310
Great Exhibition (1851) 241
Great Fire, London 182, **182–183,** 184
Great Game (conflicts with Russia) 248
Great Hunger *see* Irish Famine
Great Irish Famine *see* Irish Famine
Great Plague 182
Great Reform Act (1832) 240, 260
Gregory I, Pope 49
Grenville, Sir Richard 136, 139, **139**
Grey, Jane, Lady 108–109, **129**
Grey, Lord 260
Gunpowder Plot (1605) 149, 160,
    160–161
Gwynn, Nell **181**

H

Hadrian, Emperor (Rome) 32, **33**
Hadrian's Wall 17, 32, **32, 33**
    map 32
Haig, Sir Douglas **298,** 300
Hamilton, Lady Emma 232
Hampton Court Palace
    map 123
Hancock, John **226–227**
Hanover, House of (1714–1815) 196, **196**
Hanover, House of (1815–1914) 242, **242**
Happisburgh, Norfolk 20
Harald Hardrada, King (Norway) 58
Hardie, J. Keir 278
Hardy, Thomas 232, 276
Harold I (Harefoot), King 43, 56
Harold II, King 56, 58, 59
Harold Bluetooth Gormsen, King (Denmark) 42
Harold Godwin 43, 56
Harrying of the North (1069–1070) 72
Harthacnut, King 43, 56
Hastings, Battle of (1066) 58, **58,** 72
    map 59
Hathaway, Anne 135, 144
Hawkins, Sir John 111, 136, 139, **139,** 210, 212

Health system 293, 322, **323**
Heath, Edward 330
Henrietta Maria, Queen 149, 151, 168
Henry I, King 63
Henry II, King 63–65, 78, 80, **80**
Henry III, King 65, 74
Henry IV, King 71
Henry V, King 71, 96, **97,** 124
Henry VI, King 71, 97, 98, 103
Henry VII, King
    Battle of Bosworth 71, 112, **113**
    claim to throne 103
    exploration 136
    Ireland and 142
    Lady Chapel, Westminster Abbey **105**
    man and money 114, **114,** 134
    navy 118
    tomb **105,** 114
    trade reforms 134
    Treaty of Perpetual Peace (1502) 116
    Tudor succession and 103–104
    Yeoman Warders (Beefeaters) 74
Henry VIII, King 104, **120**
    annulment from Catherine of Aragon 104, 107,
        122
    break with Rome 104, 107, 122, **122, 123**
    destruction of Thomas Becket's shrine 78
    dissolution of monasteries 49, 124, **124**
    English Reformation 126, **126**
    Field of the Cloth of Gold **108**
    inheritance 114
    Ireland and 142
    last years 107–108
    navy 118
    succession 108
    wives 104, 107, 120, **121**
Hereford Mappa Mundi **50**
Heyrick, Elizabeth 228
High Stewards 116
Highland Clearances 264, **264**
Hill forts 17, 26, **26**
Hitler, Adolf 289, 312, 316, 320
Homo antecessor 15, 20
Homo heidelbergensis 20
Homo neanderthalensis 20
Hong Kong, British rights to **247**
Hooke, Robert 184
Hooper, John 128
Hornby, Leslie (Twiggy) 326, **326**
Howard, Thomas, Earl of Surrey 116
Hudson, Henry **155,** 164
Hudson, Thomas **129**
Hume, David 228, **228**
Hundred Years' War (1337–1453)
    Battle of Agincourt 96, **96,** 124
    Battle of Crécy 70, **70**
    introduction 67, 70
    map of campaigns 97
Hunt, Henry 260

I

Imperial State Crown **1**
Importation Act (Corn Laws, 1815) 239
Indentured servants 164
India
    as British possession 164, 194, 202, **203,** 220,
        220
    independence 293, 324, **325**
    maps 221, 267
    Raj 243, 266, 293
    uprisings 243, **246,** 266, **266**
    Industrial Revolution 214
    bridges **201, 214,** 256, **256**
    inventions 214, **215**
    Late Industrial Revolution (1860–1914) **252,**
        252–253, **253**
    Luddite riots 239
    maps 215, 253
    railroads 239
    slave trade and 212
    steam power 239, **252**
    see also Labor movement
Innocent III, Pope 86
Interregnum (1649–1660) 180
Iona abbey 46
IRA (Irish Republican Army) 294, 306, 328
IRB (Irish Republican Brotherhood) 306
Ireland
    Celtic clans 50
    Christianity 46
    conquest by Henry VIII 107
    Cromwell and 178, 179, 328
    Easter Rising 306, **306**
    emigration 264, **264**
    English Civil War 178
    famine 240, **262,** 262–263, **264**
    Georgian era 194, 196–197
    grave monuments 16
    Home Rule 240–241, 245, 274, **274, 275,**
        306
    independence 293, 306
    Irish Free State creation 274
    literature 197, 230, 276, **277**
    maps 47, 143, 179, 263, 307
    Norman conquest of 80, **80, 81**
    partition **306,** 306–307
    population 264
    prehistory 15
    railroads **255**
    revolts 152
    Tudors and 142, **142**
    Vikings 52
    voting qualifications 260
Irish Famine 240, **262,** 262–263, **264**
    map 263
Irish Question 247, 274, 328
Irish Republican Army (IRA) 294, 306, 328
Irish Republican Brotherhood (IRB) 306
Iron Age 17, 26, **26, 27**

Isabella, Queen 65, 67
Isabella I, Queen (Spain) 104
Israel
    creation 308
    map 309

J

Jacobite Rebellions 188, 193, 196, 206, **206, 207**
    map 207
Jamaican immigrants 324, **324**
James I, King (James VI of Scotland) **133,** 158, **159**
    character 158, 168
    colonies 164
    heritage 111, 116, 132, 133, 158
    receiving diplomats at court **151**
    reign 149
    religious issues and 160, 162
    Union Jack flag 149
James II, King
    Battle of the Boyne 189
    Great Fire of London 182
    introduction 156–157
    Ireland and 328
    Jacobite Rebellions 206
    religious issues and 188
James III, King see James Stuart (Old Pretender)
James IV, King (Scotland) 104, 116, 117
James V, King (Scotland) 116
James VI, King (Scotland) see James I, King
James Stuart (Old Pretender) 193, 206, **206**
Jamestown, Virginia 162, 164, **164, 165,** 212
Jane Seymour, Queen 107, 120, **121**
Jarrow (monastery) 49
Jean II, King (France) 70
Jefferson, Thomas 186, 226, **226–227**
Jenkins, Simon 224, 226
Jenkinson, Anthony 136
Jenkinson, Robert Banks, Earl of Liverpool 239
John, King (England) 65, 82, 86, **87**
John, King (Scotland) 90
John of Gaunt, Duke of Lancaster 71, 103
Johnson, Samuel 230, **230**
Jones, Inigo 158, 184
Jonson, Ben 144
Jutes 37, 44
    migration map 45

K

Keats, John 276, **276**
Keegan, John 300
Keightley, Sir Charles **325**
Kenneth mac Alpin, King (Scotland) 88
Kents Cavern, Devon 15
Kilkenny Castle, Ireland **81**
King James Bible 162, **162**
Kings and queens see Monarchs; specific individuals
Kingsley, Mary 268

Kipling, Rudyard 276
Kirk (Church of Scotland) 150
Kitchener, Lord Horatio 280, **289,** 296
Knight, Anne 228
Knox, John 111
Kolkata (Calcutta), India 220

L

Labor movement 240, 245, **247,** 278, **278–279,**
    289, 330, **331**
Labour Party 245, 278, 322
Lancaster, House of 98, 112, **112**
Lancaster, Sir James 139, **139**
Landed gentry 134
Langland, William 95
Languages
    evolution 44
    Middle English 94
    pagan linguistic legacy 46
    Viking contributions 52
Lansdown Crescent, Bath, England **190–191**
Latimer, Hugh 128
Laud, William 149, 150, 162
Lawrence, Thomas Edward (Lawrence of Arabia)
    302, **302**
League of Nations 308
Legal codes
    English common law 54
    Henry II 64
    Magna Carta 65, 86, **86, 87**
Lenthall, William 151
Leo X, Pope 126
Lindisfarne Priory
    founding 46, 49
    interior **48**
Lindisfarne Stone **52**
    ruins 46, **124**
    Viking raids 52, **52**
Lister, Joseph 272, **272**
Literature
    18th century 230, **230, 231**
    medieval 94, **94, 95**
    Victorian era 276, **276, 277**
Liverpool, Robert Banks Jenkinson, Earl of 239
Livingstone, David 246, 268, **269**
Locke, John 186, **186**
Lok, John 136
Lollards 126
Londinium (Roman capital) 18
London, England
    1960s 294, **294,** 326, **326, 327**
    Blitz **6,** 314, **314,** 315, **315**
    as capital of Roman Britain 30
    fashion 294, **294,** 326
    Georgian era **198,** 216
    Great Fire 182, **182–183**
    IRA bomb attacks 328
    labor movement **247, 278–279**

    modern era **295**
    population 252
    railroads 254, **254,** 256
    Underground **292,** 314, 318
    World War II **6,** 314, **314,** 315, **315,** 318
    Wren and 184, **184, 185**
London Bridge **182–183**
Long Parliament 150
Longbows 96, **96**
Louis XIV, King (France) 206
Louis XVI, King (France) 201
Lovat, Simon Fraser, Lord **207**
Luddites 239, 278
Luther, Martin 126
Lyell, Charles 272

M

Macdonald, Flora 208
Mackenzie, Alexander 268
Maeatae tribe 32
Magna Carta 65, 86, **86, 87**
Maiden Castle, near Dorchester, England **26**
Major, John 330
Malcom III Canmore, King (Scotland) 72, 88
Manchester, Earl of 173
Manchester, England 212, 239, **252**
Maps 138–139, 270–271
    Anglo-Saxon Britain and Ireland 36
    Antonine Wall 32
    battle for Scotland (medieval age) 89
    Battle of Agincourt (1415) 97
    Battle of Bosworth (1485) 113
    Battle of Britain (1940) 313
    Battle of Flodden Field (1513) 117
    Battle of the Somme (1916) 301
    Battle of Trafalgar (1805) 233
    Black Death 93
    Blitz 315
    Bonnie Prince Charlie 209
    Britain's Empire (1815–1901) 238, 250–251
    Britain's Empire (Georgian era) 192, 204–205
    British India (18th century) 221
    British Isles (11th–15th centuries) 62
    British Mandate (1922–1948) 309
    Caribbean and American colonial possessions 154
    Celts and Saxons 51
    colonial possessions 154, 166–167, 204–205,
        221
    Cromwellian conquest of Ireland 179
    Crusades 84–85
    D-Day 321
    Darwin's voyage 273
    early Christianity 47
    early times through the Romans 14
    Elizabethan seamen 138–139
    emigration (1821–1911) 265
    England (reign of Alfred the Great) 55
    English Civil War 171

Europe (1914) 286
Europe (beginning of Reformation) 127
Hadrian's Wall 32
Hampton Court Palace 123
Hastings, Battle of (1066) 59
Hereford Mappa Mundi 50
Hundred Years' War (1415–1429) 97
India 221, 267
Industrial Revolution 214, 253
Ireland 47, 143, 179, 263, 307
Irish Famine 263
Jacobite Rebellions 207
Mary, Queen of Scots 133
medieval age (1066–1485) 62
Middle East 309
migrations and expansions (Saxons to Normans) 45
monasteries 125
Napoleonic Wars 235
Nelson's battles 233
Neolithic period 23
Norman invasion 59
Normans 73
Ottoman Empire (1299–1922) 309
physical map of British Isles and mainland
    Europe 10–11
prehistory 14, 21
railroads 255
restoration of Stuarts and Act of Union 148
Revolutionary War (1775–1783) 225
Roman Britain 31
Scotland 89, 209
Second Boer War 281
Seven Years' War in North America 223
slave trade 211
Spanish Armada defeat (1588) 141
Troubles 329
Tudor England and Wales 102
Viking raids 53
Wars of the Roses (1455–1487) 99
World War I 299, 301, 304–305
World War II 313, 315, 321
Marcus Aurelius, Emperor (Rome) 32
Margaret, Queen (Scotland) 90
Margaret of Anjou 98
Margaret Tudor 116
Marlborough, John Churchill, Duke of 157
Marlowe, Christopher 144
Marshall Plan 322
Marston Moor, Battle of (1644) **170,** 173
Marvell, Andrew 176
Mary, Queen, consort of George V 310
Mary, Queen of Scots 132, **132**
    ascension to throne 116
    betrothal to Edward VI 107, 132
    execution 111, 116, 132
    map 133
    motherhood 132, 158
    prayer book **133**
    sanctuary with Elizabeth 111, 132

Mary I, Queen
    birth 120, 121
    exploration 136
    persecution of Protestants 109, **109,** 126, 128,
        129
    succession 108–109
    treatment of Elizabeth I 130
Mary II, Queen 156–157, 188, **189**
Mary of Guise 132
Mary of Modena, Queen 188
Mary Rose (ship) 118, **118–119, 119**
Massachusetts Bay Company 162
Matilda, Empress (Holy Roman Empire) 63
Mayflower (ship) 162, **163**
McAdam, John 228
McNeill, Sir John Carstairs **248**
Medieval age (1066–1485) 60–99
    map 62
    time line 64
Medway, Battle of the (10 B.C.–A.D. 54) 28
Meerut, India 266
Melbourne, Lord 258
Mercia (Anglo-Saxon kingdom) 38, 49
Mercia (Saxon kingdom) 39
Mermaid Tavern, London **111**
Middle East
    Britain and 308, **309**
    maps 309
Middle English 94
Middleton, Catherine **333**
Migration
    map 45
    Saxons to Normans (A.D. 410–1066) 44, 45
Milton, John **152**
Miniskirts 294, 326
Mitchel, John 262
Modern age (1914–present) 284–333
    21st century 332, **332, 333**
    1920s and 1930s 310, **310, 311**
    time line 288
Monarchs 334–335
    Act of Supremacy (1534) 107
    First Act of Succession (1534) 107
    House of Denmark 40–41, **40–41**
    House of Hanover 196, **196,** 242, **242**
    House of Normandy 68–69, **68–69**
    House of Plantagenet 68–69, **68–69**
    House of Saxe-Coburg-Gotha 242, **242**
    House of Stuart 153, **153**
    House of Tudor 106–107, **106–107**
    House of Wessex 40–41, **40–41**
    House of Windsor 290, **290**
    rival claimants 98
    Scotland 41, 69, 106
    youngest 71
Monasteries
    dissolution under Henry VIII 49, 107, 124, **124**
    map 125
Monck, George 152, 154

Montcalm, Louis-Joseph de 222
Monteagle, William Parker, Lord 160
Montgomery, Bernard Law **317**
Monymusk Reliquary **90**
Moore, Bobby **327**
More, Sir Thomas **105,** 107
Morocco
    World War I **303**
Morris, William 245
Mortimer, Roger de 67
Morton, John 124
Mount Sandel, Ireland 15
Mountbatten, Lord 325
Murrow, Edward R. 314

N
Napoleon I, Emperor (France) 201, 232, 234, 235,
    235
Napoleonic Wars 234, 239, 278
    map 235
Nasmyth, James 252
Nasser, Gamal Abdel 308, 325
National Health Service 322, **323**
Neanderthals 20
Nelson, Horatia 232
Nelson, Horatio
    Battle of the Nile 201, 232
    Battle of Trafalgar 201, **232,** 232–233
    maps of battles 233
    portrait **233**
Neolithic period
    agriculture 22
    artifacts **22, 23**
    introduction 15–16
    map 23
    monumental landscapes 22, **23, 24,** 24–25, **25**
    stone village, Skara Brae, Orkney Islands **18**
    Stonehenge **24,** 24–25, **25**
    village life 22, **22,** 24
Netherlands
    colonies 164, **165**
New Model Army 172, 173
New York (colony) 164, **165**
New Zealand, as colony 164
Newfoundland, Canada 164
Newton, Sir Isaac 186, **187**
Nightingale, Florence 242
Norfolk, Duke of 112
Normandy, House of 68–69
Normans
    conquest of Ireland 80, **80, 81**
    in England's royal bloodline 42
    invasion 58, **58**
    invasion map 59
    map 73
    origins 42
    settlement in England 72
North, Lord 199

Northern Ireland
    after Irish independence 293, 306
    creation 274, 306
    European Economic Community 306
    map of Troubles 329
    Troubles 294, 306, **328,** 328–329
Northumberland, Earl of 112
Northumberland, John Dudley, Duke of 108–109,
    126, 130
Northumbria (Anglo-Saxon kingdom) 38, 39, 49

O

Ó Donnell, Hugh Roe 142
Ó Neill, Conn 142
Ó Neill, Hugh 142, **142**
Oates, Lawrence 268
O'Connell, Daniel 306
Offa, King (Saxons) 38
Old London Bridge **115**
Old St. Paul's Cathedral **182–183,** 184
Opium Wars **247**
Oswald, King **46,** 49
Oswy, King 49
Ottoman Empire 308
    map 309
Oxford, Earl of 112

P

Paganism 46, **46,** 48
Paine, Thomas 228, 229, 230
Pakistan
    independence 293, 324
Palestine **309**
    British Mandate 308, 309
    map 309
Parfett, Ned **282**
Paris, Matthew 86
Parker, William, Lord Monteagle 160
Parliament, Houses of 56, 260
Parnell, Charles Stewart 274, **274**
Patrick, St. 46
Paulinus (monk) 49
Peasants' Revolt (1381) 71
Peel, Sir Robert 240
Pepys, Samuel 218
Peterloo Massacre (1819) 239
Petition of Right (1628) 150
Philip I, King (France) 72
Philip II, King (Spain) 109, 128, 140
Philip IV, King (France) 67
Philip V, King (Spain) 206
Picts 50
Pilgrims **157,** 162, **163**
Pitt, William, the Elder 196, 199, 222, 224
Pitt, William, the Younger 200
Plague
    Black Death **92,** 92–93, **93**

Black Death map 93
    Great Plague 182
Plantagenet, House of 64, 68–69
Plot, Ridolfi 111
Poetry 276
Political parties, origins 156
Pontefract Castle, England **60–61**
Pope, Alexander 230
Population
    1821 to 1911 264
    Georgian era 216
    Industrial Revolution 252
Potato famine *see* Irish Famine
Prehistory 20
    Bronze Age 16–17, **17**
    hunting and gathering 15, 20, **20, 21**
    introduction 15
    maps 14, 21, 23
    Neolithic period 15–16, **18, 22,** 22–25, **23,**
        24, 25
Preseli Hills, Wales 24
Pride, Thomas 152
Protestant Reformation 111, 126, **126, 127**
    map of Europe 127
Prussia
    Battle of Waterloo 234
Puritans **157,** 162, **163**

Q

Quant, Mary 294, 326
Queens and kings *see* Monarchs; *specific individuals*
Queen's House, Greenwich **158**

R

Radar 312, **312**
Railroads 239, 240, **243,** 254, **254, 255,** 256
    maps 255
Raj 243, 266, 293
Raleigh, Sir Walter 136, **137**
Ramsay, William 272
Rationalism, Age of 186, **186, 187**
Reagan, Ronald 330, **330**
Reason, Age of *see* Enlightenment; Rationalism, Age of
Reformation 126, **126**
    map of Europe 127
Restoration (return of monarchy) 154, 180,
    180–181, 181
Revolutionary War (1775–1783) **224,** 224–227
    artifacts **225, 226, 227**
    Burgoyne's surrender (1777) **200**
    causes 199
    final surrender 224
    introduction 199–200
    map 225
    Paine and 228, 230
Rhode Island (colony) 162
Rhodes, Cecil 280

Rhyl, Wales **291**
Richard I (the Lionheart), King 65, 82, **82–83, 83**
Richard II, King 71
Richard III, King 71, **71,** 74, 98, 103, 112, **113**
Richard of Shrewsbury, Duke of York 98
Richard Plantagenet, Duke of York 98
Richardson, Samuel 230
Ridgeway (ancient "road") 25
Ridley, Nicholas 128
Rizzio, David 132
Roanoke Island, Virginia 136, **136–137,** 164
Robert I (the Bruce), King (Scotland) 65, 90, **90–91,**
    91
Robert II, King (Scotland) 116
Robert of Jumièges 56
Robert of Normandy, Duke 56
Robert the Bruce *see* Robert I (the Bruce), King
    (Scotland)
Roberts, Frederick **267**
Rochambeau, Comte de 224
Roebuck, John Arthur **260**
Rolling Stones 326, 327
Roman Britain
    artifacts **31**
    baths and thermal springs **19**
    legacy 18
    maps 14, 31
    rise and fall 17–18, 30, **30**
    Roman conquest 17, 28, **28–29**
    towns 30
Rommel, Erwin 320
Roosevelt, Franklin D. 316
Rothschild, Baron Walter 308
Royal crest **75**
Royal Navy
    Battle of Trafalgar 232, **232,** 233
    beginnings **42,** 54
    Georgian era 198–199
    maps of Nelson's battles 233
    Revolutionary War 224
    Seven Years' War 222
Royal Society 186
Royal Ulster Constabulary (RUC) 328
RUC (Royal Ulster Constabulary) 328
Rump Parliament 152
Runnymede **86**
Rupert, Prince 172
Russia
    Crimean War (1853–1856) 241–242
    Great Game 248

S

Sailors 136, **136–137**
Saladin (Muslim general) 82, **82–83**
Salisbury Cathedral, Wiltshire, England **64**
Saxe-Coburg-Gotha, House of 242, **242**
Saxons
    artifacts **39, 44, 45, 51**

Celts and 37–38, **50,** 50–51
Christianity 38
colonization 50
invasion of Britain 37
last kings 42–43
map 45, 51
migration 44–45
rise of Saxon kingdoms 38–39
time line 38
warriors **34–35**
Science and learning
    Age of Empire 272, **272, 273**
    Age of Rationalism 186, **186, 187**
Scotland
    Act of Union (1707) 157
    Bonnie Prince Charlie and 208
    crisis of succession 90
    Cromwell and 178
    English Civil War 178
    Enlightenment 196, 228, **228, 228–229**
    Georgian era 194, 196–197
    Highland Clearances 264, **264**
    independence (1328) 90
    independence referendum (2014) 332
    independence struggle (1314) 65
    invasion by William I 72
    Jacobite Rebellions 188, 193, 196, 206, **206,**
      207, **207**
    kings and queens 41, 69, 106
    literature 230, **231**
    map of battles for 89
    map of Jacobite Rebellions 207
    Picts 50
    population 252, 264
    Protestant Reformation 111
    resistance to Roman conquest 28
    revolts 152
    rise of (medieval age) **88,** 88–91, **90–91**
    Vikings 52
Scott, Robert Falcon **245,** 268, **268**
Scott, Sir Walter **231**
Scottish National Covenant 150
Seaman, William **129**
Seven Years' War (1756–1763) 198–199, 222, **222,**
    223, 224
    map 223
Severus, Septimius, Emperor (Rome) 32
Seymour, Edward 108, **126**
Shackleton, Ernest 268
Shakespeare, William **111,** 135, 144, **144**
Shelley, Mary Wollstonecraft 276
Short Parliament 150
Sidney, Sir Philip 144
Simnel, Lambert 103
Simpson, Wallis 289, 310, **310**
Sinn Féin 306, 328
Sir Gawain and the Green Knight (Pearl Poet) 95
Sirāj al-Dawlah 220
Skara Brae, Orkney Islands **18**

Slave trade 164, **210,** 210–213, **211, 212, 213**
    abolition 200, 210, 212, 213, 228
    map 211
Slavery Abolition Act (1833)
    commemorative medal **200**
Smith, Adam 228
Soccer 326, **327**
Solent, Battle of the (1545) 118
Somerset, Edward Seymour, Duke of 108, **126**
Somme, Battle of the (1916) 298, 300, **300, 301**
    map 301
Sophia of Hanover 157, 193
Sophie, Archduchess (Austro-Hungarian Empire)
    296
South Sea Company 193–194
Spanish Armada **100–101,** 110, 111, 140, **140**
    map of defeat 141
Speke, John 268, 271
Spenser, Edmund 144
Squire-Brown, Ena **293**
St. Clement's Church, Harris, Scotland **2–3**
St. Paul's Cathedral, London **6,** 49, 184, **185,**
    315
Staffordshire Hoard **39**
Stalin, Joseph 316, 324
Stamford Bridge, Battle of (1066) 58
Stamp Act (1765) 224
Stanley, Henry Morton 268, 271
Stanley, Lord 112
Stephen, King 63
Stephenson, George 254
Stevenson, Robert Louis 276
Steward family 116
Stewart family 116
Stirling Bridge, Battle of (1297) **88**
Stockport, England **236–237**
Stockwell, Sir Hugh **325**
Stoker, Bram 49, 277
Stone Age *see* Neolithic period
Stonehenge **24,** 24–25, **25**
Strongbow *see* FitzGilbert, Richard
Stuarts (1603–1714) 146–189
    colonies 164, **165**
    Georgian era claims to throne 206–209
    House of Stuart 153, **153**
    map 148
    map of settlement and exploration 166–167
    origins 116
    time line 150
Sturt, Charles 268, 271
Sudan
    war (1898) 241
Suez Canal, Egypt 308, **325**
Surrey, Thomas Howard, Earl of 116
Sussex (Anglo-Saxon kingdom) 49
Sutton Hoo ship-burial, Suffolk, England **44**
Swan, Joseph 272
Swein Forkbeard, King (Denmark) 42
Swift, Jonathan 197, 230

T
Tanistry 88
Tasman, Abel 164
Tea **197,** 218
Telegraph 254
Tertullian (historian) 46
Thames Tunnel 256
Thatcher, Margaret 295, 322, 328, 330, **330, 331**
Theater **310, 311**
Thirty-Nine Articles of Religion (1562) 110
Thomas, Lowell 302
Thomas Becket 64, 78, **78, 79,** 94, 95
Thompson, David 268
Timekeeping 254
Titanic, R.M.S. 247, 282, **282, 283**
Tolpuddle Martyrs 240, 278
Tories 156
Tostig (brother of Harold II) 56, 58
Tower of London 74, **74, 75,** 98, 103, **115,**
    182–183
Trafalgar, Battle of (1805) 201, 232, **232**
Trains *see* Railroads
Treaty of Paris (1763) 199
Treaty of Paris (1783) 200, 224
Treaty of Perpetual Peace (1502) 116
Treaty of Versailles (1919) 289, 302
Tresham, Francis 160
Trevithick, Richard 254, **254**
Triple Entente 246, 296
Troubles 294, 306, 328, **328**
    maps 329
Tudor, Edmund 103, 112, 114
Tudor Britain (1485–1603) 100–145
    House of Tudor 106–107, **106–107**
    Ireland and 142, **142**
    kings and queens of Scotland 106
    land and homes 134, **135**
    map of counties 102
    money and trade 134, **134, 135**
    seamen **136–137,** 136–139
    time line 104
Tudor rose 112, **112**
Twiggy 326, **326**
Tyndale, William 122, 162

U
Union Jack flag 149, 332
Unions *see* Labor movement
United Nations Partition Plan (1947) 308, 309
Universal health system 293
Urban II, Pope 82
Urbanization 216

V
Vespasian, Emperor (Rome) 28
Victoria, Queen 240, **244,** 256, 258, **259,** 293
Victorian-era literature 276, **276, 277**

Vikings **38,** 39, 42, 52, **52, 53,** 54
  map 53
Villiers, George, Duke of Buckingham 158, 168
The Vision of Piers Plowman (Langland) 95, **95**
Voltaire 223
Vortigern, King 44
Voting qualifications 239–240, 260, **260–261,** 288

W

Wales
  as Celtic sanctuary 50
  conquest by Henry VIII 107
  map of Tudor counties 102
  population 252, 264
  resistance to Roman conquest 17, 28
Wallace, Alfred Russel 272
Wallace, William 88, **88,** 90
Walpole, Horace 222
Walpole, Sir Robert 194, 199
Walsingham, Sir Francis 132
War of 1812 200
Warbeck, Perkin 103
Wars of the Roses (1455–1485) 71, 112
  map 99
Wars of the Three Kingdoms *see* English Civil War
Warwick, Richard Neville, Earl of 98
Washington, George 199, 222, 224, **224,** 226
Waterloo, Battle of (1815) 201, 234
Watt, James 228
Webb, Beatrice 278
Webb, Sidney 278, **279**
Wedgwood, Josiah 228
Weldon, Sir Anthony 158
Welfare state 322, **322, 323**
Wellington, Arthur Wellesley, Duke of 234, **234,** 239
Wells, H. G. 276
Wentworth, Thomas 178
Wesley, John 228
Wessex (Anglo-Saxon kingdom) 38–39, 49, 54
Wessex, House of 40–41, **40–41**
Westminster, Palace of 56
Westminster Abbey **57**
  Books of Indentures **114**
  founding 56
  Lady Chapel **105**
  tombs 89, **105,** 115
  William I's coronation **72**
Whigs 156
Whitby, Synod of 49
Whitby Abbey 49, **49**
Wilberforce, William 210, **212,** 213, 228
Wilde, Oscar 276, **277**
William, Prince, Duke of Cambridge **333**
William I (the Conqueror), King
  Battle of Hastings 58, **58,** 59, 72
  castle-building 72, 74
  claim to throne 43, 56
  conquest of Scotland 88

coronation **72**
death 72, **72**
Domesday Book 76, **76,** 77
Harrying of the North 72
lineage 56
portrait **65**
reign 63, 72
William I (the Lion), King (Scotland) 90
William II "Rufus," King 63, **66**
William III, Prince of Orange 156–157, 188, **188,**
  189, 328
William IV, King 239, 240, 260
Williams, Roger 162
Willoughby, Sir Hugh 136
Wills, William John 268
Wilson, Woodrow 299
Winchester, England 54
Windsor, House of 193, 290, **290**
Wolfe, James 199, 222, **222**
Wollstonecraft, Mary 228
Wolsey, Thomas 104, 107, 122, 123, **123**
Women
  21st century 332
  1920s 310
  Enlightenment 228
  World War II 318, **318–319**
Wood, John 216
Woodville, Elizabeth *see* Elizabeth, Queen, consort of
  Edward IV
Wool 134
Worcester Priory 124
World Cup (1966) 326, **327**
World War I
  aftermath 288–289, 310
  aircraft **288**
  Battle of the Somme (1916) 298, 300, **300, 301**
  Battle of Ypres (1915) **284–285,** 300
  Battle of Ypres (1917) 300
  introduction 287–288
  map 304–305
  map of Battle of the Somme 301
  map of Western Front 299
  outbreak **296**
  Palestine **309**
  poison gas 287, 288, 300, **300**
  recruitment posters **289, 303**
  trench warfare 296, 298, **299**
  weapons **299**
  Western Front **296–297,** 296–299
  as world war 302, **302, 303**
World War II
  aftermath 287, 291, **291,** 293–294, 322–325,
    324, 325
  Battle of Britain (1940) 289, 312, **312,** 313
  Blitz **6,** 314, **314,** 315, **315**
  Caen, France **317**
  D-Day **320,** 320–321, **321**
  home front 318, **318–319**
  introduction 287, 289, 291

map of Battle of Britain 313
map of Blitz 315
map of D-Day 321
radar 312, **312**
war brides **293,** 318
Wren, Sir Christopher 184, **184,** 185
Wulfhere, King (Saxons) 38
Wyatt, Sir Thomas 109
Wycliffe, John 126, 162
Wyndham, Thomas 136

Y

Yalta Conference (1945) 316
York, House of 98
York Minster 49
Yorktown, Virginia 224, 226
Ypres, Battle of (1915) **284–285,** 300
Ypres, Battle of (1917) 300

THE BRITISH WORLD

Tim Jepson

Published by the National Geographic Society

Gary E. Knell, *President and Chief Executive Officer*
John M. Fahey, *Chairman of the Board*
Declan Moore, *Chief Media Officer*
Chris Johns, *Chief Content Officer*

Prepared by the Book Division

Hector Sierra, *Senior Vice President and General Manager*
Lisa Thomas, *Senior Vice President and Editorial Director*
Jonathan Halling, *Creative Director*
Marianne Koszorus, *Design Director*
R. Gary Colbert, *Production Director*
Jennifer A. Thornton, *Director of Managing Editorial*
Susan S. Blair, *Director of Photography*
Meredith C. Wilcox, *Director, Administration and Rights Clearance*

Staff for This Book

Barbara Payne, *Editor*
Sanaa Akkach, *Art Director*
Matt Propert, *Illustrations Editor*
Michelle R. Harris, *Researcher*
Carl Mehler, *Director of Maps*
Gregory Ugiansky, *Map Production and Research Manager*
XNR Productions, *Map Research and Production*
Zachary Galasi, *Editorial Assistant*
Marshall Kiker, *Associate Managing Editor*
Judith Klein, *Senior Production Editor*
Mike Horenstein, *Production Manager*
Constance Roellig, Galen Young, *Rights Clearance Specialists*
Katie Olsen, *Design Production Specialist*
Nicole Miller, *Design Production Assistant*
Bobby Barr, *Manager, Production Services*

For more information, please call 1-800-NGS LINE (647-5463) or write to the following address:

National Geographic Society
1145 17th Street NW
Washington, D.C. 20036-4688 U.S.A.

For information about special discounts for bulk purchases, please contact National Geographic Books Special Sales: ngspecsales@ngs.org

For rights or permissions inquiries, please contact National Geographic Books Subsidiary Rights: ngbookrights@ngs.org

ISBN: 978 1 4262 1553 7 (trade)
ISBN: 978-1-4262-1554-4 (deluxe)

Printed in the United States of America

15/RRDW-CML/1